The Greening of Dublin Castle

The Greening of Dublin Castle

The Transformation of Bureaucratic and Judicial Personnel in Ireland, 1892-1922

Lawrence W. McBride

The Catholic University of America Press
Washington, D.C.

Printed in the United States of America

The paper used in this publication meets the minimum requirements of American National Standards for Information Science—Permanence of Paper for Printed Library Materials, ANSI Z39.48-1984. ∞

Library of Congress Cataloging-in-Publication Data

McBride, Lawrence W., 1945–
The greening of Dublin Castle : the transformation of bureaucratic and judicial personnel in Ireland, 1892–1922 / by Lawrence W. McBride.
p. cm.
Includes bibliographical references.
1. Civil service—Ireland—History. 2. Judges—Ireland—History. 3. Religion and politics—Ireland—History. 4. Ireland—Politics and government—1837–1901. 5. Ireland—Politics and government—1901–1910. 6. Ireland—Politics and government—1910–1921. I. Title.
JN1448.M33 1990
354.41504—dc20 89-38830
ISBN 0-8132-0715-0 (alk. paper)

Contents

Abbreviations vii
Note on Capitalization viii
Introduction and Acknowledgments ix

I. A Different System 1

II. Cleaning Out the Castle, 1892–95 38

III. Fill Every Office in Ireland with Friends, 1895–1900 70

IV. It Dies Very Hard, 1900–1905 95

V. A Race of Officials Not Merely Irish by Birth, 1906–10 124

VI. An Efficient, Content, and Loyal Body of Officials, 1910–15 159

VII. Power without Responsibility, May 1915–December 1916 193

VIII. The Hereditary Influence of the Governing Circles, December 1916–December 1918 222

IX. A Fair and Square Fight, 1919–22 259

Epilogue 304

Bibliography 313
Index 325

Abbreviations

Libraries and Archives

B.L.	British Library (British Museum)
Bod. Lib.	Bodleian Library
C.S.O., R.P.	Chief Secretary's Office, Registered Papers
D.D.A.	Dublin Diocesan Archives
H.H.	Haddo House, Tarves, Scotland
H.L.R.O.	House of Lords Record Office
K.I.I.	King's Inns, Ireland
N.L.I.	National Library of Ireland
N.L.S.	National Library of Scotland
P.F.C.S.	Horace Plunkett Foundation for Cooperative Studies, Oxford
P.R.O.	Public Record Office, England
S.P.O.I.	State Paper Office, National Archives, Ireland
T.C.D.	Trinity College, Dublin

Collections

Ab.P.	Aberdeen Papers
Ash.P.	Ashbourne Papers
Bal.P.	Balfour Papers
Bry.P.	Bryce Papers
Cab.	Cabinet File
Cad.P.	Cadogan Papers
C-B.P.	Campbell-Bannerman Papers
D.P.	Dillon Papers
G.P.	Gladstone Papers
Gill P.	Gill Papers
Law P.	Law Papers

L.G.P.	Lloyd George Papers
MacD.P.	MacDonnell Papers
Nat.P.	Nathan Papers
O'B.P.	O'Brien Papers
P.D.	Plunkett Diary
P.P.	Plunkett Papers
Red.P.	Redmond Papers
Rip.P.	Ripon Papers
Ros.P.	Rosebery Papers
S-S. P.	Sheehy-Skeffington Papers
Strath.P.	MacPherson Papers

Note on Capitalization

In this book, *Nationalist, Republican,* and *Unionist* appear with initial capital letters and refer to indivduals who embraced the general demands or programs of these political movements. They do not necessarily refer to members of the Irish Parliamentary party, Sinn Fein, or the various Unionist parties. I have tried to use modifiers and the context of the narrative to clarify the specific use of these terms. I have also used initial capital letters to identify particular geographic administrative areas, including areas referred to colloquially as the North or the South. Elsewhere, I have tried to minimize the use of capital letters.

Introduction and Acknowledgments

The purpose of this book is to describe the transformation of the Irish civil administration and the Supreme Court of Judicature politically and religiously between 1892 and 1922. In 1892 that administration was dominated by both a bureaucratic elite and rank and file civil servants who were Unionist in politics and Protestant in religion. The same characteristics were true of the courts, from the justices of the Supreme Court of Judicature through the court's administrative officers. Thirty years later, in 1921, the administration and the court system were largely controlled by Nationalists and Catholics. This transformation was as comprehensive as it was complete because it extended across the whole spectrum of the Irish administration and judicial system from top to bottom. The transformation was effected both by the changed nature of the direct appointments that were made by the members of the Irish executive to the higher levels of the bureaucracy and the courts after 1892 and by the institution of open competition examinations for the rank and file civil servants after 1876. The most important result of this transformation is that it facilitated the smooth transfer of power from Britain to the Irish Free State in 1922, and it helps explain why the Free State was able to achieve a remarkable degree of stability in the face of severe political and economic problems after 1922.

The source material for this study includes descriptions of the civil administration and courts found in public documents, newspapers, journals, and books from the period, as well as material in the manuscript collections and memoirs of leading bureaucrats, judges, soldiers, and politicians. These sources indicate how Irish and British administrators made personnel decisions for Irish administrative departments and the courts. They often reveal how the decisions were perceived by the public at large. Contemporary writers who were interested in the bureaucracy or judiciary were aware of the broader, national context for institutional change, but when they commented on a particular appointment they often focused on the religious and political background of the candidate. Contemporary accounts are also valuable because they often provide information about a judge or bureaucrat that is impossible to find in the other primary sources: why he was appointed; what his institutional, political, and social connections were; how he performed on the bench or in public service. My one regret, as I review the manuscript for the final time, is that space constraints do not permit the inclusion of very much collateral biographical information about individual Irish civil servants and judges. Perhaps that is the way it must be in administrative history.

The growing body of scholarly work on the administrative history of Ireland has contributed significantly to this book. T. J. Barrington's *The Irish Administrative System* (1980) explains why the social and political character of public officials is important in the delivery of services to the public. R. B. McDowell's *The Irish Administration, 1800–1914* (1964), surveys the history of the bureaucracy, department by department. Leon O'Broin describes the Irish administration from 1907 to 1916 in *The Chief Secretary: Augustine Birrell in Ireland* (1969) and in *Dublin Castle and the 1916 Rising* (1966). Charles Townshend gives the Irish administration a prominent place in *The British Campaign in Ireland, 1918–1921* (1975). John McColgan describes the transfer of administrative services in *British Policy and the Irish Administration, 1920–1922* (1983). In *The Decline of the Union: British Government in Ireland, 1892–1920* (1988), Eunan O'Halpin describes how the disjointed lines of administrative authority in the Irish administration and the shifting political environment affected the creation of British policy in Ireland. The last three books, in particular, are models of archival research for administrative history. They provide exhaustive treatments of the complicated period between 1916 and 1921, which takes up the closing chapters of this book. The Bibliography includes other important secondary sources that focus on administrative and judicial history during the period, 1892–1922.

Research for this book was conducted in Ireland, England, and Scotland. I express my appreciation to the librarians, archivists, and staff members at a number of research centers for permission to consult their collections. In Ireland, I was assisted at the National Library, the National Archives, the Public Record Office, the Trinity College Manuscript Room, the Dublin Diocesan Archives, the King's Inns Library, and the Department of Education Library. In England, I was assisted at the British Library, the Public Record Office, the London School of Economics, the House of Lords Record Office, the Bodleian Library, and the Plunkett Foundation for Cooperative Studies. In Scotland, I was assisted at the National Library and at Haddo House. I want to thank the trustees of the Asquith Papers and the Strathcarron Papers at the Bodleian Library for permission to use those collections in this book.

Many people have encouraged me during the years that it has taken to complete this manuscript. Emmet Larkin at the University of Chicago is my mentor and friend. Former colleagues in Chicago also deserve thanks: Gerald A. Danzer at the University of Illinois at Chicago; Walt Kelly at Chicago State University; Art Anderson and Adrian Capehart at the Newberry Library. My current colleagues at Illinois State University have been interested in my work, and Earl A. Reitan was especially helpful in suggesting ways to shorten the manuscript and improve the prose. Earlier drafts were critiqued by Bill Murphy and Emmet Larkin at the University of Chicago and by the Catholic University of America Press's critic readers and editorial staff. An anonymous critic reader has saved me from making several embarrassing errors, particularly in the closing chapter. The manuscript was prepared at Illinois State by Todd Koehler and Sharon Hagan.

If there are remaining factual errors, I take full responsibility. The interpretations are based on my reading of the sources, many of which have been pared down to capture their most essential points. I regret any loss of nuances that may have resulted during my editing of individual sources and the manuscript. I hope that any such loss has been compensated for through the overall narration and analysis of the transformation of the bureaucratic and judicial personnel.

My wife, Sandra, has helped me throughout every stage of this project, from conducting the initial research to critiquing numerous drafts. Simply put, this book could not have been written without her support and love.

The book is dedicated to my parents, Lawrence and Anita McBride. He helped me define my teaching; she believed that I could write.

Thanks to one and all.

Lawrence W. McBride
Illinois State University

The Greening of Dublin Castle

Chapter I

A Different System

When R. Barry O'Brien began his survey of the Irish administration, *Dublin Castle and the Irish People* (1912), he placed a quote from Lord Rosebery, the Liberal prime minister, above the first page. Rosebery, who was speaking in Edinburgh about his party's program, declared that he would not have anything to say on the topic of Ireland. "In the first place," he explained, "it is a different system of administration and one with which I am not so conversant; and in the second place, this is at present a harmonious meeting and I have discovered that there is no topic so likely to terminate the harmony of a meeting as that of the administration or the government of Ireland."[1] If this humorous remark helped Rosebery finesse a serious aspect of the Irish question—the lack of public confidence in Dublin Castle, the seat of government and administration in Ireland—the comment provided the perfect foil for O'Brien's work. As the biographer of Charles Stewart Parnell, O'Brien appreciated a controversial topic when he saw one, and the story of the administration of Ireland had enough twists and turns both to satisfy his artistic talents and to sustain his readers' interest.

This opening chapter will attempt to describe the structure of that "different system" as it existed in Ireland between 1892 and 1922, and it will provide a profile of the politicians, civil servants, and supreme court justices who served there during this period. The best place to begin is at the top, with the politicians who were the executive officers

1. R. Barry O'Brien, *Dublin Castle and the Irish People,* 2nd ed. (London: Kegan Paul, Trench, Trubner & Co., Ltd., 1912), p. i. O'Brien does not supply a date for Rosebery's quote.

in Dublin Castle. The bureaucracy is next, proceeding through three levels of civil service personnel: department heads, professional staff officers, and rank and file. The structure of the supreme court is described next. A profile of the court's judicial and administrative personnel completes the overview.

The Civil Administration

The Executive

The Irish executive included the lord lieutenant (or viceroy), his chief secretary, the lord chancellor, the attorney-general, and the solicitor-general. Each was a politician who either assumed his position in the Irish administration with a change in government or was appointed by the government of the day.

The chief executive officers were the lord lieutenant and the chief secretary. With two exceptions, a Scotsman as lord lieutenant and a Canadian-born chief secretary, they were Englishmen. The lord lieutenant resided in Dublin; the chief secretary spent at least half, and usually three-quarters, of the year in London. Administrative decisions in Ireland were carried out in the lord lieutenant's name, although for most of the period the chief secretary was the actual head of the administration. This was because the chief secretary was responsible in the House of Commons for the conduct of the administration, and because chief secretaries usually had a seat in the cabinet where Irish policy was usually determined. When the lord lieutenant and chief secretary were out of the country, executive functions were assumed by three lords justices, who included the lord chancellor, a supreme court justice, and the commander of the forces in Ireland. The Irish Privy Council, an advisory body that fluctuated in size between forty-five and sixty-eight members and included prominent citizens, judges, law officers, civil servants, and unpaid commissioners and board members who were associated with the bureaucracy, issued orders-in-council that implemented certain acts of the executive.

The Lord Lieutenant. Finding a person to serve as the crown's chief representative in Ireland was not always easy for a prime minister. The seven men, four Liberals and three Conservatives, who accepted the lord lieutenancy between 1892 and 1921 approached it as a duty, rather than as a political opportunity. Part of the burden was that the lord lieutenant had to reside in Dublin most of the year. This took him away from the center of British political life, and it removed his family from the whirl of London society. Although the viceroy's residence and demesne in Dublin's spacious Phoenix Park were well appointed and manicured, the city itself was not very inviting. Dublin was plagued by urban decay, poverty, and corrupt local leadership.[2] Perhaps the lord lieutenant found some consolation in being the center of attention for Dublin's upper class. Because of that social prominence, however, the private lives of the lord lieutenant and his family members were under close scrutiny.

The major burden for the lord lieutenant was that his role was largely symbolic. Five of the seven lord lieutenants were totally subservient to the chief secretary. The two exceptions, Lord Cadogan between 1895 and 1902, and Lord French between 1918 and 1921, both held seats in the cabinet. In or out of the cabinet, all lord lieutenants expected to be informed in advance of the chief secretary's directives. Lord lieutenants were determined, moreover, to maintain their prerogatives in the area of appointments at the local level. Chief among these was the appointment of justices of the peace (there were approximately fifty-five hundred serving at a given time) and the deputy lord lieutenants of the thirty-two counties. The lord lieutenant also expected to control the appointment of his own staff. Of some forty staff positions, army officers made up the largest bloc, holding positions as aides de camp or gentlemen-in-waiting. Younger sons of great landlords from the country received appointments at nominal salaries as masters of the horse, comptrollers, stewards, or ushers. Prominent Dublin doctors and clergymen served as surgeons and chaplains to the household. The position of private secretary to the lord lieutenant was the most lucrative at over eight hundred pounds per annum in salary, and it often led to a permanent position at the head of a department in the bureaucracy.

The main Irish criterion for evaluating a lord lieutenant, however, was his largesse, not his appointments. As the highest paid official in

2. Joseph O'Brien, *Dublin: City in Distress* (Berkeley: University of California Press, 1983).

Ireland, earning some twenty thousand pounds per year, the lord lieutenant traditionally spent his entire annual salary in Ireland. The real measure of a lord lieutenant's performance, therefore, was the amount of money he spent beyond his salary. The account books of Lord Aberdeen, the most generous lord lieutenant of the period, show how he expended his salary and personal money.[3] In 1906 his salary was approximately £20,500. Aberdeen's estimate of his potential expenses was approximately £18,000:

Food	£6,486	The Castle season	
Wine and spirits	822	Music and entertainment	414
Ales	83	Viceregal entertainment	120
Beer	197	Charity	1,311
Minerals	100	Punchestown races	187
Cigarettes	20	Stables	3,733
Wages and travel;		Motorcar	736
expenses for staff	3,164	Gardens	773
	£10,872		£7,274

When his actual expenses were tallied, the figures were as follows:

Castle season	£7,800	Travel expenses	1,190
Punchestown	550	Stables	3,733
King's birthday dinner	100	Cars for touring	660
Tour of western Ireland	660	Garden	773
Cricket Week	400	Charity: donations and	
Horse Show Week	350	subscriptions	1,478
Viceregal lodge:		Personal gifts	932
ordinary expenses	7,838	Linen and service	532
			£26,996

Despite the value of a lord lieutenant's expenditure to the economy of Dublin, many observers thought the position should be abolished. Critics of the lord lieutenancy pointed out that Irish taxpayers paid over five thousand pounds each year to make up the difference between the lord lieutenant's twenty-thousand-pound salary and his staff's salaries of fifteen thousand pounds and the return of this money to the

3. Haddo House, Aberdeen, Tarves, Scotland, Aberdeen Papers, H.H. Ms. 1/41, Account Books.

local merchants.[4] In addition, many of the Irish felt a sense of grievance because the lord lieutenant, by law, could never be a Catholic.[5] The studied indifference of Dubliners when each lord lieutenant departed at the end of his tenure was, perhaps, the true indication of how the bulk of the population felt about the position, if not the man.

The Chief Secretary. The office of chief secretary was a powerful position that lured ambitious men who saw in Ireland a place to display both political acumen and administrative skill. A variety of other aims also motivated the ten politicians, six Liberals and four Conservatives, who accepted the appointment between 1892 and 1921. A prime minister might ask a follower to take the office out of personal loyalty. Family connection was sometimes an important factor. A prime minister could also use the chief secretaryship to reward a man who had rendered services in another area of government. The salary, forty-five hundred pounds, was attractive; the chief secretary's lodge in Phoenix Park was comfortable.

The chief secretaryship also carried risks. The position could make or break a reputation. Success in Ireland was a sign of ability that could be recognized with a subsequent appointment to a higher position. Failure, on the other hand, could drive a chief secretary from public life. Physical and mental exhaustion was an occupational hazard. Because assassination was a real threat, police bodyguards always accompanied the chief secretary. At one time, revolutionaries practiced military maneuvers beneath his office windows; another time, the office was dynamited.

The chief secretary had two major tasks. One was developing legislation for Ireland; the other was directing the administration of services in the country. Both tasks were challenging because many chief secretaries came to Ireland ignorant of its rousing public life. After 1892, land reform, home rule, education, and social welfare were the most difficult issues that required legislation. After 1916, the central problem was crushing out revolution. Throughout the period, the main challenge of the office grew out of the use of existing laws pertaining to

4. Jeremiah MacVeagh, *Home Rule in a Nutshell,* 4th ed., revised (Dublin: Sealy, Bryers & Walker, 1912).

5. O'Brien, *Dublin Castle and the Irish People,* p. 78.

law and order. The chief secretary could either enforce or suspend the Coercion Acts, and he could either encourage or restrain the law officers in prosecuting people who were suspected of threatening order.[6] For Nationalists, suspension of the Coercion Acts, upholding of the rights of the accused, and forbearance among the law officers were signs of statesmanship. For Unionists, implementation of the Coercion Acts and vigorous prosecutions were signs that a chief secretary was strong enough to resist intimidation by Nationalist politicians.

The chief secretary's other task was directing the administration of services. His challenge in this area was twofold: he had to learn how the bureaucracy functioned, and he had to establish a working relationship with his subordinates. Few chief secretaries, however, could master the intricacies of some thirty Irish departments (Table 1). Each had its own organization and method of operation. Moreover, the chief secretary's ability to make policy varied widely from department to department.

Eleven departments were directly controlled by the chief secretary. Eleven others were under his partial control, although in two of these he was an ex officio member. The three education departments effectively repudiated his administrative authority. In addition to the Irish departments, there were by 1912 thirteen other departments in Ireland that were branches of British departments. These were completely beyond his control. The supreme court's administrative offices, which were located about a mile north of Dublin Castle at the Four Courts, were also outside the chief secretary's jurisdiction.

The Chief Secretary's Office was at the center of the bureaucracy in Dublin Castle, although the offices of some Irish departments were located elsewhere in the city.[7] Most departments conducted their business with the Irish executive through one of the Chief Secretary's Office's three major divisions: Finance, Administration, and Judicial. Of the three, Finance was first among equals. It reviewed financial estimates before forwarding them to the Treasury Office in London,

6. The Coercion Acts permitted trial by two magistrates (instead of trial by jury), changes of venue, and indefinite prison terms for persons who refused to give evidence to investigatory tribunals convened in Dublin Castle.

7. Kieran Flanagan, "The Chief Secretary's Office, 1853–1914: a bureaucratic enigma," *Irish Historical Studies,* XXIV, no. 94 (Nov. 1984): 197–225.

Table 1. Irish Administrative Departments in 1914

Departments under the immediate control of the executive government

Inspectors of Lunatics (and the Dundrum Asylum)
Registrar-General
Dublin Metropolitan Police
Royal Irish Constabulary
General Prisons Board
Reformatory and Industrial Schools
Registrar of Petty Sessions Clerks
Loan Fund Board
Office of Arms
Resident Magistrates
Crown Solicitors
Chief Secretary's Office

Departments of which the chief secretary was president but that were not under the immediate direction of the Chief Secretary's Office

Local Government Board
Department of Agriculture and Technical Instruction
Congested Districts Board

Educational departments only partially controlled by the Irish government

Commissioners of National Education
Commissioners of Intermediate Education
Commissioners of Education (Endowed Schools)

Noneducational departments only partially controlled by the Irish government

Commissioners of Charitable Donations and Bequests
Public Record Office
Land Commission
National Gallery
Clerks of the Crown and Peace

United Kingdom departments functioning in Ireland

Admiralty
Customs and Excise
Exchequer and Audit
Friendly Societies Register
Home Office
Inland Revenue
Ordinance Survey
Post Office
Stationery Office

Table 1 continued

Board of Trade
War Office
Departments under the Treasury
Commissioners of National Health Insurance
Treasury Remembrancer's Office

Adapted from: Chief Secretary for Ireland, *Memorandum as to the organization and staff of the Chief Secretary's Office and other Departments connected with the Irish Government* (Dublin: HMSO, 1913).

which had ultimate authority over the estimates. The Judicial Division managed business that pertained to law and order. It maintained contact with the attorney-general, the heads of the Dublin Metropolitan Police and the Royal Irish Constabulary, the local magistracy, prisons, and reformatory schools. The education departments also communicated with the Irish executive through this division. The Administrative Division conducted all correspondence with English departments, although the Judicial Division corresponded directly with the Army Council and Admiralty because police business might be involved. The Administrative Division also managed personnel matters related to both paid and unpaid appointments. There were two minor divisions in the Chief Secretary's Office: the Convicts Division and the Registry Department. The former reviewed petitions from prisoners, and the latter recorded all of the office's correspondence. Because the chief secretary spent most of his time in London, the under secretary, who was the highest-ranking civil servant in Ireland, supervised the day-to-day operation of the office.

The Lord Chancellor and the Law Officers. The lord chancellor, the attorney-general, and the solicitor-general were also part of the Irish executive. All three were political appointees who changed with a change in government. A new prime minister, usually acting in concert with the chief secretary or lord lieutenant, selected the lord chancellor, who then offered his advice on the selection of the two law officers. Throughout this process the prime minister's options were restricted by tradition. These positions were always given to members of the prime minister's party or to his Irish political allies, and prior service as a law officer was a prerequisite for the lord chancellorship. When he appointed the attorney-general and solicitor-general, the prime minister was bound by the same considerations. The attorney-general had a right to return to the Law Office in Dublin Castle if he desired; the previous solicitor-general had the same right. Should the attorney-general decide not to return to the Castle, the position normally went to a former solicitor-general. The selection process could then be extended through the three sergeants-at-law, who were considered to be next in the line of succession. If no one with prior experience pressed his claim, or if the sergeants were not acceptable, political service to the party was used as a criterion for selecting candidates.

Because the law officers had to be present in the House of Commons to explain the legal aspects of Irish administration, it was also helpful if a candidate for the Law Office had experience in Parliament. The law officers usually represented Irish constituencies, although the pattern of representation in Ireland after 1886 greatly restricted their choice of seats. Unionist lawyers had a wider field than the Liberals. A safe seat could be found for them in the Unionist political strongholds in Ulster, but safe seats for Unionists in the south were limited to the two seats for Trinity College and (for a time) the St. Stephen's Green and South County Dublin seats. The Nationalists in the Irish Parliamentary party held eighty-five of the one hundred three Irish seats, including all of the other seats in the west and south. Liberals had to contest the Dublin seats or a seat in Ulster. Sometimes, the Nationalist candidate would stand aside in the North Louth constituency in order to permit the election of a law officer from the Liberal party.

The lord chancellor, attorney-general, and solicitor-general had several tasks. Specifically, the lord chancellor served as one of the appeals justices on the supreme court and as a judge in the Chancery Division (see Tables 4 and 5). He advised the lord lieutenant and chief secretary on all appointments to the Law Office, the county courts, and the supreme court, including the court's administrative staff. His knowledge of men and affairs in the country was also useful in determining local appointments, from justices of the peace and resident magistrates to the deputy lord lieutenants of the counties. The attorney-general was the chief law-enforcement officer in the administration. The solicitor-general assisted him and reviewed the legal aspects of matters that affected the various departments. The chief crown solicitor, a civil servant who, like the under secretary, was not a member of the executive, handled day-to-day questions from the justices of the peace and resident magistrates. In times of emergency, a law adviser could be appointed to the Law Office.

The law officers' political and administrative influence enhanced their position at the top of their profession. All of them were elected as benchers of the King's Inns, an inner circle of eighty of the most prominent Irish barristers. Their salaries were high: the lord chancellor received eight thousand pounds per annum, reduced in 1897 to six thousand; the attorney-general, five thousand; and the solicitor-general, twenty-five hundred. Furthermore, service to the government as lord chancellor or as a law officer virtually guaranteed promotion to the Supreme Court of Judicature in Ireland, should a vacancy occur while their government was in power. Fifteen of the eighteen individuals who served as law officers between 1892 and 1921 advanced to the supreme court, and one Irish attorney-general was appointed to a law lordship in the House of Lords. Because prior political service was a prerequisite for an appointment to the Law Office, Irish law officers were open to the charge that they were place hunters who were interested only in the spoils of office. Critics of this method of advancement to the bench claimed that Irish justices could not divorce themselves from their earlier experiences when, in private practice or as law officers, they had prosecuted individuals who might someday stand before them in court.

The Bureaucracy

The Bureaucratic Elite

The highest-ranking civil servants in Ireland were the heads of the administrative departments and the officials who occupied positions that were immediately subordinate to the department head. About 75 officials occupied these positions at any given time between 1892 and 1921. They may properly be called the bureaucratic elite. About 185 individuals were appointed to the highest-ranking positions during this period. The departments, the elite positions, and the number of officials who served in them between August 1892 and December 1921 are provided in Table 2.

As the group of officials who occupied the top positions in 1892 was slowly supplanted by new officials by 1921, the bureaucratic elite was transformed. Profound changes took place in both the religious affiliation and the political orientation of the members of the bureaucratic elite. The subsequent chapters of this book describe in detail how these transformations occurred. In broad outline, in 1892 every Irish department head, save three, was a Protestant. In 1922, after a war for independence, when the civil service was about to be divided between the Irish Free State and the government in Northern Ireland, Catholics and Protestants were serving in equal numbers as department heads. The number of Catholics increases substantially when key subordinate positions in the elite are added to the equation. Similarly, there was a significant change in the political orientation of the bureaucratic elite. Nationalists maintained that in 1892, all of the departments, save two, were directed by officials who were at least sympathetic to the Unionists and that only one home ruler was at the head of a department. When the Nationalists in Sinn Fein inherited the largest part of the Irish bureaucracy from the British in 1922, none of the department heads or their immediate subordinates was associated politically with Sinn Fein. Nevertheless, when the members of the bureaucratic elite were given a choice of where they would like to serve, forty-two of the forty-nine department heads transferred to the Free State. Five members of the elite assumed positions in departments in Northern Ireland. Ten more transferred to the imperial service.

The department heads and their chief subordinates were responsible for implementing procedures to put legislative and administrative policy into effect. To ensure the successful day-to-day administration of public services, the chief secretary had to give the department heads freedom to make decisions on how to conduct departmental policy and manage office procedure. He could not be overbearing. Should a zealous chief secretary, who was a transient, try to exercise his authority in an aggressive or insensitive manner, a department head, who was a permanent official, sent him a few large boxes of correspondence from the circumlocution files for attention and comment. Most chief secretaries recoiled from this work and, upon due reflection, asked instead to be kept generally apprised of a department's affairs through the under secretary.

Table 2. Bureaucratic Elite, August 1892 to December 1921

Department	*Position (Number of officials)*
Department of Agriculture and Technical Instruction	Vice president (3) Secretary (1) Assistant secretary (4) Deputy assistant secretary (1)
Board of Trade	Principal district officer (4) Labor Exchange and Unemployment Insurance, divisional officer for Ireland (1) Ministry of Labor, secretary (1) Ministry of Transportation, director-general (1)
Board of Works	Chairman (4) Three commissioners (5) Secretary (4) Assistant secretary (1)
Charitable Donations and Bequests	Two joint secretaries (6)
Chief Crown Solicitor	Chief crown solicitor (2)
Chief Secretary's Office	Under secretary (9) Assistant under secretary (8)
Commissioners of Education	Secretary (3)
Congested Districts Board	Secretary (4) Assistant secretary (4) Chief inspector (1)
Dublin Metropolitan Police	Chief commissioner (5) Assistant commissioner (4) Second assistant commissioner (1)
General Post Office	Secretary (4)
General Prisons Board	Chairman (3) Vice-chairman (2) Secretary (2) Inspector (6) Medical member (4)
General Registrar Office	Registrar-general (3) Assistant registrar-general (4)
General Valuation Office, Boundary Survey	Commissioner (3)
Intermediate Education Board	Two assistant commissioners (5)
Irish Lights Commission	Secretary (3)

Table 2 continued

Land Commission	Three commissioners (5) Secretary (3) Assistant secretary (4) Public trustee (1)
Local Government Board	Vice president (3) Three commissioners (9) Secretary (3)
National Education	Resident commissioner (3) Secretary (7)
National Health Insurance	Chairman (1) Deputy chairman (1) Two commissioners (2) Secretary (1) Assistant secretary (1)
Office of Arms	Ulster king of arms (2) Athlone pursuivant of arms (4)
Office of Fisheries	Inspector (3)
Office of the Inspectors of Lunatic Asylums	Resident physician and governor, Criminal Lunatic Asylum, Dundrum (2) Inspector (4)
Public Loan Fund Board	Secretary (1)
Public Record Office	Deputy keeper (4)
Reformatory and Industrial Schools	Inspector (4)
Registrar of Petty Sessions Clerks Office	Registrar (2)
Registry of Friendly Societies and Trade Unions, Building and Cooperative Societies	Assistant registrar (2)
Royal Irish Constabulary	Inspector-general (3) Assistant inspector-general (10) Deputy inspector-general (5)
Treasury Remembrancer's Office	Treasury remembrancer (4)
The National Library The National Gallery The National Museum	Directors (6)

Note: Approximately 185 individuals served in the bureaucratic elite during the period 1892 to 1921. A total of 216 officials who served in these positions is listed. The difference is due to the fact that, over time, some individuals occupied more than one position.

A department head had to have confidence in his staff, and his staff had to follow his lead. This relationship depended on a department head's ability to understand the work at hand and on his leadership skills. Irish department heads were qualified on the first point. A review of the education and professional training of eighty-five members of the bureaucratic elite, including virtually every department head, reveals that they possessed the appropriate credentials in, for example, medicine, engineering, military science, and pedagogy. The officials who performed strictly administrative duties were trained in the classics or law. (A public administration curriculum did not appear in Irish universities until late in the 1920s.) The leading bureaucrats held degrees from a number of institutions. Of the eighty-five officials under review, twenty-one graduated from Trinity College, Dublin. Nine graduated from one of the Queen's Colleges: five from the Royal University in Dublin, and two each from the Queen's College in Galway and Belfast. Three graduated from the National University after it was founded in 1908. Ten received degrees from Oxford, three from Cambridge, four from Edinburgh, and two from London University. Five had degrees from universities on the Continent. Eleven others held degrees, but the universities that they attended have not been identified. Four received private tutoring, and one was educated in a seminary. Four completed their education at small Catholic colleges in the country. Sixteen had been called to the bar; fifteen others were solicitors. Nineteen held master's degrees or other advanced degrees and certificates.

The second point, leadership, depended on the department head's ability to win the confidence of subordinates and to nurture ties of personal loyalty. The Irish department heads maintained, therefore, that they were in the best position to make recommendations to the chief secretary on the appointment and promotion of key staff members. Depending on a particular department's rules, its head could usually nominate candidates for positions directly, particularly in the case of an immediate subordinate. A department head could also use a limited competition examination, which restricted the number of candidates to those who had the prerequisites to qualify to take the examination, and which included an interview with the department head as part of the examination. Of 1,611 principal positions in the Irish administration, 622, or 39 percent, were made by direct nomination, and 766, or 48 percent, were made after qualifying examinations. The remaining 219, or 13 percent, were made after open competition examinations that admitted all candidates.[8] Thus, over time and given the opportunity provided by retirements and resignations, a department head could make a profound change in his office's character that could last for years after his own retirement.

The bureaucratic elite's place in the public eye rounds out the profile of these officials. As individuals, they do not reflect Dublin Castle's popular image of being as aloof as the statue of Blind Justice that straddled the Castle gates with her scales unbalanced and her back turned against the city. Perhaps Sir James Dougherty, the assistant under secretary between 1895 and 1908 and the under secretary for Ireland between 1908 and 1914, spoke for all department heads when he testified in 1913 before the Royal Commission on the Civil Service. Dougherty explained to the chairman of the commission, Antony MacDonnell, who had been under secretary for Ireland between 1902 and 1908, that in Ireland "we have a quasi-separate Government, and that the people of Ireland look to what they call 'The Castle,' despised as it is by many, for advice and guidance, and, above all, they make it the repository of their complaints." "You know, I am sure, my Lord," he continued, "that a great deal of time of the Under-Secretary is taken up in interviewing people who come from all parts of the country, not only those connected with the public departments, but others who have a right to be heard."[9] The stereotype of the unresponsive bureaucrat was further undermined by the obituary writers of the *Freeman's Journal, Irish Times, Belfast News-Letter,* and *London Times.* Their notices of deceased bureaucrats were always kind, and they genuinely saluted those officials who were considerate, efficient, and impartial.

The leading officials and their families were socially prominent people. They were featured by the Irish society magazines, dined with the lord lieutenant at his residence or at the Castle, and received honors

8. G. F. H. Berkeley, "The Present System of Government in Ireland," in J. H. Morgan, ed., *Home Rule Problems* (London: P. S. King & Son, 1911), p. 47.

9. Great Britain, Parliamentary Papers, 1914, Vol. XVI, *Royal Commission on Civil Service, Second Appendix to Fourth Report of the Commissioners,* Minutes of Evidence, testimony of James Daugherty, pp. 185–86.

from the crown. Salaries for department heads and their immediate subordinates were handsome, ranging from approximately seven hundred to twelve hundred pounds. Most of the leading officials lived in Dublin, although some lived in the pleasant suburbs to the north and south of the city. The most important department heads were neighbors of the law officers and judges who resided on fashionable Fitzwilliam Square or Merrion Square. Likewise, they belonged to the same clubs: Unionists joined a Masonic lodge and the Kildare Street Club; Nationalists joined a sodality and the Stephen's Green Club. Family connections bound members of the elite even closer, although charges of nepotism were rare.

Their outside interests, avocations, and professional contributions add a final detail to the group's portrait. Yachting, golf, and tennis seem to have been the preferred sports. Beyond that, individuals were engaged in all sorts of pastimes, from biking to motoring, angling to swimming, croquet to rugby. Several of the officials followed intellectual pursuits. There were classical scholars, historians, and supporters of the arts. Others published works related to their official duties. Statistical analysis in scientific journals and technical reports were the favored genres.

The Professional Staff

The second echelon of officials occupied positions that required professional training or special skills. The professional staff positions might typically include a department's inspectorate and its assistant inspectors, principal district officers, solicitors, legal advisers, registrars, or auditors.[10] At a given time, there were approximately 650 civil servants in these positions. Approximately 330 of them served in the departments under full or partial control of the chief secretary. Some 250 more served in either the Royal Irish Constabulary or the Dublin

10. The figures on the professional staff officers are extrapolated from *Government Departments Ireland, Historical Notes,* which was prepared in 1913 for the Royal Commission on the Civil Service by the Chief Secretary's Office. A copy is in the National Library of Ireland: Ir 350 C9. The document gives the number of officials and the position titles noted in Table 1. The Dublin Metropolitan Police had a complement of 1,279 men in various ranks; the Royal Irish Constabulary had 232 officers and 10,483 men in various ranks.

Metropolitan Police. Another 75 served in departments that were beyond the chief secretary's control.

Enough information is available about individuals in this category to draw some conclusions about them as a group. Professional staff officers shared one characteristic. Each of them had to come to the attention of the head of the department for appointment or promotion. A random check of the career paths of some two hundred of these officials shows that they either were directly recruited into the civil service from businesses or entered the system at a high level through a limited competition examination.[11] Less than 10 percent worked their way up through the clerical ranks to be in a position to take the limited competition examination for promotion. However, once an official joined the professional ranks, he—or she, as this group includes about a half-dozen women who were inspectors—often moved from department to department in order to assume a higher position.

A review of the career paths of the professional staff members of three departments—the Department of Agriculture and Technical Instruction, the Intermediate Education Office, and the National Health Insurance Commission—bears out the generalizations on recruitment. When the Department of Agriculture and Technical Instruction was founded in 1900, the new vice president of the department spent eighteen months personally recruiting fifteen professional staff officials. In an effort to find the best qualified candidates, he canvassed the University of Chicago, state agencies in Kentucky, and schools, colleges, and universities across the United Kingdom. He sought businessmen from private industry and commercial farmers. Only one of his eventual selections for a professional staff position had prior experience as a civil service clerk. The Intermediate Education Office can serve as another example. Under the direction of two assistant commissioners, the

11. This passage is based on the following government publications: Great Britain, Accounts and Papers: 1912–1913, Eighth Volume, *Civil Service and Revenue Departments, 1912–1913,* Vol. LVI, no. 454, "Return setting forth the Name, Age, Date of Appointment, Salary, Address at Time of Appointment, and Occupation for the Five Years preceding the Appointment, of each person appointed without Competitive Examination to any position in the Public Service during the period from the 29th day of June 1895 to the 5th day of December, 1905, with an Annual Salary of £100 and upwards, specifying separately the Appointments for England, Wales, Scotland, and Ireland"; no. 455, "Similar Return from the 5th day of December, 1905"; no. 528, "Similar Return from the 27th day of February, 1912."

office's inspectorate of six officials was largely recruited from outside the civil service in 1909. Of the six, two had teaching experience in intermediate schools and two in universities. The fifth had been an inspector of national schools and the sixth an examiner for the Irish Intermediate Education Board. The National Health Insurance Commission provides the third example. After its founding late in 1911, the chairman of the commission selected its professional staff in 1912. Of six inspectors, four came from outside the civil service, one had been a clerk in the civil service, and one had been a professional staff officer in the Department of Agriculture and Technical Instruction. Eighteen assistant inspectors were also appointed. Two had prior experience in the civil service, but the others had such diverse backgrounds as Gaelic League organizer, private secretary to the lord mayor of Dublin, *Freeman's Journal* employee, and teacher. Two others had been employees of insurance companies and five more worked for voluntary associations. Two small Irish departments, the General Register Office and the Land Registry, seem to be the only departments in Ireland that promoted professional staff members almost exclusively from their own ranks.

It is impossible to recover the religious and political characteristics of all professional staff officers. Civil service documents did not record any official's church affiliation, and the Treasury's long-standing, and enforced, regulation prohibiting public political activity by civil servants was effective.[12] There is, however, evidence in Catholic and Nationalist periodicals, such as the *Leader* and the *Irish Catholic,* that indicates that the professional staff officers in some departments were mostly Protestants. The *Leader* took an interest in the appointment of Catholic and Nationalist officials—the two variables were synonymous for this periodical—to professional staff positions. "Light on the Local Government Board," an article that appeared in January 1907, is typical of the *Leader's* investigatory reports.[13] Based on statistics compiled by the Catholic Defense Society, the *Leader* noted that of the nominated salaried posts in the board's office, Protestants held thirty-four and

12. Royal Commission on Civil Service, *Fourth Report,* "Minutes of Evidence," testimony of Sir James B. Dougherty, pp. 181–190, and testimony of William Bailey, p. 310.

13. *Leader,* Jan. 12, 1907.

Catholics held thirteen. The Protestant officials earned £22,225 compared to £7,550 for the Catholic officials. In the Board of Works, sixty-six Protestant officials earned £23,615, and forty-seven Catholic officials—none was able to reach the professional ranks—earned £9,490. Another typical article, "Bigotry in the Prison Service," reported that the four largest prisons were governed by Protestant officials and that only one of these had a Catholic serving as deputy-governor. Of the ten next largest prisons, seven had Protestant governors. In the third echelon in the prisons system, three of four governors were Protestants.[14] The principal problem that militated against the promotion of Catholic Irishmen and Irishwomen was the attitude of the Protestant department heads who acted as "croupiers for their religion." "In the past," the *Leader's* reporter observed, "the Irish were treated as nothing." "At present," he continued, referring to some new department heads,

> the spirit of serfdom and indifference which distinguished the older generation does still exercise a depressing influence over the younger men. There is a tendency with them to slip into the old groove. The great majority of the superior positions being in the hands of the anti-Irish, there is little encouragement to Irishmen, especially Catholics, to work for anything. The scepter of authority is wielded by those people as if they appeared to be convinced that the Irish are really an inferior breed, and, therefore, not supposed to look above their present level.[15]

The professional staff officers enjoyed financial security in a depressed Irish economy. They received substantial salaries, earning between four hundred and one thousand pounds per annum. A department's chief inspector, inspectors, and solicitors might earn as much as, or more than, a minor department's assistant secretary or secretary. As a group, the professionals prospered. A random check of thirty wills that went into probate reveals that seventeen officials left more than twenty-five hundred pounds to heirs, and that five others left between one thousand and twenty-five hundred pounds. Those at the top end of the salary scale maintained a life-style that was similar to their department chiefs'. They lived in suburban or city homes, held memberships in clubs, and enjoyed social and professional prominence.

14. Ibid., Mar. 11, 1905.
15. Ibid.

Competent service warranted nomination from the chief secretary for honors or induction into the Imperial Service Order or Order of the British Empire. Finally, professional staff officers could advance further in the civil service. Twenty-five members of the bureaucratic elite were promoted from the professional ranks.

The Rank and File

Approximately four thousand civil servants served in the Irish departments and some twenty-three thousand civil servants, mostly post office employees, served in the Irish branches of the English departments. Table 3 gives a list, for 1911, of the number of officials in each department.

The civil service offered an attractive career. The entry level salary for clerks was set at about one hundred pounds. A newly appointed Irish official's salary was at the national average for comparable positions in business, although because of a cost of living adjustment, Irish civil servants earned about 15 to 20 percent less than their counterparts in England.

Hundreds of Irish men and women hoped to join the civil service each year, but only a small percentage succeeded. For example, in 1908 when the Labor Exchanges were established, thirteen thousand persons in England and Ireland applied for two hundred positions. About thirty of these positions were in Ireland. In 1912, when the National Health Insurance Commission was established, over ninety thousand persons applied for thirty-seven hundred positions. About one hundred of these positions were in Ireland. Ireland's largest departments added only about ten new officials annually. By 1912 many departments in both England and Ireland stopped advertising for candidates because vacancies were so rare. The government's statistical tables on pensions indicate that Irish civil servants held fast to their positions until they reached the retirement age of sixty-seven or until ill health forced them to retire.[16] There was, however, some mobility within the system. Each year, hundreds of officials took open competition examinations for pro-

16. Great Britain, Accounts and Papers: 1912–1913, Eighth Volume, *Civil Service and Revenue Departments, 1912–1913,* Vol. LVI, no. 297, "Appendix to the Estimate for Civil Services, Class 6, pp. 76–86, Vote 1, containing a List of Superannuation and Retired Allowances payable on the 30th November, 1911."

Table 3. Officials Employed on March 31, 1911

Department	*(a) Established*	*(b) Unestablished*	*(c) Total*	*(d) No. making £160/yr or more*
Ireland				
Agricultural and Technical Instruction Dept.	285	435	720	236
Charitable Donations and Bequests Office	5	1	6	3
Chief Secretary's Office	34	15	49	21
Congested Districts Board	15	276	291	54
Crown Solicitors (including Treasury Solicitor and staff)	5	54	59	38
Deeds, Registry	68	28	96	34
Dublin Metropolitan Police	21	2	23	16
Dundrum Lunatic Asylum	47	6	53	4
Endowed Schools Commissioner	2	—	2	2
Land Commission (including Estates Commissioners)	400	286	686	197
Land Registry	23	62	85	18
Local Government Board	182	92	274	108
Lord Lieutenant's Household	1	18	19	10
Lunatics, Inspectors of	4	5	9	5
National Education Commissioners	218	50	268	118
National Gallery	4	12	16	2
Office of Arms	2	5	7	3
Prisons Board	524	84	608	42
Public Record Office	31	41	72	10
Reformatory and Industrial Schools	7	3	10	4
Registrar-General	31	14	45	11
Royal Irish Constabulary	25	2	27	13
Supreme Court of Judicature	166	65	231	118
Teachers' Pension Office	5	1	6	4
Treasury Remembrancer's Office	9	2	11	6
Valuation Office	94	84	178	64
Works (Public) Office	138	53	191	99
Total	2,346	1,696	4,042	1,240
English Branches				
Admiralty	14	8	22	15
Customs and Excise	800	76	876	413

Table 3 continued

Exchequer and Audits	15	—	15	12
Friendly Societies Registry	1	—	1	1
Home Office	6	4	10	6
Inland Revenue	141	104	245	66
Ordinance Survey	218	342	560	12
Post Office	5,922	14,519	20,441	451
Stationery Office	9	9	18	5
Trade, Board of	22	53	75	20
War Office	48	855	903	38
Woods and Forest	8	6	14	5
Total	7,204	15,976	23,180	1,008
Grand Total	9,550	17,672	27,222	2,248

Note: This list was prepared by the Treasury Office for presentation to the House of Commons on December 14, 1911. It is located in the *Parliamentary Papers,* 1912–13, Vol. 56, H. C. Paper 104. The list excludes part-time and temporary employees.

motion to higher-paying positions and tried to transfer from one department to another to further their careers.

Most Irish officials entered the civil service through the open competition examinations for second-division clerkships. About half of the candidates for examination came from rural areas. If they succeeded, the new clerks took up positions in the capital cities or other urban centers that contained branch offices of larger departments. Special rooming houses, social organizations, and friendly societies eased the transition from country to city. Women candidates took separate examinations from their male counterparts, even if they eventually assumed analogous positions, such as telegraphist or typist. Women were not permitted to compete for all positions. Certain clerkships, for example, had a five-foot height requirement that was put in place ostensibly to make sure that a clerk was tall enough to conduct business across a counter.

Second-division, or class II, candidates were usually graduates of intermediate schools. When Irish intermediate education was reformed in 1878, two years after the civil service adopted the use of competitive examinations, the school examinations were designed on the model of the civil service examinations. Many who supported the education reform in Ireland believed that successful young scholars would find useful careers in the bureaucracy.[17] Theoretically, Irish candidates competed on the examinations on an equal footing with their British and Scottish counterparts. However, the members of the Royal Commission found that both Irish and English intermediate schools lagged behind Scottish intermediate schools in preparing candidates for the civil service. The inequality among the intermediate systems, the commissioners believed, prevented the attainment of the ideal: a civil service that was equally open to qualified candidates from every class and from every locality. Among Irish candidates, graduates of Irish Christian Brothers schools, which were not included in the Irish educational reform, often achieved the highest scores on the competitive examinations.[18]

Regardless of who taught them, Irish Catholics soon began to dominate the rank and file positions in the civil service.[19] The *Leader* used statistics on this point to throw the religious and political imbalances in the professional staff positions and among the members of the bureaucratic elite into stark relief. For example, when twelve Protestants were about to be appointed as postmasters in 1903, the *Leader* observed that the positions should be filled by promoting officials from the Sorters Department, which was 90 percent Catholic.[20] The *Leader* concluded that the use of open competition examinations should be extended throughout the civil service because that was the only practical and fair method to permit Catholic officials to advance to the higher-level positions in the bureaucracy.

First-division, or class I, candidates for examination usually had attended a residential public school or a large urban day school. Those

17. Those who connected intermediate education reform to the civil service include Henry Hennessy, F.R.S., *On Freedom of Education* (Dublin: Hodges, Foster, and Figgis, 1878); Rev. Robert Rice, *The Irish Intermediate Education Act* (Dublin: Hodges, Foster, and Figgis, 1878); Lord Randolph Churchill, *Intermediate Education in Ireland: A Letter to Sir J. Bernard Burke* (Dublin: Hodges, Foster, and Figgis, 1878); "Educationist," *The Irish Intermediate Education Act of 1878* (Dublin: Ponsonby, 1878).

18. S. O. Mathuna, "The Christian Brothers and the Civil Service," *Administration,* 3, no. 2–3, (1955): 69–74.

19. James Lowry Whittle, *Freedom of Education: What It Means* (Dublin: Hodges, Smith and Co., 1866), indicated that Catholics had achieved a majority of 13,022 civil service positions to 8,520 positions for Protestants. He does not give a source for this statistic.

20. *Leader,* Nov. 28, 1903.

who succeeded on the class I examinations were virtually all university graduates: 455 of 464 class I candidates for examination between 1906 and 1910 held degrees.[21] It was difficult, although not impossible, for class II officials to advance to class I because of the competition they faced from university graduates. Oxford University graduates may have had an advantage over all candidates because Oxford's Literae Humaniores curriculum covered every subject (except political economy and history) on the examination. Cambridge's classical and mathematical tripos curriculums covered half of the examination. Of 473 successful candidates with university degrees, Oxford had 247, Cambridge had 142, and other English universities had 8. Scottish universities had 30 successful candidates. Trinity College, Dublin, had 23 successful candidates. The Royal University and the National University had a total of 14. The remainder held degrees from other European universities.

Members of the Royal Commission on the Civil Service asked S. M. Leathes, who held the position of first civil service commissioner, about the small percentage of successful candidates from Irish universities, which could not be explained by the difference in populations. Leathes testified that he had visited Ireland and Scotland, but no one in the Scottish or Irish universities objected to the examinations. Later, the commissioners took evidence from several Irish officials, including Eoin MacNeill, a former Irish civil servant who had become a professor at the National University, about the low status of Irish history and the Irish language—in terms of points awarded—on the examinations. The Irish officials indicated that knowledge of the Irish language was an obvious asset for a prospective civil servant whose duties might extend to the west of Ireland, where some 550,000 persons spoke Irish as a first language.[22]

The exercise of patronage in the lower ranks of the civil service was one of the Royal Commission's central concerns. The commissioners learned from Leathes that in some departments a letter from a member of Parliament was a passport to an appointment. He testified that de-

21. *Fourth Report of the Civil Service Commissioners,* p. 30. See also, Minutes of Evidence, Testimony of S. M. Leathes, pp. 17–18, and Appendix 11, pp. 125–133, for tables of schools and universities attended by successful division I candidates.

22. *Second Appendix to Fourth Report of the Commissioners,* Minutes of Evidence, testimony of John MacNeill, pp. 215–22.

partment heads usually selected candidates for appointment or promotion from a select list of individuals who had proved themselves to be qualified for the position. He admitted that department heads might not be impartial in making these appointments and promotions.[23] The commissioners also heard testimony on the exercise of patronage from F. H. Norman, a representative of the Association of Clerks in the Second Division. He declared that the appointment of favorites over the heads of qualified candidates resulted in inefficiency and increased costs. Although favorites who received appointments might be qualified, Norman maintained that these sorts of appointments demoralized the other clerks.[24] Norman then submitted a written statement detailing allegations of patronage in eighteen departments.[25] Five of his instances involved Irish offices. Norman objected to the employment of temporary clerks instead of second-division clerks in the Local Government Board; he also charged that there had been patronage abuses at high levels in the Board of Public Works, the General Register Office, and the Land Commission. The Land Commission allegation implied nepotism.

The commission took evidence on these allegations from Irish department heads in February 1913, but the commissioners were unable to substantiate Norman's charges. The department heads refused to comment on affairs that took place in their offices before they were in charge. Some of them indicated, however, that Treasury regulations had created a shortage of first-division clerks in the Irish system and that, as a result, second-division clerks often performed administrative tasks that might normally be undertaken by higher-ranking officials. They maintained that the hard work of second-division clerks had potential rewards, including a chance of advancement to the first division. Irish department heads also declared that when the opportunity to promote arose, a personal interview was the best way for them to judge

23. *Appendix to First Report of the Commissioners,* Minutes of Evidence, testimony of S. M. Leathes, pp. 32–34. See also *Fourth Report of the Commissioners,* Chapter VIII, sections 7–8, "Measures for bringing merit to notice," and "Conditions of Ministerial responsibility for promotion," p. 58.

24. *Appendix to Second Report of the Commissioners,* Minutes of Evidence, testimony of Frederick Harwood Norman, pp. 16–19, 21.

25. *Appendix V to Minutes of Evidence of Second Report*; see p. 486 for "Patronage in Irish Offices."

a candidate's character and potential to conduct professional responsibilities. They had a good reason for endorsing this technique. The eighteen members of the bureaucratic elite who testified all had been directly appointed to their positions.[26] Indeed, the other representatives of rank and file Irish civil servants who presented evidence about their departments admitted that personal influence had played a decisive part in their own appointments.[27]

The final report of the Royal Commission on the Civil Service as it regarded Ireland must have pleased the Irish department heads. The commissioners concluded that Treasury regulations were to blame for a scarcity of first-division clerks in Ireland, and that this shortage encouraged the exercise of more departmental patronage at lower levels in Irish departments than in Scottish or English departments. The commissioners also concluded that, overall, the use of examinations for promotion to the higher permanent positions had eliminated virtually all patronage at that level. The Irish department heads' assertion, that they were in the best position to select their immediate subordinates and professional staff officers, was not challenged.[28]

Board Members, Commissioners, and the Privy Councilors

The Irish administration also included seven commissions and boards. Each body monitored the implementation of policy in a given department and reviewed its annual reports, which were issued to the lord lieutenant and presented to Parliament in the board's or commission's name. Personnel on these bodies included twenty commissioners of National Education, ten other commissioners of education, twenty-two commissioners of Irish Lights, fourteen commissioners of the Congested District Board, twelve members of the Board of Superintendents of Dublin Hospitals, thirteen commissioners of Charitable Donations and Bequests, and fifteen commissioners of the Loan Fund

26. *Second Appendix to Fourth Report of the Commissioners,* Minutes of Evidence of Irish department heads and officials.

27. Ibid., testimony of Mr. M. Duggan, Hon. Secretary of Irish Temporary Clerks Association, pp. 340–41.

28. *Fourth Report of the Commissioners,* Chapter VIII, "Promotions," "Measures for bringing merit to notice," "Conditions of Ministerial responsibility for promotion," pp. 57–58.

Board. There were, in addition, between forty-five and sixty-eight members of the Irish Privy Council. Appointed by the lord lieutenant, they issued orders-in-council to implement administrative policy, and they considered and reviewed certain legal causes and petitions.

Generally, half of the board members and commissioners were appointed for a specific term by the lord lieutenant; the other half was selected by local agencies. After the Local Government Act of 1898 fostered the election of representative local government bodies and, after 1899, when grand juries became more representative of the communities that elected them, Nationalists began to object to the large nominated, unrepresentative element of the national boards and commissions. In 1909, for example, only eight of the sixty-eight members of the Privy Council were Catholics.[29] The *Leader* recommended that in opposing the nominated boards, "the popularly elected boards in the country could make themselves as nasty as possible to all the nominated Castle boards of all kinds—education, local government, and the rest . . . with any and all weapons that are effective and that are calculated to do a maximum damage to Dublin Castle boards and a minimum amount of damage to the popular bodies."[30] Change on the boards' personnel was slow. The average tenure of board members and commissioners (in 1906) was about twelve years. Individual commissioners served much longer, with the Lights Commission commanding unusual loyalty from the retired navy officers and merchant marine captains who served on it.

About twenty of the commissioners and board members were also members of the administrative and judicial elite. Virtually every supreme court justice served on a commission. Several places were reserved on the appropriate commissions for such department heads as the resident commissioner of National Education, the secretary of the Congested District Board, and the inspector of Reformatory and Industrial Schools. The chief secretary and under secretary served on two commissions each. At any given time between 1892 and 1921, approximately fifteen members of the Privy Council also served on boards and commissions. The remaining sixty commissioners or board

29. O'Brien, *Dublin Castle and the Irish People,* p. 79.
30. *Leader,* Sept. 23, 1905.

members, both elected and appointed, included bishops and other members of the Catholic clergy, bishops of the Church of Ireland, clergy from other Protestant denominations, as well as barristers, landlords, businessmen, county court judges, and university professors.

The Privy Council, commissions, and boards gave their members an opportunity to offer public service to Ireland by participating in business that was especially important to them. One commission and one board can serve as examples. In 1901 the twenty commissioners of National Education were appointed by the lord lieutenant and elected by the local school boards in equal numbers. The commissioners were divided equally between Catholic and Protestant members. Because education was an issue of great interest to the clergy, six of the ten elected members and five of the ten nominated members were clergymen. The Loan Fund Board, the second example, conducted business with loan societies located throughout the country. In 1903 nine of its ten board members were either deputy lord lieutenants of their counties or justices of the peace. The tenth member was a clergyman.

The Supreme Court of Judicature

The Irish took particular pride in the Supreme Court of Judicature because it had not been abolished by the Act of Union in 1801. After some seventy-six years, however, the Judicature Act of 1877 reorganized the structure of the court into two parts: a Supreme Court and a High Court of Justice (Table 4).

Between 1877 and 1897 the Supreme Court had two divisions: a Court of Appeal and the Lords Justice of Appeal. The High Court of Justice had six divisions: Chancery, Queen's Bench, Exchequer, Probate and Matrimony, Admiralty, and Bankruptcy. The Land Commission was also part of the High Court of Justice. A total of fifteen justices and the lord chancellor, who was also a member of the executive in Dublin Castle, served on the High Court. The lord chancellor, lord chief justice, master of the rolls, chief baron of the Exchequer, and two lords justices of appeal served on the Supreme Court. In addition, the judicial land commissioner and two additional land commissioners were usually counted as justices. Two nonjudicial commissioners also served on the Land Commission, although they were not usually included on lists of

Table 4. Structure of the Irish Supreme Court of Judicature, 1877–97

Supreme Court	
Court of Appeal	*Lords Justice of Appeal*
Ex officio judges	Two justices
Lord chancellor	
Lord chief justice	
Master of the rolls	
Chief baron of the Exchequer	
High Court of Justice	
Chancery Division	*Queen's Bench Division*
Lord chancellor	Lord chief justice
Master of the rolls	Five other justices
Vice-chancellor	
Land court judge	
Exchequer Division	*High Court of Admiralty*
Chief baron of the Exchequer	One justice
Two other barons	
Probate and Matrimony Division	*Bankruptcy Division*
One justice	One justice
Land Commission	
One judicial commissioner	
Two additional commissioners	
Two nonjudicial commissioners	

Adapted from: V. T. M. Delany, *Christopher Palles: Lord Chief Baron of Her Majesty's Court of Exchequer in Ireland, 1874–1916* (Dublin: Allen Figgis & Co., Ltd., 1960).

supreme court justices. The total number of justices was seventeen, although the number fluctuated during the time it took to fill vacancies. When the lord chancellor and the three land commissioners are included, the total number of personnel rises to twenty-one.

The structure of the Supreme Court of Judicature was reformed in 1897 (Table 5). The reform simplified the court's structure by reorganizing the High Court of Justice into two divisions: Chancery and Queen's (or King's) Bench. It created an immediate reduction in personnel by abolishing two positions and provided for an additional reduction when the vice-chancellor retired. However, with the creation

Table 5. Structure of the Irish Supreme Court of Judicature, 1897–1921

Supreme Court

Court of Appeal	*Lords Justice of Appeal*
Ex officio judges	Three justices
Lord chancellor	Two justices (after 1906)
Lord chief justice	
Master of the rolls	
Chief baron of the Exchequer (until 1916)	

High Court of Justice

Chancery Division	*Queen's Bench Division*
Lord chancellor	Lord chief justice
Master of the rolls	Chief baron of Exchequer
Vice-chancellor (abolished 1904)	Eight other justices
Land court judge	
Chancery judge (after 1918)	

Land Commission

Two judicial commissioners
Three estates commissioners (after 1903)
Two nonjudicial commissioners

Adapted from: V. T. M. Delany, *Christopher Palles: Lord Chief Baron of Her Majesty's Court of Exchequer in Ireland, 1874–1916* (Dublin: Allen Figgis & Co., Ltd., 1960).

of the Estates Commission and the reorganization of the Land Commission in 1903, and with the abolition of the chief baron's position in 1916 and the appointment of an additional Chancery judge in 1918, the Supreme Court of Judicature came to have nineteen positions: fifteen justices, the lord chancellor, and three estates commissioners.

Supreme Court Justices

In 1892 there were eighteen justices, the lord chancellor, and three land commissioners. By 1921 seventeen of the twenty-two individuals who had served as law officers or lord chancellors in the Irish executive had advanced to the Supreme Court of Judicature. Three other individuals were appointed directly to the bench without serving first as law officers. These appointments bring the total number of men appointed to the Irish Supreme Court of Judicature after 1892 to twenty. In addition, three new judicial land commissioners were appointed after 1892, and four estates commissioners served on the Estates Commission after it was established in 1903. This brings the total number of new judicial personnel to twenty-seven, for a grand total of forty-nine justices and land or estates commissioners when the twenty-two individuals who were already sitting in 1892 are included.

Like the bureaucracy, the Supreme Court of Judicature was transformed in terms of the both religious affiliation and the political orientation of its personnel, although the figures are less dramatic. In August 1892, eighteen of the justices and land commissioners, and the lord chancellor were Protestants, and three were Catholics. In 1914, the judgeships were equally divided between Catholics and Protestants, and the lord chancellor was a Catholic. Two of three estates commissioners were Protestants. In 1921, there were eight Catholic justices and estates commissioners and ten Protestants, including the lord chancellor. The figures are identical for the judges' political orientation for the same dates. In 1892, eighteen of the justices were Unionists and three were Liberals. In 1914, the bench was evenly divided between Unionists and Liberals; and the lord chancellor was a Liberal. In 1921, there were seven Liberals, including the lord chancellor, and eight Unionist justices.

Apart from the two variables of religious affiliation and political orientation, the judges and land commissioners had similar social backgrounds and legal training.[31] Their fathers were primarily landlords, lawyers, ministers, or businessmen. As undergraduates the justices matriculated at Trinity College, Dublin, by a two to one margin over the other Irish universities. Those who did not attend Trinity graduated from one of the Queen's Colleges: eight from Belfast, and three each from Galway and Cork. Four received their bachelor of arts from the Royal University in Dublin. Two graduated from Oxford, where one was president of the Oxford Union, and one graduated from London University.

After taking professional preparation at the King's Inns in Dublin and being called to the bar, they usually began private practice in Ireland. Eleven of them, however, were also called to the bar in En-

31. F. E. Ball, *The Judges in Ireland, 1221–1921*, Vol. 2 (London: John Murray, 1926), pp. 331–87.

gland. Four began their careers as teachers in universities or at the King's Inns. Typically, twelve to fifteen years elapsed before they took silk as Queen's or King's counselors, although there were extraordinary cases of future judges who had achieved this distinction after six or seven years at the bar. It was often said that barristers and solicitors who later moved into public service first rose to prominence while practicing on the Munster circuit.[32] That circuit was attractive because it yielded higher fees than the other five circuits. The northeast circuit was, perhaps, second in order of remuneration, although many barristers preferred the home circuit because it was close to Dublin. Lawyers often gained both recognition from the supreme court judges on assize and public notoriety in trials that had political overtones. Friendships forged in school or on a circuit could pay a handsome dividend if one's friend became a law officer, or better, lord chancellor.

The Irish judges were competent and knowledgeable. Two measures of their competency and knowledge are the soundness of their judgments and their contributions to legal theory. On occasion, even the greatest justices had a decision reversed on appeal, but the Irish justices appear to have had a good overall record in this regard. There were three reasons for this. First, a unique feature of Irish trial procedure in civil cases helped the justices prevent mistakes that could lead to reversals. After a justice explained the law to a jury and sent them to deliberate, counsel on either side had the opportunity to meet with the justice and object to the charge to the jury. If the justice realized that he had erred, he could call the jury back, correct his mistake, and give them further directions. Second, justices of average ability worked hard and were prepared for trial. The skill of the master of their courts to rule correctly in advance of a trial on the admissibility of testimony and evidence was a particularly important part of pretrial preparation that could also reduce the grounds for complaint. Third, and most important, the justices knew the law. Unsound rulings were bound to be detected by the legal community, and certainly by the lord justices of appeal in Ireland, who were among the greatest jurists to serve on the bench in the nineteenth and early twentieth centuries.[33]

32. Maurice Healy, *The Old Munster Circuit* (Dublin and Cork: The Mercier Press, 1979); Delany, *Palles,* p. 30. See also Daire Hogan, *The Legal Profession in Ireland, 1789–1922* (Dublin: Incorporated Law Society of Ireland, 1986), pp. 143–57, 158–64, for the social background of lawyers and the state of the profession in 1900.

33. Delany, *Palles,* p. 158.

All of the Irish judges contributed to the literature in their fields. Their publications on criminal and civil law covered such topics as probate, admiralty law, divorce, and registration of deeds and titles. Land law was of particular interest to a number of the justices. As lawyers many of them had trial experience in this area and they maintained an interest in land law after they had advanced to the bench. Perhaps they took special pride in one area of Irish law that was able to withstand the onslaught of English legal precedents.[34] Lord Chief Baron Christopher Palles's contributions to the elaboration of case law, especially in the law of torts, made him one of the most respected authorities in British legal history.[35]

The supreme court judges were associated with the executive and the bureaucracy in a number of ways. Most important, service in the Law Office in Dublin Castle was a prerequisite for appointment to the supreme court. Family connections among judges, and between the bench and the bureaucracy, were important because they brought the members of the bureaucratic and judicial elites together on a personal level. Ten of the justices were related to one another. Generally, the family ties spanned generations, father to son, although two justices were brothers. Fourteen of the justices had relatives who were either members of the bureaucratic elite or professional staff officers in the civil service. Two justices had relatives both in the civil service and on the bench. Another typical family connection, within the court system, was the marriage of a justice's daughter and a master of the court.

The justices often advised the civil government in administrative matters. About half of the justices at a given time served on the Irish Privy Council. One Irish justice was a member of the English Privy Council. Half of the justices served as nominated members of boards and commissions. During the period 1890–1921, for example, between two and four of twenty places on the Commission of National Education were occupied by justices. Justices occupied two of ten places as commissioners of intermediate education. One or two justices served as commissioners of education and as commissioners of charitable bequests. This public service brought them into contact with department heads and professional staff officers who might be present at commis-

34. New Ireland Forum, *The Legal Systems, North and South* (Dublin: The Stationery Office, 1983), pp. 10, 24.

35. Delany, *Palles,* pp. 158–73.

sion and board meetings, and with influential citizens who also served on these bodies.

A brief description of the justices' place in Irish society rounds out the profile of judicial personnel. The judges enjoyed great prestige in Ireland. Until 1906 all but one of the justices were members of Dublin's most exclusive social organization, the Kildare Street Club. Indeed, when a suit was brought against the club around 1905, only one justice could be found who could not excuse himself on grounds of a conflict of interest. Eight justices were members of Dublin's Molesworth Street Masonic Lodge. The Liberal justices joined the St. Stephen's Green Club. The Royal St. George's Yacht Club was another organization that claimed some judges as members. The University Club, the Carlton, the Reform, and the Athenaeum were other favorites among the judges. Those who preferred to live in the city maintained residences in its most exclusive areas. Seventeen of them lived on Merrion Square. The justices' salaries put comfortable homes within easy reach. The lord chancellor earned eight thousand pounds per annum (lowered in 1897 to six thousand pounds). The justices earned between thirty-five hundred and five thousand pounds. The judicial commissioners earned two thousand pounds (raised in 1903 to thirty-five hundred pounds). The justices also contributed to Ireland's intellectual life. One was a Shakespearean scholar. Three wrote history. One of the judicial land commissioners hosted a literary salon that was frequented by devotees of the Irish literary revival. He eventually became a trustee of Dublin's famed Abbey Theater and a governor of the National Gallery. Another judicial commissioner, who was the only Englishman among the entire group, spearheaded scientific and technical innovations in agricultural and livestock production. And there were, of course, some colorful and eccentric justices who were good subjects for Dublin's humorists and caricaturists.

The Administrators of the Supreme Court of Judicature

Between 1892 and 1921, a total of forty men administered business for the supreme court. At a given time, there were about twenty-five officials at the top of the court's administrative system. Although some titles changed when the court's structure was reorganized in 1897, the officials included the masters and registrars of the Queen's or King's

Bench Division, registrars of the Court of Appeal, and masters and registrars of the Probate and Matrimony, Exchequer, Admiralty, and Bankruptcy branches. In the Chancery Division, the officials included the permanent secretary to the lord chancellor, who was also the clerk of the crown and hanaper; the secretary to the master of rolls; and the registrar of the Land Judge Department. After 1903, the registrar of the Estates Commission and the registrar of titles joined this small group of court administrators. The three taxing masters completed the court's leading administrative personnel.

Typically, the administrators of the courts were sons of solicitors or barristers. They attended Trinity College, Dublin, by a two to one ratio over the other Irish universities. All of them became solicitors or barristers, and five moved to the first rank of the profession as queen's or king's counselors. The average duration between their careers in private practice and their appointment to the court system was about ten years.

Each supreme court justice filled the vacancies that occurred on his court's administrative staff. The lord chancellor and the law officers were consulted about these appointments and they could bring suitable candidates to the particular justice's attention. Service as private secretary to the lord chancellor offered a quick route to the top of the court's administrative system for two of the registrars. Four justices employed their own sons. One of the branches was bound by tradition. The Yeo family provided masters of the court of the lord chief baron for three generations. After they had been appointed, the court's top officials remained firmly in place until they decided to resign or until they reached retirement age.

Top judicial administrators enjoyed considerable financial and social benefits. Salaries ranged from seven hundred to fifteen hundred pounds. This was equivalent to the salaries of the members of the bureaucratic elite. However, only two of the court's administrators lived in exclusive areas in Dublin. Four were married to daughters of other judicial administrators, thereby tying this small group even closer together. Most of them belonged to the fashionable clubs, including the Fitzwilliam Lawn Tennis Club and the University Club. Like their counterparts in the bureaucratic elite, they had a variety of outside interests. There were hunters, rugby players, golfers, and rowers. Several followed intellectual pursuits. One wrote a college text for logic courses. Another was vice president of the Royal Irish Academy.

No official documents recorded the political affiliation or religious orientation of the court's administrative officers. Of twenty court administrators whose religion has been determined from other sources, Protestants outnumbered Catholics, seventeen to three. The *Irish Catholic,* which had as deep an interest in judicial appointments as the *Leader* had in administrative appointments, identified two reasons for the imbalance that existed in 1906.[36] First, among the seven hundred lawyers in Ireland, Protestant lawyers outnumbered Catholic lawyers by a three to one margin. Of forty-four benchers of the King's Inns, only nine were Catholics. Second, and more important, when judges and law officers made appointments, they favored Protestant lawyers over Catholic ones.[37] The *Irish Catholic* maintained that as a result Protestant lawyers were favored by a seven to one ratio over Catholics for local, county, and other regional judicial appointments. Referring specifically to the discrimination in the top administrative positions on the supreme court—the masters, registrars, receivers, and taxing masters—the *Irish Catholic* observed, "Religion is never inquired into when making these appointments. Why should it? . . . when all the Law Officers of the Crown, as far back as the eye can see, are of the dominant creed. At their head you have an Attorney General and a Solicitor General, both of them remarkable for their hostility to Catholics, ready to step on to the Bench and to administer justice to the people whose interests they have hitherto been trampling under their feet."[38] In 1909 the *Irish Catholic* reported that Protestants outnumbered Catholics twelve to seven on the county court bench; Catholics held only twenty-two of sixty-five positions as resident magistrates; there were twelve Protestants and eight Catholics serving as sessional crown solicitors; ten Protestant district probate court registrars and only one Catholic occupied this position. "No one," the *Irish Catholic* concluded, "will need to be told that these figures indicate the existence of a scandalous

36. *Irish Catholic,* Jan. 20, 1906.

37. The number of lawyers practicing in Ireland is taken from the *Annual Directory, 1900, of the Incorporated Law Society of Ireland.* A complete set of the directories is in the King's Inns Library, Dublin.

38. *Irish Catholic,* Jan. 20, 1906.

favoritism, a favoritism having its origin in religious prejudice which the present government have given absolutely no earnest desire to correct."[39]

Rank and File Staff in the Supreme Court of Judicature

The judicial system's administrators supervised about two hundred workers. Throughout most of the nineteenth century, the justices and court administrators selected the entire staff of their courts, from clerks to train bearers and messenger boys. As such, the administration of the Supreme Court of Judicature was much more open to the exercise of patronage than the civil bureaucracy. Open competition examinations, which were authorized for the court in 1897, were not used to select clerks until 1903 because vacancies were infrequent. When the examinations came into regular use, patronage ceased, and Catholic civil servants were singularly successful.[40] In time, Catholics began to fill the courts' lower offices, just as they had filled similar positions in the civil administration.

39. Ibid., Nov. 6, 1909.

40. *Leader,* Jan. 10, 1903. See also Dublin Diocesan Archives, Walsh Papers, Palles to Archbishop William J. Walsh, Nov. 2, 1897. Palles described the reduction in clerical staff and the justices' loss of their authority to make appointments after the introduction of competitive examinations and the reorganization of the courts' structure in 1897.

Chapter II

Cleaning Out the Castle, 1892-95

After the general election of July 1892, William E. Gladstone, the leader of the Liberal party, became prime minister for the fourth time. He hoped to introduce a home rule for Ireland bill in Parliament in the spring session of 1893, but he realized that his home rule proposal would have to overcome three obstacles. The first was the House of Lords, which was dominated by Conservatives who opposed home rule. The Liberal party's overall majority of forty votes in the House of Commons was too small to coerce the House of Lords, should that body reject the bill. Gladstone did not expect that the electorate would support him if he attempted to reform the House of Lords. Gladstone's second obstacle was in Ireland, where bitter political feuding continued between Parnellite and anti-Parnellite factions in the aftermath of the death of the Irish Nationalist leader, Charles Stewart Parnell, in 1891. Of the eighty-one Irish Nationalist members of Parliament (MPs) elected, the anti-Parnellites claimed seventy-two, but they were themselves divided. John Dillon led the larger faction, Timothy Healy the smaller one, although both recognized Justin McCarthy as their titular leader. The Parnellites, who numbered nine, were led by John Redmond. The anti-Parnellites were loyal to their alliance with the Liberal party, but Redmond's group rejected it for the position of independent opposition. Gladstone's third obstacle, also in Ireland, was that a substantial minority of the Irish population, centered mainly in the Protestant sections of northeast Ulster but scattered throughout the rest of Ireland as well, did not want home rule. Known as Unionists, they feared that they would be discriminated against by a home rule government that was bound to be dominated by representatives of the

Catholic Nationalist majority in Ireland. Unionists, and their Conservative party allies and supporters in Britain, also held that home rule legislation was a direct violation of the Act of Union of 1801, which had established the United Kingdom.

Undaunted, Gladstone began to prepare the way for home rule by devising an alternative plan for Ireland that included reform of the Irish administration.[1] Gladstone knew that successful reform would depend largely upon the ability of the minister responsible for Ireland, the chief secretary. Gladstone offered the position to John Morley, who accepted. Morley had some knowledge of the Irish situation, having served as chief secretary for a few months in 1886 when Gladstone made his first attempt to secure home rule. His experience had convinced him that the Irish administration was not sympathetic to the needs of the Catholic Nationalists in Ireland. Like Gladstone, Morley was determined to remedy the situation, but he wanted to be sure that he had in his own hands the means to reach the desired end. In particular, Morley wanted to prevent any appearance of divided authority in Dublin Castle. Therefore, he asked to play a part in the selection of the titular head of the Irish government, the lord lieutenant.[2]

Morley's request posed a problem for Gladstone because during the previous Liberal administration, John Campbell, Lord Aberdeen, had served as lord lieutenant. Many observers assumed that he would be appointed again. Morley, however, did not want to work with Aberdeen, although he knew that Aberdeen was anxious to serve. Gladstone turned for advice to Earl Spencer, who had been lord lieutenant between 1880 and 1886. Gladstone, thinking that Spencer might be induced to return to Ireland, wrote to him, explaining that he and Morley had prepared an alternate plan for Ireland. "I daresay you remember a declaration of Harrington's," Gladstone began, referring to their former political colleague, "to the effect that 'Dublin Castle' must be fundamentally recast. This would require a strong hand." "One of the principal subjects of thought in coming weeks or months," Gladstone continued, "is how far it can be done; and when the time comes, no

1. B.L., G.P., Add. MS. 44774, ff. 35–46, n.d.

2. B.L., Hamilton Diaries, Add. MS. 48658, July 22, 1892; ibid., G.P., Add. MS. 44256, f. 214, Morley to Gladstone, July 9, 1892.

one can speak on it with such authority as you."[3] The prime minister then wrote to Morley and asked him to consult Spencer about the lord lieutenancy. "I have said nothing as to himself," Gladstone declared, "and do not know whether he has any determined wish. If he has it ought to receive the utmost possible consideration."[4] Gladstone reassured Morley that as chief secretary and a member of the cabinet, he alone would conduct business with Irish Nationalists.

Morley was pleased that he had Gladstone's confidence—in fact, he was eager to meet with John Dillon to discuss legislative priorities—but he had a different perspective on the personnel for the Irish executive. Morley warned Gladstone, "The first impressions of the country will depend on the personnel of the new government looking fresh and unhackneyed."[5] Morley also presented his ideas to Aberdeen. Then, in a letter to Gladstone that summarized the interview, Morley pointed out that he had made it plain to the former viceroy "that we should do better to start the new system with a new lord lieutenant."[6] Morley readily admitted that Aberdeen had been a very popular viceroy, "But I am sure that he will understand that this alone does not of itself meet all the objects with which I shall start on this difficult passage." The prime minister finally accepted his chief secretary's viewpoint, and he offered Spencer and Aberdeen other positions.

Although Earl Spencer accepted the position of first lord of the Admiralty, Lord Aberdeen balked at the offer of the governor-generalship of Canada. Lady Ishbel Aberdeen, who preferred Ireland and its people, felt that it was her duty to tell Gladstone of her husband's and her own desire to serve in Ireland. She countered the chief secretary's point about having an unknown man for lord lieutenant by emphasizing the value of experience and qualifications. She pointed out their personal interest in the Irish home industries movement and their Presbyterian church connections, which were an important asset in satisfying Ulster's Liberals, many of whom were of that faith. "Aberdeen and government," she assured Gladstone, "would rest wholly in the hands of the Secretary, and I think you can trust him to be loyal in things, great

3. B.L., G.P., Add. MS. 44314, ff. 32–35, Gladstone to Spencer, July 13, 1892.
4. B.L., G.P., Add. MS. 44256, ff. 215–16, Gladstone to Morley, July 17, 1892.
5. B.L., G.P., Add. MS. 44256, ff. 217–19, Morley to Gladstone, July 19, 1892.
6. B.L., G.P., Add. MS. 44256, ff. 231–32, Morley to Gladstone, Aug. 13, 1892.

and small."[7] Gladstone, however, resisted the plea.[8] The lord lieutenant was to be the youthful and politically inexperienced Lord Houghton.[9]

While the prime minister and chief secretary were settling the matter of the lord lieutenancy, they were searching for a lord chancellor for Ireland and for candidates for Dublin Castle's Law Office: the attorney-general, the solicitor-general, and a sergeant-at-law. They did not, however, have as free a hand in making these appointments as they had in selecting the viceroy. Legal protocol required that law officers who had served past governments should receive first consideration, and practical politics required that these men should be acceptable to the government's Irish allies. The three candidates with the strongest claims were Samuel Walker, who had already served twice as attorney-general; Hugh MacDermott, who had prior service as solicitor-general; and Charles Hemphill, who had prior service as sergeant-at-law. All three had been retained by the Nationalists during the land war of 1880–82 to represent evicted tenants.[10] Both MacDermott and Hemphill were discreet contributors to the Irish Parliamentary party fund; the latter, who had been the president of the Protestant Home Rule Association, was a close friend of Redmond's.[11] Walker accepted the lord chancellorship; MacDermott and Hemphill accepted the offices of attorney- and solicitor-general, respectively. In rounding out the legal appointments, Gladstone and Morley selected William Dodd for sergeant-at-law. He was a Liberal from Ulster, a Presbyterian, and had served as editor of the leading Presbyterian journal, *The Banner of Ulster,* in which he had advocated land reform and the cause of the tenants.[12]

The chief secretary turned directly to administrative reform when the staffing of the Irish executive was completed. There were two ways to proceed. First, drafting the administrative clauses of the home rule bill provided him an opportunity to plan for significant adjustments in the bureaucratic system. Under home rule, the departments that were

7. B.L., G.P., Add. MS. 44090, ff. 203–6, Lady Aberdeen to Gladstone, Aug. 13, 1892.

8. B.L., G.P., Add. MS. 43515, ff. 73–77, Gladstone to Lord Ripon, Aug. 21, 1892.

9. Charles O'Mahoney, *The Viceroys of Ireland* (London: John Long, Ltd., 1912), pp. 305–6.

10. *London Times,* Feb. 8, 1904; *Belfast News-Letter,* Aug. 14, 1911; ibid., Mar. 4, 1908.

11. T.C.D., D.P., H. H. MacDermott to Dillon, June 10, 1894.

12. *Belfast News-Letter,* Mar. 18, 1930.

responsible to the chief secretary as well as the branch offices that were under the control of English departments would report to the members of an Irish ministry. Second, Morley hoped to break the stereotypical image of the Irish bureaucrat, which conjured up an underworked official who took a lackadaisical approach to official duties. Morley wanted to appoint new officials and promote able ones from the ranks to positions of authority. Energetic leadership at the head of a department, he hoped, would cause subordinate officials to work harder. In this area, he knew that he would be limited by the number of vacancies that would occur during his term. Because civil servants served until they retired, his hope for the development of a more disciplined civil service over time depended largely on how he made appointments and promotions when the opportunity arose. This made each vacancy a matter of major concern.

Morley's first opportunity to make a high-level appointment occurred in September 1892 when one of three judicial commissionerships on the Irish Land Commission became vacant after the death of M. G. F. McCarthy. The position was equivalent in salary to a supreme court justiceship and carried almost as much prestige. Morley was anxious to make judicial appointments of all types, especially at high levels. In 1881, the bench had been evenly divided between Catholics and Protestants, but Conservative chief secretaries and lord chancellors had used their power to put the bench in Protestant and Unionist hands.

The steps taken to fill this vacancy may serve as a useful case study for Morley's term and for scores of other high-level appointments that were made between 1892 and 1921. Morley made his view of the candidates clear in a letter to the prime minister.[13] "I need not tell you," he began, "that the flies cluster pretty thick about such a pot of honey as this. The clergy are for Judge Waters, but he is not a fit man in any way. One Nationalist group is for Morrough O'Brien, now a valuer or inspector in the department. Another is for George Fottrell—thoroughly competent but not popular. Much interest is being made for Thomas Dickson, but not in Ireland, and his appointment would never do." "There are many others," Morley concluded, "but not very suit-

13. B.L., G.P., Add. MS. 44256, ff. 241–42, Morley to Gladstone, Sept. 15, 1892. The salary was two thousand pounds.

able. I incline to Fottrell—on the whole. It should be either him or M. O'Brien." Hoping to make some economies in the administration, Morley regretted the cost involved in filling the vacancy, which he mistakenly thought carried a three-thousand-pound salary. He realized, however, that he had to fill the position. "The late commissioner," Morley explained to Gladstone, "was the only active representative of the tenants in the department."

The *Irish Figaro,* a weekly journal published in Dublin, kept the closest watch on the politics of appointments in 1892. On September 24 it reported that Morley was being besieged by the applicants for the Land Commission.[14] The *Figaro* began its review of possible successors to McCarthy with Dickson, the former Liberal party member of Parliament for Stephen's Green, Dublin. He was, the *Figaro* maintained, without qualifications and without a public record. Indeed, the *Figaro* dismissed Dickson as a disturbing element in the political life of the country and hoped that Morley would have more respect for the administration of justice than to appoint a person with no legal standing to the office. The weekly then noted that George Fottrell was being pushed for the position, although it did not comment on his qualifications. The *Figaro*'s favorite candidate was Edward Greer, who had served ably on the Land Commission since its inception in 1880. Observing that he deserved some consideration, the weekly noted that Greer not only enjoyed the confidence of the people of Ulster but also had a thorough knowledge of the duties of the commissioner. The *Figaro* followed this opinion a week later when it countered the *Manchester Guardian*'s support for Dickson by declaring that Morley would not do this "bad job" and concluded in support of Greer, "if the appointment was an English one, the Government would not hesitate to recognize merit and service, and do what is right."[15]

Morley hoped to bring the various nationalist parties into negotiations with him about all types of appointments. The chief secretary had already begun to include the anti-Parnellites in his decisions. He worked with John Dillon and with Dillon's associate, William O'Brien, in appointing personnel to serve on a viceregal commission to inves-

14. *Irish Figaro,* Sept. 24, 1892.
15. Ibid., Oct. 8, 1892.

tigate the problems of evicted tenants who had lost their holdings during the land war.[16] During the exchange of letters about the viceregal commission, Morley learned that Dillon had confidence in Morrough O'Brien as a potential land commissioner. But after Morley interviewed William O'Brien, the chief secretary wrote to Dillon complaining that O'Brien, "with characteristic simplicity," had recommended the former Fenian revolutionary and former Land League president, Michael Davitt, for the position.[17]

Morley also tried to involve the Parnellites in appointments. He invited Redmond to visit him in the chief secretary's lodge, but the Parnellite leader declined. Redmond declared that he would only agree to meet Morley at the lord chancellor's home, or at any of the law officers' residences, or if Morley preferred, at Morrough O'Brien's.[18] Lord Chancellor Walker eventually negotiated a site, and he, Morley, and Redmond met in mid-October. Redmond's memorandum of this meeting sheds light not only on this particular appointment but on his approach to all appointments.

Morley asked me for suggestions on this subject. I said I could only offer one suggestion, namely to shake himself clear of all placehunters, to give it to some independent man qualified for the position, absolutely disregarding all men having so-called political claims on the Liberal Party.

M. Would you call Morrough O'Brien a placehunter?

R. No.

M. Or George Fottrell?

R. I am in a difficulty in speaking of Fottrell with whom I am very friendly and whom I regard as a most competent man—but he does not in my opinion stand as clear as Morrough O'Brien.

M. Would you suggest a name?

R. No, that is a responsibility I cannot take.[19]

Redmond did not initiate meetings and he did not nominate candidates for positions, but he did not object to the appointment of suitable candidates for positions that were vital to his party's interests.

16. T.C.D., D.P. See correspondence of William O'Brien, Dillon, and Morley, August and September 1892.

17. T.C.D., D.P., Morley to Dillon, Sept. 23, 1892.

18. N.L.I., R.P., MS. 15207(1) Redmond to Morley, Sept. 28, 1892.

19. N.L.I., R.P., MS. 15207(1) "Memorandum of a meeting with the Chief Secretary and Lord Chancellor, Oct. 17, 1892."

The appointment went to Morrough O'Brien. He enjoyed the confidence of both anti-Parnellite and Parnellite leaders, who must have been pleased that Morley had only seriously considered two Nationalists. Everyone, however, could not be satisfied. The *Figaro*'s favorite candidate was not mentioned in Morley's letter to Gladstone, and the weekly had not even identified O'Brien as a possible candidate. The clergy also had a candidate, but the reasons for their support and their reaction to this appointment have not been recovered.

Two weeks later, in October, Morley had another opportunity to accommodate Nationalists in appointment matters when a vacancy occurred on the Congested Districts Board. The five permanent members of the board, which had a large measure of independence from Dublin Castle, provided funds from an annual budget of approximately eighty-five thousand pounds for relief works and for agricultural and industrial improvements in the congested districts in the west of Ireland. "It is," O'Brien wrote to Dillon in reference to the vacancy, "an opportunity which ought not to be neglected. Burdensome task as it would turn out to be, I think you ought to press Morley to appoint some thoroughgoing friends."[20] Dillon replied that it would be up to Morley to approach him, and he added that he (Dillon) would not take a seat on the board under any circumstances.[21] Before Morley could make the appointment, a second permanent position on the board opened. Morley selected for one of the places the youngest of the Catholic bishops, Patrick O'Donnell, bishop of Raphoe. He was an ardent Nationalist, a friend of Dillon's, and the leading financial expert among the Irish hierarchy.[22] A few months later, Morley filled the second place by appointing Denis O'Hara, a Catholic priest whose parish of Kiltimagh was in a congested district in East Mayo, Dillon's constituency. O'Hara, a fast follower and friend of Dillon's, was an active participant in Nationalist politics at the local level. The two new board members quickly became the dominant members on the board. "I have little doubt," wrote W. L. Micks, the board's secretary and historian, when he recalled these appointments many years later, "[that] Mr. Morley was influenced

20. T.C.D., D.P., O'Brien to Dillon, Oct. 15, 1892.

21. T.C.D., D.P., Dillon to O'Brien, Oct. 16, 1892.

22. F. S. L. Lyons, *John Dillon: A Biography* (Chicago: University of Chicago Press, 1968), p. 259.

by the advice he received from Mr. John Dillon M.P., who, like most of his colleagues, was most friendly to the Board."[23] Dillon, however, would neither confirm nor deny this, even thirty-three years later when Micks, who was writing a book about the board, asked him about these appointments.[24]

Dillon's refusal to discuss a particular appointment some thirty years after the fact is not surprising. Nationalist politicians were always sensitive about rumors that they used their influence to help friends obtain government positions. In spite of Morley's eagerness to involve Nationalists in his decisions, the members of the various factions of the Parliamentary party were wary of cooperating with him on appointments. Their reasons were rooted in the past. The members of the Parliamentary party pledged, each year, that they would not accept positions in the Irish administration and declared that it would be improper and inconsistent for them to use influence, direct or indirect, to secure the appointment or promotion of any other person in a paid government position.[25] The pledge protected party members from charges that they were mere place hunters, and it insulated them from the demands of Nationalist supporters who wanted help in gaining access to careers in public service. By prohibiting meddling in patronage, the pledge also kept party members out of the potentially awkward position of

23. W. L. Micks, *An Account of the Congested Districts Board for Ireland from 1891–1923* (Dublin: Easton & Son, Ltd., 1925), p. 177.

24. T.C.D., D.P., Micks to Dillon, Nov. 22, 1925.

25. The party's pledge was apparently devised around 1845 by Charles Gavan Duffy, a leader of the Young Ireland movement. Young Ireland was short-lived, but in 1850 the Independent Irish party adopted Duffy's idea of a pledge as a means to unify its members. Within two years, two of the party's key members, William Keogh and John Sadlier, had taken office in the administration. A dozen other party members soon followed them into public service. The party disintegrated by 1860, but Sadlier's and Keogh's apostasy had long-term consequences. Their acceptance of office showed how easily party leaders could be corrupted by the lure of patronage. In the 1870s Isaac Butt, the founder of the home rule movement, used the pledge to unify the members of the Irish Parliamentary party. Butt's successor, Charles Stewart Parnell, expanded the pledge in 1885 to provide a further measure of party discipline by prohibiting members from influencing appointments and promotions. This brief outline of the history of the pledge, through 1892, is based on Charles Gavan Duffy, *Young Ireland* (Dublin: M. H. Gill & Son, 1884), esp. Part II, pp. 60–64; J. W. Whyte, *The Independent Irish Party* (Oxford: Oxford University Press, 1958); Conor Cruise O'Brien, *Parnell and His Party, 1880–1890* (Oxford: Oxford University Press, 1957).

having to defend an official of their choosing who might have to take an action that was detrimental to Nationalist interests. Most important, the pledge was a sign of independence from British politicians; as such it promoted the party members' dignity and standing.

William O'Brien, who had been eager to cooperate with Morley during the first three months of the chief secretary's term, now tried to check potential charges of pledge breaking before they started. In an article provocatively titled "Cleaning Out the Castle," which appeared in the November 1893 issue of *The Nineteenth Century,* O'Brien maintained that Nationalists could surely administer Dublin Castle's departments as correctly and as well as they had administered local government bodies in Ireland since the early 1880s. "But," O'Brien wrote, "a Nationalist will no more enter Dublin Castle until an Irish Government possesses the keys than he will go by choice to reside in a cholera hospital. Even with a Home Rule Chief Secretary at the helm, the place is in quarantine."[26] O'Brien admitted it was perverse for Nationalists to attack officials from the platform and then refuse to help Morley supply better administrators. Nevertheless, O'Brien concluded, the chief secretary would have to find his own way when he made administrative appointments and would, in fact, probably wrack his brains trying to find Nationalists who would enter public service.

Irish Parliamentary party members could, however, nominate candidates for appointment to the local magistracy without breaking the pledge. The Irish executive officers appointed approximately 225 local justices of the peace each year. Nationalist politicians took an active interest in these positions. An appointment as a justice of the peace was important for an individual because it confirmed his status in the community and carried with it important responsibilities, including hearing civil cases and working with local government bodies to secure assistance and contracts. These appointments were also important for Nationalists as a group. Local offices provided an opportunity for Nationalists to prove that they were competent administrators. This helped them combat Unionist charges that they did not have the ad-

26. William O'Brien, "Mr. Morley's Task in Ireland," *Fortnightly Review,* Nov. 1892; reprinted in William O'Brien, *Irish Ideas* (London and New York: Longmans, Green, and Co., 1893).

ministrative ability or preparation to deliver services at the national level.

The party leaders, particularly the anti-Parnellites, urged their members to submit the names of suitable candidates for the justiceships of the peace to James Deasy, the party whip, for transmission to the chief secretary and the lord chancellor.[27] Deasy, Dillon, Davitt, and Healy met frequently with Morley to discuss these appointments. In fact, Lord Chancellor Walker, who made these appointments on the chief secretary's advice, could not act quickly enough for several eager anti-Parnellites, who perhaps had made too many promises to their constituents. Redmond, who remained aloof about high-level appointments, did not hesitate to take Morley to task over men the Parnellite leader termed "local Healys" and "bitter partisans" who were appointed justices of the peace at "the behest of Davitt and the priests."[28] When Morley tried to enlist Redmond's help on local appointments, however, the Parnellite leader was diffident. "He said he was going to appoint a batch of R.M.s [resident magistrates]," Redmond noted of Morley in a memorandum, "and said he would appoint one Parnellite barrister if I would name one. I said I could not do so. He asked me if I knew Miles and Dan Kehoe and were they Parnellites? I said yes."[29]

This cat and mouse game added to the complications that normally accompanied the scores of local appointments. Morley wrote to his colleague, Lord Rosebery, "If I please Dillon I displease Healy, and vice versa. I cut the knot by pleasing myself. This delights the Parnellites and the Tories who applaud my firmness in order to insult the Nationalists."[30] Nevertheless, Morley was determined to change, as far as possible, the overall religious and political character of the fifty-five hundred Irish magistrates, who were then overwhelmingly Protestant and Unionist. During his tenure, Morley appointed 554 Catholics to the

27. N.L.I., MS. 5834, *Minute Book of the Committee of the Party,* Vol. II, Sept. 1892–Jan. 1893. See entries for Sept. 27, Oct. 29, and Nov. 1, 1892; T.C.D., MS. 6501, *Irish Parliamentary Party Minute Book.* See entries for Jan. 31, 1893, and Mar. 21, 1894.

28. N.L.I., R.P., MS. 15207(1), "Memorandum of a meeting with the Chief Secretary and Lord Chancellor, Oct. 17, 1892."

29. Ibid., MS. 15207(1), Memo of Redmond's after meeting with Morley, Feb. 19, 1894.

30. N.L.S., R.P., MS. 10046, ff. 70–72, Morley to Rosebery, Sept. 18, 1892.

magistracy of a total of 637 appointments.[31] His appointees were soon known derisively in unionist circles as "Morley Magistrates." Unionists complained that the "Morley Magistrates" were inferior in respectability and ability.

Although Morley tried to enlist Nationalist help during the autumn of 1892, the chief secretary took matters into his own hands when he focused his attention on the chief permanent civil servant in Ireland, the under secretary, Sir Joseph West Ridgeway. Ridgeway was identified with the coercive policies of a former chief secretary, Arthur Balfour, during his Conservative administration of 1886–91. He was looked upon as a marked man, because, in 1887, Balfour had removed a Liberal under secretary, Robert Anderson, and some other Liberal officials from Dublin Castle because they were sympathetic to home rule.[32] A clash with Ridgeway over candidates for the evicted tenants' commission gave Morley the occasion he needed to act. He wrote to Gladstone that it was impossible to expect Ridgeway to "zealously forward those changes in policy and *personnel* which the new system demand." "Moreover," Morley added, "so long as he remains where he is, every subordinate in the government of the country, down to the common constable, will be apt to fear that any zeal in carrying out my views and wishes will entail a black mark in Ridgeway's book—to be followed by penal results whenever I disappear."[33] Gladstone advised Morley to seek advice on how to proceed from Lords Houghton and Spencer. He also stated that the cabinet must be informed of the urgency of the situation and that its members must be asked to locate alternative employment for Ridgeway.[34]

Ridgeway had no desire to leave Ireland. He knew that his position was bound to be uncomfortable, but on October 15 he wrote to Balfour explaining that there were political and administrative reasons why he must resist Morley's attempt to remove him.[35] "Morley wants an under secretary who is in political sympathy with him. When Parliament meets he cannot leave me, who was so identified with the last regime,

31. John Morley, *Recollections* (London: Macmillan and Co., Ltd., 1921), 2:23; 1:308–9.

32. *Irish Figaro,* Aug. 20, 1892.

33. B.L., G.P., Add. MS. 44256, ff. 245–46, Morley to Gladstone, Sept. 22, 1892.

34. B.L., G.P., Add. MS. 44256, ff. 250–51, Gladstone to Morley, Sept. 23, 1892.

35. B.L., B.P., Add. MS. 49812, Ridgeway to A. Balfour, Oct. 15, 1892.

to administer his country." "This is the pretext," he elaborated, "but the real reason, I believe, is that Tim Healy insists on my going." Healy, Ridgeway added, was being assisted by W. L. Micks, whose appointment in 1891 as secretary of the Congested Districts Board he had opposed. Ridgeway also believed that Micks had blocked the appointment of the Conservative land commissioner, Frederick Wrench, to the evicted tenants' commission. All of this, however, was only part of a larger issue. Ridgeway deprecated Morley's argument about Castle officials who feared reprisals after changes in governments, noting that if the Liberals "removed permanent officials, your side would probably retaliate, and our civil services would be Americanized." Without reliable and non-partisan advice, Ridgeway observed, a chief secretary might "be for a time in a fool's paradise, but he will come to grief."

Morley and his cabinet colleagues searched for a suitable position for Ridgeway throughout October and November. Ridgeway rejected at least one offer, an appointment in Australia, but he considered a temporary solution early in December—a six-months leave of absence on full pay with no prejudice to his position as under secretary. Morley presumed that during the next six months his colleagues would find a permanent post for Ridgeway. Before Ridgeway would finally agree to this arrangement he wrote to Balfour asking whether his former chief and colleagues in the late Conservative government would consider his departure from Ireland "a desertion of his post in time of need."[36] When Balfour assured him that this would not be the case, Ridgeway left for temporary consular duty in Tangier, Morocco.

Morley, hoping that he had seen the last of Ridgeway, immediately began to search for a new under secretary. He asked a former chief secretary, now secretary for war, Henry Campbell-Bannerman, whether he knew of a military man with experience in intelligence work who might be available for the position.[37] Before Campbell-Bannerman could find anyone, Morley changed his mind. He wrote again on January 9, 1893, explaining, "We must have an Irishman—on Home Rule principles."[38] His choice was David Harrel, the chief commissioner of the

36. B.L., B.P., Add. MS. 44812, Ridgeway to A. Balfour, Dec. 4, 1892.

37. B.L., C-B. P., Add. MS. 41223, f. 12, Morley to Campbell-Bannerman, Jan. 3, 1893.

38. Ibid., f. 13, Morley to Campbell-Bannerman, Jan. 9, 1893.

Dublin Metropolitan Police. During the land war, when Harrel was a magistrate in County Roscommon, his evenhanded judgments won him the respect of all local parties. Later, in 1883, as chief commissioner of the Dublin police, he earned a national reputation when the assassins of Chief Secretary Frederick Cavendish and Under Secretary Thomas Burke were brought to justice in the Phoenix Park murder trial.[39] Ridgeway, who kept abreast of Irish affairs from north Africa, cared neither for Morley's choice of his successor nor for the subsequent police appointments. "The appointments which Morley has been making in Ireland," he explained to Balfour, are "very bad and ought to be undone when a Unionist Government comes into power." "Jones," he noted, referring to J. J. Jones of the Royal Irish Constabulary, "who was removed from a troubled county in your time for laziness and diffidence is head of the Metropolitan Police. The Nationalists, I dare say, insisted on this, and that is why they were glad to get rid of Harrel."[40]

Morley's appointment of Nationalists at the local level and in the central administration also worried Irish Unionists and their British sympathizers. By spring 1893 they were especially alarmed because Gladstone and Morley had completed work on their second home rule bill, a measure that had the potential to turn the bureaucracy over to a Nationalist ministry. Few Unionists feared actual persecution because of their religious beliefs, but they did fear discrimination in administrative matters. They expected that their Protestantism would be a disqualification from participation in public life.[41] A spate of anti-Catholic, anti-Nationalist writing expressed this fear in 1892 and 1893. Such publications as *Does Home Rule Mean Rome Rule?; Mr. Gladstone's Home Rule Bill: "The Great Betrayal": A Forecast of Evil to the British Empire; Rome Rule in Ireland and Civil War;* and *The Priest in Politics* played on fears of a Roman Catholic ascendancy that would seek vengeance against its enemies.[42] A satire, complete with a zany cartoon

39. *Times,* May 13, 1939; *Belfast News-Letter,* May 15, 1939.

40. B.L., B.P., Add. MS. 49812, Ridgeway to A. Balfour, June 10, 1893.

41. Patrick Buckland, *The Anglo-Irish and the New Ireland, 1885–1922* (Dublin: Gill and Macmillan, 1972), p. xxiii.

42. R.J.S., *Does Home Rule Mean Rome Rule?* (London: Harrison and Sons, 1892); William Wileman, *Rome Rule in Ireland and Civil War* (London: William Wileman, Publisher of Gospel and Protestant Literature, 1892); Philip H. Bagenal, *The Priest in Politics* (London: Hutchinson and Co., 1893); P. V. M. Filleul, *Mr. Gladstone's Home*

cover, written by "Phineas O'Flannagan" characterized a potential Nationalist administration as priest- and bishop-ridden, corrupt, incompetent, and unable to function in the interests of the people.[43] The opinions of the scholar A. V. Dicey, however, could not be easily dismissed. Dicey, like most Unionists, was not as concerned about a Nationalist-dominated legislature as he was about a Nationalist-controlled administration and judiciary.

> Again, we are so used to the preservation on the part of the Executive and the Courts of an attitude of perfect impartiality and to the extension of their aid to all citizens alike, that we can hardly even in imagination conceive, what would be the condition of things if the public administration favoured particular classes and looked askance on the rights of one class, whilst it enforced with vigour the rights of another.
>
> Let us consider for a moment a few of the things which the Irish Cabinet might do if it chose. It might confine all police, administrative, or judicial appointments to Nationalists, and thus exclude Loyalists from all positions of public trust. It might place the Bench, the magistracy, the police wholly in the hands of Catholics. . . .[44]

Irish bureaucrats were also concerned about what might happen to them under home rule. Representatives of the four thousand permanent civil servants in Ireland formed a committee to review those clauses of the bill that affected their pensions, salaries, and tenure. At the heart of their concern lay the understanding that a civil servant had entered into a contract with the government. These civil servants feared that a Nationalist government would try to break that contract. Those in elite and professional staff positions, many of whom had abandoned professional careers for state service, felt most threatened. Others who had no professional training or preparation for alternative employment

---

Rule Bill: "The Great Betrayal": A Forecast of Evil to the British Empire (Weston-Super-Mare: R. E. M. Lawrence and E. A. M. Lawrence, 1893).

43. "Phineas O'Flannagan," *Ireland a Nation! The Diary of an Irish Cabinet Minister: Being the History of the First (and only) Irish National Administration, 1894* (Belfast: Olley & Company ([Ltd.]), 1893). Nationalist and Catholic propagandists, Jeremiah Mac Veagh and J. A. Fox, in the Home Rule Union countered with pamphlets and leaflets titled *Protestant Ascendancy in Ireland: What Orangeism Means: An Object Lesson in Irish Politics*; *Irish Catholics—The Persecuted, not the Persecutors*; and *Orange Ascendancy in Ireland.*

44. A. V. Dicey, *A Leap in the Dark or Our New Constitution* (London: John Murray, 1893), p. 72.

faced financial ruin if adequate pension benefits were denied them. Advancing age and poor prospects of professional employment in Ireland were frightening propositions. The provision that no pension was to exceed a maximum of two-thirds of an official's salary, instead of three-fourths, meant the reduction of the modest goals that every civil servant presumed a career in government service guaranteed—a secure retirement and perhaps a small inheritance for survivors.

When members of the committee met with Morley in spring 1893, they assured him that their position was one of perfect neutrality toward the bill. Their sole object was to safeguard their own interests. They recalled that when they were similarly organized in 1886, their attitude was misconstrued as hostility.[45] In a memorandum they presented to the chief secretary, the civil servants identified provisions in the bill that they thought would have a deleterious effect on them. These provisions included one that awarded pensions at a sliding rate of approximately one-seventh to two-thirds salary according to years of service. Another provision gave no compensation for years of employment that might be lost for civil servants who chose to retire because of a change in government. The committee members feared the new government might demand that a civil servant retire without showing cause. The committee recommended that civil servants who were dismissed should receive a pension of three-fourths salary, and a full year's salary bonus, if they had fewer than twenty-five years' service, and a pension that was equal to a full salary if they had over twenty-five years' service. Further, the committee recommended that those who voluntarily retired should receive from one-half to three-fourths of their salaries and compensation for lost employment. The committee also wanted the Treasury to guarantee the salaries and pensions of civil servants who remained in Ireland. If a civil servant decided to leave Ireland, he or she should be able to use special transfer procedures and receive moving expenses. This provision would help them find positions in other imperial departments.[46] In short, the permanent civil servants wanted protection from two possible eventualities: either find-

45. *Irish Figaro,* Mar. 18, 1893.

46. *Supplementary Statement on behalf of the Permanent Civil Services of the Crown Serving in Ireland, with Suggested Amendments to the Government of Ireland Bill, 1893.* N.L.I., Ir. 3511, c. 11.

ing themselves in working conditions that were so untenable under a Nationalist-controlled government that they must resign or facing a politically motivated purge of the bureaucracy by a Nationalist executive. On the basis of their representations to Morley, the Irish civil servants were not yet willing to serve, without reservation, under any legitimate Irish government. Clearly, they did not have confidence in the integrity and goodwill of the Nationalist party leaders.

The second home rule bill included a series of clauses that reserved parts of the administration to imperial control and other clauses that restricted the power of the Irish legislature and executive. Gladstone hoped to prevent a reaction both in the country and in the Liberal party like the one that wrecked the first home rule bill in 1886. He also hoped to relieve Unionist and Conservative party anxiety about the protection of minority rights in Ireland. Gladstone highlighted these features of the bill when he introduced it in the House of Commons on February 13, 1893. Irish representation, set at thirty-four members, was to be retained at Westminster. The proposed Irish legislature was to be denied lawmaking power that would deprive Irish minorities of equal protection under the law. The bill temporarily reserved some financial powers, including levying and collecting taxes, to the imperial Parliament. After six years all taxation except customs and excise would revert to Irish control. The Irish post office, another important source of revenue, was reserved for six years. The bill also included checks on the Irish legislature's and executive's control over its bureaucracy and judiciary. The appointment of justices to the Irish Supreme Court of Judicature was to be reserved to the imperial government for six years. Appeals of decisions in the Irish courts could be made to the Judicial Committee of the English Privy Council. Two Exchequer Court judges who would be appointed by the imperial government would adjudicate questions that were beyond the purview of the Irish legislature. Control of the two police forces was permanently reserved. Civil servants were given a five-year transition period to determine whether they would choose to continue to serve in Ireland. The Irish government would assume financial responsibility for officials who were dismissed.[47]

47. Erskine Childers, *The Home Rule Bills of 1886 and 1893 Compared and Explained* (Westminster: The Irish Press Agency, 1893).

The bill advanced through its first and second readings by a narrow margin. During the committee stage that followed the second reading, the Conservative and Unionist members tried to place additional checks on the executive by introducing both specific and wide-ranging amendments. This allowed them to attack the bill's details as well as its spirit. The line-by-line amending process was also an oblique attempt to enumerate, and thereby further restrict, the powers of the Irish executive. The Liberals employed a twofold defense. They professed their faith in the Nationalists' integrity, and pointed out the bill's safeguards, and cited administrative precedents in the empire that protected minority rights. The Nationalists, who wanted the bill to pass as quickly as possible, introduced only a few amendments.

Clause v, which dealt with the lord lieutenancy, was debated on July 3. The 1886 bill had done away with the religious qualification for the office. The 1893 bill depoliticized the office further by fixing the viceroy's tenure in office at five years, rather than changing with the ministry. Unionists wanted to know who would be responsible to the House of Commons for Irish matters, and they hoped to increase the viceroy's ability to act independently by defining his veto power over legislation passed by the Irish Parliament. They introduced approximately one hundred amendments to this clause alone, which they used to vent their distrust of Nationalists. For example, Joseph Chamberlain, member for Birmingham and leader of the Conservative party opposition, read portions of speeches Nationalist MPs delivered during the land war in Ireland to support his allegation that they would turn the forces of law and order against "enemies of the people," that is, against Unionists and landlords.[48] H. O. Arnold-Foster, Unionist MP for West Belfast, claimed that the Nationalist executive would appoint fugitives who were wanted for murder to important government offices.[49] D. R. Plunket, the Unionist MP for Trinity College, Dublin, best summarized Unionist fears. "We want to have restrictions put upon the executive power, which we fear more than the legislative power, restrictions analogous to those which have already been adopted in regard to the property, and liberty, and lives of the minority in Ireland." "What we

48. *Parliamentary Debates,* House of Commons, Fourth Series, 1893, 14:715.
49. Ibid., 769.

want to ask," he concluded, "is how are we to have any remedy against the executive power being used to injure the minority?"[50]

Clauses xxviii and xxix, which concerned the tenure of Irish judges and civil servants, were debated on July 17–19. The former clause had a smooth passage, although Thomas Sexton, the anti-Parnellite member for Kerry and the only Nationalist to play a significant part in any of the debates relating to the administration, objected that the Irish land commissioners were to remain imperial officers. Sexton pointed out that they might be prohibited from acting on land legislation enacted by the Irish Parliament.[51] Morley replied that the Land Commission was bound to interpret and enforce any new Irish land legislation and that barring a successful motion of removal in both houses of Parliament, or the removal of the commissioners by the lord chancellor on the grounds of misbehavior, the commissioners would continue to sit until they chose to retire.[52]

Clause xxix treated the civil service. In his introductory remarks, Morley gave a vote of confidence to officials serving in Ireland, many of whom, he admitted, did not agree with his policy. He stated that the clause protected them from capricious dismissal and from alterations in their tenure, salary, gratuities, rank, and pension. He hoped the safeguards would prevent sullen behavior by officials that would hamper the new government. At the same time, he continued, the clause protected the Irish government from a resignation en masse. Moving to specifics, Morley called attention to the five-year transition period that permitted the new government and its officials to become acquainted. Morley then outlined the transfer procedures that civil servants could use if they voluntarily left the Irish service. The government would help in a search for a new post but would not pay any expenses. He also explained the compensation scheme for those officials who might be dismissed. The maximum pension was set at two-thirds, short of the suggestions made to him by the civil servants but an equitable balance between the needs of the officials and the requirements of the new government. Morley concluded by declaring that the government took care to prevent anything like a vindictive clean sweep, which, however, it did not anticipate.[53]

50. Ibid., 750–51.
51. Ibid., 1714–17.
52. Ibid., 1717–18.
53. Ibid., 1779–84.

The debate turned on the belief that there would, in fact, be many changes in civil service personnel. Redmond had already set the tone for Nationalists during his speech on the second reading. "Large masses of the Protestants are, no doubt, frightened by the Bill. I do not wonder at it. They have had in their hands for generations a monopoly of all power and place and patronage."[54] Redmond had touched on the part religion played in the Irish administration, but Conservatives and Unionists, who denied that a Protestant ascendancy existed in Ireland, contended that under home rule the Nationalists would use the civil service for political ends. Arthur Balfour began the committee debate by declaring that the House was not dealing with a simple departmental reorganization but with a great official and social revolution. He said he understood why the Nationalists made provocative remarks years earlier during the land agitation, when they threatened retribution against the police. He was alarmed, however, by William O'Brien's *Fortnightly Review* article that demanded a clearing out of the Castle. This signaled a premeditated policy against the civil service. He asked, "Is it to be supposed that it is in human nature that when these gentlemen have the power they will not deal with those gentlemen, according to their own statement, of what they deserve?"[55] Whether the Nationalists were motivated by revenge or by a desire for economy, Balfour believed there was bound to be an enormous number of dismissals.

Gladstone replied that "Clearing the Castle" meant simply altering a system, but he admitted that the alteration could involve dismissals at high levels. It was, he said, important for both the House of Commons and the Irish civil servants to trust the proposed Irish executive. Gladstone then turned directly to the pension scheme. He declared that no one had any cause to complain about the unprecedented liberality of the financial provisions of clause xxix. It was ludicrous, he concluded, to assume that the Irish executive would engage in wholesale dismissals, if only because of the financial burden this would place on the Irish government, which had to pay the pensions of dismissed officials.[56] Nevertheless, Lord Randolph Churchill, Conservative MP for

54. Cited in Denis Gwynn, *The Life of John Redmond* (London: George C. Harrap & Co., Ltd., 1932), p. 80.

55. *Parliamentary Debates,* House of Commons, Fourth Series, 1893, 14:1787–88, 1844–49.

56. Ibid., 1849–58.

South Paddington, predicted there would be dismissals on a large scale.[57] The Ulster Unionist member for South Tyrone, T. W. Russell, forecasted sweeping changes in the Land Commission.[58] Lord Randolph then rose again to ask whether the Liberals knew "that many of the prominent men in Ireland have claims upon [the Nationalists] that they cannot fail to recognize, and have established over them an influence which must make them provide offices for them?" "That is why I hold the Irish Government will make many vacancies in the Civil Service. They are bound to provide for their own friends."[59] After Henry Labouchere, radical MP for Northampton, declared that Irish officials who resigned or retired would receive too much money,[60] J. J. Clancy, anti-Parnellite MP for County Dublin and a leading financial expert among the Nationalists, added that it was unfair to burden the Irish government with the payment of the pensions because the Irish civil service was overmanned and too expensive.[61] Balfour countered by demanding an assurance that positions abolished on economic grounds would not then be opened to Nationalist supporters.[62] In closing the debate, J. J. Clancy and L. P. Hayden, anti-Parnellite MP for South Roscommon, declared that the Irish government would work well with its officials; that it would be liberal and generous; and that Nationalists did not have the slightest hostile intention toward the members of the Irish civil service.[63]

The debates on the clauses concerning the administration contained little that was statesmanlike. Tempers were short and members on both sides frequently made personal comments about their opponents. Although the Nationalists said very little, the Unionists made it clear that they considered the judiciary and civil service to be a bulwark against the Nationalists' power in the country. The Unionists feared that a Nationalist executive would break that bulwark, thereby curtailing Unionist influence in Dublin Castle and further undermining their power in the country. The Unionists and their Conservative party allies were, however, unable to amend these clauses.

The home rule bill passed its third reading on September 1, 1893, by a majority of thirty-four votes.[64] One week later, as expected, the

57. Ibid., 1855–62.
58. Ibid., 1865–67.
59. Ibid., 1891–92.
60. Ibid., 1859–62.
61. Ibid., 1911–13.
62. Ibid., 1912–13.
63. Ibid., 1908–9 (Hayden); 1911–12 (Clancy).
64. Ibid., 16: 1839.

House of Lords rejected home rule by the overwhelming margin, 419 votes to 41. Gladstone had won in the House of Commons, but he had not overcome Irish Unionist and British Conservative opposition. There was to be no social and political revolution in the Irish administration. Any changes in personnel would have to occur one at a time as vacancies appeared. The debates on clauses v, xxviii, and xxix signaled that each new appointment would be closely watched by Nationalists and Unionists alike.

The defeat of home rule by the House of Lords ended the high politics in Parliament, and Morley returned to the lower order of administrative business in Dublin Castle. There, he had to contend with a problem that was largely of his own making. Sir Joseph West Ridgeway's leave of absence was about to expire, and he wanted to return to Dublin Castle as under secretary. No alternative position had been found for him. Morley, however, refused to account for two under secretaries, either to the Treasury or to the opposition. Morley's chief difficulty was that he had no charge to bring against Ridgeway, and to remove a civil servant because his political views were suspect was a serious matter, especially in the light of the recent committee debates on civil service personnel. "I am," he wrote to Gladstone on September 24, "at the end of my resources. I have pressed the case on my colleagues for a whole year, both privately and formally in Cabinet, but my representations have now come to naught." "The ceaseless vexations and anxieties of Irish administration," he continued, "are sufficient burden themselves—to say nothing of a Home Rule Bill thrown in—and if a quarrel and a scandal about Ridgeway is to be cast upon me as well, the Cabinet will really be riding the willing horse to death. Only the horse happens to have come to the end of his willingness, and that is what I now—with infinite reluctance—write to say."[65] Morley also wrote to Lord Rosebery, indicating that he was tired of the chief secretaryship. "I have had such a long spell as supplicant," he declared, "that I have tried a change of position, and I shall now have to be supplicated. Or perhaps I shall not be. And that will suit me better still."[66]

Gladstone had held continually that Ridgeway must go as part of the

65. B.L., G.P., Add. Ms. 44257, ff. 126–27, Morley to Gladstone, Sept. 24, 1893.
66. N.L.S., R.P., Ms. 10046, ff. 148–49, Morley to Rosebery, n.d.

administrative reform policy. He redoubled his effort to assist Morley. Gladstone explained to Lord Kimberly, the secretary of state for India, that the chief secretary could not continue with Ridgeway as his right-hand man. "In this there is much reason to suppose him right, for what is required is very nearly to turn topsy-turvy the Balfour-Salisbury methods." "But in any case," Gladstone concluded, "I conceive Morley's title to be relieved of an impossible condition is absolute."[67] But the cabinet was preoccupied by internal intrigue caused by the prospect of Gladstone's retirement, and his ministers responded sluggishly to pleas on Morley's behalf.[68] Those positions that were eventually suggested were either unsuitable in themselves or financially unsatisfactory to Ridgeway.

Gladstone hoped to extend Ridgeway's leave, and he searched for a technicality that could put an end to the matter. In a letter to Morley he suggested that if Ridgeway might be declared "incapacitated from the performance of his duties as they are estimated by his official superior, is there not then a moral right and with it moral duty to dismiss him?" "It seems to me," Gladstone observed, turning the problem back over to Morley, "that you are the person necessarily most responsible for establishing the fact of incapacity."[69] Morley's own probity, however, would not permit a dismissal on such transparent grounds.

Morley's refusal to act finally began to try the prime minister's patience. "It is incredible, though true," Gladstone wrote to Spencer on October 16, "that a man of his high character and admirable qualifications should so strangely misapprehend the position and duties which it entails." "Meanwhile, I shall continue to speak plainly to him. He may, if we do not take care, overset the coach."[70] Morley was unconcerned about the threat to the ministry. "Mr. Gladstone," he wrote to Rosebery, "says that I shall upset the coach. The gentleman with the reins should have kept the vehicle out of this . . . rut."[71] Morley played a double game, first threatening resignation and then castigating his colleagues who would not help him. Gladstone wrote to Rosebery, "I

67. B.L., G.P., Add. Ms. 44549, ff. 135–36, Gladstone to Kimberly, Sept. 30, 1893.

68. Peter Stansky, *Ambitions and Strategies: The Struggle for Leadership in the Liberal Party in the 1890's* (Oxford: The Clarendon Press, 1964).

69. B.L., G.P., Add. Ms. 44549, ff. 136–37, Gladstone to Morley, Oct. 3, 1893.

70. B.L., G.P., Add. Ms. 44549, f. 143, Gladstone to Spencer, Oct. 16, 1893.

71. N.L.S., R.P., Ms. 10046, ff. 150–51, Morley to Rosebery, Oct. 15, 1893.

nevertheless understood him to adhere to his almost incredible resolution to remove *himself* at all hazards unless Ridgeway is provided for by the end of this month."[72]

Eventually, the governor-generalship of the Isle of Man was offered to Ridgeway. Morley feared that the necessary financial arrangements, which he called "fishy smelling," would prompt embarrassing questions in the House of Commons that he would refuse to answer.[73] Ridgeway thought Balfour should raise a question about the matter, if only to reassure Dublin Castle officials.[74] Balfour, however, did not want to make an issue of the under secretaryship. The memory of the Conservatives' similar treatment of Sir Robert Anderson in 1886 had not yet faded. He advised Ridgeway to accept the governor-generalship.[75] Ridgeway followed the advice and the matter was closed. Gladstone and Morley had intended to clean out the Castle by removing officials who were hostile to home rule. Their first operation had been as prolonged as it was distasteful.

Morley was, in fact, about to be on his own in trying to effect a change in the Castle system. Gladstone, who had been Morley's friend and mentor, was now eighty-four years of age. The prime minister wanted "to go to the country" on the issue of the House of Lords' veto, but he did not have the full support of his cabinet or the force of British public opinion behind him. Moreover, he was isolated in the cabinet on national defense issues, which became his new priority after the defeat of home rule. Therefore, in March 1894 Gladstone retired from public life. Lord Rosebery succeeded him. Morley hoped for a transfer to the Foreign Office, but when Rosebery offered him the Home Office instead, he decided to remain Irish secretary.[76]

When the new prime minister spoke in the House of Lords on March 12, 1894, it was clear that Morley's position was fundamentally altered. Rosebery declared that England, as the predominant partner in the three kingdoms, would have to be convinced of home rule's justice and equity before a measure of self-government would be granted to

72. B.L., G.P., Add. Ms. 44549, f. 145, Gladstone to Rosebery, Oct. 23, 1893.
73. N.L.S., R.P., Ms. 10046, ff. 157–58, and ff. 159–60, Morley to Rosebery, Nov. 18, 1893.
74. B.L., B.P., Add. Ms. 49812, Ridgeway to A. Balfour, Nov. 29, 1893.
75. B.L., B.P., Add. Ms. 49812, A. Balfour to Ridgeway, Nov. 29, 1893.
76. Morley, *Recollections,* 1:367–69.

Ireland. The speech strained the anti-Parnellite–Liberal party alliance and signaled a turning away by the Liberals from home rule toward the solving of other problems. Morley urged Rosebery to rectify what he tactfully called the "false impression" the speech made in Ireland, but Rosebery did not respond. Morley soon discovered that this silence underlined the new prime minister's apparent lack of interest in Ireland.[77]

Morley wanted to continue his administrative reforms, but he knew his time to act was limited. The government's small majority in the House of Commons would not last much longer. Morley began to affect the administration's tone by exacting maximum efficiency from its officials. When Ridgeway returned to Ireland for a brief visit, he was struck by the changes he saw.

> Morley [he wrote to Balfour in May 1894] is a veritable pedagogue. He rules all the officials with a rod of iron. *All,* . . . have to keep fixed hours and work done or not, dare not leave their office till the clock strikes the prescribed hour. To prevent their disobeying with impunity they have to sign attendance books and if a day is required for rest or hunting, it is deducted from the annual leave. Morley's minutes are stinging—not merely tart! He flagellates all. All work is done by him—work which used not to be seen even by the Under Secretary. . . . I guess that the Nationalists insist on this and examine him occasionally to see whether he is keeping his promise. All or nearly all the Castle officials appear to be in a state of sullen discontent.[78]

Morley also tried to expand the sphere of his administrative authority. He interfered in the Law Office by trying to prevent prosecutions and was rebuked by the press when he interfered in the business of the courts.[79] When he attempted to place the Congested Districts Board under his control, W. L. Micks informed him that the statutes that governed the board only gave the chief secretary ex officio member status, even though the chief secretary was responsible for the board in Parliament.[80] Morley also hoped to influence personnel decisions on the

77. F. S. L. Lyons, *The Irish Parliamentary Party, 1890–1910* (London: Faber and Faber Ltd., 1950), p. 48.

78. B.L., B.P., Add. Ms. 49812, Ridgeway to A. Balfour, May 6, 1894.

79. *Irish Figaro,* Nov. 18, 1893.

80. Micks, *History of the Congested Districts Board,* p. 176.

Treasury-controlled Irish Board of Works. However, when the Treasury ignored him and extended the retirement age of the board's chief commissioner, George Sankey, for two years, Morley was unable to convince Lord Rosebery to intervene on his behalf. Morley had hoped to use the expected retirement of this official to bring new officials into the bureaucracy, but Treasury officials maintained that Sankey's retention was vital for the successful completion of a new railway system in the west of Ireland.[81]

Morley's administrative style and his attempt to concentrate authority in his own hands were due, perhaps, to his mistrust of officials who he thought meant well, but who had bad habits and required incessant vigilance.[82] When Morley's health broke down—an occupational hazard in Dublin Castle—he was not able to stop working even when he was recuperating at Cannes. "Who will administer Ireland in my absence?" Morley asked Rosebery, rhetorically. "Who administers Russia when the Czar goes to Yalta? He leaves behind him a body of faithful *chinovniks* with steady instructions as to course, compass, and chart—and a telegraphic cypher."[83]

During the closing months of his chief secretaryship, however, Morley had three opportunities to make important personnel changes. First, he waged a six-month long battle over retirement technicalities in an effort to dismiss Charles Bourke, the chairman of the General Prisons Board. Morley was ready to fight out Bourke's case on the floor of the House of Commons, if necessary, because he thought that Bourke was incompetent.[84] Morley knew that political service and family connections within the bureaucratic elite had often been routes to an appointment in the office. Private secretaries to the lord lieutenant were frequently appointed commissioners instead of experienced professionals.[85] Morley wanted to break away from this method of advancement. After he eventually secured Bourke's retirement, he appointed a new chairman, James Gibbons, a county inspector in the Royal Irish

81. N.L.S., R.P., Ms. 10046, ff. 230–32, Morley to Rosebery, June 14, 1894; ff. 245–46, Morley to Rosebery, July 28, 1894.

82. B.L., G.P., Add. Ms. 44257, ff. 148–49, Morley to Gladstone, Jan. 25, 1894.

83. N.L.S., R.P., MS. 10047, ff. 42–43, Morley to Rosebery, Dec. 19, 1894.

84. N.L.S., R.P., Ms. 10047, ff. 46–48, Morley to Rosebery, Jan. 2, 1895. See also, C.S.O., R.P., 1912, no. 4259 for Bourke's file.

85. *Irish Figaro,* Aug. 6 and 13, 1892.

Constabulary, over the heads of the commissioners.[86] Morley immediately informed the new chairman of working conditions in the Castle. On his first day at his new post Gibbons received a crisp memorandum: The Prisons Board "will be able to arrange their work so that, subject to exceptional circumstances, the members of the Board shall be habitually found upon their duties at Headquarters."[87]

Morley's second opportunity occurred when the other Catholic member of the bureaucratic elite, P. J. Keenan, retired after serving nearly twenty-five years as the resident commissioner of the National Board of Education. Although the resident commissioner never gained the influence over the National Education Board's commissioners that comparable bureaucrats had over their respective boards, Morley understood that this position was both important and sensitive. The board, which included ten Protestant and ten Catholic commissioners, dispensed £1.8 million in grants-in-aid to approximately eighty-two hundred national schools. The resident commissioner supervised the operations of the schools from a beautifully appointed office in the Beresford mansion, incongruously located in the slums near Marlborough Street. Assisted by two secretaries—one Catholic, the other Protestant—the resident commissioner managed a staff of 150 clerks and also guided the board when it appointed examiners and school inspectors. The chief educational concerns of the resident commissioner involved curriculum and evaluation. Low teacher salaries were also a continuing concern. The position called for religious and political sensitivity, too, because the great majority of the 500,000 students who attended the national schools were Catholics and the system was supported entirely by public funds.[88]

Morley did not allow his own agnosticism and opposition to denominational education to interfere in this appointment. His immediate concern was to find an educational administrator who could put the office on a more businesslike footing because during Keenan's long tenure the staff had grown lethargic. Morley wanted his new man to be a Catholic and a Nationalist. He selected Christopher Redington, the

86. *Irish Times*, Apr. 6, 1914.

87. C.S.O., R.P., 1912, no. 4259. Memorandum, Mar. 3, 1895.

88. *Fourth Report of the Royal Commission on the Civil Service*, Minutes of Evidence: 288–91 and 423–31.

vice-chancellor of the Royal University in Dublin. Redington was an outspoken home ruler who had impressed Morley as a member of the Congested Districts Board and as a commissioner in the inquiry into the problems of the evicted tenants. Redington's work habits were exactly what Morley wanted. His broad educational training at Christ Church, Oxford, and a chivalrous personality set the proper tone in the office, and his example as an indefatigable worker had a stimulating, but short-lived, effect on his subordinates.[89]

The third position Morley filled was the assistant under secretaryship. It was an important administrative post and, depending upon the occupant, could also be politically important. The assistant under secretary, Sir William Squire Baker Kaye, retired at age sixty-five, but he wanted to continue his public service career in another capacity. Nationalists wanted him out of Ireland because he worked with the administration that had attempted to connect Parnell to the infamous Phoenix Park murders. Morley wanted to help Kaye but he proceeded carefully. "He is one of the very best of fellows in the world—kindly, genial, and causing no friction," Morley told Lord Ripon. "It would please our political friends here, who—most unjustly—dislike Kaye." "It would not do," Morley warned Ripon, "to send him to a colony where Irish abound."[90]

Edward Ennis, a former reporter on the Nationalist daily paper, the *Freeman's Journal,* who was serving as Lord Chancellor Walker's secretary and as a liaison between the Four Courts and the anti-Parnellites, hoped to succeed Kaye. He wrote to Dillon, on May 2, 1895, asking for assistance, mindful of Ridgeway's fate but observing that the next change of government would stop short of the assistant under secretary. If appointed, he could be a permanent influence in the Castle. "It has been represented to me," he suggested, "that a Catholic should fill it and especially one who would be more or less agreeable to the Church. If necessary I could possibly win more Bishops and priests than any other likely candidate."[91] Ennis also canvassed Walker and Morley, but when Dillon would not sanction his candidature, Ennis let the matter drop.[92]

89. *Belfast News-Letter,* Feb. 7, 1899; *London Times,* Feb. 7, 1899.
90. B.L., R.P., Add. MS. 43515, f. 79, Morley to Ripon, Oct. 23, 1894.
91. T.C.D., D.P., Ennis to Dillon, May 2, 1895.
92. T.C.D., D.P., Ennis to Dillon, May 13, 1895.

Morley appointed James Dougherty, a Presbyterian clergyman from Londonderry and professor of logic and mathematics at Magee College, as assistant under secretary. Dougherty was a Liberal home ruler who had been defeated in a recent Londonderry city election. Perhaps the appointment was a compensation for his loss. In addition to his home rule sympathies, he was not an unknown quantity to Castle officials, because he had served as a commissioner of education and on the Educational Endowments Board.[93] Dougherty quickly made one important change in Dublin Castle procedure. He disregarded precedent and adopted the first-person singular when he replied to queries addressed to Dublin Castle. This innovation disturbed Dublin Castle's older and stodgier officials, but in time it became Dougherty's hallmark.[94]

In June 1895, during the closing weeks of his administration, Morley turned to the annual Irish honors list. For three years Unionists and Nationalists alike had been dissatisfied because Irishmen had been omitted from honors lists, which included only English professionals. They blamed Morley for this apparent indifference and, in fact, Lord Houghton and Morley had asked for honors only twice in three years.[95] Lord Houghton had no names to suggest, an accurate measure of his isolation as viceroy. Healy observed that Houghton attracted only Tories, but they were attracted more to the lord lieutenant's position than to his personality.[96] Most wealthy Unionists would not attend his social functions because of the government's home rule policies, and Houghton had nothing in common with those who did attend. Irish Liberals found him too imperious, and he did not gain the trust of the Nationalists. Even the viceroy's entourage of young soldiers and private secretaries, who had traditionally played an active part in Dublin's social circles, suffered from the general disfavor that centered on Houghton.[97] Nevertheless, Morley magnanimously recommended Houghton, whom

93. Henry Robinson, *Memories: Wise and Otherwise* (London: Cassell and Company, Ltd., 1923), p. 219, wrote that Dougherty was not well known.

94. *Belfast News-Letter,* Jan. 3, 1934. Leon O'Broin, *The Chief Secretary* (Dublin: Chatto and Windus, 1969), p. 17. *London Times,* Jan. 4, 1934.

95. N.L.S., R.P., Ms. 10047, ff. 54–55, Morley to Rosebery, Jan. 2, 5, and 11, 1895.

96. T. M. Healy, *Letters and Leaders of My Day* (London: T. Butterworth, Ltd., 1929), 2:383; Robinson, *Memories: Wise and Otherwise,* pp. 106–7.

97. O'Mahoney, *The Viceroys of Ireland,*pp. 305–8.

he had treated as a mere figurehead, for an earldom. He also asked for a baronetcy for his own private secretary, but he did not ask for usual honors for either the bench or the civil service.[98] If Morley thought Rosebery was going to add the names of some Irishmen to the list, he was wrong. On June 27 he wrote in exasperation to Rosebery, "If you tell me that this is still to be refused, it will prevent me from the only form of recognition that is available for our few supporters among the professional classes in Ireland."[99] Rosebery finally suggested that John Franks, the secretary of the Land Commission who had been appointed during a Conservative administration, should be made a Companion of the Bath. Because Franks was a Unionist, this was an impossible choice from Morley's point of view. But he did not have the will to exhort Rosebery any longer. Morley simply replied, "this would do one much harm."[100]

It is easy—and incorrect—to regard John Morley's chief secretaryship as a failure. Home rule was by far the greatest disappointment, and two land bills he prepared also failed to reach the statute book. These failures in the legislative sphere, however, have obscured Morley's successes in the administrative sphere. The latter was an important test of a chief secretary's ability and the real foundation of his reputation in Ireland.

From the outset Morley wanted to control the entire administrative system and make it respond to his commands. He complained when his legal advisers vacillated when they were told to prosecute Nationalists. He criticized judges who made political speeches to juries, or worse, passed political intelligence to former Irish law officers who were on the opposition front bench.[101] He tried to influence departments that were beyond his immediate control. Initially, department heads were suspicious of him, and many rank and file civil servants who were worried about their security in Ireland in the event of a home rule government's coming to power must have shared the anxieties of their superiors. He listened to the complaints of the permanent civil servants regarding tenure, benefits, and pensions, but the clauses

98. N.L.S., R.P., Ms. 10047, ff. 103–4, Morley to Rosebery, June 24, 1895.
99. N.L.S., R.P., Ms. 10047, ff. 103–4, Morley to Rosebery, June 24, 1895.
100. N.L.S., R.P., Ms. 10047, f. 107, Morley to Rosebery, June 26, 1895.
101. Morley, *Recollections,* 2:22–23.

of the Home Rule Bill were largely designed to keep them in their places. His authoritarian style also had an effect on the country. In terms of dealing with agrarian unrest, one test of administrative ability, Ireland was quieter than at any time since 1876, although it is difficult to judge whether this was due to Morley's administrative style or the forbearance of the Nationalists.[102] Although Dublin Castle was dynamited in 1894 by a clandestine group of Irish revolutionaries, it may have been his success in the country that caused the radical Nationalists to resort to physical force to affect political change.

Morley used two methods to initiate reforms in the administrative system. First, he served notice on the department heads that they must begin to act in a professional manner. If he could not change the attitude of individuals, he could insist upon diligence, and he set the standard by his example. In time, he won their respect. Morley was pleased to tell Rosebery, in 1897, that Irish officials received him with "immense cordiality" upon a return visit to Dublin Castle.[103] David Harrel noted in his memoirs that Morley also had a softer side to his personality that could inspire real affection, recalling the concern and encouragement Morley expressed to him when he was seriously injured in a coach accident.[104] Second, Morley began to meet one of the fundamental objections of Nationalists to Dublin Castle. Morley succeeded as far as was possible in appointing Catholics and Nationalists, in spite of William O'Brien's intimation that Morley would wrack his brains in a vain attempt to find Nationalists who would serve in Ireland. His success in this area, however, was necessarily limited by retirements, resignations, and deaths. For example, at the end of the Liberal government's tenure, Lord Chancellor Samuel Walker advanced to the supreme court as lord justice of appeal when Justice John Townshend of the Bankruptcy Court retired. However, Attorney-general MacDermott, who also desired a judgeship, was effectively blocked by Justice John Monroe. Although he was very ill, Monroe's Unionist friends convinced him not to resign until after the government changed hands.[105]

102. Thomas W. Heyck, *The Dimensions of British Radicalism: The Case of Ireland, 1874–95* (Urbana: University of Illinois Press, 1974), pp. 221–24.

103. N.L.S., R.P., Ms. 10047, ff. 117–18, Morley to Rosebery, Dec. 31, 1897.

104. London School of Economics, Manuscript Collections, David Harrel, Memoir, *Recollections and Reflections*, p. 111.

105. T. M. Healy, *Letters and Leaders of My Day*, 2:407.

Nevertheless, the few appointments Morley made in the central administration represented a new departure. His appointments to the Congested Districts Board, in particular, made it the only board that enjoyed the widespread confidence of Irishmen. In local administration, Morley reduced the number of Protestants in the magistracy from between three and four positions to one, to a proportion of rather more than two positions to one.[106] Where he could not appoint men in complete sympathy with the majority of the Irish people, he tried to appoint men who would command respect.

Morley's appointments demonstrated that the political alliance between the Liberal party and anti-Parnellites could yield important results outside the legislative sphere. Cooperation on appointments, however, cut two ways. On the one hand, the Nationalist leaders were pulled toward a system they denigrated when they were drawn into negotiations on appointments. They were put into the ambiguous position of having responsibility without power. On the other hand, those Nationalist supporters who took up positions—local or central—became part of the Dublin Castle system. Nationalist officials were susceptible to attack if public policy or its implementation ran counter to Nationalist expectations. This conflict of interest between the party's official position on appointments and the participation of those who were generally believed to be its nominees for positions in the Irish administration was to plague Nationalist politicians until their downfall in 1918 and, in fact, would play a significant part in that downfall.

106. Morley, *Recollections,* 1:308–10.

Chapter III

Fill Every Office in Ireland with Friends, 1895-1900

A Conservative government assumed power in August 1895 with a commanding overall majority of 152 seats in the House of Commons. In Ireland the Parnellites and anti-Parnellites shared eighty-one seats, the Unionists held twenty-one seats, and there was one Liberal-Unionist. Lord Salisbury, prime minister for a second time, hoped his majority would support a more constructive approach to administering Ireland than his prior, and largely unsuccessful, policy of "Coercion and Conciliation." The new policy included reform legislation as well as administrative action to redress the grievances of Irish Catholics, especially those who were also Unionists. Salisbury realized that the change of front would not please all of the Conservative party's Unionist allies in Ireland and that it would not be embraced by every Conservative party supporter in Britain. "The party will have to make mutual concessions," Salisbury observed while discussing this potential problem with his cousin, Lord Cranbrook, "and there will be plenty of carping critics in and outside of it."[1]

The shape of the new Irish executive did not prefigure a reform administration. As Salisbury selected his personnel, he altered the relationship that had existed between recent chief secretaries and lord lieutenants. He described the new arrangement when he offered the lord lieutenancy to Lord George Cadogan. Salisbury explained, "You would be a member of the Cabinet, and the question of the Irish secretary must be settled with you if you accept. I [would rather have]

1. Cited in Robert Taylor, *Lord Salisbury* (New York: St. Martin's Press, 1975), p. 155.

an Irish secretary who is not in the Cabinet."[2] Cadogan accepted these terms and Salisbury then selected Gerald Balfour, Arthur Balfour's younger brother and his own nephew, for chief secretary. Balfour had neither administrative experience nor special insight into Irish administration, although he could expect to receive assistance from his brother, a former chief secretary who was leader of the Conservative party in the House of Commons. Under the new arrangement, Balfour would explain Irish policy in the House, but he would not be in the cabinet, where that policy was created. Cadogan would largely control appointments.

Salisbury followed precedent, however, when he appointed the lord chancellor and law officers. Lord Ashbourne, who had been lord chancellor in the previous Conservative administration, was reappointed. He was also given a seat in the cabinet. Ashbourne enjoyed the confidence of Unionists and landlords and the respect of some Nationalists because of the modestly successful Land Purchase Act he introduced a decade earlier. Salisbury also reappointed John Atkinson, reputedly the best lawyer in Ireland, to his former position as attorney-general.[3] The last Unionist to hold the solicitor-general's position was Edward Carson, MP for Trinity College, Dublin. Because his legal career in England was flourishing, he did not press his claim for office in Ireland.[4] This gave Salisbury and his colleagues in Dublin Castle an opportunity to launch the new conciliatory policy in the area of appointments. The choice of candidates for solicitor-general was quickly narrowed to Dunbar Plunket Barton, the nephew of the Protestant archbishop of Dublin, and William Kenny, a Catholic and prominent Liberal-Unionist lawyer. Gerald Balfour preferred Barton, although he thought that Kenny's past services to Unionists gave him precedence with regard to any judgeships, should one become available.[5] Cadogan and Ashbourne both favored Kenny, and even Barton's prior service as Ashbourne's private secretary was not enough to tip the scales in his favor.[6]

Once at full strength, the members of the Irish executive prepared

2. H.L.R.O., CAD/663, Salisbury to Cadogan, June 27, 1895.
3. H.L.R.O., CAD/670, Ashbourne to Cadogan, June 27, 1895.
4. H. Montgomery Hyde, *Carson* (London: William Heineman Ltd., 1953), p. 144.
5. H.L.R.O. CAD/699, G. W. Balfour to Cadogan, Aug. 7, 1895.
6. H.L.R.O. CAD/707, Ashbourne to Cadogan, Aug. 10, 1895.

the government's legislative program for Ireland. Gerald Balfour studied land reform and local government reform. Cadogan appointed several commissions of inquiry, and he welcomed the formation of a nonpartisan body, which became known as the Recess Committee. Under the leadership of Horace Plunkett, a proponent of the cooperative agricultural movement in Ireland and the Unionist MP for South County Dublin, the committee investigated Irish local government and land purchase legislation. Meanwhile, Lord Chancellor Ashbourne made plans to reorganize the structure of the Supreme Court of Judicature. The ultimate success of their ambitious reform program would depend in large part on the officials who would implement the new laws and policies.

Gerald Balfour's land bill of 1896 was the first of four major pieces of legislation that the Conservative government eventually introduced for Ireland. The negative reaction to the bill from Unionists demonstrated that Salisbury was correct in anticipating opposition to his reforms. Nineteen Irish Unionist members in the House of Commons followed Edward Carson into the opposition lobby when the House divided on the measure. Lord Londonderry, a former lord lieutenant for Ireland, led the opposition to the measure in the House of the Lords. Unionists opposed the bill because it incorporated parts of John Morley's two ill-fated land bills and was based on the recommendations made in the final report of Morley's Evicted Tenants Inquiry. Balfour overcame the opposition, and approximately 36 million pounds in land purchase money was advanced to the tenants. This amount was larger than any previous allocation. Interest rates were lowered and mortgage repayment time was extended. The act also called for a new determination of what constituted fair rent for land. This, in turn, determined the purchase price ultimately paid by the tenants.

Because Irish landlords believed that they would not receive a fair price for their property, they turned their attention to the selection of Land Commission personnel who would assess land values. The appointment of these officials also concerned the Nationalists, who charged that in the years after the commission was founded in 1880, its officials had favored the landlords. Balfour tried to obviate complaints from both Irish landlords and Nationalists by making changes in personnel and policy. After 1896 all clerical appointments in the commission's offices had to be filled through competitive examinations.[7] The professional staff positions, however, would continue to be filled by means of limited competition examinations and an interview with the land commissioners. These seventy staff officials, mostly land inspectors and surveyors, determined land value. Over the next five years landlords monitored these appointments and looked for evidence that the Conservative administration was wavering in its traditional commitment to them. The duke of Abercorn, the son of a former viceroy and a leading Unionist who owned some sixty thousand acres in Counties Tyrone and Donegal, became the most outspoken critic of the Land Commission appointments. "It is beyond comprehension," the duke complained to Cadogan when the Land Act took effect, "how Gerald Balfour could have selected [for land valuer] such a man as Mr. Teeling, who is an acknowledged Home Ruler with very advanced principles."[8] The government had a simple rebuttal. Unionists who felt a sense of grievance were told to think about what the Land Commission would be like under a Nationalist home rule government.[9]

In the area of judicial reform, Lord Chancellor Ashbourne took the lead. He told Cadogan that moderation was of the utmost importance and that no judicial reform would be popular in Ireland unless the savings were redirected for use in Ireland.[10] He hoped to abolish two supreme court judgeships and redistribute the work load. His initial figures projected an immediate annual savings of over £11,600 in salaries alone.[11] Ashbourne was also eager to develop other judicial reforms. He planned to reduce his own £8,000 salary by one-fourth and to reorganize the Land Court and the Land Commission.[12]

Several factors, however, acted as brakes on Ashbourne's enthusiasm. Many Irishmen took pride in the supreme court because it was a reminder of the legal system that existed before the Act of Union of 1801.

7. *Fourth Report of the Royal Commissioners on Civil Service, with Minutes of Evidence and Appendices.* See testimony of Justices Wylie and Bailey, pp. 298–312.

8. H.L.R.O., CAD/1011/1, Abercorn to Cadogan, Jan. 11, 1897.

9. See, for example, B.L., B.P., Ms. 49853, Arthur Balfour to Lady Gosford, Jan. 26, 1899.

10. H.L.R.O. CAD/744, Ashbourne to Cadogan, Nov. 6, 1895; CAD/750, Ashbourne to Cadogan, Nov. 14, 1895.

11. H.L.R.O. CAD/793, Ashbourne to Cadogan, Dec. 29, 1895.

12. H.L.R.O. CAD/744, Ashbourne to Cadogan, Nov. 6, 1895.

Moreover, Irish justices resisted reform initiatives that threatened their interests, and in any case, the Judicature Act of 1877 gave them the right to initiate judicial reform when they deemed it necessary. Salaries and continued employment prospects for court officials were factors, too. Irish justices were the highest salaried public servants in Ireland, and each judge controlled the appointments to his staff, from the well-paid master of the court to the meanest functionary. Court officials were not protected by civil service regulations, but they maintained they had the same rights to secure tenure as civil servants claimed for their positions. Finally, the Irish administration of the day was always under pressure from its supporters to recognize lawyers who expected rewards for political services, and from the time of the Act of Union the courts ably served to meet that need.

Lord Ashbourne worked to overcome the emotional, financial, and political obstacles, but it was the death of four justices between 1895 and 1897 that smoothed his way. The first vacancy was created by the sudden death of Michael Harrison of the Queen's Bench in September 1895. A few days later John Monroe of the Land Court tendered his expected resignation. Attorney-General Atkinson, according to protocol, had the first opportunity to take or refuse promotion to the bench, but he did not want either position. Some Unionists who were prepared, within limits, to support the administration's attempt to conciliate Catholics thought that Solicitor-General Kenny should be offered the position.[13] But Gerald Balfour looked beyond the individual vacancy, realizing that the executive had the opportunity to address a larger question. "I think," he wrote to Cadogan, "we should be making a great mistake now if we fill up Judge Harrison's place. This vacancy is a windfall, which coming at the very beginning of our period of office, ought, in my opinion, to be utilized for the purpose of making a highly desirable reform."[14] The press of business in the Land Court, however, could not permit any delay. Several Unionists expressed an interest in the position. Lord Abercorn wrote to Cadogan on January 21, 1896, in support of John Ross, who had represented landlords during the 1880s but had lost his seat in Parliament for Londonderry

13. H.L.R.O., CAD/734, Archbishop Plunket to Cadogan, Oct. 10, 1895.
14. H.L.R.O., CAD/735, G. W. Balfour to Cadogan, Oct. 14, 1895.

in the general election. Abercorn told Cadogan that a man should be chosen who has fought and sacrificed for his [here the word *country* is crossed out] party, who has shown his own personal worth by his political actions, in preference to others who have been the happy possessors of safe seats and whose abilities and eloquence have been extolled by an admonitory and greedy lot of Dublin lawyers and officials."[15] Abercorn added that Cadogan would "gratify a very large amount of Presbyterians in the North of Ireland by selecting Mr. Ross for the vacancy." Ross, whose father had been moderator of the General Assembly of the Presbyterian Church in Ireland, was eventually appointed. At age forty-one, he was the youngest supreme court justice serving in either England or Ireland, and he was the only Presbyterian on the bench.[16] In May 1897, Stearne Ball Miller of the Bankruptcy Court and Charles Barry, lord justice of appeal, died within two weeks of each other. After listening to the claims put forth by Justice Peter O'Brien on behalf of a Catholic Liberal-Unionist barrister named Stephen Ronan, Cadogan and Ashbourne promoted Justice Hugh Holmes of the Queen's Bench Division to the appeals position.[17] Then they transferred Justice Walter Boyd, who had been Miller's colleague in the Bankruptcy Court to the Queen's Bench, thereby abolishing the Bankruptcy Court's separate jurisdiction.

Ashbourne incorporated these changes into the judicial reform legislation that Gerald Balfour introduced in the House of Commons in July. Balfour told the House that the Supreme Court of Judicature (Ireland) Bill would reduce the court from four divisions—Chancery, Queen's Bench, Exchequer, and Probate and Matrimony—to two divisions, Queen's Bench and Chancery. This would be accomplished by merging the Exchequer Division, the Court of Bankruptcy, and the Probate Court with the Queen's Bench Division. In addition, Balfour announced that the government had decided not to fill the vacancy created by Justice Harrison's death. The net result was a reduction of three justices and their respective staffs. (See Chapter I, Tables 4 and 5, for the structure of the Supreme Court of Judicature, 1877–97 and

15. H.L.R.O., CAD/829, Abercorn to Cadogan, Jan. 21, 1896.
16. *Belfast News-Letter,* Aug. 16, 1935; *Irish Times,* Aug. 17, 1935.
17. H.L.R.O., CAD/1113, Atkinson to Cadogan, June 3, 1897; CAD/1114, O'Brien to Cadogan, June 6, 1897; CAD/1119, Salisbury to Cadogan, June 9, 1897.

1897–1921.) Balfour expected to save seventy-five hundred pounds per annum in judges' salaries alone. These savings would be applied to any specific purpose that the Irish members of Parliament might suggest or to a separate credit for Irish purposes that might be determined by Parliament.[18]

Nationalists gave the bill a mixed reception. John Dillon, the anti-Parnellite leader, remarked that the judges' high salaries were the greatest abuse in the Irish judicial system. He pointed out that under the proposed reorganization, Justice Boyd's salary would actually increase by over one thousand pounds. Dillon claimed that it was a reward for the political services Boyd rendered to landlords during the land war. Dillon then called for a more substantial reorganization because business in the courts had fallen by 70 percent over the last twenty years.[19] Timothy Healy, who had become Dillon's archrival within the anti-Parnellite movement, welcomed the bill. Healy was well informed on matters affecting the courts and the legal profession in Ireland, and he also respected Irish legal traditions. Healy defended the salaries on the ground that the justices must be above suspicion of corruption. He also defended Boyd, who had served as counsel for William O'Brien in 1885 against the administration during a trial that helped to bring down a scandalous Conservative administration in Dublin Castle.[20]

Dillon carried his criticism into the committee stage. He objected to a clause that called for the chief baron of the Exchequer, Christopher Palles, to yield precedence to the chief justice of the Queen's Bench, Peter O'Brien. Dillon ridiculed O'Brien's judicial ability and recalled O'Brien's record as Irish attorney-general in Arthur Balfour's administration. In 1888, O'Brien, one of the few Catholics then serving in the administration, had been given the nickname "Peter the Packer" by Irish Nationalists because he allegedly packed juries with Unionists and Protestants who would convict Nationalist agitators.[21] Dillon then returned to the extent of the reform. Joined by Michael Davitt, member for South Mayo, Dillon complained that there were too many justices

18. Great Britain, *Parliamentary Debates,* Fourth Series, House of Commons, 1897, 51:732–33.

19. Ibid., 1189–91.

20. Ibid., 1191–94.

21. Ibid., 52:22–25.

in Ireland and that the cost of the judicial administration, approximately £2 million, was far out of proportion to the demands made by the Irish crime and litigation rates.[22] Davitt proposed reducing the number of justices to eight or ten and reorganizing their work schedules.[23] Other Nationalist members charged that the bill perpetuated Dublin Castle jobbery. Arthur Balfour warned them that if they engaged in obstruction, the government could not complete the legislation in that session, or in any future session. The debate closed with Dillon fighting to safeguard the interests of the officials whose courts were to be dissolved.[24] Dillon recalled how the Conservatives had argued for pensions and bonuses for officials during the home rule debates in 1894. Finally, Sir Michael Hicks Beach, the chancellor of the Exchequer, stated that he thought the court officials would be retained in the reorganized system, but if they were not, he promised that the government would be as generous as possible. The bill was read a third time, on August 5, and received the royal assent the following day.[25]

With the judicial reform concluded, Gerald Balfour piloted the administration's third major piece of legislation, the Local Government Act, to the statute book. The legislation, enacted in 1898, established a new administrative system in local government by forming elective county councils, urban district councils, and rural district councils. These representative bodies replaced the grand jury system that had been dominated by both centrally appointed and local ex officio members. For decades, the old system kept the greater part of the country's local affairs under the control of the landlords. The act largely broke their grip on local government and gave the new bodies fiscal and administrative responsibilities, including power to make scores of local appointments.

Nationalist leaders welcomed the legislation because Nationalists were certain to dominate all of the elected councils outside northeast Ulster. John Redmond, the Parnellite leader, believed the measure gave Nationalists an opportunity to demonstrate their capacity for intelligent administration.[26] Healy was also pleased, declaring, "Mr. Gerald Balfour, splendidly aided by Mr. John Atkinson, has laboured faithfully and

22. Ibid., 28–31.
23. Ibid., 31–34.
24. Ibid., 163–68.
25. Ibid., 377, 509.
26. Gwynn, *Life of John Redmond,* pp. 90–91.

well to overcome the obstacles of Castle environment."[27] Dillon contributed constructive criticism during the committee stages of the bill's passage.[28] On the other hand, the Unionists realized that the legislation further undermined their authority in the country. Having now lost local power, one Unionist maintained, "It is surely the duty . . . of the so-called English garrison in Ireland to retain its hold, to leaven society with its hopes and aspirations that their common country may never become the plaything of a base political clique, whose ambition would be . . . to see an Ireland in the grip of a Tammany Hall administration, where mendacity would flourish, corruption would be rampant, and industry would decay."[29]

The immediate concern for Unionists and Nationalists alike was the selection of personnel who would serve the Local Government Board and administer the act throughout the country. Several staff and executive positions were available. The transition period from the old system to the new one was stressful. The board's secretary had a nervous breakdown and retired; several clerks also cited broken health and disability as the reason for their retirement. The vice president of the board, George Morris, reached retirement age just before the legislation took effect, and the medical commissioner on the board, Dr. F. X. MacCabe, retired a few weeks later.[30]

With several key positions vacant, the administration had an opportunity to make the board's personnel more reflective of the people who were going to control the local bodies. In filling the vice presidency Gerald Balfour turned to Henry Robinson, an Englishman with ten years' experience as a commissioner of the Local Government Board in Ireland. Robinson had helped Balfour draft the measure and had acted as a liaison to Lord Cadogan during the bill's passage. A Unionist who was on good personal terms with many Nationalists and Catholic priests in the country, Robinson recalled in his memoirs that the task of breaking up the old system "was considered such a hazardous job that there were no applicants for the post of Vice-President."[31] In fact,

27. The *Nation,* Aug. 20, 1898.
28. Lyons, *Irish Parliamentary Party, 1890–1910,* p. 68; Lyons, *Dillon,* p. 188.
29. Patrick Buckland, *Irish Unionism,* 1:xxi-xxii. This opinion was expressed by J. M. Wilson of County Wexford.
30. Robinson, *Memories: Wise and Otherwise,* pp. 127–28.
31. Ibid.

his experience and mastery of the measure's details probably guaranteed his promotion. His comment that the task at hand was "a hazardous job" may have been made for effect. By 1898 Nationalists were already entrenched at several levels of local government, including the elected Boards of Poor Law Guardians, which they had occupied since the 1880s.[32] In large part Robinson would be working with established vested interests, not breaking them up. Perhaps he would have been more correct if he had called the job "infuriating." He was a stickler for proper procedures, and for the next twenty-two years he demanded them in the proposals and petitions that local government bodies sent to his offices in the Custom House. In time this led to charges from Nationalists that he was not responsive to the needs of the people.

As vice president of the board, Robinson oversaw the appointment of the board's commissioners and its important staff members. When the Royal Commission on the Civil Service took evidence in Ireland in 1913, he reflected on the Unionist principles that guided him when he made appointments in 1898 and in subsequent years.

> Politics and religion find their way into many matters of local government in some parts of Ireland, and as things stood then our staff was nearly all Irishmen and knew almost too much of the political and religious aspects of affairs. I was therefore very anxious to leaven them if I could with a few Englishmen and Scotchmen. . . . I have seen the characteristics of the three, English, Irish, and Scotch, and, working together, they make a really perfect combination. The Englishmen we have had from the upper division examination have been stolid, sensible, highly competent persons. The Scotchman is a rock of common-sense, accurate, and cautious. The Irishman is brilliant, resourceful, and quick, but he is rather impulsive and wants the steadiness of the English and Scotch. An office with all three nationalities represented is perfectly equipped.[33]

Unionists hoped that more men like Robinson would be placed in positions of responsibility on the board. They wanted Robinson's commissionership to be filled by a Mr. Willis instead of the Nationalist candidate, W. L. Micks, the secretary to the Congested Districts Board.

32. William L. Feingold, *The Revolt of the Tenantry: The Boards of Poor Law Guardians in Ireland* (Boston: Northeastern University Press, 1983).

33. *Fourth Report of the Royal Commission on the Civil Service,* Minutes of Evidence, pp. 199–209.

The duke of Abercorn was worried, however, that Gerald Balfour was falling victim to Nationalist pressure. "I believe," Abercorn wrote to Cadogan, "that you personally are not adverse to the appointment, beyond the fact that Mr. Willis has been closely connected with the landed interest in Ireland. This, with a Radical Government, might stand as an objection, with a Conservative one, however, I should have thought it would have been rather in his favour." Abercorn then noted, "Mr. Gerald Balfour is determined to appoint Mr. Micks to the vacant Commissionership. If antecedents are to be taken into consideration, Conservatives might object to the appointment of a Home Ruler, for I am told that those originally were Mr. Micks' political opinions, whatever they may be at the present time."[34] After receiving more letters and some deputations supporting Willis, Cadogan sent the duke a terse reply. "It is unfortunate," Cadogan wrote, "that at a time when proposals for effecting great constitutional changes in Ireland are under consideration, we are confronted, as usual, with a *personal* difficulty which appears to absorb the attention of those to whose guidance and advice in more important matters it would be natural to look."[35]

The chief secretary submitted the names of the new commissioners to the board for the lord lieutenant's review on April 29, 1898. They included Robinson, Micks, and Dr. T. J. Stafford, a son-in-law of the Unionist landlord Colonel King-Harmon.[36] The Treasury also sanctioned the appointment of a temporary commissioner, Richard Bagwell. He was a landlord and historian and a founder of the Unionist organization, the Irish Loyal and Patriotic Union. George Swain, the new secretary for the board, satisfied the Unionists' demand for an experienced official. He had twenty years of experience in poor law administration at the time of his appointment. There were, in addition, other important positions, including four appeals commissioners who, working in conjunction with the vice-president of the board, were to settle conflicts between local bodies. Balfour tried to strike a balance by appointing two Nationalist members of Parliament: one was a follower of Dillon, the other a follower of Healy. The other two, Balfour told Cadogan, must be Unionist and Protestant.[37]

34. H.L.R.O., CAD/1326, Abercorn to Cadogan, Mar. 24, 1898.
35. H.L.R.O., CAD/1329, Cadogan to Abercorn, Mar. 27, 1898.
36. H.L.R.O., CAD/1342, G. W. Balfour to Cadogan, Apr. 29, 1898.
37. H.L.R.O., CAD/1375, G. W. Balfour to Cadogan, July 27, 1898; CAD/1376, Ca-

The Agricultural and Technical Instruction Act, which reached the statute book in 1899, was the government's final major piece of reform legislation. Based on the findings of the Recess Committee of 1896, the act centralized the bureaucratic functions surrounding agricultural production and education. Merged into a new department, aptly called the Department of Agricultural and Technical Instruction (DATI), were the Veterinary Department of the Privy Council, the Office of Inspectors of Irish Fisheries, and several educational institutions, including the Royal College of Science, the Metropolitan School of Art, and several public museums and art galleries. The act designated the chief secretary as the president of the department and a vice president of the department as director of its affairs. "The Department," as it was called, was represented in Parliament by the vice president, who was also given junior ministerial rank in the Irish administration. DATI was controlled, in part, by a council of agriculture and by two advisory boards. One-third of their members were nominated by the department and two-thirds by local administrative bodies. The council and boards had to concur before the department expended monies out of its £2 million endowment fund. The inclusion of these representative bodies gave the department a unique status vis-à-vis the rest of the bureaucracy. When the nominating bodies made their selections for the council and boards in 1899, Nationalists were heavily represented.[38]

Nationalist and Unionist observers alike recognized that if the department were to realize its full potential, much would depend on the quality of its officials. Unionists and landlords, who blamed Balfour for destroying their power in local government, were especially alarmed by the chief secretary's statutory precedence in the new department, which they interpreted as a blatant move for more power.[39] The Healyite newspaper, the *Nation,* warned Balfour that in making appointments to the department, he must be guided solely by a sense of personal fitness. The slightest taint of jobbery or partiality in the selection of its officers was the one thing certain to ruin it.[40]

---

dogan to G. W. Balfour, Aug. 1, 1898; CAD/1385, G. W. Balfour to Cadogan, Aug. 30, 1898; CAD/1404, G. W. Balfour to Cadogan, Oct. 17, 1898.

38. Earnest Barker, *Ireland in the Last Fifty Years* (Oxford: Clarendon Press, 1917), pp. 75–77.

39. *Irish Figaro,* July 29 and Oct. 28, 1899.

40. *Nation,* July 2, July 22, 1899.

Horace Plunkett, who had labored so diligently on behalf of Irish agricultural reform, was the obvious choice for vice president of the department that had been his handiwork. Indeed, he had received applications for positions in the department months before the bill reached the statute book.[41] In the autumn, Plunkett began to exercise the traditional prerogatives of an Irish department head by selecting his three chief subordinate officers: the permanent secretary and two assistant secretaries, one for the Agricultural Division and one for the Technical Division. Plunkett had long favored T. P. Gill for the secretary's post. Gill, who had been a prominent Nationalist MP in the 1880s, was a journalist and an expert on agricultural questions. He had been Plunkett's secretary during the Recess Committee's work and had compiled its report. Many observers believed that Gill would be appointed, and he, too, began to receive applications for positions in the department before the bill became law.[42] Plunkett knew that the appointment of a home ruler was bound to be challenged by Unionists, and he also knew that Balfour did not favor Gill. Plunkett began his campaign for Gill by writing to Lady Betty Balfour, the chief secretary's wife, with whom he was on friendly terms. On October 3, he unfolded a strong defense of Gill, who had just written some articles attacking the government's Transvaal policy. Plunkett explained that Gill's political past had shaped his current opinions on the Boer War, and he went on to state, "I don't think Gill has an 'anti-English' craze or even conscious bias." "I suppose," Plunkett elaborated, "a man of his origin and history must have a virulent nationalist bacillus in his blood which becomes active whenever he breathes an atmosphere in which such bacilli thrive." Plunkett then noted, "Gill does not seek a Government appointment, though he has the best right of any man living to be offered it and longs for this means of silencing cruel slander." "It is most honourable," Plunkett continued, "though, I admit, exasperating to us, that he does not allow his own interests to affect his position as a journalist."[43]

41. N. L. I., Gill P., Ms. 13494 (5), Plunkett to T. P. Gill, Feb. 10, 1899. See also P. F. C. S., P. D., Oct. 23, Oct. 25, 1899.

42. N. L. I., Gill P., Ms. 13509 (14) Gill to Plunkett, Nov. 28, 1899.

43. P.F.C.S., P.P., BAL. 49, Plunkett to Lady E. E. Balfour, Oct. 3, 1899. See also P.D., Oct. 26, 1899.

In December, Plunkett traveled to Belfast to discuss the staffing of the department with several Ulster Unionist leaders. He then relayed their reaction through Lady Betty to her husband. "Their final decision, speaking for the North," Plunkett explained, referring to the two assistant secretaryships, "is that there must be a Catholic in one of the posts."[44] The Belfast Unionists would not stand for Gill's occupying the assistant secretaryship of the Technical Division, Plunkett continued, but the Unionists agreed "that, putting the religious question aside, Gill is by far the best qualified person for the chief post." Plunkett concluded with another personal endorsement of Gill, declaring that he was indispensable to the reform effort. "With Gill under me I can do it," Plunkett explained, "[With] the pick of the entire Irish officialdom, I could not even explore it."

Meanwhile, other Ulster Unionists hoped that Lord Cadogan would somehow prevent Gill's appointment. "G. Balfour undertook in the House that these places should be filled by men who were purely selected for their merit," one writer began, "and certainly it was never intended that the holding of any particular 'faith' was to be a qualification. I hear privately that G. Balfour was not in favour of Gill, but if he is to go contrary to Plunkett he will, I think, require to have his hands strengthened. I think to put forward a Fenian and a *pro-Boer* now would be most detrimental."[45] Cadogan then met Plunkett at the department's new offices in Merrion Square, but he could not sway the vice president. Ten days later, Gerald Balfour tried his hand at negotiating with the junior minister. Afterward Plunkett thought that he had brought the chief secretary around to his way of thinking, but he also noted in his diary on January 4, 1900, "I am quite ready to resign my post if I don't get the appointment of my own staff into my own hands."[46]

Gill had some initial misgivings that his appointment might jeopardize the success of the new department, but he eventually decided to advocate his own case. On January 2 he wrote a letter to Plunkett and sent a copy to his friend, John Redmond. Gill explained that his appointment would certainly call attention to a celebrated comment

44. P.F.C.S., P.P., BAL. 55, Plunkett to Lady Balfour, Dec. 21, 1899.
45. H.L.R.O., CAD/1710/3, J. Hogg to Viscount Duncannon, Dec. 23, 1899.
46. P.F.C.S., P.D., Jan. 4, Jan. 14, 1899.

Arthur Balfour made when he was chief secretary—that "there were no Catholic Irishmen sufficiently educated and qualified for government posts." Gill then observed that his appointment would serve the useful purpose of blunting ill-advised criticism from Catholics of the appointment of qualified Protestants to the other important positions. Gill also wrote that he had resolved a potential problem that was related to his accepting such an appointment. When he was a Nationalist MP, Gill had pledged not to seek or accept office, but he assured Plunkett that he had received "an adequate representation of those who would take the most sensitive view of the pledge" that they would not block his way. Gill then concluded with a direct challenge to the administration's policy of conciliation. "I should have thought, indeed, so understand the position, that it was not in spite of, but rather to a considerable extent because of my political past that my services are held to be of some special use to a Department which had its origin in a non-party movement and which is dependent not only for its successful working, but for its actual power of motion upon the goodwill and confidence of the masses of the people, who are to elect 2/3 of its purse-controlling Board."[47]

Plunkett's determination was strong enough to secure Gill's appointment. Reaction followed on predictable lines. The *Irish Catholic* observed in February that because the president and vice president of the department were Protestants, Gill's appointment gave special satisfaction. "The new Department would not begin under a cloud of suspicion and distrust and this to us is a hopeful augury for the efficiency and popularity of the new Government Department." The *Irish Catholic* went on to hope "that in the disposal of the other office connected with it, the claims of Catholics will be fully recognised."[48] Unionists in the House of Commons suggested that the Irish Parliamentary party had acquiesced in Plunkett's appointment in return for the appointment of Nationalists to other positions.

After the struggle to secure Gill's appointment, Plunkett was determined to avoid anyone who was involved in political affairs when he selected his other subordinates. Although he was not going to avoid

47. N.L.I., Red. P., Ms. 15190 (2), Gill to Plunkett, Jan. 2, 1900.
48. *Irish Catholic,* Feb. 10, 1900.

Catholics, Plunkett advised Gill in February that he saw "difficulties in overdoing the Catholic Nationalist appointments."[49] Plunkett looked to academe for the two division chiefs. At Leeds University he secured the services of John Campbell, a young professor from Scotland for the agricultural side.[50] He found the other man he wanted, William Somerville, at the head of Cambridge University's new Agricultural Department. Gerald Balfour was also impressed by Somerville's credentials, and Plunkett asked Arthur Balfour to assist them in obtaining the professor.[51] Somerville deliberated but decided that the university had greater claims on him.[52] Captain T. B. Shaw, whom Plunkett had recruited from the London Board of Education and the South Kensington Science and Art Department to assist in shaping DATI's Science and Art Section, then agreed to assume the additional duties of head of the Technical Instruction Division. Plunkett hoped that, in time, he could promote a departmental inspector from the ranks to the position.[53]

With the top echelon filled, Plunkett and Gill searched for the best qualified candidates for the other leading positions in the department's varied divisions. They recruited personnel from faculties in England, Scotland, and the United States; they also recruited outstanding graduates of Irish colleges and universities. Many experienced officials transferred from departments that were merged with the new department. The Office of Fisheries Inspectors remained under the leadership of Rev. William Spottswood-Green, a Protestant clergyman who had a worldwide reputation as an expert in the field. The museums, libraries, and other educational institutions also transferred some of their professional and clerical staffs.[54]

Over the years, Gill developed a unique point of view among Irish bureaucrats on the qualities he looked for when he selected staff officials. He liked to promote from the ranks and opposed the selection of even high-ranking clerks only on the basis of competitive exami-

49. N.L.I., Gill P., Ms. 13495 (1), Plunkett to Gill, Feb. 9, 1900; see also P.F.C.S., P.D., June 22, 1900.
50. P.F.C.S., P.D., June 5, 1900.
51. B.L., B.P., Ms. 49792, Plunkett to Balfour, Feb. 9, 1900.
52. P.F.C.S., P.P., BAL. 80, Plunkett to Lady Balfour, Feb. 22, 1900.
53. N.L.I., Gill P., Ms. 13495 (2), Plunkett to Gill, Feb. 13, 1900.
54. *Fourth Report of the Royal Commission on the Civil Service,* Minutes of Evidence, see testimony of T. P. Gill, pp. 223–40.

nation scores. He feared that the examinations might create a caste system within the Irish bureaucracy. He gave his opinion to the Royal Commission on the Civil Service in 1913.

I attach myself more importance to rearing and breeding than to subsequent education. I mean if they come from a good home, from a decent stock of people with right traditions, you will have a chance of getting better original material; and when I speak of decent traditions, I am not speaking of aristocratic traditions, though I include them in my idea. I think the home of a farmer or a working-class home, in which independence, religion, honesty, truthfulness, loyalty, and these old principles were not merely names, but were revered and practised, would be just as likely to give you the original qualities. . . . I don't think that merely putting in a few years in a university and letting a man pass a brilliant examination at the end will make him a much better man for exercising control over a staff and for getting the best qualities out of a staff.[55]

Although the four legislative measures effected significant changes in the bureaucracy, the Irish executive in Dublin Castle also had to manage the normal course of appointments between 1895 and 1900. Leading positions in some minor departments, the Irish Public Record Office, for example, were filled by promoting officials from the ranks. Two county court judgeships were filled by appointing a Catholic Liberal-Unionist and one of Lord Ashbourne's brothers-in-law.[56] Cadogan and Ashbourne also had to attend to the appointment of local magistrates. During the viceroy's seven-year tenure in Ireland, he appointed approximately 1,270 justices of the peace. Only some 250 of these were Catholics, a sharp reversal of Morley's creation of Catholic magistrates.[57]

Judicial appointments at the highest level proved to be the major concern. One month after the judicial reorganization took effect, Judge Robert Warren of the Probate Court died. Accordingly, that court was merged into the Queen's Bench Division. Solicitor-General Kenny decided that he would now advance to the supreme court. One never knew when a given opportunity to move to the bench would be one's

55. Ibid., p. 227.

56. H.L.R.O. CAD/1428, Atkinson to Cadogan, Dec. 21, 1898; CAD/1434, Atkinson to Cadogan, Dec. 27, 1898; CAD/1385, G. W. Balfour to Cadogan, Aug. 30, 1898; CAD/1431, G. W. Balfour to Cadogan, Dec. 25, 1898.

57. *Leader,* Nov. 8, 1902.

last, and Attorney-General Atkinson, who was not interested in Warren's position, still had the first option to exercise if a better vacancy occurred. A political problem, however, complicated matters in this instance. The successor to the solicitor-generalship would have to face a by-election after receiving a government appointment. This concerned the Conservative party's leaders because their victory in the 1895 general election had not touched Ireland; in fact, the Unionists lost a seat to the Nationalists in that election. Moreover, Conservative party organizers warned Cadogan that Kenny's parliamentary seat in Dublin was not safe from the Parnellites in the event of a by-election.[58] The problem was solved when Dunbar Barton, who held a safe seat in Mid-Armagh, was named as Kenny's successor.[59]

Later that year, Lord Ashbourne's brother-in-law, Justice Edmund Bewley, became deaf and resigned from the Land Court. The Nationalists were especially interested in this vacancy. They thought that Bewley, although a Conservative, had been fair, but they thought that Ross had been a disappointment. Bewley's successor was R. E. Meredith, whose appointment was at least as surprising as Ross's had been the previous year. He was forty-one and had achieved Queen's Counselor rank only four years earlier. The *Nation* declared that the appointment was made on political grounds and predicted that Meredith was certain to favor the landlords.[60] The charge of bias was premature. Meredith was the only justice who did not join the Kildare Street Club, membership in which symbolized support for the Protestant ascendancy in Ireland.[61] Meredith did, however, exercise one prerogative of a supreme court justice: he appointed his two sons to important staff positions in the court's office.

There was yet another appointment to the supreme court late in 1899. Pressure began to build when rumors spread that Justice William O'Brien, one of only four Catholics on the bench, was about to retire. The most provocative letter Cadogan received about this imminent vacancy came from The O'Conor Don, a Nationalist landlord. After

58. H.L.R.O., CAD/1041–43; CAD/1048; CAD/1052; CAD/1104.

59. H.L.R.O., CAD/1210, Kenny to Cadogan, Oct. 15, 1897; CAD/1269, Barton to Cadogan, Dec. 22, 1897.

60. *Nation,* Jan. 8, 1898.

61. *Irish Times,* Jan. 28, 1916.

summarizing the religious and political imbalance on the supreme court, O'Conor Don advised, "In England and Scotland the government have lately shown that in making Judicial appointments, party and political considerations have been represented as of secondary importance."[62] He then asked, "Why should not the same principle be applied to Ireland?" "There can be no doubt," he continued, attempting to help the viceroy find an answer, "that putting party considerations aside, the late Attorney-General McDermott is at the head of the profession. . . ." Meanwhile, a letter appeared in the *London Times* that supplemented O'Conor Don's comments. "Vigil" noted in his open letter that in 1881 there had been an equal number of Protestants and Catholics on the supreme court, but by 1886 the composition of the bench stood at twelve Protestants and six Catholics. Lately, "Vigil" observed, there were fourteen Protestants against four Catholics, and now the Catholic component was threatened by further reduction. "Vigil" realized that a Unionist government could not be expected to appoint lawyers who had identified themselves with separatist schemes. "Nevertheless," "Vigil" concluded, "it seems clear that if there are men of distinction at the Irish Bar, born and bred in the faith of the majority, of whose fidelity to the cause of law and order there can be no doubt, and there certainly are such men, it would be expedient to choose Mr. Justice O'Brien's successor from among them."[63]

According to protocol the attorney-general had the first opportunity to accept or reject the post. This time Atkinson was interested, and he deliberated for almost a month.[64] Meanwhile, a group of Unionists, including a deputation from Ulster, pressed Cadogan and Ashbourne to appoint J. H. M. Campbell, the Unionist MP for St. Stephen's Green in Dublin, to either the bench or the Law Office.[65] Ashbourne admitted that Campbell had served his party well but would have to wait his turn behind the attorney-general and the solicitor-general.[66] Ashbourne

62. H.L.R.O., CAD/1671, The O'Conor Don to Cadogan, Dec. 3, 1899.

63. H.L.R.O., CAD/1688/2, *Times* (London) clipping, n.d.

64. H.L.R.O., CAD/1715, Atkinson to Cadogan, Jan. 2, 1900; CAD/1701, G. W. Balfour to Cadogan, Dec. 26, 1899.

65. H.L.R.O. CAD/1678, Duke of Dufferin and Ava to Cadogan, Dec. 7, 1899; CAD/1681, W. Q. Ewert to Cadogan, Dec. 8, 1899; CAD/1682, Lecky to Cadogan, Dec. 8, 1899; CAD/1686, H. W. Young (of Antrim) to Cadogan, Dec. 10, 1899; CAD/1687, H. O. Arnold-Foster to Cadogan, Dec. 11, 1899.

66. H.L.R.O., CAD/1685/1, Ashbourne to Cadogan, Dec. 10, 1899.

pointed out that Stephen Ronan, the Catholic Liberal-Unionist lawyer, had already been disappointed twice, but his real concern centered on Campbell's seat in Dublin. Instead, Ashbourne proposed George Wright, the senior crown prosecutor, who had also been passed over several times for the Law Office. Ashbourne explained to Campbell that he could have Wright's position and keep his seat. Ashbourne thought this plan was attractive because the senior crown prosecutorship was worth nearly fifteen thousand pounds, but Campbell was not interested. Campbell, who aspired to the lord chancellorship, wanted to start his public career in Dublin Castle. He maintained that his Dublin seat was safe and even had the temerity and foresight to warn Ashbourne that if he were passed over again, his friends would be so angered that possibly two Unionist seats in Dublin would be lost at the next general election.[67]

Atkinson eventually refused the judgeship, and Gerald Balfour was pleased that the attorney-general decided to remain in Dublin Castle.[68] Two days later Solicitor-General Barton exercised his option and took O'Brien's place on the bench. The viceroy then wrote to the prime minister and reviewed the candidates for solicitor-general. Cadogan told Salisbury that Ronan was not being pressed by Catholic interests, but he favored him. Balfour, he warned, was very much opposed to Ronan, and he added that Atkinson would probably resign if Ronan were appointed.[69] Nationalist opinion, if it was considered at all, opposed Ronan's appointment. He had served as junior counsel for the London *Times* during the Pigott forgery case, which failed to implicate Parnell in the Phoenix Park murders. With so many factors working against him, Ronan was passed over again, and Wright, who wanted the position, became the new solicitor-general.[70]

The executive's last important appointment was made in February 1899, when Christopher Redington, the resident commissioner of national education, died suddenly after surgery. The vacancy attracted a good deal of attention. Protestant leaders were especially concerned because in 1897 Cadogan had passed over Protestant educators and

67. H.L.R.O., CAD/1688/1, R. W. Middleton to Cadogan, Dec. 11, 1899.
68. H.L.R.O., CAD/1716, G. W. Balfour to Cadogan, Jan. 2, 1900.
69. H.L.R.O., Ash. P., B. 22/14, Cadogan to Salisbury, Jan. 18, 1900.
70. H.L.R.O, CAD/1720, Geo. Wright to Cadogan, Jan. 15, 1900.

selected two Catholics to serve as presidents of the Queen's Colleges in Galway and Cork. Church of Ireland opinion on the resident commissionership was mustered by two Protestant bishops who declared in a letter to Cadogan that it was time to appoint a Protestant to the position.[71] The bishops pointed out that there were already more Catholics than Protestants in important staff positions in the office and that the two previous resident commissioners had both been Catholic.[72] Meanwhile, the Committee of the General Assembly of the Presbyterian Church of Ireland, acting through its moderator, William Beatty, suggested to Cadogan that the resident commissioner should be appointed on a rotating basis and that it was now a Presbyterian's turn. The only Presbyterian ever to hold the post, Beatty informed Cadogan, was the first resident commissioner, some sixty years ago.[73] The leading Catholic on the board, the archbishop of Dublin, William J. Walsh, did not give Cadogan any lead. He wrote to Cadogan stating only that the quasi-interregnum between the old and new resident commissioners was a suitable time to secure competent secretaries and expert advisers for the board.[74]

Cadogan, however, was determined to appoint a Catholic educator as resident commissioner. He favored Dr. William Starkie, a moderate Unionist, who was the recently appointed president of Queen's College, Galway. Starkie also received support for the commissionership from two influential sources: W. E. H. Lecky, the Unionist MP for Trinity College, Dublin, and Justice Gerald FitzGibbon.[75] FitzGibbon agreed that Starkie was the best candidate and advised Cadogan that Starkie was willing to take the position.[76] After Starkie was appointed, Cadogan garnered several letters of approval, including one from the Protestant archbishop of Dublin, who thanked Cadogan for explaining the exceptional circumstances of the case.[77] Archbishop Walsh assured the vice-

71. H.L.R.O., CAD/1490/1, Peacocke to Cadogan, Feb. 15, 1899.

72. H.L.R.O., CAD/1490/1, Archdall to Cadogan, Feb. 15, 1899.

73. H.L.R.O., CAD/1496, William Beatty to Cadogan, Feb. 17, 1899.

74. H.L.R.O., CAD/1488, Walsh to Cadogan, Feb. 12, 1899.

75. H.L.R.O., CAD/1489, W. E. H. Lecky to Cadogan, Feb. 13, 1899.

76. H.L.R.O., CAD/1485/1, Fitzgibbon to Cadogan, Feb. 12, 1899; CAD/1486/2, Starkie to Fitzgibbon, Feb. 10, 1899; and CAD/1491, Fitzgibbon to Cadogan, Feb. 16, 1899.

77. H.L.R.O., CAD/1500, Archbishop Walsh to Cadogan, Feb. 18, 1899. See also Miller, *Church, State and Nation in Ireland,* pp. 5–6.

roy that the selection gave general satisfaction and noted optimistically that Starkie was a strong advocate of the reform of Irish intermediate education, which, along with university reform, was an issue of great importance to the Catholic hierarchy.[78]

During his administration of 1895–1900, Lord Salisbury and his advisers on Irish matters hoped to "kill home rule with kindness." They devised a strategy of legislative reforms and conciliatory administrative policies that was rooted in two principles: one traditional, the other progressive. The former principle was the Conservatives' standing commitment to continued rationalization of management and finance in public administration. This guided the Irish administration when it reformed the Irish supreme court. The government also maintained continuity with established policy in its Irish land legislation. The Land Act of 1896 followed the pattern of offering easier land purchase terms for tenants. The progressive element, on the other hand, was evident in the appointments that followed the creation of the Department of Agriculture and Technical Instruction and the local government board. The administration was abreast of contemporary thinking on the importance of employing certified professionals in public administration. Unionists, however, believed that the personnel changes in the bureaucracy were made at their expense. Their complaints notwithstanding, the government had in fact implemented the conciliatory strategy at a politically opportune time. Since the fall of Parnell in 1891, the various Nationalist factions had been in disarray. Parnellites and anti-Parnellites fought over control of newspapers and Irish Parliamentary party funds, assessed blame for Parnell's fall, and vied for authority in the country by championing the cause of the tenants.[79] They also used charges of place hunting to impugn their rivals' integrity and to demonstrate their own independence from British governments and their exponents in Dublin Castle.

The Parnellites used the topic of patronage to attack those Irish Parliamentary party members who brought their leader down. Parnellites believed that Gladstone's threat in 1891, that he would abandon home rule if Parnell continued to lead the Nationalists, was tied to a promise

78. H.L.R.O., CAD/1500, Walsh to Cadogan, Feb. 18, 1899.
79. Lyons, *Dillon,* pp. 179–206.

that he would give Nationalists positions in the Irish administration if they would abandon their leader. Slowly, the theory took root in the Irish imagination. Some Unionists, including the editors of the *Dublin Evening Mail,* were among the first to adopt the theory that Parnell had been the victim of a conspiracy of greedy place hunters.[80] Stanzas of panegyric poetry, "The Muses Tribute to Parnell," published in 1895 in Arthur Griffith's newspaper, *The United Irishman,* alluded to the link between Parnell's fall and the promise of patronage.[81] Parnell's reputation for being independent of British politicians and his disdain for the lure of Dublin Castle patronage became important components of the myth that developed after his death.[82] His opponents in the Nationalist movement were portrayed as petty and corrupt. Indeed, the dry rot in the movement seemed so pervasive that one of the party organizers in James Joyce's short story "Ivy Day in the Committee Room," which was set in Dublin in this period, could remark casually that even half of the hillsiders were in the pay of Dublin Castle.[83]

Timothy Healy had played a leading role in deposing Parnell. After splitting with Dillon in 1894, he portrayed himself as a watchdog on appointments. Dillon, he charged, only supported the Conservative party's legislation for Ireland in return for patronage favors. Healy also demonstrated his independence by periodically castigating Dublin Castle bureaucrats in his faction's newspaper, the *Nation.* Healy distanced himself still further from the Dillonites, late in 1896, when he accused them in his newspaper of making a profit through jobbery during the Rosebery administration.[84] This serious charge clearly implied that Dillon and his followers had violated the party's pledge. Three of the accused quickly defended themselves and their leader in letters to the *Nation.*[85] P. G. Phelan tried to turn the tables on Healy and make explicit what many Nationalists were now thinking about accepting appointments. "The information [on patronage] could be got much nearer

80. *Dublin Evening Mail,* Oct. 6, 1892.
81. *United Irishman,* Oct. 5, 1895.
82. William Murphy, *The Parnell Myth and Irish Politics, 1891–1956* (New York: Peter Lang, 1985).
83. James Joyce, "Ivy Day in the Committee Room," *Dubliners* (Middlesex, England: Penguin Books, 1975), pp. 113, 116–33.
84. *Nation,* Sept. 19, Sept. 26, Oct. 3, 1896.
85. Ibid., Oct. 10, 1896.

home than from me," Phelan began, alluding to Healy. "Try the medium through which a Crown Solicitor and a Resident Magistrate were made in Dundalk, a Crown Solicitor in a midland County, and magistrates galore in North Louth and other places." "Bear in mind," he admitted, "that I find no fault with the influential person who secured those offices for his political friends. On the contrary, I approve of his action, and only regret he did not succeed in making more." Phelan then warned Healy, "according to your views, all public offices in Ireland should go to the Unionists, and Nationalists allowed to remain the hewers of wood and drawers of water in their own country. I join issue with you on that, and boldly say that I would fill every office in Ireland with friends rather than foes." "I regard officialdom a greater enemy to Home Rule than landlordism," Phelan concluded, explaining, "the first is a living and growing power, the second a dying one."[86]

The debilitating arguments over jobbery and the government's successes in securing useful Irish legislation forced the Nationalist leaders to put an end to their feuds. Late in 1899 the followers of John Dillon and John Redmond finally recognized that the Irish Parliamentary party had to present a united front in the country because it was apparent to all observers that the Conservative government would again be returned to power after the general election, which was scheduled for late summer 1900. Should the Irish Parliamentary party remain divided for five more years, its position in the country would certainly be undermined by more conciliatory legislation, and the demand for home rule might indeed be compromised. And no one in the Nationalist movement had anything to gain from leveling more charges of place hunting at his opponents. This only called into question the integrity and judgment of all of the party members. By April 1900 the Irish Parliamentary party had closed ranks and selected Redmond as chairman. Healy refused to resolve his differences with the reunited party, although after his recent allegations of corruption it would have been difficult for many Nationalists to welcome him home.

During the general election Salisbury and his Irish advisers remained confident. The strategy of "killing home rule with kindness,"

86. T. W. Healy, *Why Ireland Is Not Free* (Dublin: Printed at the *Nation* offices, 1898), p. 99.

however, had not yet eroded the demand for home rule. It had, in fact, alienated some of their Unionist allies and helped to unite the Irish Parliamentary party. Nevertheless, Conservative party leaders planned to introduce more reform legislation in their next administration and to continue to prove that the union could work in the interest of all.

Chapter IV

It Dies Very Hard, 1900-1905

The Conservative government returned to power with an overall majority of 134 members in the House of Commons, more than enough to continue the conciliatory policy in Ireland. There was no change in the overall political division of the 103 seats in Ireland, although the Unionists' seats in Dublin and County Dublin were lost.[1] The personnel serving in the Irish executive remained unchanged, with one notable exception. Gerald Balfour resigned as chief secretary and became president of the Board of Trade with a seat in the cabinet. Balfour had been seriously ill in 1898, and he may have suffered a nervous breakdown in 1899. Moreover, his working relationship with other members of the Irish administration had deteriorated during 1900. Reaction to his departure was mixed. Some Irish observers thought that Lord Salisbury removed Balfour to pacify those Unionists who blamed the chief secretary for the administration's conciliatory policies toward Catholic Nationalists and tenant farmers.[2] Nationalists, recalling Balfour's work in land purchase legislation and his local government and grand jury reforms, thought that Balfour ranked among the greatest of all chief secretaries.[3] Unionists, recalling the same actions, thought that he had betrayed them.[4]

Balfour was succeeded by George Wyndham. In many ways Wyndham epitomized the talented, aristocratic Englishman who had chosen politics as a career. Thirty-seven years of age, Wyndham had advanced

1. Lyons, *Irish Parliamentary Party, 1890–1910,* p. 130.
2. P.F.C.S., P.P., BAL. 61, Plunkett to Lady Balfour, June 19, 1900.
3. Healy, *Letters and Leaders of My Day,* 2:435–37; Gwynn, *Redmond,* p. 98.
4. O'Mahony, *Viceroys of Ireland,* p. 315.

rapidly from the position of private secretary to Arthur Balfour, when Balfour served as chief secretary in 1886, to Parliament in 1889, to under secretary of war in 1898, and finally to chief secretary for Ireland. His appointment had some appeal to Irish sentiment because his mother was born in Athlone and his ancestors included a leader of the United Irishman Rising of 1798 who had been killed during the rebellion. Although he was not admitted to the cabinet, Wyndham made no complaint. Indeed, he was soon writing cheery letters from Dublin Castle to his family and friends about Ireland's bewitching atmosphere.[5]

Wyndham was convinced he could solve the Irish question. He thought a new and more comprehensive land purchase act could be the centerpiece of a Conservative party legislative program, which would also include university reform in the interest of Irish Catholics and administrative reform of Dublin Castle. However, an agrarian agitation in the west of Ireland posed a threat to his long-term plans. He made two personnel changes in the police departments. Colonel Neville Chamberlain, an Englishman, was appointed inspector-general of the Royal Irish Constabulary; John Ross of Bladensburg, an Irishman, was named chief commissioner of the Dublin Metropolitan Police.[6] Chamberlain was among the first of a number of soldiers who transferred from South Africa to assume police and civil service positions in Ireland. Ross, a convert to Catholicism and to unionism, had served in several Irish administrations between 1878 and 1885. He left retirement in 1898 to volunteer for South African duty but had recently returned home. The new police officials pleased the new chief secretary, who reported to Arthur Balfour that Chamberlain was preparing the constabulary for any eventuality.[7] In December the constabulary took the field, but the use of coercion against the tenant farmers did not stop the agitation. By 1902 nine counties had been proclaimed.[8]

The implementation of coercion worried Lord Cadogan, who had

5. See J. W. Mackail and Guy Wyndham, *Life and Letters of George Wyndham,* 2 Vols. (London: Hutchinson & Co., 1925), for his correspondence.

6. *New Irish Jurist and Local Government Review,* Dec. 27, 1900; *Belfast News-Letter,* July 10, 1926.

7. B.L., B.P., Add. Ms. 49803, Wyndham to Balfour, Nov. 26, 1900.

8. Michael Davitt, *The Fall of Feudalism in Ireland* (Dublin: MacMillan & Co., 1904), pp. 699–701.

only remained in Ireland out of personal loyalty to Salisbury. In cabinet meetings, Cadogan maintained that in areas where coercion was necessary, the chief secretary's use of the constabulary was ineffectual.[9] Wyndham argued in a letter to Arthur Balfour that the viceroy was not capable of comprehending his point of view. Wyndham stated that in the future his communications with Cadogan would only be conducted within the minimum bounds of ordinary politeness and loyalty. He concluded by asking Balfour "not [to] hold me responsible for Cadogan's views, and, still less, for his versions of mine."[10]

In this deteriorating personal situation both Cadogan and Wyndham became difficult colleagues. Cadogan tried the patience of Henry Robinson of the Local Government Board and Horace Plunkett of the Department of Agriculture and Technical Instruction.[11] Wyndham was equally difficult. Plunkett, who had initially welcomed Wyndham's appointment, told Lady Betty Balfour that Wyndham always seemed to be struggling for effect and that he was too much concerned about receiving the credit for reforms.[12] Eventually, Plunkett had qualms about making his regular visit to America because he feared what the "ingenious" and "heartless" Wyndham might do in his absence.[13] Wyndham brought much of this ill will upon himself. He once wittily observed that the government of Ireland seemed to be conducted by continuous conversation, but this pejorative assessment may have been at the root of his difficulties.[14] He was impatient with Dublin Castle officials, who were often bewildered when he held forth in conference. Wyndham complained to his father on Christmas Day 1901 that his subordinates rarely showed initiative or assumed any responsibility. "They watch your every gesture as a dog does instead of going in the direction you point out. In the end you must go yourself."[15]

Relations between Wyndham and Cadogan continued to deteriorate throughout 1901 over the issue of how to suppress agrarian outrages.

9. B.L., B.P., Add. Ms. 49803, Wyndham to Balfour, Sept. 20, 1901.

10. Ibid.

11. Robinson, *Memories: Wise and Otherwise,* pp. 137–41.

12. P.F.C.S., P.P., BAL. 64, Plunkett to Lady Balfour, Jan. 2, 1901; P.D., Nov. 13, 1900; Jan. 5, 9, May 27, 1901.

13. Digby, *Plunkett,* p. 91. P.F.C.S., P.D., Sept. 24, Nov. 5, 1902.

14. Mackail and Wyndham, *Life and Letters of George Wyndham,* 1:99; 2:407.

15. Ibid., 2:434.

Slowly, Wyndham isolated the lord lieutenant. Cadogan tried in vain to recapture the allegiance of those officials whose loyalty Wyndham had won.[16] Tension in Dublin Castle was finally relieved when Lord Salisbury retired from public life in July 1902. A few days later, Arthur Balfour, Salisbury's successor as prime minister, received news of the viceroy's resignation.[17] The new viceroy was Lord Edward Dudley, a wealthy young Conservative whose only previous experience in government was at the Board of Trade with Gerald Balfour. Dudley did not receive a seat in the cabinet, which went instead to Wyndham.

Although Cadogan was not consulted about his successor, his sense of duty demanded as he prepared to leave Ireland that he must give Wyndham a vote of confidence. Nevertheless, he could not refrain from noting in a final letter to Lord Ashbourne that Wyndham had so completely undermined his influence that not a single pen had been raised in his defense.[18] Cadogan expected, and perhaps deserved, a farewell salute because his effort to implement his government's policy in Ireland had been a success. In addition, as lord lieutenant he enlivened the social life of Dublin after the dull years of John Morley's and Viscount Houghton's tenure. He had worked hard to arrange the visits of the queen and members of the royal family to Ireland, and he secured honors and awards for judges and civil servants. Apparently no one in his entourage warned him that Dubliners watched all lord lieutenants, even the best of them, depart with a studied indifference.

Shortly after Cadogan announced his resignation, David Harrel, the under secretary, became severely ill. He explained to Wyndham that continued service in Dublin Castle would place his health in further jeopardy and as a consequence he too wished to resign.[19] Wyndham had anticipated his under secretary's resignation, and he had already begun to search for a replacement. Candidates for the position included Henry Robinson, Sir Joseph West-Ridgeway, and Walter Laurence, a civil servant with colonial experience. Wyndham was more impressed, how-

16. H.L.R.O., Ash. P., B. 22/39, Cadogan to Ashbourne, May 4, 1902. Healy, *Letters and Leaders of My Day,* 2:457, noted that Wyndham was worried about the undermining of his influence over Dublin Castle officials. Healy did not think Cadogan was instigating this intrigue.

17. H.L.R.O., B. 22/41, Cadogan to Ashbourne, July 15, 1902.

18. H.L.R.O., Ash. P., B. 22/43, 44, Cadogan to Ashbourne, July 28, Aug. 25, 1902.

19. Harrel, *Recollections and Reflections,* pp. 162–63.

ever, by Sir Antony MacDonnell, who was recommended to him by two Unionists, Lord Lansdowne, a former viceroy of India, and George Hamilton, president of the India Council. MacDonnell, an Irishman and a Catholic, had recently completed a distinguished career on the subcontinent, and he had expressed a desire to return to Ireland to do something for his native land.[20]

Wyndham wrote to Balfour about MacDonnell on August 25, 1902, explaining that it would be impossible to find a man as experienced as the former lieutenant-governor of the Northwest Province of India.[21] Balfour urged the chief secretary to exercise caution because MacDonnell was a Liberal and he did not want a home ruler for under secretary.[22] Wyndham made inquiries on this point and interviewed MacDonnell. He was relieved to learn that MacDonnell's interpretation of home rule extended only as far as a convention that would discuss local legislation. He also discovered that MacDonnell was opposed to extreme measures of coercion but that they were in accord on the issues of land legislation, university reform, and administrative reform.[23]

MacDonnell, meanwhile, conducted some interviews of his own. At the urging of his brother, Dr. M. A. MacDonnell, the Irish Parliamentary party member of Parliament for Queen's County, Sir Antony met with the party's leaders.[24] John Redmond and John Dillon were eager for the famous civil servant to join their ranks and were prepared to offer him a safe seat in Parliament. MacDonnell, however, was an administrator, not a politician. Besides, MacDonnell objected to taking the party's oath, which bound all of its members to the will of the majority. When Redmond and Dillon could not persuade MacDonnell to join them, they encouraged him to take the under secretary's position, and they backed up their words by criticizing Harrel's record in order to hasten his

20. Mackail and Wyndham, *Life and Letters of George Wyndham,* 1:79–81, 2:752–63.

21. CAB/37/75/00065, Wyndham to Balfour, Aug. 25, 1902.

22. Ibid., Balfour to Wyndham, Aug. 26, 1902.

23. Ibid., Wyndham to Balfour, Sept. 1, 1902. See also, N.L.I., Bryce Papers, Ms. 11014(2), Memorandum of Oct. 22, 1906, from MacDonnell about his political attitudes, citing letters from MacDonnell to Lansdowne, Sept. 13, 1902, and referring to a letter to Wyndham, Sept. 22, 1902.

24. Gwynn, *Life of Redmond,* pp. 100–101.

resignation.[25] MacDonnell also met with Liberal party leaders because he was worried about serving in a sensitive position in a Conservative administration. He explained to his confidant, Lord Ripon, that the under secretaryship afforded him an opportunity to reform Dublin Castle.[26] Ripon urged MacDonnell to be cautious, just as Balfour had urged Wyndham. Ripon noted that the Irish under secretary had occasionally assumed a political posture that was alien to the position of a regular civil servant. If this was to be the case again, he advised MacDonnell to obtain an assurance that he would be in a position to influence administrative policy. He also told MacDonnell that he must be equally certain of succeeding in his conciliatory schemes.[27]

MacDonnell weighed Ripon's advice and then wrote to Wyndham along the lines suggested.[28] MacDonnell expected to be treated as a colleague who would have government support for his work. Wyndham agreed to these conditions in a letter on September 25, 1902.[29] A form of assurance was also arranged. MacDonnell was promised a seat on the India Council that could serve as an escape route from Ireland if he found himself in an untenable situation.[30] When Harrel resigned in October, the government, by prearrangement, borrowed MacDonnell from the council for service in Dublin Castle.

Wyndham and MacDonnell began to work on their top priority—land purchase legislation. Wyndham grasped the essentials necessary to the ultimate solution of the land question: advancement of purchase money by the Treasury to the tenants at low interest rates, longer repayment time, and proper administration. His desire for a successful land act was given a boost by a roundtable conference that convened in Dublin in December. The tenants were represented by Redmond, William O'Brien, T. C. Harrington, and T. W. Russell, an independent Unionist member of Parliament from North Tyrone who had just won a narrow by-election victory by campaigning on the issue of compul-

25. Harrel, *Recollections and Reflections,* pp. 162–63.
26. B.L., Rip. P., Add. Ms. 43542, ff. 85–88, MacDonnell to Ripon, Sept. 17, 1902.
27. Ibid., ff. 89–91, Ripon to MacDonnell, Sept. 20, 1902.
28. Mackail and Wyndham, 2:760–61. See also N.L.I., Alice Stopford Green Papers, Ms. 15089(2), MacDonnell to Green, Oct. 30, 1902.
29. Ibid., p. 762.
30. CAB/37/75/00065, Wyndham to Lansdowne, Sept. 22, 1902; Wyndham to Balfour, Sept. 24, 1902.

sory sale of entire estates. The landlords were represented by Lord Dunraven, who took the chair, and by a number of other landlords. Leaving the administrative details of land purchase to the government, the participants reached agreement on three principles that they thought should frame new land legislation: new owners were entitled to a fair start and a reasonable prospect of success; landlords were to receive some special inducement to sell; and income from the sales should continue to be expended in Ireland.[31] Following the lead of the conference, Wyndham introduced a land bill in March 1903 and carried it triumphantly through Parliament. Known as the Wyndham Act, the legislation called for the compulsory sale of entire estates if three-fourths of the tenants on a given estate agreed to the purchase price. The state advanced the entire purchase price at 3 1/4 percent interest, to be repaid over 68 1/2 years. Landlords who sold their entire estates were given a 12 1/2 percent bonus from the Treasury based on the total sale price.[32]

Wyndham was determined to remedy the administrative failings that hindered previous purchase schemes. He began by appointing new personnel to positions that were created by the legislation. The new officials and positions were prompted as much by the increased work that would fall on the Land Commission as by Wyndham's lack of confidence in the current land commissioners. Wyndham did not believe that two of the Land Commission's three judges would negotiate sales with equity in terms of the landlords' interest. He thought Judge Richard Meredith had lost his nerve, and he called Judge Morrough O'Brien "a crank" with "disloyal proclivities."[33] Only John Wrench won the chief secretary's confidence, although Wyndham also formed a high opinion of John Franks, the commission's chief permanent official.

Three positions as estates commissioners, that is, land commissioners who would confine their business to the purchase of entire estates rather than to individual parcels of land, were created. Because the three new commissioners had judicial and administrative power to make rules governing land transactions and prices, these appointments were important to landlords and tenants alike. One appointee was one

31. Lyons, *Ireland Since the Famine,* pp. 218–19.
32. Ibid., p. 219.
33. B.L., B.P., Add. Ms. 49803, Wyndham to Balfour, Nov. 26, 1900.

of the current land commissioners, John Wrench, who was transferred within the commission to the new position. The second appointee, Michael Finucane, was probably recommended by the under secretary, who knew of his administrative record in India. Finucane, if unknown personally, was from a well-known Catholic Nationalist family. The landlords presumed that the third appointee would swing the balance of power among the estates commissioners in their favor. This did not happen. The position was given to William Bailey, who was promoted from the rank of assistant land commissioner. Bailey joined with Finucane to set prices that favored the tenants and, as a result, lowered the landlords' bonuses. Landlords and Unionists complained to Bailey, but he ignored them.[34]

The estates commissioners took the lead in staffing the new division within the Land Commission. The number of officials in the field—subcommissioners, land valuers, and surveyors—did not increase greatly, but the clerical staff had to be enlarged to cope with the massive transfer of land. Applicants brought letters of reference, some carrying political overtones, to the commissioners when they conducted their interviews. When the Royal Commission on the Civil Service asked Bailey about staffing procedures in 1913, he said that these letters had no bearing on hiring. New officials were trained on a complicated pending matter to determine their ability.[35] Most of the higher-ranking clerks who joined the Estates Commission transferred from other Irish departments. This rankled lower-ranking officials in the Land Commission Office who thought that their prior experience warranted their promotion to the new division. They hoped to take advantage of the extraordinary expansion in their own department because under ordinary circumstances there were not many opportunities for rapid advancement in the Irish civil service.[36]

Meanwhile, interest in the quality of administration in Ireland, an issue hitherto overshadowed by the land question, was building. Con-

34. J. G. Swift MacNeill, *What I Have Seen and Heard* (London: 1925) for correspondence between William Moore and Estates Commissioner Bailey.

35. Royal Commission on the Civil Service, 1914, (Cd. 7340), *Second Appendix to the Fourth Report of the Commissioners,* "Minutes of Evidence," Testimony of W. F. Bailey, C. T. Beard, and J. T. Drennan, Feb. 27, 1913: 298–312.

36. Ibid., pp. 312–19, for testimony from representatives of second division clerks and assistant clerks in the Land Commission.

cerns about patronage, place hunting, and maladministration were voiced with increasing regularity between 1900 and 1904. Dublin Castle's most extreme critic was Arthur Griffith, a Dublin journalist whose newspaper, *The United Irishman,* and organization, Cumann na nGaedheal, advocated exclusive use of Irish manufactured goods and resistance to anything that resulted in the anglicization of Ireland. He developed the so-called Hungarian policy, which was influenced by Francis Deák's withdrawal of Hungarian representatives from the imperial diet at Vienna, Austria, in 1867 and the subsequent reestablishment of a separate parliament in Budapest. Similarly, Griffith called for noncooperation with the British government, urging the withdrawal of Irish members from Westminster and the reconstitution of the Irish Parliament in Dublin. Griffith also called for the creation of a nationalized civil service that would compete with Dublin Castle's officials. In time, he maintained, British control of the Irish administrative machinery would loosen and wither away.[37] These ideas were incorporated into the political philosophy of the Belfast Dungannon Clubs, which were founded in 1904 by Bulmer Hobson and Denis McCullough. Both men were members of the secret physical-force organization the Irish Republican Brotherhood. Dubbed *Sinn Fein* (literally, "ourselves") in 1905, Griffith's self-reliance policy began to catch the imagination of some Irish men and women.[38]

Exponents of the exclusive use of Irish manufactured goods and the encouragement of the Gaelic Irish cultural heritage, referred to as the Irish-Ireland movement, were championed by D. P. Moran, editor of the influential Dublin weekly, the *Leader.* First appearing in September 1900, the *Leader* became a focal point for Irish-Ireland ideas, which Moran put into a Catholic and Nationalist context. For Moran, to be Irish was to be Catholic, and he had little tolerance for things non-Irish and non-Catholic in Ireland, including Dublin Castle administration. Few of its departments were spared from inquiry by the *Leader's* investigative staff. Moran substantiated his charges of bigotry in the administration with statistics showing the number of Catholics and Protestants in a given department or court. Moran differed from Grif-

37. Arthur Griffith, *The Resurrection of Hungary: A Parallel for Ireland* (Dublin: James Duffy & Co., Ltd., 1904).

38. Lyons, *Ireland Since the Famine,* p. 255.

fith and the supporters of Sinn Fein in one important respect. He did not believe that Irish Catholics could afford the luxury of ignoring Dublin Castle. On the contrary, he believed that Catholics should take every opportunity to join the civil service and police, and he congratulated those Irishmen who succeeded in advancing in the system. Moran thought that a great change for the better had occurred in the Irish bureaucracy's second division as a result of the competitive examinations.[39] He was, therefore, especially concerned about the high-level positions, which in the Indian and English civil service were filled through examinations. This was not the case in Ireland, and he believed that the use of open competition examinations for all civil service positions was the only way that Catholics could secure their fair share of appointments. Moran's fundamental optimism on this point helps to explain why he monitored high-level appointments so closely and why he treated the appointment or promotion of "foreigners" and Anglo-Irish Protestants over the heads of qualified Irish-born Catholic officials with such ridicule and scorn that it became his trademark as a journalist.

Irish Catholic interests also received attention from the *Irish Catholic.* Owned by Timothy Healy's friend the influential Dublin businessman William Martin Murphy, the *Irish Catholic* held that even enlightened Protestantism would not redress the inequities in the civil administration as they affected Catholics. The paper encouraged the formation of the sectarian Catholic Association, a layman's organization that sought a fair share of profit and preferment for Catholics in all areas. The newspaper took a special interest in issues related to Irish education and in the officials who operated in that sphere. Catholic newspapers such as the *Irish Catholic* and periodicals such as the *Irish Rosary,* as well as lay Catholic spokesmen, demanded that discrimination against Catholics must stop. They thought Catholics had been patient too long, and they were tired of the arrogance and bigotry of Dublin Castle officials who confronted them every day.[40]

The Catholic bishops were, of course, the most important spokesmen for the interests of Irish Catholics. While there was a chance that the

39. *Leader,* Jan. 10, 1903.
40. Healy, *Letters and Leaders of My Day,* 2:463; Miller, *Church, State and Nation in Ireland,* pp. 97–99.

Conservatives might solve the Irish university question, the bishops as a body would not undertake an unrestrained attack on the Irish administration. Indeed, the university question was closely linked to the question of administrative reform because the establishment of a Catholic university in Ireland would ensure that Catholic professional men could no longer be ignored in high-level administrative appointments on the ground that they did not have the proper educational qualifications. In addition, the administration in Dublin Castle pleased the bishops when it took action to improve intermediate education in Ireland. The number of commissioners was expanded in August 1900 from seven to ten and was made more representative of Catholic interests. In April 1901 Swift Paine Johnson was selected to fill the assistant commissionership in the Intermediate Education Office, which was reserved for a Protestant. Johnson was a leading educational reformer in Ireland and an expert in modern pedagogical theory. Of the eighteen candidates for the position, he was the only one who had an endorsement from the Catholic bishops.[41] Finally, the bishops exercised restraint because they did not want to lend credence to the anticlerical literature of the period that charged that the civil administration was already intimidated by the power of the priests, as one critic put it, "from the clerk of the petty sessions to the judge on the bench, from the sergeant of police to the highest permanent official in Dublin Castle."[42] Individual members of the hierarchy, however, occasionally spoke out about the Castle's discrimination against Catholics. The *Leader* repeated their comments in some of its articles and periodically recalled a quaint phrase Cardinal Michael Logue once used, that in the area of administrative appointments, Catholics never seemed to walk on the sunny side of the street.[43]

The bishops' general rule of silence on appointments was broken after the Conservative government announced in February 1904 that it

41. S.P.O.I. Registered Papers/1901/File no. 7430; S.P.O.I. Registered Papers/1901/File no. 7726, Johnson to Harrel, Apr. 18, 1901, and J. P. O'Farrell to Lord Plunkett (Cadogan's private secretary), Apr. 20, 1901.

42. Michael J. F. McCarthy, *Priests and People in Ireland* (Dublin: Hodges, Figgis & Co., Ltd., 1902), p. xii; see also, M. J. F. McCarthy, *Five Years in Ireland* (London: Simpkin, Marshall, Hamilton, Kent & Co., Ltd., 1901).

43. *Leader,* Nov. 21, 1903. See also, *Freeman's Journal,* Feb. 13, 1899; *Freeman's Journal,* Feb. 11, 1902.

would not proceed with university reform. At their annual spring meeting at Maynooth Seminary, Rev. John Hogan, the editor of the *Irish Ecclesiastical Record,* reported that Catholics were completely excluded from several administrative departments and that there was a disproportionate number of Protestant officials in many others. Then, in a discussion at the same meeting on the various education departments, the bishops scoffed at Wyndham's preliminary education reform proposal—the creation of a single Department of Education that would coordinate the different parts of the Irish education system—because in the prevailing administrative scheme of things, it would only mean the creation of "another outwork of Dublin Castle and a further opportunity of practical ascendancy for a favoured sect."[44] Dr. Hogan's paper and the discussion of the proposed department were a prelude to two resolutions concerning the administration. One took note of "the practical exclusion of Catholics and of others who are known to entertain popular sympathies from public offices and employments in the gift of the Government" and called this "a flagrant abuse of governmental power worthy of the worst days of ascendancy." Next, the bishops resolved that they were not in favor of excluding Protestants, or anyone else, from positions to which they were justifiably entitled; rather, they wanted fair play for Catholics in appointments and promotions. The resolution went on to encourage the concentration and attention of public men, the press, and the full force of enlightened public opinion on "the indefensible system . . . until the monopolists are compelled to stand on exactly the same footing as the rest of their fellow countrymen in public opportunities and advantages."[45]

Protestant opinion responded to the points that were being raised by the Catholic Nationalist writers and the bishops. Rev. John Mahaffy, the provost of Trinity College, Dublin, set the pace for his coreligionists in the article "The Romanizing of Ireland," which appeared in *The Nineteenth Century and After* in July 1901.[46] Dr. Mahaffy pointed out that in the two years since Gerald Balfour's local government reform, Catholic officials had become so dominant in all but two Irish counties

44. *Leader,* July 2, 1904.
45. Ibid.
46. J. P. Mahaffy, "The Romanization of Ireland," in *Nineteenth Century and After,* 50 (July 1901), 31–43.

that everything from local appointments to business contracts had been awarded in the Catholic interest. He warned Ulster Unionists not to be lulled into a false sense of security by their geographic isolation, because if Catholics gained control of the central administrative apparatus, the entire bureaucracy and judiciary would be turned against Protestants everywhere in Ireland. Likewise, he warned Presbyterians, Methodists, and Quakers who cooperated with Catholics to gain redress of their own grievances to beware of the Catholics' strategy to divide and conquer Protestants of all denominations. Mahaffy went on to predict that unless Protestants were vigilant even the independent-minded Catholic bureaucrats who were not yet under the control of the Catholic hierarchy and priests would be purged from public service. Mahaffy also declared that the time might come when knowledge of the Irish language would supersede professional qualifications for administrative positions.

For those who thought along the lines laid down by Dr. Mahaffy, control of the administration was a matter of "winner take all." Protestant Unionists were already frightened by the sweeping personnel changes that occurred in local government, on grand juries, and, to a lesser extent, in the local magistracy. The Conservative administration's appointment of twelve Catholics, of a total of fifty-seven high-level appointments in Ireland between 1895 and 1901, alarmed them. In 1902, the new solicitor-general for Ireland, John Campbell, publicly criticized the Catholic Association's demands for preferment of Catholic officials.[47] Protestants in Ulster were on the alert for any evidence that the administration was undermining their position. They objected vigorously in summer 1903 when Antony MacDonnell removed a Protestant constabulary officer allegedly because the parish priest complained to him that the officer was about to marry a local Catholic woman.[48] In 1904 Protestant leaders in Dublin responded to the Catholic bishops' resolutions. Under the headlines WAR AGAINST PROTESTANTS and STARTLING SPEECHES BY R.C. PRIESTS, the *Daily Express* warned Protestants, "Their Lordships speak out with bitterness and arrogance which plainly ex-

47. *Leader,* June 18, 1904. Campbell succeeded Wright in 1901.

48. Alice Stopford Green, "The Case of Sir Antony MacDonnell," *The Independent Review,* 6 (July 1905), 22–23.

presses the determination 'to get on top' as if they had taken that phrase as the text of their discourse."[49]

The Irish administration could have used some support from individuals who occupied the middle ground between Catholic Nationalists like Griffith and Moran and Protestant Unionists like Mahaffy. Such support was not forthcoming. Indeed, the administration was criticized by moderates both within its ranks and outside them. A county court judge, William O'Connor Morris, declared in print that although the bureaucratic regime in Ireland maintained order and remained imposing, it was an essentially weak government, resembling the French system that Tocqueville exposed as a factor in bringing on the French Revolution. Judge Morris also thought that the Conservatives were not doing enough for Catholics and Nationalists in terms of appointments.[50] Antony MacDonnell complained about how the Irish administration was largely closed to Catholics. He confessed to his wife shortly after his arrival in Ireland that he was amazed at the bigotry he encountered among the bureaucrats.[51] Six months later in a speech after a dinner honoring the lord lieutenant, MacDonnell said that he had been told when he returned to Ireland that sectarian animosity was on the wane. If so, he said bluntly, "it dies very hard."[52]

Moderate Irish Unionists and some English observers called for an end to the Protestant ascendancy's control of the Irish bureaucracy. R. J. Smith advised in 1903 that since Catholics had become the ascendancy party after the Local Government Act of 1898, it was now in the Protestants' best interest to reconcile themselves to this fact and voluntarily put an end to their collective conceit. Smith singled out for special criticism a clique of Freemasons who blocked Catholics from their fair share of official appointments and commercial advantages.[53] If it became necessary to curb the ascendancy, other writers suggested that abolishing the lord lieutenancy would be a good place to start. Filson

49. *Leader*, July 2, 1904.

50. William Morris, *Present Irish Questions* (London: Grant Richards, 1901), pp. 11, 20, 28, 31; 190–99.

51. Bod. Lib., MacD. P., e. 216, ff. 11–22, letters from MacDonnell to his wife, Nov. 1902.

52. *Leader*, May 16, 1903.

53. R. J. Smith, *Ireland's Renaissance* (Dublin: Hodges, Figgis & Co., Ltd., 1903), pp. ii–iii, 313, 343.

Young maintained that the lord lieutenancy was an outmoded institution. He explained that of the viceroy's court, "its officials and entourage—are not Irish, but friends and relations of the English viceroy. [They were] a little glittering cloud of parasites, invested with a mimic dignity, and often impudent and intolerant in their public behavior. . . ."[54] An anonymous pamphleteer, "A Constitutional and Loyal Home Ruler," looked to the king to breathe a new spirit into the Irish administration. He urged the king to encourage MacDonnell's reform efforts and summarily to replace the decadent ascendancy officials in Dublin Castle.[55]

Wyndham did not do much between 1901 and 1904 to blunt the criticism from Catholics. When Solicitor-General Wright succeeded Justice James Murphy on the Queen's Bench Division in October 1901, John Campbell, a Protestant Unionist who was hated by the Nationalists, was appointed solicitor-general. In November 1901 the *Leader* reported that all six of the recently appointed intermediate education inspectors were either Englishmen or Scots and as such, the *Leader* contended, were not qualified to examine Irish students in courses with an Irish content.[56] The *Leader* also criticized Horace Plunkett's selection of experts in the Department of Agriculture and Technical Instruction, deriding them as foreigners and scholastic dilettanti.[57] Several of Wyndham's appointments smacked of nepotism and favoritism. Harrel's son was promoted to the assistant commissionership of the Dublin police in January 1902; Wyndham's private secretary, Philip Hanson, a Protestant Englishman, was appointed commissioner in the Board of Public Works, a position that had been held by a Catholic Irishman.[58] One Catholic Nationalist who received a high-level appointment, as secretary of the General Prisons Board, was the son of The MacDermott, the former Liberal attorney-general for Ireland.[59] Lord Londonderry, the

54. Filson Young, *Ireland at the Crossroads: an Essay in Explanation* 2nd ed. (London: Grant Richards, 1904), pp. 140–41.

55. A Constitutional and Loyal Home Ruler, *A New Spirit in Irish Administration, and the King* (Westminster: P. S. King & Son, 1903), pp. 12–13.

56. *Leader,* Nov. 2, 1901.

57. Ibid., Feb. 9, 1901.

58. Harrel, *Recollections and Reflections,* p. 154.

59. The son of the chief crown solicitor for Ireland, Sir Patrick Coll, replaced young MacDermott in the Inland Revenue Department.

postmaster-general who oversaw the Irish General Post Office and its twenty thousand employees, did not help Wyndham later that year when he appointed seven Englishmen to head Irish postal stations.[60] In 1903 all twenty-one of the assistant land commissioners appointed to administer the new land act were Protestants.[61] Plunkett added to Wyndham's woes in 1904 when he maintained in his book, *Ireland in the New Century,* that Ireland's economic troubles could be traced to the Catholic church's role in Irish education and to certain defects in the Irish Catholic character.[62] With one stroke the so-called junior minister (who had lost his seat in Parliament in the general election but remained in his position of vice president of the Department of Agriculture and Technical Instruction) brought the thunder of the church down upon himself, and he alienated the entire spectrum of Nationalist opinion that had encouraged his work in agricultural reform.

The questions raised by critics both inside and outside the Irish administration helped the Irish Parliamentary party. The party took advantage of the reports of religious and political imbalances in personnel to maintain that under a home rule administration these imbalances would be corrected—not in the interest of party, but rather in the interests of equity, fair play, and sound administration. The party also began to repair the damage caused by the charges of place hunting and pledge breaking that had been hurled about during the split. The party needed to take action because potential political rivals such as Griffith denounced party members as "green-liveried henchmen of the British connection who were interested only in the spoils of office."[63] James Connolly, the leader of a small group of socialists in the Irish labor movement, made similar charges in his pamphlets.[64]

The Irish Parliamentary party and its supporters began their offensive against Dublin Castle in 1903 when Thomas Addis Emmet, a collateral descendant of the celebrated Irish hero Robert Emmet, wrote a two-volume history of the Irish administration.[65] Emmet charged that

60. *Leader,* Sept. 13, 1902.

61. Ibid., July 23, 1904.

62. Horace Plunkett, *Ireland in the New Century* (New York: E. P. Dutton and Company, 1904).

63. Cited in Lyons, *Ireland Since the Famine,* p. 249.

64. James Connolly, *Erin's Hope* (Dublin: 1897).

65. T. A. Emmet, *Ireland Under English Rule, or A Plea for the Plaintiff,* 2 Vols. (New York and London: G. P. Putnam's Sons, 1903).

the bigoted Orangemen, or Unionists, who currently held office acted with the tacit support of the government to ensure steady support for themselves and their friends at the expense of the country at large. Moreover, Emmet was not convinced that those few Catholics who had been appointed to office were all the best possible men. "While there have been some notable exceptions and some most estimable Irishmen selected as Catholics to hold office under the British Government in Ireland," Emmet explained, "there have been too many chosen who were not shining lights as Catholics and who were as little interested afterwards in the welfare of the country at large as any other English office holder." To substantiate his charges of bigotry, Emmet included an appendix with statistics illustrating religious imbalances in several departments. Emmet contended the figures demonstrated that every public office where appointments were made by nomination was crammed with Protestants. In the lower divisions of the bureaucracy, however, Emmet observed large numbers of Catholic officials who had obtained positions because they had succeeded in the open competition examinations. This differentiation between competitive and nominated positions in the same department concerned Emmet. "The higher posts are usually filled by Protestants; for examination only insured fair play in the first step, and 'Preferment goes by letter and affection.'" "One is sometimes driven to the conclusion," Emmet declared, "that a little less forbearance on the part of the majority would more speedily realize the condition of simple equity, which is what Catholics desire."[66]

In November 1903 William Field, one of the party's experts on government finance, began a three-part series in the *New Ireland Review* that called attention to the waste of Irish monies by the British-controlled parts of the Irish bureaucracy. Field did not enter into the personnel question. For him, Dublin Castle's maladministration involved problems of efficiency, public utility, contracts, and finance. The competent administration of local government under the recently elected councils supplied Field with the evidence he needed to claim that Ireland's financial affairs would be ably administered under Nationalist

66. Ibid., 2:324. Emmet employed statistics from the *Freeman's Journal* and from John F. Taylor, K.C., "Downtrodden Irish Protestants: An Appendix to Mr. Mahaffy's Paper in the July Number of this Review," in the *Nineteenth Century and After,* 1901.

leadership.[67] Working from that premise and maintaining that Ireland could be administered by Irishmen without any increase in expenditure, Field declared that the Irish civil service departments that were under direct imperial control by the Treasury and by British department heads in London should be transferred to Irish control in Dublin.[68] In his third essay he noted that imperial regulations on the Irish post office savings banks drained £30,000 annually from the country and that an additional £10,800 was lost in stamps and postal orders. Further, Ireland lost £10,000 in Exchequer and audit fees, and between £23,000 and £46,000 to the London Stationery Office. The Civil Service Commission took £18,000 each year, and Field could not even begin to estimate the revenue that was lost in the Irish portion of taxes paid to support the Board of Trade and the Admiralty.[69]

Field's research in administrative finance was an important departure for the Irish Parliamentary party. It allowed the party leaders to concentrate on management issues as opposed to personnel issues, which often lead to charges of place hunting. Using Field's data, Redmond could argue that a home rule government under his leadership would put an end to the waste of Ireland's tax revenue. During his speeches Redmond first entertained crowds with anecdotes about the Board of Public Works' macadamite roads that connected unimportant towns and its wharves that crumbled into the sea before he went on to explain the up-to-date statistics and figures that pertained to public administration.[70]

By 1904 conditions seemed right to initiate a comprehensive administrative reform in Ireland. The lead was taken by Lord Dunraven, who intended to organize a roundtable conference to study this problem in 1902, but the land purchase conference took priority. MacDonnell and Wyndham, however, kept the issue alive and periodically discussed administrative reform with Dunraven in 1903. In his book, *The Outlook in Ireland* (1904), Dunraven called attention to the need for better

67. William Field, "How Ireland Suffers Under Centralized Departments," in *New Ireland Review* 20, (Nov.–Dec., 1903).

68. Ibid., Jan. 1904.

69. Ibid., Feb. 1904; see pp. 338–348.

70. John Redmond, *Ireland's Financial Relations with England: An Address to the Young Ireland Branch of the United Ireland League delivered in the Mansion House, January 26, 1905*. N.L.I., Ir. 94108, p. 16.

administrative coordination by describing some sixty-seven departments that operated in Ireland. Hoping once again to rally both Nationalists and Unionists, Dunraven invited various political leaders to attend a roundtable conference to prepare the way for administrative reform. This time the leaders of the Irish Parliamentary party refused to participate. Redmond and Dillon were determined to pursue an independent course of action that excluded cooperation with Unionists on anything that might undermine the demand for home rule. Among Nationalists only William O'Brien, who resigned from the Parliamentary party on the issue of cooperation with Unionists, supported the new conference.[71]

On August 31, 1904, Dunraven's group, known as the Irish Reform Association, issued a short preliminary report calling for the devolution to Ireland of a larger measure of self-government than the country currently possessed. The association wanted to alter the administrative procedures for spending the annual development grant for Ireland by constituting a deliberative body in Ireland that would act in much the same way that a similar body operated in India. As work on elaborating the preliminary report proceeded, MacDonnell wrote to Wyndham, who was away on holiday, and to Lord Dudley, who took a keen interest in the proceedings, to inform them that he was collaborating with Dunraven. The more detailed scheme, which was probably drafted by MacDonnell, was published on September 26, 1904.[72] It called for the devolution of Irish financial affairs and legislative business to two local councils. The Financial Council, half of whose members would be elected and the other half nominated, would administer the general public finances of Ireland. The other council, to be known as the Statutory Body, would be constituted of Irish peers, Irish members of Parliament, and members of the Financial Council. It would promote legislation for purely Irish purposes.

Official reaction to devolution was as quick as it was decisive. The

71. Lyons, *Dillon,* pp. 231–43; N.L.I., Wm. O'B. P., Ms. 10496(5) and Ms. 10496(12). O'Brien stated, "There is absolutely nothing left to hope for except a wobbling Party slowly but surely losing the confidence of the country and getting replaced by Heaven only knows what crew of 'Cawtholic' placehunters or Unionists."

72. Correspondence relating to devolution is in Mackail and Wyndham, *Life and Letters of George Wyndham,* 1:91–107; 2:764–82. See also, N.L.I., Green P., Ms. 15089(3), MacDonnell to Green, Sept. 1, Sept. 12, 1904.

day after the more detailed proposal appeared, Wyndham wrote a letter to the London *Times* repudiating it as contrary to Unionist principles. He was supported by speeches from both Attorney-General Atkinson and Solicitor-General Campbell. Atkinson probably spoke for many Unionists—and perhaps unwittingly for some Nationalists as well—when a few days later he called devolution a "weak and silly attempt to grant home rule on the sly."[73] After meeting with the chief secretary, MacDonnell wrote to Dunraven and severed his connection with the Irish Reform Association.

The proposal gave the Nationalist press an opportunity to address issues directly related to administration and home rule. The *Freeman's Journal* focused on the Parliamentary party's current emphasis on administrative finance. It asked why financial administration, expenditure, and taxation were not included under the cognizance of the statutory body.[74] A week later, the *Leader* welcomed the proposal, but Moran raised questions about executive power. "In plain words," his editorial asked, "what about Dublin Castle? Who is to be in power there? Who will appoint the judges, high court and county court? Who will appoint the higher government officials? Who will control the police?"[75] Although devolution was null and void without Wyndham's support, the Nationalists nevertheless touched on the conditions that would have to be met before they could confidently take control of the Irish administration: clear responsibility for, and the power to shape, policy and its implementation.

Unionist opposition to devolution centered on the proposal's political implications.[76] It was for them also a question of power. Unionists believed that they would be in a minority on both councils, just as they had become on the local government bodies. Ulster Unionists were convinced that the Conservative government had broken faith with them on preserving the union. They identified MacDonnell, who they suspected of being devolution's chief architect, as well as Lord Dudley

73. *Irish Times,* Oct. 13, 1904.

74. *Leader,* Oct. 1, 1904; Lyons, *Dillon,* p. 274.

75. *Leader,* Oct. 1, 1904.

76. For Unionist party reaction to devolution see Lyons, "The Irish unionist party and the devolution crisis of 1904–5," *Irish Historical Studies,* 6, no. 21 (Mar. 1948): 1–22; and N.L.I., Chief Secretary's Office, Dublin Castle, *Irish Newscuttings, with some annotations,* 1880–1920, Vol. I, "Devolution Scheme, Irish Reform, 1904."

and other anonymous Dublin Castle officials as leaders of a plot against their hegemony. Exasperated by what they perceived as the government's latest attempt to conciliate Nationalists, several Ulster Unionist organizations joined forces to form the Ulster Unionist Council in December 1904. Although the Nationalists were quite willing to let devolution pass into oblivion, the Ulster Unionist party was determined to drive the people responsible for the proposal out of public life.

Wyndham and Balfour expected hostile questions from Ulster Unionists about both devolution and MacDonnell's position in Dublin Castle when Parliament opened in 1905. MacDonnell, who was at first shaken by the vehemence of the Ulster Unionist criticism of his actions, quickly decided that he would not yield to political pressure, and in any case, the place on the India Council that was to serve as his route of escape had been filled by another man. Besides, he did not think that he had done anything untoward.[77] Wyndham admitted to Balfour on November 24, 1904, that should a debate centering on MacDonnell's conduct arise, he could not say that MacDonnell had ever disobeyed instructions or acted disloyally. Wyndham declared further that if he could not justify the retention of MacDonnell to his fellow Conservatives on the merits of the case, he would resign.[78]

The cabinet met in a special session on December 10 to discuss the devolution scheme and MacDonnell's role in its formulation. The cabinet yielded to pressure from Ulster Unionists and decided to give a "measured censure" to MacDonnell; that is, the government declared that he had overstepped his bounds, but he was not to be charged with any disloyalty to his superiors. The next day, Wyndham, following the lead of the cabinet, told MacDonnell that as a result of the censure he would be unable to defend him when the House of Commons convened in February.[79] The under secretary bristled at the implication that he had acted improperly by assisting Dunraven. He reminded Wyndham that he had informed both of his superiors in writing about his actions, and he recalled the special conditions of his appointment, which although undefined, promised him freedom of action and rea-

77. Bod. Lib., MacD. P., e. 216, ff. 70–71, MacDonnell to Lady MacDonnell, Oct. 11, 1904.

78. Mackail and Wyndham, 2:766–68; see also 1:98.

79. Lyons, "The Irish unionist party and the devolution crisis of 1904–5," p. 14.

sonable prospects of success. Because Wyndham had misplaced the relevant correspondence on these points, he was at a severe disadvantage as he prepared his explanation of his own knowledge of events in Ireland and a description of the lines of authority that governed the activities of his subordinate civil servants.[80]

When the House of Commons met on February 16, 1905, Charles Craig, the Unionist party MP for South Antrim, asked Wyndham to explain MacDonnell's relationship to devolution. Wyndham told the House that the under secretary had assisted Dunraven in shaping the scheme; that the government believed MacDonnell had acted honestly but erroneously; that he (Wyndham) had no knowledge of MacDonnell's activity in drafting Dunraven's second report; and that MacDonnell had been appointed to the under secretaryship on a temporary basis at the chief secretary's request.[81] The following day in the House of Lords, Lord Lansdowne spoke in support of Lord Dunraven and Lord Dudley, who was under fire from Ulster Unionists because he supported devolution. The major part of his speech gave an exposition of the special terms of MacDonnell's appointment and his role in assisting the Irish Reform Association.[82] The majority of the Irish Unionists in both Houses of Parliament expressed amazement that an irregularly appointed civil servant was engaged in what appeared to them to be a conspiratorial attack on the union, with the knowledge of his superiors to boot.

Eager to take advantage of the trouble in the Unionist ranks, Redmond moved an amendment to the opening address: "that the present system of government is in opposition to the will of the Irish people." Only six Irish Unionists voted with the government, and three of them were law officers. Members of the Parliamentary party then demanded to know why MacDonnell had been censured if Wyndham had appointed him as a colleague rather than as an ordinary public servant.[83]

80. Mackail and Wyndham, *Life and Letters of George Wyndham,* 2: Appendix A, 771–88.

81. Great Britain, *Parliamentary Debates, House of Commons,* Fourth Series, 141 (Feb. 16, 1905), 324–26.

82. Ibid., House of Lords, Feb. 17, 1905: 455–66. Dunraven spoke earlier (pp. 432–37) to rebut Edward Carson's allegation "that a permanent civil servant retained under a Unionist Government at Dublin Castle had himself evolved a policy which had been disavowed by the Prime Minister and the Chief Secretary for Ireland."

83. Lyons, *Dillon,* p. 245.

Neither Wyndham nor Balfour was able to reconcile their previous statements that MacDonnell had exceeded his authority as a mere temporary civil servant with Lansdowne's exposition of the special conditions of the appointment. As the minister responsible, Wyndham resigned when he found himself in an untenable position on both the terms of the appointment and his admitted lack of knowledge of what he had called erroneous activities.

Ulster's Unionist leaders were not satisfied with blocking devolution and driving Wyndham from public life. During 1905, they demanded Dudley's and MacDonnell's removal, too, but both remained in place.[84] Balfour hoped to restore the confidence of his Irish Unionist allies when he selected a new chief secretary. His first choice was the solicitor-general for England, Edward Carson. Carson was willing to accept, on the condition that all official communications would pass directly to him rather than through the hands of the under secretary, whom Carson did not trust.[85] But an obstacle arose when Carson decided that he could not be senior to Attorney-General Atkinson, who had been his senior in the Law Office during Arthur Balfour's chief secretaryship. This consideration caused Carson to withdraw. Atkinson, who stated that he was a lawyer and not a politician, also refused the post. Horace Plunkett and Henry Robinson were other possible choices, but Balfour eventually selected Walter Long, the president of the English Local Government Board.[86] Like several of his predecessors in the Chief Secretary's Office, Long had some Irish relatives. It was his attitude, however, that most pleased the Unionists. Long's view was straightforward: he would "endeavor to govern in accordance with the fundamental principles and accepted policy of the Unionist Party" during the few months that were thought to be left to the government.[87]

The new chief secretary's first priority was to define his working relationship with his under secretary, who Long discovered had earned widespread respect. They conferred in March 1905 and both men came away from the briefings believing that they could work together.[88] Long

84. B.L., Bal. P., Add. Ms. 49802, letters of Dudley to Balfour, Feb. 2, Feb. 25, Feb. 26; Mar. 7, Mar. 11, Mar. 15, 1905.

85. Hyde, *Carson,* p. 209.

86. P.F.C.S., P.D., Mar. 11, 1905.

87. Cited in Gwynn, *Redmond,* p. 111.

88. N.L.I., A. S. Green Papers, Ms. 15089(5), MacDonnell to A.S. Green, dated by

soon developed a sympathetic opinion of MacDonnell's part in the devolution episode, although he informed Balfour in April that the hostility to MacDonnell was continuing unabated in Ulster.[89] MacDonnell's chief concern was to prevent Long from yielding to demands of landlords who wanted the administration to suppress tenant farmers who had begun to agitate for lower land purchase prices. He made trips into the country accompanied by bishops, priests, and local politicians in an effort to calm the tenants.[90] However, the under secretary was soon hospitalized and underwent surgery, and the subsequent period of recuperation prevented him from performing his duties for several months. Without MacDonnell's restraining influence Long eventually used the constabulary to curb the agrarian agitation.

Long also had to define his relationship with Lord Dudley. Reaching an accommodation with him was not so easy. Difficulties centered on appointments. Dudley wanted to continue to implement the conciliatory policy toward Catholics and Nationalists and Long wanted to act in the Protestant and Unionist interest.[91] Both men were quick to criticize the other's decisions. Dudley complained to Long and Balfour when they ignored him during appointment decisions for the commissioners of National Education and the Royal University in Dublin; Long complained to both Dudley and Balfour when the viceroy appointed the son of a late Nationalist MP to the viceregal household.[92]

The chief secretary explained his view of the proper distribution of authority in the Irish administration to Balfour on July 31. He asked Balfour to make it clear to Dudley that the minister responsible to the House of Commons must be the head of the government in Ireland, regardless of previous relationships between viceroys and chief sec-

---

Green "after MacDonnell's first meeting with Long." B.L., B.P., Add. Ms. 49766, Long to Sanders (Balfour's private secretary), Mar. 15, 1905.

89. Ibid., Long to Cabinet Colleagues, Apr. 28, 1905. See also, CAB/37/75/00065, Memorandum of meeting of Ulster Unionist Members of Parliament, March 30, 1905: unanimous resolution that MacDonnell is a "standing menace" to Unionist interests and their regret that he had not yet been transferred out of Ireland.

90. N.L.I., A.S. Green Papers, Ms. 15089(5), MacDonnell to Green, Apr. 12, 1905; B.L., Rip. P., Add. Ms. 43542, ff. 149–54, MacDonnell to Ripon, May 5, 1905.

91. Gwynn, *Redmond*, p. 111; Robinson, *Memories: Wise and Otherwise*, pp. 164–66; Charles Petrie, *Walter Long and His Times* (London: Hutchinson & Co., 1936), pp. 90–91.

92. B.L., B.P., Add. Ms. 49776, Long to Balfour, July 31, Aug. 25, 1905; Long to Sanders, Aug. 10, Aug. 21, Aug. 25, 1905.

retaries.[93] A few days later Long took the opportunity of a question that Dudley raised about the proper office procedure to follow in making appointments to tell the Lord Lieutenant the same thing. "Policy," Long explained, "is often indicated by the appointments made; this is especially the case in Ireland and if I, as the Minister responsible for the Government of Ireland, come, after careful and full consideration, to the conclusion that the selection of a particular individual is necessary, I must ask you to be so good as to act upon my advice unless you can show me that some other individual would be a better selection and would represent the same principle."[94] Dudley was not prepared to accept this explanation; and Balfour was asked to settle the dispute. On August 15, the prime minister replied to Dudley's direct question: whether it was Balfour's wish that "the views of the Chief Secretary should always prevail." After quickly reviewing the history and constitutional status of the Irish lord lieutenancy, Balfour declared, "I can only answer *yes.* There can be but one head of the Irish administration."[95] Dudley conceded but his relationship with Long did not improve. Within weeks Dudley complained to Balfour again that Long was ignoring him in matters both large and small. He told the prime minister that he found himself "completely out of sympathy with Long's policy and with many of his acts." "He seems," Dudley explained, "to be allowing himself to be advised by the extreme Unionist and Protestant section of the Irish community and to be departing entirely from the conciliatory spirit of Wyndham's regime." "I cannot make a speech," Dudley continued, "except on most unimportant matters, because nothing would induce me to adopt the tone that Long affects, whereas to take the line I did while Wyndham was secretary would immediately precipitate a crisis between Long and myself."[96]

During the government's final weeks in power, ill will continued. When he looked ahead to the eventual change of governments, Long asked Balfour not to transfer Dudley to a prestigious post such as the vacant governor-generalship of Madras because Irish Unionists would interpret this as an endorsement of the lord lieutenant's behavior on

93. Ibid., Long to Balfour, July 31, 1905.
94. Cited in Petrie, *Walter Long and His Times,* pp. 94–95.
95. B.L., B.P., Add. Ms. 49802, Balfour to Dudley, Aug. 15, 1905.
96. Ibid., Dudley to Balfour, Oct. 8, 1905.

devolution.[97] A decision also had to be made on Attorney-General Atkinson's future. He had passed up numerous opportunities to advance to the supreme court because Lord Cadogan had promised him an appointment as lord of appeal in the House of Lords. Long discovered, however, that Lord Ashbourne was pressing the English lord chancellor to block the appointment. This alarmed Unionists because Ashbourne's candidate for the prestigious position was Justice FitzGibbon, who they suspected might be a home ruler.[98] Long was worried, too. He pointed out to Balfour that FitzGibbon would be a powerful advocate for home rule in the House of Lords.[99] Balfour honored the long-standing commitment made to Atkinson and at the same time allayed Unionist fears about Fitzgibbon. Campbell, the solicitor-general, was promoted to the vacant attorney-generalship, thereby establishing his claim on the position and, ultimately, on a promotion to the supreme court bench when the Conservatives next returned to power. Balfour and Long refused to succumb to eleventh hour Ulster Unionist pressure to appoint as solicitor-general the outspoken Ulster Unionist member of Parliament for South Belfast, William Moore. With only a few days remaining for the Conservative government, that position was left vacant.

The Irish executive was at the center of two Conservative governments' attempts to "kill home rule with kindness." It was the agent that implemented conciliatory programs that changed the shape of the Irish administration by creating new, and somewhat decentralized, departments and by expanding the number of officials. Between September 1895 and November 1905 significant legislation reorganized the structure of the Irish Supreme Court of Judicature, established the Department of Agriculture and Technical Instruction, and created the Estates Commission. Legislation affecting grand jury and local government reform in 1898 and land purchase legislation in 1903 greatly increased the work load of the Local Government Board, the Congested Districts Board, the Land Commission, the Registry of Deeds, and the Chief Secretary's Office. The Land Commission officials' ability to manage the administrative details attendant to the massive transfer of land was especially remarkable. The commission averaged about fifty purchases

97. B.L., B.P., Add. Ms. 49776, Long to Balfour, Oct. 23, 1905.
98. Ibid., Long to Balfour, Nov. 12, Nov. 26, 1905.
99. Ibid., Gerald Arbuthnot to Sanders, Nov. 26, 1905.

per working day between 1904 and 1914. Officials in the Agriculture and Technical Instruction Department collected data and conducted useful field work. At the Local Government Board the increased amount of paperwork pressed its staff to process some twenty thousand pieces of correspondence per year. Overall, the number of civil servants increased by about twelve hundred, mainly in the Land Commission and Department of Agriculture and Technical Instruction, rising by about 30 percent to approximately forty-three hundred officials in 1905.

Not only did the number of bureaucrats increase as a result of conciliatory policy. There was also a slight change in the type of officials who were appointed to leadership positions in the bureaucracy, and there was a significant change in the type of officials who were entering the system's lower and middle levels. The latter phenomenon was the result of two processes that after twenty-five years were beginning to produce observable changes in the bureaucracy's personnel. The first was the use of competitive examinations to fill vacancies in the bureaucracy; the second was intermediate education reform that benefited Irish Catholic students, making them more competitive in many walks of life, including public service. These two processes coincided as the generation of officials who had administered services in Ireland under the unreformed administrative system before 1876 began to reach retirement age. While these two processes were having a predictable outcome, the Conservative government and its Irish executive officers were selective when they made appointments at the highest levels. Although Catholics and Nationalists remained outnumbered by wide margins on the bench and in most departments in 1905, the appointment of fifteen Catholics, mostly Unionists but some Nationalists, too, out of approximately seventy high-level appointments that were made between 1895 and 1905, augmented the small number of Catholic Nationalists who were holdovers from John Morley's term.

The policy of "killing home rule with kindness" in general, and the administrative aspects of the policy in particular, affected the Unionists and Nationalists in very different ways. Moderate Unionists, centered largely in the southern counties, believed that the union could produce tangible benefits for all Irishmen. They accepted reform of local government councils and grand jury selection procedures, where their authority was already eroded, and they accepted land purchase legislation, for a price. They were prepared to admit, within reason, that Catholic and Nationalist candidates for judicial, legal, and administrative positions should not be excluded for preferment on grounds of religious belief or political orientation. They encouraged the rationalization of the Irish administration through a plan of devolution that would take fiscal responsibility for the bureaucracy from Dublin Castle and transfer it to more representative Irish councils. However, the more conservative Unionists, centered largely in Ulster, did not want to alter Ireland's relationship with the United Kingdom. Although they lost no appreciable power in local government in their province after 1898, and like the landlords to the south, benefited from the bonus clause that was attached to the Wyndham Act, they believed that the administrative plan to loosen imperial control of Dublin Castle posed a potential threat to the union. They linked the trend toward popular control of local institutions to the proposal to reform the central administration, which they feared was a prelude to further measures of home rule. Devolution was beyond what Ulster Unionists would tolerate from their Unionist allies at home and from their Conservative allies in Britain.

The Conservatives' conciliatory policies presented an interesting challenge to the Nationalist leaders. They cooperated with Conservatives and Unionists on legislation that benefited the Irish Parliamentary party's constituents: local government reform, supreme court reorganization, creation of the Department of Agriculture and Technical Instruction, and land purchase legislation. They would not cooperate on devolution. Two popular Nationalists, Timothy Healy and William O'Brien, broke with John Redmond on the issue of continued cooperation with the Unionists and Dublin Castle, thereby calling into question the even larger issue of the party leaders' authority to determine the most advantageous route to home rule.

During the decade of Conservative administration, Nationalist observers began to believe that a reform of Dublin Castle's employment practices would somehow promote efficiency and promise a better delivery of services. Of course there was no proof that Catholic Nationalists were better administrators than Protestant Unionists. D. P. Moran was on firmer ground when he exposed the bigotry and discrimination against Catholic and Nationalist officials and candidates for appointment and promotion. But the personnel issue was an especially difficult one for Redmond. He had little, if anything, to gain by calling continual attention to the religious and political imbalances in the administration. The place hunter label had to be avoided at all costs. He turned instead to finance and management issues to offer a more statesmanlike argument for home rule, but he would not cooperate to formulate administrative and financial devolution. That might undermine the demand for full home rule, and in any case there was no guarantee he would have power over, and responsibility for, a devolved administration. Nationalists of all stripes wanted a government in Ireland with a responsible executive and a bureaucracy that would reflect the composition of, and respond to, the citizens of the nation. That point of view was perhaps best summarized in 1905 in an open letter to the lord lieutenant from the Parliamentary party's ablest publicist, R. Barry O'Brien:

> It is notorious that the highest positions in the government of Ireland have been and are filled by Protestants, almost wholly to the exclusion of those who professed the religion of the nation. There is nothing bigoted in calling attention to these facts. The Irish do not want a Catholic Government. They want a National Government. Of course a National Government in a country like Ireland must, from the nature of the case, be in the main a Catholic Government because Ireland is in the main a Catholic nation. It has well been said that the government of a country must partake of the character of the people.[100]

100. R. Barry O'Brien, *England's Title in Ireland: A Letter Addressed to His Excellency the Lord Lieutenant of Ireland* (London: T. Fisher Unwin, 1905), pp. 36–37.

Chapter V

A Race of Officials Not Merely Irish by Birth, 1906-10

When the Liberal party prepared to take power in December 1905 its leaders reordered the country's priorities to concentrate on social welfare legislation and defense. Home rule was placed in a subordinate position, although Henry Campbell-Bannerman, the new prime minister, decided to pursue a step-by-step legislative program to prepare the way.[1] John Redmond had no difficulty in reaffirming his party's alliance with the Liberal party, but until home rule regained its position at the top of the Liberal party agenda, he wanted the Liberals to consult him about the conduct of Irish affairs. Therefore, when Campbell-Bannerman was shaping his ministry in December 1905, Redmond wrote to him expressing the hope that Nationalists would see a new spirit instilled into Irish government. He stated that the appointment of the chief secretary, lord lieutenant, and law officers was particularly important, and that so far he was unimpressed with the candidates he had seen mentioned in the press.[2]

In selecting his Irish executive, Campbell-Bannerman tried to reassure Irish Nationalists about his own commitment to home rule by appointing enthusiastic home rulers. He appointed his fellow Scotsman and former lord lieutenant, Lord Aberdeen, as viceroy, and he appointed James Bryce, a distinguished historian and a native of Belfast, as chief secretary. Campbell-Bannerman followed the traditional course

1. John Wilson, *C-B: A Life of Sir Henry Campbell-Bannerman* (London: St. Martin's Press, 1973), pp. 435, 456.

2. B.M., C-B. P., Add. MS 41238, ff. 129–30, Redmond to Campbell-Bannerman, Dec. 5, 1905.

by reappointing Samuel Walker as Irish lord chancellor, the position he had held between 1892 and 1895 in John Morley's administration. Walker had also served as Irish attorney-general in 1885 when Campbell-Bannerman had been chief secretary for Ireland. A week later Campbell-Bannerman distributed the law offices, using a plan devised by Bryce, Walker, and Antony MacDonnell, who, as a civil servant, had not vacated his position as under secretary with the change in government. The plan deviated from the traditional procedures. C. H. Hemphill, the former Liberal solicitor-general, was given a peerage; William Dodd, the Liberal sergeant-at-law who was next in line for promotion, was promised the next vacancy on the Irish Supreme Court of Judicature if he would not now claim a law office.[3] This permitted the appointment of two new law officers, and R. R. Cherry and Redmond Barry were named attorney- and solicitor-general, respectively. Cherry was an expert on land law; Barry was a highly respected Catholic barrister. The final decision on appointments concerned the so-called junior minister, Horace Plunkett. He expected that the Nationalists would demand that he be replaced as vice president of the Department of Agriculture and Technical Instruction. To his surprise, MacDonnell convinced the lord lieutenant and chief secretary to retain Plunkett provisionally, until the Irish administration could be reorganized or until the department could be assessed by a committee of inquiry. In return, Plunkett understood that he was to take a strictly nonpartisan approach in his official duties.[4]

Campbell-Bannerman's appointments did not give the Parliamentary party leaders satisfaction. Dillon called Walker an "old Whig," and Healy aptly characterized Aberdeen as "a decoy duck who carried no guns."[5] The retention of Plunkett, whose controversial book on Irish education had recently appeared in an inexpensive popular edition, annoyed both the party's clerical allies and those Nationalists who did not endorse his policies for improving life in the countryside.[6] The law offi-

3. Ibid., Add. MS. 41211, f. 321, Bryce to Campbell-Bannerman, Dec. 13, 1905.

4. P.F.C.S., P.D., Dec. 13, 1905; P.P., Bal. 73, Plunkett to Lady Balfour, Dec. 15, 1905; B.M., C-B. P., Add. MS. 41211, ff. 322–24, Bryce to Campbell-Bannerman, Dec. 15, 1905.

5. B.M., C-B. P., Add. MS 41211, ff. 331–32, Bryce to Campbell-Bannerman, Dec. 20, 1905; Healy, *Letters and Leaders,* 2:475–76, letter of T. M. Healy to his brother, Dec. 12, 1905.

6. *Leader,* Dec. 23, 1905; Jan. 6, 1906.

cers, however, did commend themselves to the Parliamentary party. Barry, a Liberal, was vigorously supported by the party when he fought a close election in the North Louth constituency. Cherry, on the other hand, was not liked by Irish Unionists, who criticized his radical politics throughout his career.[7]

The most important new official was Bryce, and Redmond was not happy about this choice. He doubted Bryce's administrative ability, which would be severely tested in Dublin Castle, and he felt that Bryce did not command much respect in the House of Commons.[8] Dillon, however, thought that it would be difficult to find anyone better, and on December 19, 1905, he sent Bryce a letter with advice about what the Liberals should do while home rule was pending. They "ought to govern the country, so far as the present system allows, in accordance with Irish ideas—ascertaining those ideas from the representatives of the majority of the Irish people."[9] If the Liberals were attacked in the House or in the press on their Irish policy, he advised Bryce to declare that "the great evil of the present system is that under it, it is not possible to carry out fully the government of Ireland because the men who are entitled to speak for the Irish people cannot be fixed with the responsible and sobering influence of power." Bryce forwarded the letter to the prime minister and replied to Dillon that he agreed "with most, perhaps indeed with all" of the letter.[10] Dillon took advantage of this opening and sent Bryce an agenda that included land legislation, agricultural laborers legislation, and repeal of the Coercion Act. He also suggested close consultation with party leaders on Irish finance, on the position of Horace Plunkett, on the use of the Irish language in the national schools, on the evicted tenants problem, and on the appointment of personnel to the Land Commission.[11]

Bryce, in turn, found that he had something to offer Dillon and Redmond. His under secretary, MacDonnell, was busy working on a new plan to reform Dublin Castle's administrative system. Although

7. B.M., Bal. P., Add. MS 49776, Long to Balfour, Jan. 3, 1906.

8. J. O. Baylen, "'What Mr. Redmond Thought': An Unpublished Interview with John Redmond, December, 1906." *Irish Historical Studies,* 19 (Sept. 1974), 185. N.L.I., Red. P., MS. 15182(8), Dillon to Redmond, Dec. 12, 1905.

9. B.M., C-B. P., Add. MS 41211, ff. 333, Dillon to Bryce, Dec. 19, 1905.

10. T.C.D., D.P., Bryce to Dillon, Dec. 25, 1905.

11. Lyons, *Dillon,* pp. 281–83.

they were not yet prepared to offer any detailed plan, both officials promised to keep the Parliamentary party leaders informed. Meanwhile, Bryce began to prepare for a legislative program by appointing commissions of inquiry for the Department of Agriculture and Technical Instruction, the Belfast Police Department, railways, canals and waterways, Trinity College, Dublin, forestry, arterial drainage, the poor law system, and the congested districts. Bryce followed the precedent set by John Morley in 1892 by consulting Redmond on the staffing arrangements, but he did not always take Redmond's advice on commission personnel or on the terms of reference. Dillon was particularly unhappy about the selection of the commissioners. He concluded that the key officials in the Irish executive were too concerned about conciliating Unionists and landlords.[12] Bryce took a different point of view. He explained to MacDonnell that with so many commissions to be arranged and so many interests to be satisfied, it might seem as if he were acting contrary to Redmond's wishes, but actually he was trying to appoint balanced commissions whose reports would not be dismissed out of hand.[13] Redmond and Dillon continued to object. In May Redmond repudiated the Trinity College, Dublin, inquiry, and in July he and Dillon were disappointed with the personnel selected to serve on the congested districts inquiry, which was the only commission they had expressly requested. Dillon was always concerned when anyone beyond his control took an interest in the problems of Irish tenant farmers. He was worried because MacDonnell placed himself on that commission and selected the former Conservative lord lieutenant, Lord Dudley, to serve as its chairman.[14]

With the commissions of inquiry under way, Bryce and MacDonnell turned to another area that concerned the Parliamentary party leaders, the personnel on the Irish Land Commission. Redmond and Dillon had pledged during the general election that they would seek personnel changes at all levels on the commission, alleging that the assistant land commissioners and land valuers, who were charged with fixing fair

12. Ibid., Red. P., MS. 15182(10,11), Dillon to Redmond, Mar. 25, Apr. 4, June 30, July 6, July 9, July 11, 1906.

13. N.L.I., Bry. P., MS 11013(1), MacDonnell to Bryce, May 15, May 17, May 20, 1906.

14. Ibid., Red. P., MS. 11013(3), Redmond to Bryce, July 10, July 17, 1906.

prices for farms, had maintained a prolandlord bias. They looked to Bryce to correct the imbalance. Bryce was in a position to satisfy the Nationalists because in March 1906 all twenty-seven assistant commissioners came up for an annual review. He turned the review over to MacDonnell, who invited the land and estate commissioners to join in the process. MacDonnell first recommended eight new appointments—all Nationalists, he thought—but he then reduced the number to five.[15] Dillon was furious when he saw the list. He wanted twenty new officials, and he could only express his satisfaction with two of the five new men. He concluded that MacDonnell must have ignored the advice of the Nationalist commissioners, Bailey and Finucane. Dillon wrote to Redmond on March 29 and observed that because Bryce and MacDonnell knew the importance Nationalists placed on the personnel of the Land Commission, their decisions were all the more ominous.[16] Redmond agreed, and in his reply to Dillon he warned that if the party acquiesced or showed weakness by failing to remonstrate in Parliament, their credibility in Ireland would be threatened.[17] When they raised the issue during the debates on the Irish estimates in April, however, Bryce told both the Parliamentary party members and the Unionist party members, who challenged the five new men, that the appointments were final.[18]

Frustrated on this front, Dillon and Redmond turned from the assistant land commissioners and land valuers to the larger and more complicated question of appointing new land and estates commissioners. Their plan was based on the hope that either Justice Richard Meredith or Justice Gerald Fitzgerald would agree to move from the Land Commission to the supreme court. Bailey, the estates commissioner who had Redmond's and Dillon's complete confidence, could then be shifted from the Estates Commission to the Land Commission, where he could concentrate on settling some four thousand appeals cases brought by new proprietors who were in arrears of payment for their farms. A new estates commissioner could then be appointed in Bailey's place to hear

15. N.L.I., Bryce Papers, MS. 11012(3), MacDonnell to Bryce, Mar. 16, 31, 1906.

16. Ibid., Red. P., MS. 15182(10), Dillon to Redmond, Mar. 29, 1906.

17. Ibid., Dillon to Redmond, Mar. 31, Apr. 1, Apr. 9, 1906; T.C.D., D.P., Redmond to Dillon, Apr. 3, 1906.

18. Great Britain, *Parliamentary Debates* (House of Commons), Fourth Series, 155(1906), 1319–46.

the cases of thousands of prospective proprietors who were seeking lower purchase prices. Political, administrative, and financial considerations would all affect the outcome of this plan. The transfer of Meredith to the King's Bench Division of the court would be a serious breach of faith with Dodd, who had been promised the first promotion only three months earlier. In addition, the Treasury was certain to balk at filling a supreme court vacancy, and there was disagreement in legal circles in Ireland about the amount of time and personnel necessary for completing the Land Court's business.[19]

MacDonnell was the pivotal figure in resolving the issue. He delayed action on the appointments throughout the summer by raising questions about Bailey's qualifications for the position of judicial land commissioner.[20] Then, in August, he and Lord Chancellor Walker began to look for other candidates. Their first choice was Matthew Bodkin, who had been an Irish Parliamentary party MP for North Roscommon between 1892 and 1895. He left Parliament in 1895 to take up a career as a journalist on the *Freeman's Journal* and became the newspaper's expert on land law. Walker, however, could not arrange the retirements and transfers that were necessary to permit the appointment because none of the Unionist judges would resign for Bodkin's benefit.[21] Walker and MacDonnell found a second candidate for the Land Court, Charles O'Connor, a Nationalist barrister who worked in the Sergeants-at-Law Office, and they were able to obtain some movement when A.M. Porter retired as master of the rolls.[22] Porter had been in ill health since the unexpected death of his sons, one in 1901 and the other in 1903. Meredith left the Land Court to succeed Porter. Dillon, who wanted Bryce to follow his advice, then told Bryce that O'Connor's appointment to the Land Court would be completely unsatisfactory to the Parlia-

19. Red. P., MS. 15182(10), Muldoon to Dillon, Mar. 26, 1906; Dillon to Redmond, Mar. 29, 1906.

20. Bry. P., MS. 11012(3), MacDonnell to Bryce, Mar. 6, 1906; MS. 11012(4), MacDonnell to Bryce, Apr. 2, 1906.

21. Bod. Lib., MacD. P., MS. Eng. hist. c. 350, ff. 27–28, Bryce to MacDonnell, Aug. 13, 1906; N.L.I., Bodkin Papers, MS. 10702(1), Bryce to Bodkin, [Aug. or Sept.] 11, 1906.

22. N.L.I., Bry. P., MS. 11014(1), Walker to Bryce, Sept. 17, 1906; MacDonnell to Bryce, Sept. 19, 1906. B.M., C-B. P., Add. MS 41211, ff. 340–43, Bryce to Campbell-Bannerman, Oct. 5, 1906.

mentary party.[23] A third candidate, James Wylie, was then identified by Bryce. Wylie had been one of the first legal assistant commissioners appointed under the Land Act in 1881. An Ulsterman, he stood for election unsuccessfully as a Liberal in North Armagh in 1885 and in North Tyrone in 1886. He had a sound reputation at the Four Courts as both a lawyer and a legal scholar. After Bryce advised Redmond of his intention, Wylie was appointed.[24] Neither Dillon nor Redmond objected to Wylie's selection as judicial commissioner, but after the appointment had been made, Dillon complained to Bryce about the lack of consultation with the Parliamentary party leaders earlier in the summer. He wrote to Bryce on October 17 declaring that Bailey was the obvious choice for the position and that the opinions the chief secretary had received from MacDonnell about Bailey's lack of qualifications and about O'Connor's acceptability to Nationalists were not only inaccurate but deliberately deceptive.[25]

Redmond's and Dillon's disenchantment with the chief secretary and under secretary continued into the autumn. Redmond found it increasingly uncomfortable even meeting with Bryce. There had been no coordinated effort between them in the House during 1906, and they did not meet to discuss long-range legislative plans. The Parliamentary party discovered that much of the social welfare legislation that was fashioned for England was not suited to Irish conditions. The legislation that enabled local authorities to provide meals to needy schoolchildren seemed to be based on socialist philosophy, and as such it alarmed Catholic clerics and Catholic school officials. The legislation designed to provide housing for the urban poor in England was unsuited to Ireland because Irish municipal corporations were unable to pay for or borrow their share of the cost.[26] It became apparent to Redmond that until Bryce's numerous commissions of inquiry reported, there could be no action on the Parliamentary party's own legislative program. As far as legislation was concerned, 1906 was turning out to be a very disappointing year in Ireland.

23. N.L.I. Bry. P., MS. 11014(2), Dillon to Bryce, Oct. 14, 1906.
24. Ibid., Bryce to Redmond, Oct. 16, 1906; Redmond to Bryce, Oct. 17, 1906.
25. Ibid., Dillon to Bryce, Oct. 17, 1906.
26. Joseph O'Brien, *Dublin: City in Distress* (Sacramento: University of California Press, 1983). See chapter 5, "Housing," pp. 126–58.

Bryce was disappointed that his relationship with Redmond had not been amicable. Still, he hoped that MacDonnell's plan to reorganize the Irish administration would win him favor in Nationalist circles.[27] Redmond and Dillon were not optimistic. MacDonnell had dashed their hopes on the appointments to the Land and Estates Commissions, and it was evident to them that he had captured Bryce and did not care to take them into his confidence.[28] Moreover, MacDonnell had promised to consult with Redmond about the details of his work on administrative reform, but the only prominent Nationalist he consulted was the independent William O'Brien.[29] As early as June 1906, when the cabinet reviewed a preliminary draft of the plan, Redmond worried that he might be held responsible in Ireland for a scheme that he knew nothing about.

Redmond finally received a draft of the proposal in October.[30] He learned that MacDonnell envisioned an Irish council that would manage Irish administrative affairs. The council would have fifty-five members: two-thirds elected triennially by the county councils, the remainder nominated by the lord lieutenant. The under secretary would act as an ex officio council member. The lord lieutenant would have absolute control, through the council, of all matters concerning the registrar-general, the Public Works Board, primary and secondary education, reform and industrial schools, the Local Government Board, the Department of Agriculture and Technical Instruction, and the Congested Districts Board. Individual committees of the council would oversee each of these administrative areas. The council's administrative costs would be met by a special fund granted by the imperial Exchequer. There were no provisions for control of the police forces or the judiciary; there were no provisions for revenue raising.

Bryce and MacDonnell believed that the proposal had merit on both

27. B.M., C-B. P., Add. MS 52518 (unbound), Bryce to Campbell-Bannerman, Aug. 19, 1906. "The thing one might fear," Bryce told the prime minister, "is that the Nationalists will be disappointed when they find how far from the Home Rule Bill of 1886 is that which we propose to give them. Still, they will be fools if they don't take it."

28. J. O. Baylen, "'What Mr. Redmond Thought,'" pp. 183–86.

29. Joseph V. O'Brien, *William O'Brien and the Course of Irish Politics, 1881–1918* (Berkeley: University of California Press, 1976), pp. 168–69.

30. A. C. Hepburn, "The Irish Council Bill and the Fall of Sir Antony MacDonnell, 1906–1907," *Irish Historical Studies,* 17 (1971), 474–75.

administrative and political grounds. MacDonnell made an ingenious effort to decentralize a large part of the administrative machinery of Dublin Castle. He thought that careful attention to the selection of the personnel who would serve on the small committees would place individual departments closer to the people because the majority of the council members would be selected by the county councils. Bryce thought the proposal had merit on political grounds. It was consonant with the Liberal party's strategy to move step-by-step toward home rule. For him, the council was a logical interim measure. At the same time, he believed that a reform of the Irish administration would pass in the House of Lords, whereas home rule was sure to fail.

If Bryce hoped for vindication through the creation of an Irish council, he did not receive it. The Nationalists wanted home rule, not halfway measures. Redmond told Dillon the proposal was beneath contempt.[31] From Redmond's perspective, MacDonnell's design for a new mode of administration in Ireland had two fundamental defects. First, the council was too small and the method of indirect election of council members could have unpredictable results. For example, the Parliamentary party might be expected to return approximately twenty-six of the thirty-two county council representatives, but an improper distribution of the nominated council members could leave the Nationalists without a working majority. Redmond preferred a council constituted of all the Irish MPs elected by existing constituencies. This, in large measure, would look something like an Irish representative body. The second defect was that the relationship between the council, the lord lieutenant, and the Irish executive on the one hand, and the imperial Parliament on the other was not well defined. MacDonnell, an able administrator who was not a student of constitutional relationships, had not addressed the problem of who would be responsible to Parliament when the council wielded its administrative powers. Under the proposal, the council would have de jure authority in the prescribed administrative areas without being responsible to an Irish legislature in a home rule government. Moreover, there was no guarantee in the proposal that the majority party on the council would have de facto control over the administrative departments. The plan did not

31. T.C.D., D.P., Redmond to Dillon, Oct. 8, 1906.

give the council the power to appoint department heads, and these officials would influence the committees that would advise the council. Redmond also had another concern. He told Bryce that the Parliamentary party's freedom to criticize the Irish administration would be circumscribed if it participated in the proposed council, which, he felt, did not bring the party any nearer to its ultimate goal.[32] In short, the proposed administrative reform had some of the trappings of home rule, but it did not guarantee that Redmond would have the two essential elements of power over and responsibility for the Irish government.

Bryce was now as disappointed as he was frustrated in trying to please his Irish allies.[33] Nothing he had done gained their approval. Campbell-Bannerman was aware of the chief secretary's frustration. In November he offered him the ambassadorship to the United States. Bryce decided to resign, although he delayed the formal announcement one month until some of his committees of inquiry could issue their reports. Bryce had been an early and eloquent supporter of the home rule movement. His reputation as a historian and political theorist gave his support added weight. But Bryce was not a good politician. When he came to Dublin Castle, he had one goal: to implement his party's step-by-step approach to home rule. Although he asked for advice from Dillon on how to proceed, he followed instead the lead of his under secretary, an administrator who now seemed to be impervious to the opinions Irish politicians held on Irish issues. As the Parliamentary party leaders criticized Bryce, he turned inward and communications broke down, preventing the consultation on Irish affairs that Redmond had demanded earlier in the year.

Redmond took his grievance to Campbell-Bannerman, who consulted Redmond and Dillon directly when he selected the new chief secretary. Bryce, John Morley, and T. P. O'Connor, the Irish home ruler who sat for Liverpool, were also involved in the discussions. By the end of December 1906 the field of six interested candidates had been narrowed to Augustine Birrell, the minister for education. Birrell was

32. B.M., C-B. P., Add. MS. 41211, ff. 344–46, Bryce to Campbell-Bannerman, Oct. 8, 1906.

33. B.M., C-B. P., Add. MS. 41211, ff. 351–52, Bryce to Campbell-Bannerman, Oct. 10, 1906.

looking for a new position because his recent work on a comprehensive educational reform had just been wrecked by the House of Lords. O'Connor raised a question about Birrell's ability to control MacDonnell, but Morley told him confidentially that the under secretary had approached him about leaving Ireland and claiming his seat on the India Council.[34] On January 1, 1907, Morley forwarded to Campbell-Bannerman some information that enhanced Birrell's chance for the appointment. O'Connor had reported to him that the Irish Catholic bishops respected Birrell's attempt to protect Catholic interests in his ill-fated education bill, and he concluded they would not oppose the appointment.[35] This was important because Birrell, who was a well-known essayist, maintained a secular and agnostic perspective on life that might have alarmed the bishops. Birrell's appointment was formally announced on January 24, 1907, but not before rumors were afloat that MacDonnell, who decided to stay in Ireland, had been offered the position.

Soon after the new chief secretary arrived in Ireland, Redmond informed him that MacDonnell's administrative reform proposal was unsatisfactory. Redmond also used the memorandum to recapitulate his unhappy relationship with Bryce, identifying the lack of consultation as the root of the difficulty.[36] Birrell was determined not to follow in Bryce's path. He began to establish his authority over the under secretary by questioning the merits of the council scheme in several cabinet meetings. In February 1907 a cabinet committee considered the proposal and conceded the direct election of members of the council, which was expanded to twice the size specified by MacDonnell's October 1906 draft. MacDonnell wrote to his wife observing bleakly that the most active members of the committee (Birrell and Morley were now committee members) capitulated to Nationalist demands on the constitution of the council and control of appointments.[37]

On March 9 the entire cabinet formally considered the proposal. The under secretary, who still considered himself a colleague and not a

34. T.C.D., D.P., O'Connor to Dillon, Dec. 28, Dec. 31, 1906.
35. B.M., C-B. P., Add. MS. 41223, ff. 207–8, Morley to Campbell-Bannerman, Jan. 1, 1907.
36. Gwynn, *Life of Redmond,* pp. 141–42.
37. Bod. Lib., MacD. P., MS. Eng. hist., e. 217, f. 5, Feb. 23, 1907.

subordinate, submitted a lengthy memorandum. He proposed a politically independent lord lieutenant who would hold office for a definite term; retention of the existing tenure from the crown for civil servants, rather than patronage residing in the elective council; and a council of about 55 to 60 members instead of the 120-member council suggested by the cabinet committee.[38] Birrell also submitted a memorandum. He argued that the Irish Parliamentary party must have effective control of both the council and the administrative areas designated for council control. He endorsed Redmond's position on the need for a large elective element in the council, and he maintained that the question of appointments was closely tied to the question of effective control of the council:

> A good deal may be made of the argument that it is proposed to hand over the Civil Service in Ireland practically to the Irish Nationalist Parliamentary party, who will become, in the American phrase, the "'boss' of the whole machine."
>
> Personally, I do not see how this argument can be met, and its effect is the same whatever is the nature of the Council that is set up—either we are prepared to give this control to the dominant party in Ireland or we are not.[39]

In the remainder of the memorandum, Birrell gave his view of what he thought the Liberals' long-range political strategy should be. If they produced a strong measure that turned the Irish administration over to the Nationalists, the House of Lords was certain to throw it out. When that happened the Liberal and Parliamentary parties could fight the lords together and in harmony. For the short term, he believed that offering a generous measure now would at least be an act of faith in home rule that would restore the Parliamentary party's faith in the Liberal party.

The cabinet was not completely convinced by either Birrell or MacDonnell. It followed MacDonnell's suggestion on reducing the size of the council and Birrell's on retaining the direct election of the council members. It also decided to keep Redmond, Dillon, and MacDonnell

38. Cabinet Files, CAB/37/87/00069, Irish Office [MacDonnell] memorandum, Mar. 2, 1907. See also B.M., C-B. P., Add. MS. 41239, ff. 234–35, MacDonnell to Ponsonby (Campbell-Bannerman's private secretary), Mar. 25, 1907.

39. CAB/37/87/00069, Birrell memorandum, Mar. 6, 1907.

involved in refining the details of the measure. As a result, the council assumed a bewildering array of shapes during March and April when the Parliamentary party leaders, cabinet members, Birrell, and MacDonnell all tried to create a council that matched their predilections.[40]

Negotiations continued until the Irish Council Bill was introduced by Birrell in the House of Commons on May 7. The bill had not yet been drafted, in this instance a sign that no consensus had been reached. As Birrell spoke it was clear that the cabinet had not met Redmond's objections on either the constitution, method of selection, and size of the council or the locus of responsibility.[41] Redmond identified these weaknesses in his speech and refused to take any responsibility for the measure. He told the House that his party supported the introduction of the bill but that he would submit the measure for approval to the Irish National Convention, which was scheduled to convene in Dublin in two weeks.[42]

The Conservative and Unionist party members criticized the bill on several points. Arthur Balfour, now the leader of the opposition, praised the existing administrative system. He stated that Birrell's hostile introductory comment, that "Dublin Castle was switched off from the current feeling in Ireland," was not justified and only served to prejudice the debate. Turning to the proposed council, Balfour observed, "A more preposterous way of attempting to carry out the local government of a country surely was never conceived." Balfour then focused on the county councils' role in selecting members of the proposed council. He told the House that the Nationalist-controlled county councils could not be trusted to operate democratically.[43] William Moore, Unionist MP for North Armagh, maintained that the Unionist minority in Ireland would not be safe or fairly represented. To prove his point, he explained that in the entire province of Connaught only 2 of 144 county councilors were Unionists, and, he added, Unionists were completely excluded from the County Councils Association. Moore then expressed concern that the Nationalists would carry out an unwar-

40. Hepburn, "The Irish Council Bill and the Fall of Sir Antony MacDonnell," pp. 484–87.

41. *Parliamentary Debates* (House of Commons), Fourth Series, 174(1907):78–103.

42. Ibid., 112–28.

43. Ibid., 103–12.

ranted amalgamation of various portions of the administrative system, and he noted ominously that Nationalists had criticized Protestant clerks on Dublin Castle boards.[44] James Campbell, the former Irish attorney-general who was now Unionist MP for Trinity College, Dublin, was also concerned about potential sectarian appointments by the Irish council. He cited a resolution from the Claremorris District Council that "no man was to be appointed unless he brought a certificate from his priest," and then he read a letter that Michael Davitt had written to the *Freeman's Journal* in 1904, in which Davitt complained about interference from Catholic priests in education matters.[45]

T. W. Russell, a former Unionist who had become a Liberal MP for South Tyrone, spoke in favor of the bill. He admitted that Ulstermen would not vote for home rule, but he was confident that Ulster Protestants would support this bill because it abolished the power of Dublin Castle and transferred it to the representatives of the Irish people. He then explained why Irish Unionists opposed the bill:

> From the magistrates up through the whole gamut of officials these gentlemen have occupied posts for the whole period of the Union. They oppose the Bill because they see that their privileges—they have no rights in the matter—are in danger. It is because the old system is going—the system of administration by patronage and jobs; that is the sole ground upon which they can logically oppose the Bill.[46]

The reaction in Ireland to the Irish Council Bill was predictable, especially at the opposite ends of the political spectrum. At one end, some Unionists raised the familiar cry of "Rome Rule," claiming that an elected council would be controlled by Catholic Nationalists.[47] Walter Long, now the chairman of the Irish Unionist Council, and without a seat in Parliament, declared that any reform that placed more power in the hands of the Parliamentary party would not end agitation but would instead lead "in the direction of their one and only goal, Home Rule."[48] Some of Dublin Castle's Unionist officials feared that their

44. Ibid., 130–44.
45. Ibid., 167–78.
46. Ibid., 144–46.
47. "Devonia," *The Irish National Ideal: An Open Letter* (London: "Grievances from Ireland Office," 1907), p. 68.
48. "The Outlook," *National Organizations in Ireland: Their Origin, Development, and Aims: With An Introduction by the Rt. Hon. Walter Long, M.P.* (London: Offices of "The Outlook," 1907), p. 2.

positions might be jeopardized. Horace Plunkett noted in his diary that moderate Unionists thought the bill might develop into a useful piece of legislation upon amendment, but he saw no prospect for efficiency in Irish administration under the proposed system. He called the financial provision "a bribe thrown in in order to supply the drain which will be caused by the ensuing waste and jobbery."[49]

At the other end of the spectrum, the Sinn Fein theoretician Bulmer Hobson called the bill an insult to the Irish people. "It is not Home Rule," he declared. "It is a stupid scheme, absurd, unworkable—a scheme to trap the Irish people and further tighten the grip of England on this country."[50] Hobson also pointed to the proposed powers of the lord lieutenant and to the council's lack of control over police, judiciary, and prisons as specific weaknesses. He concluded by turning to domestic politics, charging that Redmond was guilty of complicity with Ireland's enemies and nothing less than a betrayal of the Irish nation. The *Leader,* which usually maintained that Nationalists should take whatever benefits they could obtain from any government, thought the measure was too feeble to support.[51] One exception to these opinions was taken by Padraic Pearse, the editor of the Gaelic League newspaper, *An Claidheamh Soluis.* He was pleased by the prospect of popular control of Irish education boards.[52] *Sinn Fein Weekly* was another exception. It was pleased by the increased stature of the county councils.

The Parliamentary party's principal organ, the *Freeman's Journal,* and Nationalist newspapers in the country also opposed the measure. So did the majority of the county councils. Numerous party members wrote to Redmond stating that the bill was unsatisfactory; only a few advised him to seek amendments.[53] Nationalist civil servants were not enthusiastic. T. P. Gill of the Department of Agriculture and Technical Instruction told Redmond that the scheme displayed fear and distrust of the Irish people.[54] The Catholic bishops opposed the measure be-

49. P.F.C.S., P.D., May 7, 1907.

50. Bulmer Hobson,*The Creed of the Republic* (Belfast: The Republican Press, 1907), pp. 34–38.

51. *Leader,* May 17, 1907.

52. *An Claidheamh Soluis,* May 18, 1907.

53. Hepburn, "The Irish Council Bill and the Fall of Sir Antony MacDonnell," pp. 488–93.

54. N.L.I., Gill P., MS. 13484(6), Gill to Redmond, Feb. 9, 1907.

cause it posed a potential threat to their de facto control of primary and intermediate education.[55] Nationalist opposition to the measure proved so overwhelming that Redmond and Dillon were left with very little room in which to maneuver. They could either move for an outright and total rejection of the scheme at the convention or ask the convention to send the bill back to Parliament for amending by the House of Commons and an ultimate defeat by the House of Lords.

Redmond knew this was no time for grand strategy. When the Irish National Convention met on May 21, 1907, he recommended that the body reject the bill. He explained that the Parliamentary party was not committed to the bill, that the framers of the bill had entirely refused his advice, and that the bill was not even an advance on Lord Dunraven's devolution scheme. He observed that the council was inadequate from an administrative point of view because its financial base was weak and its attempt to control the Irish departments through committees was awkward at best. Redmond objected to the lord lieutenant's power to appoint committee chairmen and veto council recommendations. He was especially concerned that the lord lieutenant could create new departments, perhaps in education, without reference to the council. Finally, he told the convention that the constitution of the council would not reflect the interests of the overwhelming mass of the Irish people. He warned, "There would be the greatest possible danger that the council would constitute a sort of rival body to the Irish National party, which, as I have said, I believe to be the greatest weapon, with an organized country behind it, which Ireland has in her possession."[56] The seven hundred members of the convention then unanimously rejected the bill.

Each of Redmond's points had merit, save one. He and Dillon were consulted several times on the details of the measure. They simply did not get what they wanted and were, of course, never in a position to dictate terms to the cabinet. He was correct on all the other points. Conceptually, democratic control of the Irish administration through the county councils held great emotional appeal. The potential gains from this interesting feature, however, would be handicapped both by

55. Miller, *Church, State and Nation, 1898–1921,* pp. 184–88.
56. Gwynn, *Life of Redmond,* pp. 147–48.

the committee system that was to oversee department heads and by the lord lieutenant's veto power. Administration apart, Redmond also identified two areas that violated the fundamental political principles that guided the Parliamentary party. First, the party could not support anything that endangered the Catholic bishops' hold on Irish education and thereby placed its relationship with the Catholic church in jeopardy. Second, step-by-step administrative reform was no substitute for home rule. When he chided his English allies by observing that the Unionists' devolution proposal was at least equal to the Liberals' ill-considered measure, he called to mind the Unionists' recent attempt to undermine home rule by reform. He could not permit his own allies to move in this direction. By waiting two weeks for a reaction to the obvious threats to party principles to build, he was able to make this point all the more emphatically to the Liberal party leaders.

As the Irish Council Bill met its demise, Birrell was starting to take action on the legislative agenda that Dillon outlined for Bryce in 1906. He secured legislation to aid evicted tenants and to enable the Congested Districts Board to purchase and distribute land. Birrell and Lord Chancellor Walker took action to solve the problem facing thousands of farmers who were behind in their land payments. Ignoring charges that the bench was overstaffed, they appointed Sergeant-at-Law Dodd directly to the supreme court and assigned these cases to him.[57] They replaced Dodd with Charles O'Connor, a Catholic Nationalist official who worked in the Sergeant's Office and won the approval of the Catholic press.[58] Birrell also conducted the annual review of the assistant land commissioners. Redmond sent him a copy of a Parliamentary party resolution that called for the appointment of "capable and impartial men who by their antecedents may be expected to approach their duties in a sympathetic spirit and with a sound knowledge of the value of Irish land."[59] After Birrell made fourteen new appointments, Dillon wrote to Redmond, stating that he was very satisfied with four or five of the new men and, overall, knew of only two objectionable appointees. Dillon did complain that MacDonnell had continued to use

57. *Parliamentary Debates* (House of Commons), Fourth Series, 169 (1907), 1358–59.

58. *Irish Catholic,* Mar. 2, 1907.

59. N.L.I., Red. P., MS. 15169(1), Redmond to Birrell, Feb. 19, 1907.

secretive techniques,[60] but Redmond replied that Birrell had not promised to submit a list for their prior approval, although he added that this time Bailey and Finucane had been kept apprised.[61]

Birrell's next problem involved Horace Plunkett, the vice president of the Department of Agriculture and Technical Instruction. Plunkett was still in the anomalous position of being a Unionist minister without a seat in Parliament serving in a Liberal administration. Birrell was eager to replace Plunkett, who complained to Bryce that Birrell was entirely out of sympathy with his work "and appears to look at it from the point of view of John Dillon, which I need hardly tell you is not friendly."[62] The matter came to a head in the House of Commons on April 24, 1907, when several Parliamentary party members, including Dillon, called Plunkett's work and politics into question. When Birrell responded he praised the vice president, explaining that he had remained in office at the request of the Liberal government. Nevertheless, Birrell indicated that the inquiry commission on the department would recommend that the vice president should be a member of the House of Commons and he declared that the new vice president would be a Liberal.[63] A few weeks after that inquiry made its recommendations, T. W. Russell was named as Plunkett's successor.

Meanwhile, Birrell launched his own agenda with a major piece of legislation, the Irish University Bill. In drafting the measure, Birrell worked closely with the archbishop of Dublin, William J. Walsh, and with Dillon, the Parliamentary party's expert on Irish education. They disregarded Bryce's and MacDonnell's plan to establish a separate Catholic college inside Trinity College, Dublin, a plan that had support from some bishops, including Walsh, and turned in a direction most of the clergy had dismissed only eighteen months earlier as too good to be hoped for.[64] They decided to establish an independent National University for Ireland. Birrell introduced the bill in March 1908 and it was enacted later that year. It abolished the Royal University and raised Queen's College, Belfast, to independent university status. The other

60. Ibid., Dillon to Redmond, Apr. 9, 1907.
61. Ibid., Redmond to Dillon, Apr. 10, 1907.
62. Bod. Lib., Bryce Papers, UB. 22, Plunkett to Bryce, Mar. 13, 1907.
63. *Parliamentary Debates* (House of Commons), Fourth Series, 173 (1907), 161–70.
64. Miller, *Church, State and Nation in Ireland, 1898–1921,* pp. 162–63.

Queen's colleges at Cork and Galway were affiliated with the new university college in Dublin. In order to make the National University system nonsectarian, Birrell included a clause that prevented ecclesiastics from enjoying a guarantee of representation on the governing body. This made the appointment of the thirty-five-member university senate and a smaller body known as the statutory committee, which was to frame the rules of the university and appoint the professors, very important. The fear of some Catholic observers of clerical displacement by secularist laymen proved to be unfounded, and those Catholics who feared that Protestants would dominate the university's governing bodies found that the senate, the statutory committee, and the professors who were eventually selected gave almost universal satisfaction to Catholic interests.[65]

The National University was important to Catholic laymen seeking training for the professions, including public administration. In the past, English politicians, including even such Liberal allies as Morley and such friendly Conservatives as G. W. Balfour, held that Irish Catholics did not have the requisite educational training to warrant high-level appointments. Nationalists of all stripes believed that the new university would provide the solution to this charge.[66] They hoped that National University graduates who entered the civil service in high-level staff positions would bridge the gap between the mostly Protestant administrative elite and the clerical ranks where Catholic Irishmen with intermediate educations continued to succeed in the competitive examination process.[67] Irish Nationalists and Catholics now believed that graduates from the National University would compete on an equal footing with English candidates for the limited competition and purely nominative positions, and that, in time, the entire administrative system would be in sympathy with the great majority of the Irish people.[68]

65. *An Claidheamh Soluis,* Apr. 11, Apr. 18, Apr. 25; Aug. 22, 1908.

66. *Freeman's Journal,* Oct. 23, 1907; *Irish Catholic,* July 13, 1907; *An Claidhmeamh Soluis,* Dec. 19, 1908, Oct. 30, 1909.

67. Michael Tierney, *Eoin MacNeill: Scholar and Man of Action, 1867–1945,* ed. by F. X. Martin (Oxford: Clarendon Press, 1980), p. 9, for MacNeill's perspective, in 1907, on Dublin Castle and Four Courts' offices in terms of religious and national characteristics of personnel.

68. Michael Hayes, "Contribution of University College, Dublin, to the National Struggle, 1916–1921," and "Contribution of University College, Dublin, to the Building of the New State 1919–1935," in *The Easter Rising, 1916, and University College, Dublin,* ed. by F. X. Martin (Dublin: Browne & Nolan, Ltd., 1966), pp. 109–20.

However, a university degree only gave a candidate an equal chance for an interview with the head of a department. Significant and lasting change in the religious and political complexion of the Irish bureaucracy at the highest levels depended on the character of the members of the bureaucratic elite.

The creation of the National University was perhaps Birrell's most significant legislative accomplishment as chief secretary. The resolution of this issue also marked the end of Antony MacDonnell's personal agenda for Ireland. After his appointment as under secretary in 1902, he had pursued reforms in land purchase, university education, and administration. In his own estimation, he succeeded only on the first point. On the second point, he concluded that the Catholic hierarchy foiled the creation of the university system that he thought was best. MacDonnell maintained that Birrell's lack of imagination and his capitulation to Redmond, as well as the cabinet's indecision, robbed him of success on the third point. When he submitted his resignation, he told his friend Alice Stopford Green that he departed from "the field broken in hopes and in health because his brother Irishmen mistrusted him and denied him their support."[69]

MacDonnell would not admit that he brought some of the mistrust on himself. When he returned from India to Ireland in 1902, his reputation as one of the ablest civil servants in the empire helped him secure the confidence of Nationalists and Unionists alike. His desire to solve the three most politically sensitive questions of his day was certain to involve him in Irish politics. The special terms of his appointment in 1902 recognized this, but the dual role of neutral civil servant and politician courted disaster. Two of his chief secretaries, George Wyndham and James Bryce, were hounded out of office by their former political allies, whereas MacDonnell, the principal architect of the programs that caused their respective downfalls, was protected by his civil servant status. Nevertheless, he had been a man with ideas and, as such, he earned respect even if he proved to be a very troublesome friend, first to Nationalists and then to moderate Unionists and Liberals.

Speculation about MacDonnell's position was rampant. At least six men were rumored to be in the running for his place. All six were

69. N.L.I., A.S. Green P., MS. 15089(12), MacDonnell to Green, May 10, 1908.

"THE SAXON SHILLING."

JOHN REDMOND—"For the sake of the Cause, Tommy, can't you keep the birds in the yoke until we pass this place? Haven't I enough to do to keep the baste in the shafts?"

Mr. SEXTON—"Don't blame me, Johnny, I can't prevent them, it's their nature. I never had one of 'em but tried to get into the gate beyant. It's the good feedin' they smell. It's betther thin I can give them, and me thryin' hard to pay a dividend."

[Several members of the *Freeman* staff have obtained jobs from that "base, brutal, and terrible institution, The British Government."]

Charges of patronage create problems for Parliamentary party leaders.
Courtesy of the National Library of Ireland.

Irishmen with important supporters. In the face of so many expectations, Birrell promoted James Dougherty, the assistant under secretary. Dougherty was succeeded by Edward Ennis, a Catholic Nationalist who was persona grata to the Parliamentary party and supported by the lord chancellor.[70] He had waited over fifteen years for the assistant under-secretaryship; unfortunately, he was killed in a coach accident after serving only a few months at his new post. After a long delay, which caused concern in Catholic Nationalist circles, Edward O'Farrell succeeded Ennis.[71] O'Farrell was a Catholic official who had served on

70. *Irish Catholic,* May 23, 1908.
71. Ibid., July 25, 1908.

both the Land and Estates Commissions. His most recent position was registrar in the Chancery Division of the supreme court.

In 1907 and 1908 Birrell also appointed men who were clearly identified with the Parliamentary party to the middle echelon of the civil service and to the county court system. Seven of his appointees in 1907 were former reporters and editors of Nationalist newspapers, including the *Freeman's Journal* and the *Evening Telegraph.* Two of them, Matthew Bodkin and Richard Adams, received county court judgeships. Other Nationalists, including some members of the Standing Committee of the United Irish League, received positions as inspectors in the Local Government Board. In addition, Redmond's son-in-law, Max Sullivan Green, was appointed private secretary to the lord lieutenant, a position that traditionally led to higher and more important office.

These middle echelon appointments were a function of the close relationship that developed between Birrell and Redmond in 1908. They worked together to guide several pieces of land legislation through Parliament, in effect completing the legal framework that created a peasant proprietorship in Ireland. Other legislation raised salaries for national schoolteachers and provided funds for the improvement of school plant. Birrell guided legislation through Parliament to repeal the Arms and Coercion Acts that, more than anything else, symbolized past Irish executives' lack of trust in the law-abiding character of the Irish population at large. Finally, Birrell and Redmond collaborated in Parliament to adapt social welfare legislation to Irish conditions. The Old Age Pensions Act of 1908 made a wide impact on all of Ireland, especially in the rural west.

The appointments and the legislation led most Nationalists and Liberals to conclude that Redmond had captured Birrell just as surely as MacDonnell had captured Bryce and that in fact this was just the way it should be. For example, the highly respected and outspoken Liberal journalist W. T. Stead wrote in 1907, "The new Chief Secretary . . . ought to regard himself as Mr. Redmond's man. Mr. Redmond himself ought to be Chief Secretary, but as he is precluded . . . the new Chief Secretary ought to do what Mr. Redmond tells him. For Mr. Redmond if Home Rule were granted, would be Prime Minister of Ireland."[72]

72. Warre B. Wells, *John Redmond: A Biography* (London: Nesbit & Co., Ltd., 1919), pp. 79–80.

The Parliamentary party could not openly endorse this line of reasoning, particularly where appointments were concerned, because each of its members took the annual pledge not to champion the cause of any one individual or become involved in any appointment process.[73] Politicians who broke their word lost the confidence of constituents who valued the independence of their representatives. Indeed, Matthew Bodkin's appointment created consternation in Nationalist circles. He had been out of Parliament for twelve years when Birrell named him to the county court in Clare, yet some Nationalists maintained he was still bound by the pledge.[74] At a less sophisticated level, casual observers took it for granted that no one could obtain any office in Ireland without the exercise of political influence. People who had connections with Dublin Castle also thought that patronage was being distributed in the interest of the Parliamentary party. For example, in March 1909 J. B. Skeffington launched a campaign to gain an appointment as a commissioner of national education. He was an expert in languages and had worked for several years as an examiner for the intermediate schools. Skeffington obtained letters of reference from Catholic bishops, schoolmasters, professors, teachers, and former students and sent the correspondence to Birrell, Redmond, and nearly twenty other Parliamentary party members. "But I am sorry all their trouble is likely to be lost," he wrote to his son, Francis, on May 2 when he ended his pursuit of the unpaid position, "as I learn (through Joe Devlin) that Dillon is pushing a Connaught priest . . . and as you know Dillon is personally and *indirectly* all powerful in that—also I learn that J. Redmond is not interfering—no doubt to give Dillon a free hand."[75]

At the same time, many Nationalists began to doubt the wisdom of continuing to restrict the Parliamentary party in the matter of appointments. D. P. Moran summed up his feelings in a blunt editorial in the *Leader* in April 1908. He noted that Dublin Castle was extravagant and objectionable, but the fact remained that Irish affairs had to be admin-

73. N.L.I., MS. 12081, *Irish Parliamentary Party Minute Book,* Feb. 14, 1906.

74. *Leader,* Nov. 23, 1907.

75. N.L.I., Sheehy-Skeffington Papers, MS.21,632 (iv), J. B. Skeffington to Francis Sheehy-Skeffington, correspondence of Mar. 24, Mar. 25, Mar. 29, Mar. 31, Apr. 2, Apr. 3, Apr. 4, Apr. 6, and May 2, 1909.

istered. He declared that the self-denying pledge played directly into the hands of Unionists. He suggested that the Parliamentary party and its organization, the United Ireland League, "make an onslaught on the administration and get in as many Nationalists as possible in every position of administrative power in the country. Such a plank as this, of fighting for administrative power in the Irish party programme, would win the approval of commonsense men who want to see this country march."[76] Between 1907 and 1909, Moran, assisted by his political writers "Chanel" and "Imaal" and by numerous letter writers, continued to expose cases of religious bigotry in the appointment, salaries, and promotion of Catholic officials in Dublin Castle and the Four Courts. In 1909 the *Irish Independent* came into line with the *Leader.* A. M. Sullivan, one of Timothy Healy's in-laws, wrote that holding Nationalist political beliefs should not disqualify a person from holding office. "So long as they apply directly or solely on their own merits, Irishmen play an honourable part in seeking positions for which they are qualified. This is not placehunting. We may say at once that we do not subscribe to the doctrine that Nationalists should not accept Government posts. . . ."[77] Other Nationalists agreed. James Larkin, the Irish labor leader, declared that the labor movement should have its fair share of any appointments that were going;[78] the Irish women's movement demanded the appointment of female officials in several departments.[79]

The independent Nationalist William O'Brien, however, criticized Birrell's lopsided selection of Catholic Nationalists. He said that the recent appointments were the result of improper pressure from Nationalists in general, and from Joseph Devlin's Nationalist political as-

76. Ibid., Apr. 4, 1908.

77. *Irish Independent,* Sept. 27, 1909.

78. Emmet Larkin, *James Larkin: Irish Labour Leader: 1876–1947* (Cambridge, Mass.: MIT Press, 1965), pp. 25–74.

79. Andree Sheehy Skeffington, *Votes for Women* (Dublin: Andree Sheehy Skeffington & Rosemary Owens, 1976). An exhibition of documents and mementos relating to the Irish suffrage movement held at Trinity College, Dublin, in October 1975 included letters to Dublin Castle on this issue. The indices to the Registered Papers in the State Paper Office in Dublin indicate that individual women and women's organizations took a keen interest in Civil Service vacancies during Birrell's chief secretaryship. Unfortunately, these manuscripts are not yet available to researchers.

sociation headquartered in Belfast, the Ancient Order of Hibernians, in particular. Under the rule of the Hibernians, O'Brien claimed, "no Protestant could be admitted in the National movement, be a member of a public board, or be a public contractor, obtain a position in the gift of a public body, or even get the Catholics' custom in his shop. . . ."[80]

Radical Nationalists in the Sinn Fein party also turned Birrell's appointments against the Irish Parliamentary party, and criticism of the Irish administration became a stock part of their political strategy. *Sinn Fein Weekly* monitored the Parliamentary party leaders for evidence of place hunting and belittled the complaints of more moderate Nationalists about the religious and political imbalances in Irish departments. *Sinn Fein Weekly* warned the Parliamentary party, "While Dublin Castle can buy in the public market the men who yesterday followed you implicitly, Dublin Castle is the ruler and dictator of your policy."[81] Other Sinn Fein writers called the acceptance of appointments a national weakness. Placing the issue in historical perspective, they traced the malady back to Daniel O'Connell's emphasis on securing the appointment of his followers in the 1830s and 1840s.[82] Sinn Fein's two leading theoreticians recommended a cure: the youth of Ireland must be imbued with the spirit of nationality. In 1906 Arthur Griffith advanced the idea of establishing a nationalized Irish administration in *Sinn Fein Policy,* the party's political manifesto. Griffith wanted patronage to be exercised in the interest of the nation, not in the interest of the individual. The native-born Irish officials in a nationalized system would know the land, the language, and the history of the country.[83] In 1909 Bulmer Hobson observed in *Defensive Warfare* that constitutional agitation and moral force had failed to win freedom for Ireland and that strict noncooperation was now the only way to defeat England.[84] Hobson argued that noncooperation by local bodies against Dublin Castle would financially and jurisdictionally bankrupt the administration. Both men urged the formation of local arbitration courts. Hobson went further and urged jurors to refuse to serve on all civil cases and to return "not guilty" verdicts in all criminal cases and thereby break up the

80. *Cork Accent,* Jan. 1, 1910.
81. *Sinn Fein Weekly,* Oct. 2, 1909.
82. Ibid., Mar. 2, Mar. 9, Mar. 16, 1907.
83. Griffith, *Sinn Fein Policy* (Dublin: James Duffy & Co., Ltd., 1906), pp. 21–23.
84. Bulmer Hobson, *Defensive Warfare: A Handbook for Irish Nationalists* (Belfast: The West Belfast Branch of Sinn Fein, 1909), pp. 41–49.

legal system. In 1911 Padraic Pearse, writing in *An Claidheamh Soluis,* adopted the idea of a nationalized civil service. Pearse reasoned that if a knowledge of things Irish were mandatory for officeholders, the Irish administration would be purified of corruption and rid of obsequious foreign and native officials who would hamper self-government.[85]

Anticlerical writers in Ireland utilized the appointments of friends of the Parliamentary party as evidence to support their periodic expositions of so-called backstairs Catholic influence in Dublin Castle. One anticlerical writer, F. H. O'Donnell, a former Parliamentary party MP, explored in his books, *Paraguay on Shannon: The Price of a Political Priesthood* (1908) and *Political Priests and Irish Ruin* (1910),[86] the relationship among the Ancient Order of Hibernians, Catholic priests, and Catholic civil servants in Dublin Castle. The books carried suggestive chapter titles: "The Political Sacristy and the Ribbon Lodge: The Congested District Board and the Ribbon Platform," "The Universality of the Clerical Grab—Grabbing the Local Boards," and "The Congested District Board and the Ribbon Lodge—The Robespierres of the Sacristy." An appendix to the former text, "Government Places for the Clerico-Jacobin Press," was designed to demonstrate that after home rule, "no Protestant or Unionist need apply."[87] Another anticlerical writer, M. J. F. McCarthy, denigrated a statement Redmond often made, that Protestants had nothing to fear from home rule, by asking rhetorically in *Home Rule and Protestantism* (1910) whether the Protestants Redmond had in mind were Protestant Nationalist MPs or Protestant officials who owed their positions to the influence of the Catholic bishops.[88] McCarthy predicted in *Irish Land and Irish Liberty* (1911) that a Nationalist government under home rule would appoint priests as justices of the peace and bishops as lord lieutenants of the counties.[89] For the anticlerical writers, appointments were one part of a closed

85. *An Claidheamh Soluis,* Feb. 25, 1911, Nov. 12, 1910, and May 6, 1911, for articles on a nationalized civil service.

86. F. H. O'Donnell, *Political Priests and Irish Ruin: Paraguay on Shannon up to Date* (London: P. S. King & Son, 1910), p. 139.

87. F. H. O'Donnell, *Paraguay on Shannon: The Price of a Political Priesthood* (Dublin: Hodges, Figgis & Co., Ltd., 1908), pp. 101–16, 134–48, 217–30, 231–32.

88. M. J. F. McCarthy, *Home Rule and Protestantism* (Glasgow: Scottish Protestant Alliance, 1910), pp. 3, 12.

89. M. J. F. McCarthy, *Irish Land and Irish Liberty: A Study of the New Lords of the Soil* (London: Robert Scott, 1911), pp. 209, 392.

system, created by Birrell and Redmond, in which the priests and bishops were *de facto* rulers.

The *Irish Catholic* was usually a voice for the interests of Catholic Nationalists. Under the editorship of Healy's political ally, W. F. Dennehy, the weekly exposed imbalances in civil service and judicial departments. But sometimes, when he did not like the Catholic Nationalists who were appointed, Dennehy took Redmond and Birrell to task. "We are back again," the *Irish Catholic* observed in 1909, "just where Sadlier and Keogh left us in the Fifties of the last century, when the strangling grasp of Whiggery threatened to extinguish the last remnants of National aspiration and National life. The position is a shameful one, but Mr. Redmond admits no sense of humiliation. He has taken his place in the ranks led by the planners of the new jobbery in Ireland."[90] As for Birrell, "Bad as things were under the long spell of Tory domination," the *Irish Catholic* concluded, "they have become infinitely worse under the present Non-Conformist administration."[91]

The Irish Unionists also watched Birrell's appointments with great interest. Unionist newspapers, such as the *Belfast Newsletter* and the *Irish Times,* as well as Irish Unionist party publications concentrated on two points: that the appointment of Nationalists was blatant, politically motivated jobbery, and that the Nationalists who were appointed were not competent to hold administrative or judicial positions. Bryce's appointment of a few Nationalist land valuers in 1906 gave the Unionists their first opening to bring up the jobbery issue.[92] In 1907 they used the Irish Council Bill to build on the theme that a home rule administration would be dominated by Catholic officials. One Unionist publicist portrayed Lord and Lady Aberdeen's vacation visit to Rome, in January 1907, as a precursor of "Rome Rule" in Ireland.[93] Unionist civil servants also doubted the Parliamentary party leaders' competence to manage Ireland's administrative system. After he retired as registrar of deeds and titles in 1908, Brougham Leech made speeches and wrote

90. *Irish Catholic,* July 10, 1909.

91. Ibid., Nov. 6, 1909.

92. Great Britain, *Parliamentary Debates* (House of Commons), Fourth Series, 155 (1906), 1319–46.

93. O'Mahoney, *The Viceroys of Ireland,* pp. 332–33. Buckland, *Irish Unionism,* 1:9–10.

articles opposing home rule that he eventually summarized in a *Handbook for Unionist Speakers.*[94]

The Irish Unionist Alliance made the most concerted effort to attack Birrell and the Parliamentary party on the patronage issue. Its publications criticized Catholic officials who served on local government bodies and implied that the patronage they dispensed in the interest of other Catholics at the local level would spread to the national level.[95] The alliance's pamphlets often included a cartoon or illustration that lampooned Birrell's administration. One of the most telling of these appeared in 1909. Birrell was characterized as the RCA Victor dog, peering into a Nationalist victrola filled with money from the United States. A United Irish League flag fluttered over a Union Jack that was draped on the ground at the dog's rear end. A line from a speech John Redmond gave in New York in October 1908 was placed under two captions, "A REDMOND 'RECORD'" and "HIS MASTER'S VOICE." The line was, "We maintain in Dublin an office within whose walls, practically speaking, the government of Ireland is carried on."[96] This statement, made to an impressionable Irish-American audience for fund-raising purposes, was music to the Unionist caricaturist's ear.

Of course, the members and supporters of the Parliamentary party were also experienced in attacking Dublin Castle. As long as they were not responsible for shaping or implementing Irish policy, they did not feel constrained from criticizing the Irish administration, even when it was controlled by a good friend like Birrell. For example, T. P. O'Connor, in a speech in London that was reported in the *Freeman's Journal* in October 1907, argued that home rule was the only remedy for the ills of the Irish administration. He cited an unnamed Dublin Castle official, possibly Birrell, who complained that anti-Irish officials obstructed every proposal designed to benefit Ireland. "Until they had in Ireland," O'Connor declared, "a race of officials not merely Irish by birth, but Irish in the sense that they loved Ireland above all things,

94. H. Brougham Leech, *Handbook for Unionist Speakers* (Dublin: Hodges, Figgis & Co., 1910).

95. Irish Unionist Alliance, *"Clericalism" and the Irish Local Councils; Catholic-Educated Candidates for Offices of Trust.* Pamphlet no. 68 (Dublin: Irish Unionist Alliance), 1907.

96. See *Irish Unionist Alliance Pamphlets Nos. 67–121* for the period 1907–09.

and Irish in the sense that the Irish nation was their master, and an Irish Parliament their paymaster, such things would continue."[97]

In the House of Commons, Parliamentary party members used the annual debates on the financial estimates for Ireland to discuss the Irish administration. During question time they inquired about particular problems concerning the chief secretary's or Irish attorney-general's domain. Party members might also interject a comment about the Castle in debates that did not directly concern Irish affairs. The tone of these remarks varied from Redmond's seriousness, to Dillon's aggressive questioning, to Healy's blend of humor and sarcasm. Publications written by party supporters supplemented the party members' criticisms of the bureaucracy. The most comprehensive statement about Dublin Castle was R. Barry O'Brien's book, *Dublin Castle and the Irish People.*[98] It first appeared in 1909 and went into a second edition in 1912. Largely anecdotal, the 430-page text included descriptions of Irish departments, central administration, and Irish finance.

As the chairman of the Parliamentary party, John Redmond was the chief spokesman for Nationalists. His treatment of the administration during a speaking tour in Ireland in autumn 1907 is an excellent example of his method of using official figures and a quotable epigram to attack the Castle. The *Freeman's Journal* carried the full text of every speech, and in 1908 the speeches were compiled in a handsome bound edition entitled *Some Arguments for Home Rule.*[99] After establishing the guiding principle for all of his speeches on the tour—"That no ameliorative reforms, no number of land acts, or labourers' acts, or education acts, no redress of financial grievances, no material improvement or industrial development, can ever satisfy Ireland until Irish laws are made and administered upon Irish soil by Irishmen"—Redmond correlated the extravagant cost of the Irish administration with its size, at Drumkeerin, on October 27. "We are," he maintained, "cursed with the most inefficient and, at the same time, the most costly Government in the whole world." He charged that administrative officials, from the

97. *Freeman's Journal,* Oct. 14, 1907.

98. R. Barry O'Brien, *Dublin Castle and the Irish People* (London: Kegan Paul, Trench, Trubner & Co., Ltd., 1909).

99. John Redmond, *Some Arguments for Home Rule: Being a Series of Speechs Delivered in the Autumn of 1907* (Dublin: Sealy, Bryers and Walker, 1908), pp. 237–45.

lord lieutenant down to the meanest official, were overpaid and that every department, save education, was overstaffed. The prospect of inheriting an unviable fiscal situation concerned him because the recent increase in Irish revenue, from approximately £7,570,000 in 1893–94 to £9,490,000 in 1906–7 was absorbed by the increased cost of the administration, which rose from approximately £5,600,000 in 1893–94 to £7,680,000 in 1906–7. Redmond believed that this lost revenue, if it could be retained, would ensure the future financial success of Ireland under home rule. Ireland gained nothing from the increase in administrative monies, he added, "because as the Government in this country becomes more expensive, it becomes, if anything, more inefficient and bad." Redmond also drew attention to the fact that there were in Ireland over 100,000 public employees at all levels (including public school teachers) who received £3 million in salaries, gratuities, and pensions. He concluded that over the years a dependency on government-funded positions had been created and maintained by England to subvert the Irish national spirit through a wholesale system of bribery.

On November 10 at Birr, in King's County, his topic was the administration of justice. He began by declaring that the courts were almost universally distrusted in Ireland. "This distrust," Redmond observed, "is the surest and greatest of all marks of bad government, and is the greatest of all arguments in favour of Home Rule." He traced the distrust to two sources. One source was "the fact that the laws under which we live in Ireland are foreign laws, made by a foreign Parliament. But most of all this distrust springs from the manner in which the criminal laws are administered in Ireland, and from the character of the tribunals which administer them." He went on to complain about justices who were appointed for political purposes. "In England, when a politician is promoted to the Bench," Redmond explained, "he leaves his politics behind him; but in Ireland, all through the century, and down to this very moment, the Irish people are familiar with the political judge, the partisan on the Bench, with the inevitable result that the mass of the people have no confidence whatever in the impartiality of the tribunal."

Redmond contrasted the extravagance of the administration and the distrust of the judicial system with the successful working of the Nationalist-controlled local government bodies on November 17, at Ennis in County Clare. The Nationalists' successful record in the administration of local government proved, Redmond believed, that Nationalists were prepared to administer at all levels. After citing laudatory statements Gerald Balfour and George Wyndham had made about the good quality of local government in Ireland, Redmond declared that funds had been "expended by the representatives of the people efficiently, economically, and honestly." He then repudiated a statement Arthur Balfour had made to a deputation of Irish Unionists, on March 8, 1907, "Where Catholics and Nationalists are in a majority, the Protestant and Unionist minority is oppressed and ill-treated." Redmond explained that where Catholics were in a majority, the county councils were Nationalist and Catholic because the councils generally took the complexion of the constituents they represented. He maintained that Unionist charges of Nationalist intolerance were absurd and dishonest. A truer picture, he claimed, was presented by four Ulster counties, Armagh, Antrim, Fermanagh, Tyrone, where Nationalists accounted for 40.1 percent of the population but held only 12 percent of the counties' salaried appointments. He contrasted this situation with counties Clare, Galway, Cork, Westmeath, and Kings, where Protestants accounted for less than 7 percent of the population but held 23.8 percent of the salaried positions.

Attacking Dublin Castle in speeches, however, was not a completely satisfactory method of defending the party against charges of place hunting. Perhaps there was no adequate defense, except to continue the practice of taking the historic pledge and resolving that it would be improper and inconsistent for any party member to use his influence, direct or indirect, to secure the appointment or promotion of any person to a paid government position. When critics alleged that the pledge had been broken, the party's leader denied it outright. Speaking to a group of Liberals in Manchester late in 1908, Redmond declared flatly that in his twenty-five years of public life he was proud to say, "No single member of his Party has ever violated that pledge or has accepted any honour, office, or employment for himself or his friends."[100]

100. *Freeman's Journal,* Nov. 13, 1908.

What is remarkable about the attack, defense, and counterattack in the matter of appointments after 1906 is that the initial focus was on a few Catholic Nationalists who were selected for minor administrative positions and middle-echelon judicial positions. Yet the Parliamentary party's critics seized upon these appointments as a means to damage its image as the independent voice of Irish Nationalists. They used Birrell's appointments and apparent Parliamentary party complicity in those appointments to expose some greater supposed corruption. This may have affected Birrell, who followed a more balanced course when he filled vacancies in the smaller administrative departments. Late in 1908 Sir Arthur Vicars resigned (after first seeking Redmond's counsel) from the tiny Office of Arms when an investigation into the mysterious theft of the so-called crown jewels of Ireland found him negligent.[101] Birrell replaced him with N. R. Wilkinson, a soldier who knew nothing about genealogy but who, according to local lore, was appointed because the king thought he was an honest man. Wilkinson learned new skills on the job and in time became a well-respected antiquarian. Later in 1908, when Brougham Leech resigned as registrar of deeds and titles, Birrell replaced him with another Unionist, Richard Maunders. Birrell knew that Maunders was an able official on the basis of his work for him as parliamentary draftsman in the Irish Office in London. In 1909, Birrell again took an eclectic approach when he filled the key positions in the Registrar-General's Office. In April, he appointed a new assistant registrar-general, Daniel Doyle, a Catholic solicitor in Dublin. Later that year, he appointed a new registrar-general, Sir William Thompson, a distinguished physician and associate of Lord and Lady Aberdeen in their anticonsumption (tuberculosis) work. Dr. Thompson had served as president of Ireland's Statistical and Social Inquiry Society. He was a Methodist and was popular in Dublin's social circles, factors that may have had a collateral bearing on his appointment.[102]

The appointment of Augustine Birrell as chief secretary in January 1907 was one of the most important events in the slow transformation of the Irish administration. He made the best of the Liberal party's step-

101. Leon O'Broin, *The Chief Secretary: Augustine Birrell in Ireland* (London: Chatto & Windus, 1969), p. 26.
102. Robinson, *Memories: Wise and Otherwise,* pp. 226–28.

by-step approach to home rule by developing an active legislative program and an innovative administrative policy. After the Irish Council Bill was dropped, Birrell went on to make significant advances in Irish agrarian and educational matters. His legislation effectively achieved two of the Parliamentary party's historic aims: first, the creation of a National University that had the approval of the Catholic church, and second, the creation of a nation made up largely of peasant proprietors. In fact, during Birrell's administration, which would continue until 1916, an average of five pieces of legislation for Ireland per year reached the statute book, making him the most productive chief secretary between 1801 and 1922.[103]

Birrell's administrative policy deserves to be called innovative because he based his decisions on the belief that Irish Nationalists deserved to receive more evenhanded treatment from Dublin Castle. He underlined this belief by suspending the Coercion and Arms acts that were annually invoked in Ireland. Birrell also acted on the belief that the administration must be readied, in terms of personnel, for control by the leaders of the Parliamentary party in a home rule government. He underlined this belief—and gave great impetus to the transformation of the administration—by appointing several well-known Parliamentary party favorites to bureaucratic and judicial positions in 1907. He hoped that these appointments would help to make the administration's leading personnel more representative of the population in terms of religious belief and political affiliation.

When Nationalists received these appointments, however, critics of the Parliamentary party assumed that its leaders must have violated the pledge that prohibited them from interfering in appointments. Initially, this was the kind of embarrassment most Nationalists probably thought they could withstand because their supporters had been shut out of the administration of the country for so long. They were wrong. Nationalists who opposed the Parliamentary party compared the appointment of former Parliamentary party officials and publicists to the politically motivated appointments of members of Daniel O'Connell's Repeal party of the 1840s and to members of the Independent Irish party in the 1850s who had first taken the pledge not to assume gov-

103. O'Broin, *The Chief Secretary,* pp. 1–41.

ernment offices as a sign of their independence. Redmond denied that anyone in his party had broken the pledge. There is no direct evidence to cast doubt on this. There are very few letters of any sort from Birrell to either Redmond or Dillon in the manuscript collections of the party leaders. Indeed, there are very few extant letters from Birrell to any politician for the period 1907–14. No collection of correspondence that might shed light on appointments has been discovered for Sir James Dougherty, the under secretary. In any case, if letters concerning appointments were exchanged, it is unlikely that they would have remained private for very long, particularly in an era when politicians were bound to produce correspondence on demand when a controversy arose. Of course, it is possible that appointments were quietly discussed in the hallways and meeting rooms of the House of Commons or during social occasions.

Birrell did not, however, have to depend solely on advice from Redmond or Dillon on appointments. There were officials in the administration who could help him identify Nationalist candidates for office. He could obtain the Liberal perspective from Lord Chancellor Samuel Walker, or the Unionist perspective from Henry Robinson of the Local Government Board, or the Nationalist perspective from Land Commissioner William Bailey, or the administrative perspective from James Dougherty. As he gained experience in Dublin Castle, he learned for himself which candidates were most suitable for appointment.

There was another aspect of Birrell's chief secretaryship that complemented his administrative activities. He may have been the chief secretary who most enjoyed his tenure in Ireland. Birrell especially liked to leave the capital and motor through the country with a small entourage of Irish officials. He enjoyed meeting the Irish people and recommended a tour in the country for visiting dignitaries and British officials newly assigned to Ireland. Birrell usually called on Robinson, Bailey, and Henry Doran, the secretary of the Congested Districts Board, to serve as guides.

Birrell's administrative style and decisions pleased Nationalists, but rankled Unionists. They thought he did not take his responsibilities seriously and that when he set policy, he did so only at Redmond's bidding. Unionists maintained that the chief secretary's choices of new officials and judges were made more to please Nationalists than to reward men of talent. Unionists eventually coined a term, *Birrellism,* to describe their view of what they charged was a biased and incompetent administration.

Birrell, who did everything the Nationalists could have expected, could not hasten the introduction of home rule. Ironically, the British social welfare legislation, which was generally unsuited to Irish needs, provided the occasion that brought home rule back to prominence. In April 1909 the House of Lords took an unprecedented step and vetoed the finance bill that included the so-called People's Budget. This action provoked a constitutional crisis that could only be resolved by a general election on the questions of the propriety and extent of the House of Lords' veto and on the British electorate's commitment to the welfare state. The former question had a direct bearing on Ireland, because the upper House would probably veto future home rule legislation just as it had in 1894. The prospect of a general election early in 1910 gave the Nationalists the opportunity to learn where home rule stood on the Liberals' legislative agenda. On November 27, 1909, Redmond wrote to John Morley, the former chief secretary who was on close terms with the Liberal prime minister H. H. Asquith, who replaced Campbell-Bannerman in 1908. Redmond wanted his Liberal party allies to make a strong declaration in favor of home rule. This was important because it would demonstrate to the general electorate that the Liberal party leadership was committed to home rule, and it would demonstrate to the British electorate in particular that the Nationalists were an important factor in maintaining the welfare state program. Asquith abandoned the step-by-step approach to home rule in a speech at the Albert Hall on December 10, 1909, and declared that home rule was now the only solution to the Irish question.[104]

No one expected the Liberals to maintain their 130-seat majority in the House of Commons, but few observers expected the general election results to be as close as they were. The Liberals and the Conservatives finished the contest in a virtual deadlock. The Irish Parliamentary party held the balance of power in the House of Commons.

104. Gwynn, *Life of Redmond,* p. 166–67.

Chapter VI

An Efficient, Content, and Loyal Body of Officials, 1910-15

In a speech in Dublin on February 10, 1910, John Redmond gave an ultimatum to the Liberal government. Holding the budget in the balance, he declared that if the veto power of the House of Lords were not curtailed in a manner that would allow the enactment of home rule, his party would vote with the Conservative party and defeat the budget.[1] This action would inhibit the government's ability to provide essential public services and would block its plans to sustain the social welfare program. After two months of negotiations between the Parliamentary party leaders and Prime Minister Herbert Asquith, the cabinet decided to ask the House of Lords to accept three resolutions that would restrict the House of Lords to a limited veto power. If these were rejected, Asquith was to ask Edward VII for a dissolution of Parliament, call for a new election, and announce to the country that the king would create a sufficient number of peers (thought to be between three hundred and five hundred) to change the Conservative political character of the upper House, if the Liberals were again returned to power. Redmond was satisfied and the 1909 budget passed in April 1910.

Irish Nationalists now believed that the passage of a home rule bill was just a matter of time. But parliamentary activity ceased for a time with Edward's untimely death on May 7, 1910. His successor, George V, was prepared to "pack" the House of Lords, and the Liberal and Conservative party leaders began to discuss ways to reform the upper House. By July twelve conferences had been held. Throughout the dis-

1. Lyons, *Dillon,* pp. 313–20; Gwynn, *Life of Redmond,* pp. 167–86.

cussions the Liberals remained committed to home rule, which they maintained must follow a reform of the House of Lords. This prevented them from reaching an accord with the Conservatives, who, discounting Irish votes in Parliament, maintained that the Liberals' narrow margin in the House of Commons did not give them a mandate to proceed with either parliamentary reform or home rule.[2] Irish Unionists, meanwhile, insisted that they were victims of a conspiracy. In their view, home rule was being foisted upon them by the Liberals as part of a crude political bargain: home rule for Ireland in return for Irish Parliamentary party votes for the welfare state budget and a constitutional reform.[3]

The Liberals called another general election in December 1910 to settle these issues. The election did not alter the balance of power in the House of Commons or the Conservatives' insistence that the Liberals did not have a mandate to proceed with either reform. Nevertheless, Asquith introduced the Parliament Bill in the spring session of 1911. The bill completely removed the House of Lords' ability to reject all financial measures, and it limited the Lords' ability to reject nonfinancial legislation, a category that included home rule, by providing that if nonfinancial legislation were passed unaltered by the Commons in three successive sessions, it would become law after the measure's third passage, even if it were rejected by the Lords. The lower House concluded its debate on May 11. When the upper House met ten weeks later, a combination of Liberal and Conservative peers and bishops approved the bill, 131 to 114. Home rule would be introduced in 1912, and observers assumed it would reach the statute book in summer 1914.

These constitutional developments provided the backdrop for Chief Secretary Augustine Birrell's administration in Dublin Castle between 1910 and 1914. During this period he continued to prepare the Irish bureaucracy and judiciary for Nationalist control. He began in 1910 with the Supreme Court of Judicature, where Protestant and Unionist judges still outnumbered Catholics, Liberals, and Nationalists, eighteen to three. On the eve of the first general election in 1910, the politically

2. Lyons, *The Irish Parliamentary Party, 1890–1910,* pp. 130, 136.

3. David W. Miller, *Queen's Rebels: Ulster Loyalism in Historical Perspective* (Dublin: Gill and MacMillan, 1978), pp. 96–97, 102–4.

appropriate time for making judicial appointments, Justice Gerald FitzGibbon, one of the Protestant Unionist justices, retired as the lord justice of appeal for Ireland because of ill health. Richard Cherry, the attorney-general, succeeded him. This allowed Redmond Barry and Charles O'Connor, who were both Catholics, to advance to the attorney- and solicitor-generalships, respectively. Birrell subsequently appointed three Catholic barristers as sergeants-at-law to ensure that they would be in line for promotion when the next opportunity arose. The new sergeants were John F. Moriarty, Ignatius O'Brien, and Thomas F. Malony. O'Brien was on close terms with Redmond, Dillon, and several Catholic bishops; the other two were also firm home rulers.[4] The *Irish Catholic* was delighted to report in May 1911 after Malony's appointment as third sergeant, "The Irish Law Officers of the Crown for the first time in the history of the United Kingdom [have] become Catholic to a man—a proud professional preferment when the proportion in Ireland of Catholic lawyers—perhaps not more than a third of the whole—is borne in mind."[5] The preferment continued when Attorney-General Barry succeeded the lord chancellor, Samuel Walker, who retired in summer 1911. Barry was only the third Catholic to attain that preeminent position in three hundred years. His promotion allowed Birrell's other recent appointees to move a step closer to the bench. Charles O'Connor became attorney-general; Ignatius O'Brien became solicitor-general. But Birrell followed up these appointments in his own way when he appointed the new third sergeant, Charles L. Matheson, the brother of the registrar-general and a Protestant Unionist. Perhaps Birrell used this appointment to allay the concerns of Protestants about the consecutive Catholic appointments, and perhaps he also wanted to reassure the old guard that family connection did not bar a talented family relation from an appointment.

The unexpected number of judicial vacancies and Law Office promotions continued through 1912 and into 1913. Birrell kept pace, al-

4. King's Inns Library, Dublin, *"The Reminiscences" of Lord Shandon, Lord Chancellor of Ireland* (Ignatius O'Brien), pp. 345–50, 360.

5. *Irish Catholic,* May 13, Dec. 16, 1911. The *Irish Catholic* was also pleased that of 438 new justices of the peace, 257 were Catholics. Of the 181 Protestant appointments, 67 were not Church of Ireland members. The religious breakdown of JPs in 1911 was 3,598 Protestants (2,825 of these were members of the Church of Ireland); 2,275 were Catholics.

though vacancies and promotions came so fast that some of his appointees advanced from sergeant, to solicitor-general, to attorney-general, to the supreme court bench in less than one year. New sergeants included A. M. Sullivan, the son of a well-known independent Nationalist journalist, and George McSweeney, a former Parliamentary party official who changed careers to become a public servant. Charles O'Connor became the master of the rolls, and Ignatius O'Brien, who succeeded O'Connor as attorney-general in 1912, became lord chancellor in 1913 when Redmond Barry suddenly resigned as a result of ill health. Peter O'Brien, the lord chief justice, was the next notable justice to retire in this busy period. Cherry succeeded him. Birrell also took care to satisfy Irish Liberals and religious non-conformists by selecting Jonathan Pim, a member of the Society of Friends, for the solicitor-generalship. This disappointed some Nationalists who had become convinced they would receive places almost as a matter of course.[6] Nevertheless, the Parliamentary party leaders now had their personal favorite, Ignatius O'Brien, at the head of the legal establishment and a battery of loyal supporters in position to advance to the Law Office and courts.

There was less activity in administrative appointments in 1910 and 1911. Birrell only had the opportunity to promote department heads in two minor departments. He promoted from the ranks in each case. H. E. Pittman and J. R. O'Brien were appointed supervisor at the Stationery Office and secretary at the Congested Districts Board, respectively. Later that year, Colonel D. E. Flinn, who had served as the medical inspector on the Local Government Board, was appointed medical member on the General Prisons Board. He was also assigned the additional duties of the chief inspector of the Reformatory and Industrial Schools. With Flinn's appointment, Birrell satisfied long-standing Nationalist expectations that a Catholic should hold the latter position. He followed the same course when he appointed R. M. Sweetman as secretary of the Charitable Donations and Bequests Board, and when he named yet another Catholic, William Butler, to fill a vacancy as one of the two assistant commissioners of the Office of Intermediate Education. Birrell rounded out the year by appointing his private secretary,

6. T.C.D., D.P., Redmond to Dillon, Aug. 23, 1911.

Charles Beard, a Protestant, as secretary to the Land Commission in place of John Franks. The chief secretary was not afraid to reward personal loyalty, even when the position was politically sensitive.[7] Two positions not in Birrell's gift were filled in 1911 by Lord Chancellor Walker just before he retired. He appointed W. R. Dawson, M.D., and T. I. Considine as inspectors of lunatic asylums. Dawson, an Ulsterman, was a distinguished physician and was soon elected president of the Medico-Psychological Association of Great Britain and Ireland. Considine, whose father was deputy inspector-general of the Royal Irish Constabulary, had risen through the ranks and had been governor at Dundrum Criminal Lunatic Asylum since 1894.

Birrell also made personnel changes in the prisons system, which was typical of several departments in which officials in the lower echelon were predominantly Catholics and Nationalists and executive officials were Protestants and Unionists. The *Leader* estimated in 1910 that in seventeen of eighteen prisons, 70 percent of the staff officers were Catholics, but there were only five Catholic governors.[8] Of the three leading prison administrators, the chairman of the Prisons Board, James Gibbons, was a Protestant Unionist, and the vice-chairman, John Mulhall, was known as a "Castle Catholic." Gibbons was openly hostile to the third leading official, the inspector of prisons, The MacDermott, a Catholic who was an outspoken supporter of the Parliamentary party. When Gibbons's position fell vacant in 1912, MacDermott sought it through official and unofficial channels.[9] However, Redmond's son-in-law, Max Sullivan Green, who had engineering experience in the prisons' service before he began serving as Lord Aberdeen's private secretary in 1907, received the appointment. Green's family connection never seems to have been raised against him or Redmond, at least in public. A few weeks later MacDermott was promoted to the vice-chairman's position in place of Mulhall, who retired because of failing eyesight. Birrell went into the field for his next appointment. He named Lieutenant-Colonel A. F. Owen-Lewis, a Liberal home ruler who had

7. *Leader,* Aug. 6, 1910.

8. *Leader,* Sept. 10, Sept. 17, Sept. 25, Nov. 5, Dec. 17, 1910; Apr. 29, May 6, May 13, 1911.

9. C.S.O., R.P., 1912, no. 14533, MacDermott to Dougherty, July 29, 1912. See also no. 17690, Memorandum of Lord Aberdeen, Aug. 13, 1912. T.C.D., D.P., Charles and Frank MacDermott to Dillon, Aug. 23, Aug. 26, 1912.

served in South Africa and as governor of the prisons at Dundalk and Mountjoy, to succeed MacDermott. Owen-Lewis was from a family whose connection to home rule stretched back to the 1870s when Isaac Butt founded the movement. Birrell also began to appoint Catholics as governors of the prisons, naming two in 1912.

There were several departments in the Irish bureaucracy that Birrell did not control and where appointments were not in his gift. In the Irish General Post Office, for example, an English Catholic, Reginald Egerton, had held the top position as secretary since 1898. Nationalists expected that James MacMahon, a Catholic who was the assistant secretary of the General Post Office, would be promoted when Egerton resigned in 1910. But Post Master-General Herbert Samuel had his own patronage needs, and he named instead A. H. Norway, an Englishman with thirty years' postal experience. There were many precedents for one Englishman succeeding another Englishman in Irish departments that were beyond the chief secretary's control, as Maurice Headlam did in 1910 when he replaced Thomas Hewby as Irish Treasury remembrancer. Nevertheless, there was an outcry from Nationalists who were amazed that with home rule approaching, an Englishmen could now supersede qualified Irishmen. *Sinn Fein Weekly,* which did not usually comment on appointments, called Norway's appointment "one of the grossest jobs yet perpetrated" and "an insult to every Irishman in the Post Office."[10] Timothy Healy concluded that Norway's appointment meant that the Liberals did not believe home rule would ever become law. But he was especially interested in this appointment for another reason. Many of his friends in the Catholic hierarchy, and Cardinal Logue in particular, were close friends of MacMahon's. Healy informed his brother that the bishops had urged Redmond to protest against Samuel's action and that Redmond had, in fact, met several times with Samuel.[11] These visits may have had some effect because when the appointment was officially announced, Samuel stated that Norway would only hold the post until home rule reached the statute book.

10. *Sinn Fein Weekly,* Aug. 10, 1912; see also the *Leader,* Aug. 17, 1912, for protests by local government bodies.

11. Healy, *Letters and Leaders of My Day,* 2:508, Healy to his brother, Aug. 16, 1912; T.C.D., D.P., Bishop O'Donnell to Dillon, July 23, 1912.

Redmond and Dillon accepted this assurance, but many Nationalists continued to criticize the party for acquiescing. Dillon responded to the critics in a letter to the Urlingford Board of Guardians in October 1912. He pointed out that the party bore no responsibility for appointments made under the present system of government. He disagreed with the local government resolutions that declared the appointment of any Irishman was preferable to the appointment of an Englishman. He did not believe the party should insist, even if it could, that the higher positions in the Irish civil service should be closed to Englishmen, because if a similar policy were adopted in England against Irishmen, it would produce a terrible injury to Irish-born officials who had been successful in the English Civil Service.[12]

The *Leader* reprinted Dillon's letter but called his explanation "thin." The *Leader* asked rhetorically whether the party had stood by silently during the recent appointment of Nationalists in the civil service and Law Office. The weekly used the occasion of Norway's appointment to launch a series of articles focusing on religious imbalances and disparities in salaries in the departments that were beyond the chief secretary's control.[13] The *Leader* finally concluded in October 1913, "The permanent officials of Dublin Castle remain in their jobs whether a Coercionist or a Home Rule Government is in power," adding wearily that it was no use even commenting on an institution like Dublin Castle. "It is doomed; but no doubt it will do mischief in Ireland while it lasts."[14]

The passage of the National Health Insurance Act late in 1911 gave the Liberal government, acting through the Treasury, the opportunity to select the executive officers for the Irish branch of an entire department, the National Health Insurance Commission. The first chairman was Joseph Glynn. He had been educated by both the Christian Brothers and the Jesuits and was a graduate of the National University. A home ruler and Gaelic Leaguer, Glynn was a solicitor at the time of his appointment. He was also the chairman of the Galway County Coun-

12. *Leader,* Oct. 5, 1912.

13. Ibid. The following issue (Oct. 12) reported that 80 percent of the post office staff was Catholic and Nationalist, but in positions worth over £260, there were sixteen Protestants and nine Catholics earning £5,300 and £2,700, respectively.

14. *Leader,* Oct. 18, 1913. See issues of Jan. 25, Feb. 1, Feb. 8, Feb. 15, Mar. 29, May 31, June 21, and June 28, 1913.

cil.[15] The disappointed candidate for the position, P. J. O'Neill, who was also a Nationalist, was the chairman of the Dublin County Council and the General Council of County Councils, the chief representative local government body in Ireland. A Liberal, Walter Kinnear, who was appointed deputy chairman, had several years' experience as a manager of the Royal Exchange Assurance Company in Dublin. The two commissioners appointed under the act were William Maguire, M.D., a Catholic Nationalist from Belfast, and Mary Dickie. Dickie began her career as a temporary lady inspector in the Local Government Board in 1902 and was promoted to lady inspector in 1906. She held a master's degree and was the first woman to achieve executive rank in an Irish civil service department. The secretary and assistant secretary, George Houlihan and Pierce Kent, filled the other top positions. Houlihan was a career civil servant who transferred to Ireland from the War Office. Kent was also a career civil servant. He began as a clerk in the Irish Public Record Office and had experience in the Local Government Board.

The second echelon in the Insurance Commission office was the inspectorate. All twenty-two of these officials were to be selected from candidates who were successful on the limited competition examinations. This worried some Nationalists, who thought that unfriendly officials in the Irish Labour Exchange Office were intent on influencing the Treasury's decisions.[16] The concern proved unfounded, however, as Catholic Nationalist candidates virtually monopolized the inspectorate, much to the chagrin of the Unionist press in Belfast.[17] The clerical appointments were filled by open competitive examination. Approximately thirty-seven hundred candidates took the examinations, in which all individuals competed on an equal footing for three hundred positions. Finally, sixty staff positions were filled without competitive examinations, by an equal number of career civil servants who transferred to the new department and by people who left the private sector to begin a career in the civil service.

As Catholic Nationalists moved into important judicial and bureaucratic positions between 1910 and 1913, critics of the Parliamentary

15. *An Claideamh Soluis,* Feb. 3, 1912.
16. *Leader,* Jan. 6, Jan. 20, 1912.
17. *Leader,* Jan. 20, Feb. 17, 1912; *Belfast Weekly Telegraph,* Aug. 2, 1913.

party continued to allege that the party had used its influence to affect personnel changes. William O'Brien, who moved in and out of the Parliamentary party during this period, was one such critic. His comments were especially troubling because neutral observers, particularly in Britain, might have assumed that his past membership in the party gave him special insight on this issue. He began a typical speech in Cork in 1910 by claiming that Nationalists "had obtained for themselves or their dependents fifty Dublin Castle jobs or offices for every office bestowed on Sadlier and Keogh." "Many of these extreme Nationalists of *The Freeman's Journal* had obtained Government offices," he maintained, "and the innocent Mr. Birrell tells us he had not the smallest suspicion of their connection with the organ of the Irish Party. It was all a fortuitous concourse of atoms migrating from Prince's Street to Dublin Castle." Following up his allusion to *The Freeman's Journal* office, O'Brien concluded, "In all the annals of political corruption there never was such open, shameless barter and sale in the market of political prostitution. Before there can be any hope for the country, this new crop of Castle hacks must go, and with them the whole system of self-seeking and corruption which was eating into the very heart of the National movement."[18] O'Brien was convinced that Unionists were being systematically excluded from government positions and that they were sincerely worried about how a Nationalist executive would treat them under home rule. Hoping to cooperate with the moderate Unionists as he had in 1904 on the devolution scheme, O'Brien began to devise ways in which the Civil Service Commission could review any Irish appointment with a salary of over one hundred pounds to ensure that Catholic Nationalists would not monopolize the administration.[19]

While independent Nationalists attacked the Parliamentary party from one side, radical Nationalists attacked it from the other. *Sinn Fein Weekly* never questioned the competence of the new Nationalist officials, and in J. A. Glynn's case the weekly newspaper admitted that his appointment had been warmly received by the local Nationalists who elected him to lead his county council.[20] As always, however, *Sinn Fein*

18. *Cork Accent,* Jan. 1, 1910.

19. All-For-Ireland-League, *Home Rule by Consent, Speeches by Dunraven, O'Brien, Healy in City Hall, Cork, March 1, 1913.*

20. *Sinn Fein,* Dec. 23, 1911.

"CLOVER."

WILLIAM—"There's a nice crop, bedad; they thrived well out of it."

THE LEPRACAUN—"An' be the same token, William, you'll find a few of your own growin' there."

["These Irish Liberals had obtained for themselves or their dependents fifty Dublin Castle jobs or offices for every office bestowed on Sadleir and Keogh. Three-fourths of the mischief of the past seven years was done by the writers in *The Freeman's Journal.* Many of these extreme Nationalists of *The Freeman's Journal* had obtained Government offices, and the innocent Mr. Birrell tells us he had not the smallest suspicion of their connection with the organ of the Irish Party. It was all a fortuitous concourse of atoms migrating from Prince's Street to Dublin Castle (laughter). In all the annals of Irish political corruption there never was such open, shameless barter and sale in the market of political prostitution. Before there can be any hope for the country, this new crop of Castle hacks must go, and with them the whole system of self-seeking and corruption which was eating into the very heart of the National movement."—*Mr. William O'Brien, M.P., speaking at Youghal.*]

The Leprecaun calls William O'Brien's credibility as a critic of the Irish Parliamentary party into question.

Courtesy of the National Library of Ireland.

hoped that the independence and integrity that characterized Parnell's leadership would not be debased by Dublin Castle patronage. *Sinn Fein* editorialized in December 1911, "He who accepts British patronage in Ireland implies by his action that it is not with the British government in Ireland but with the administration of that government that any cause of quarrel exists. His action is a tacit declaration that if the British Government positions in Ireland were filled with men of his kidney that Ireland would be satisfied and peaceful. The one security Ireland has is the incorruptibility of her public men. The British Government is always ready to buy any man of intellect and character from the Irish side." The people must see to it too," the editorial concluded, "that those they elect to represent them on public boards are also unpurchaseable. If they condone placehunting, they will write the epitaph of the Home Rule movement."[21] One anonymous pamphleteer traced the source of the corruption to the negotiations that took place between the Liberal party leaders and the Parliamentary party leaders in 1907 and 1908 when the Irish Council Bill was under consideration. "Red Hand" wrote:

> The Government threw open the floodgates of corruption in Ireland. Hunger for office of every kind swept through the country like a moral contagion. It ate the heart out of the National movement. It transformed a noble sentiment into greedy and clamorous self-seeking of the ugliest kind. At one blow all the safeguards established by Mr. Parnell to preserve the integrity of the Irish representation and save it from becoming the mere tool of an English Government in exchange for a liberal mess of official patronage was swept away. For years the whole country has been ringing with stories of the shameless scramble for place and office that went on, and, at the seat of patronage stood some of the principal members of the Irish Party. It was through their hands the filthy stream flowed which threatened to contaminate every living thing in this island.[22]

While critics of the Parliamentary party focused on the issue of pledge breaking and corruption, Irish Unionists were completely frustrated by Birrell. They sniped at his appointments and policies in the traditional ways: outraged editorials, cartoons, pamphlets, and speeches

21. Ibid.
22. "Red Hand," *Through Corruption to Dismemberment: A Story of Apostacy and Betrayal* (Derry: Jos. Chambers, 1916 [?]), pp. 10–11.

in and out of Parliament. His appointments continued to be so lopsidedly weighted in the Parliamentary party's favor that the Unionists were convinced that he was deliberately wrecking the Irish administration by appointing incompetent officials. Convinced that their grip on Dublin Castle had been loosened, if not totally undermined, the Unionists prepared to fight against the impending home rule bill and the potential home rule government. If the Unionists had little faith in the competency of Birrell's appointees, they had even less faith in the Nationalist politicians' competency to manage Dublin Castle and the Four Courts.

Edward Carson became the Unionist party leader in February 1910 when Walter Long accepted a seat in Parliament for London. Carson and the Unionists believed that the Liberals and Nationalists were engaged in an illegal conspiracy against the Act of Union.[23] Unionists who were spread thin in the southern counties became concerned about the militance of Carson's followers in Ulster, and they were especially alarmed about the talk of Ulster's somehow opting out of home rule.[24] Carson denigrated these rumors, but in the Unionist party strongholds in northeastern Ulster the talk of separation, and the preparation for the use of military force, came to a head soon after the reform of the House of Lords was completed. At a meeting of 100,000 Unionists at Craigavon, near Belfast, on September 23, 1911, Carson declared, "We must be prepared, in the event of a home rule bill passing, with such measures as will carry on for ourselves the government of those districts of which we have control. We must be prepared—and time is precious in these things—the morning Home Rule passes, to become responsible for the government of the Protestant Province of Ulster."[25] Carson's plan was audacious. A week after the Craigavon demonstration he met in Belfast with four hundred representatives of various Unionist organizations. The delegates appointed a five-man commission and gave it a mandate to frame and submit a constitution for a provisional government of Ulster, having due regard to the interest of the Unionists in other parts of Ireland.[26]

23. Ian Colvin, *Carson: The Statesman* (New York: The Macmillan Company, 1935), pp. 42–65.
24. Buckland, *Irish Unionism,* I:18–21, 27.
25. Colvin, *Carson,* pp. 77–79.
26. Ibid., p. 82.

The component parts for the making of an administrative system that could serve a provisional government were already in place. Most of the people serving on Ulster's local government boards and most of the local magistrates were Protestants and Unionists. Carson could also rely on men with experience in central government. Birrell's recent appointee, Sergeant-at-Law Charles Matheson, as well as a former Irish attorney-general, James Campbell, publicly supported Carson's call for separation. At an Ulster Unionist Council meeting in September 1912 a former lord lieutenant, Lord Londonderry, moved for the adoption of a covenant that pledged its signatories to defend themselves "using all means which may be found necessary to defeat the present conspiracy to set up a Home Rule Parliament in Ireland. And in the event of such a Parliament being forced upon us, we further solemnly and mutually pledge ourselves to refuse to recognise its authority."[27] The covenant was signed by some 471,400 people, 447,000 of whom were Ulster men and women. Unionist organizations also formed volunteer military forces that could give force to the decisions of a provisional government.[28]

The cabinet analyzed pessimistic reports from Birrell about Unionist activity and informed Redmond that special treatment for Ulster under home rule might be necessary.[29] Asquith and Birrell decided to emphasize the permanence of the imperial connection in the Home Rule Bill. To reduce Unionists' apprehensions about their security under a Nationalist government, foreign policy and colonial matters would be retained by the imperial Parliament, as they had been in the 1886 and 1893 bills. Ireland was to return forty-two representatives to Westminster to participate in business common to both countries. Several powers were withheld from the Irish administration to allay Unionist fears that the bureaucracy, judiciary, and police might discriminate against them.[30] Asquith explained these features when he introduced the Government of Ireland or Home Rule Bill on April 11, 1912.[31]

27. Ibid., p. 144.
28. Ibid., pp. 109–10.
29. O'Broin, *The Chief Secretary,* pp. 53–54. Jenkins, *Asquith,* pp. 276–77.
30. Lyons, *Dillon,* p. 327.
31. *Parliamentary Debates,* House of Commons, Fifth Series, Vol. XXXVI, Apr. 11, 1912, for speeches of Asquith, Carson, and Redmond. (All citations from the debates in the following section are from Commons, Fifth Series, 1912.)

Carson rejected the measure. The Unionists, he declared, could not accept the principle of home rule, which they considered unconstitutional because it violated the Act of Union. Redmond welcomed the bill. Although the proposed Irish Parliament was denied full responsibility for Irish finance, at least the financial clauses ensured that the home rule government would be launched on a sound financial basis. Those clauses included a provision that directed the imperial Treasury to pay for the administration of the reserved services and for the Irish social welfare benefits, pensions being the most costly. The bill's financial scheme allowed for a small annual surplus in Irish revenue of approximately £500,000 and for Irish control over some customs and excise revenue and post office revenue. Redmond was also pleased that the Irish government was to be given administrative control over approximately twenty-five thousand civil servants, including the officials who were employed in the reserved services.

The composition and potential conduct of the future Irish ministers were important to the Unionists. James Craig, Unionist member for East Down, and Arthur Balfour, leader of the Conservative party, expressed concern about the likelihood of Nationalist jobbery. Other Unionists raised questions about potential discrimination in the Estates Commission Office, the Congested Districts Board, and the National University senate.[32] Redmond, Dillon, and Healy answered the Unionists at different points in the initial debate, declaring that Protestants would play a full role in the new government.[33] William Moore, the Unionist member for North Armagh, was not satisfied by their assurances or by the safeguards, which he termed "as good as possible, although ridiculous." It was not legislation, Moore declared when he introduced the theme Unionist members would develop during the committee debates, so much as administration that could be used to oppress a minority.[34] He predicted that Protestant civil servants would be "retrenched" if they disagreed with the Catholic power brokers in the administration.

The committee stage began in the summer, but the clauses relating to the Irish bureaucracy and judiciary were not debated until December. Clause xxvii, which concerned the appointment of supreme court

32. Ibid., XXXVII: 1477–78.

33. Ibid., XXXVIII: 104–7, 116–20.

34. Ibid., 121.

and county court judges, opened this phase of the bill's passage. The Parliamentary party members rarely spoke, preferring instead to let the Liberals take the lead in the discussion. The Unionists were not so reticent. Carson said opponents of the bill in Ireland resented this clause more than any other. He maintained that the ordinary citizen in the north of Ireland would say, "'I object to my life and my liberty and my property being subject to a number of people whom I look upon as absolutely unfitted to be put over me in relation to the adjudication of any such judicial matters as may have to come before them.'"[35] He told the House that Unionists would not submit cases to the courts for adjudication. Turning next to the appointment of judges, Carson said that although he had no objection to Birrell's recent selection of Catholic judges who were popular with Nationalists, he would only admit that they were proper appointments because they were imperial appointments. "I believe," he concluded, "if these same appointments were made under an Irish parliament with a permanent majority, as must be the case in the Irish house, of one particular persuasion, the appointments would be not merely criticised, but objected to, and looked upon as the engine of oppression."[36] In rebuttal, Healy reminded Carson that during 1906 and 1907 several Protestants had been appointed as law officers and that other Protestants had been promoted to the bench. Healy used these appointments to counter the prediction of Nationalist bigotry by frankly admitting that those men would not have been appointed if the Parliamentary party had objected. He explained that the recent Catholic appointments were inevitable because of the long history of Protestant appointments, but he concluded by denying that the selection of any future judge would be based on a religious test.[37] After a speech by William Moore, who declared flatly that law and order would break down under a Catholic-controlled home rule administration just as it had broken down in areas under Catholic-controlled local government, the clause giving complete control of the entire Irish judicial system to the Irish Parliament was passed by a vote of 320 to 193.

Clause xxviii, which established an appeal process from Irish courts

35. Ibid., Vol. XLIV (Dec. 3, 1912), 2137–41.
36. Ibid.
37. Ibid., 2153–58.

to the Judicial Committee of the English Privy Council, was passed, 316 to 192, without a debate on December 3, 1912. Two days of debate followed on clause xxix, which allowed the lord lieutenant to submit Irish legislation to the Judicial Committee of the English Privy Council to determine whether the Irish Parliament had exceeded its constitutional powers. The Ulster Unionists believed that because the lord lieutenant and his representative in the Irish Parliament would both be political partisans, neither could be relied upon to decide impartially whether a given measure should be submitted for review. Basing their argument on the hypothetical use by Nationalists of patently unconstitutional legislation designed especially for use in Ulster, they wanted to ensure that all measures likely to cause controversy would be submitted for review before their introduction in the Irish Parliament. James Craig submitted an amendment designed to give individual citizens the same right of prior appeal as the lord lieutenant.[38]

Although the amendment was rejected, Craig succeeded in underlining the Unionists' lack of confidence in the ministers who would advise the lord lieutenant. Sir Edward Hildred Carlile, Conservative MP for Hertfordshire, then submitted an amendment designed to permit the lord lieutenant to override his ministers by appealing their administrative decisions to the English Privy Council. Unionist members who spoke in support of Carlile maintained that an individual should also be able to bypass the Irish courts and appeal administrative actions directly to the English Privy Council. Again, Carson and the other Unionist speakers said that they feared the administrative power of the Nationalists far more than the legislation of an Irish Parliament and they believed that the right to appeal administrative actions would safeguard Unionist interests.[39] Thomas Scanlan, the Parliamentary party member for Sligo, defended the future Irish ministers. He thought that appeals of administrative acts by individuals would paralyze the executive's ability to govern the country.[40] After David Lloyd George alarmed Unionists by realistically observing that the lord lieutenant would inevitably be a partisan who would undoubtedly act in a partisan manner, the committee divided in favor of the clause, 315 to 186.[41]

38. Ibid., Vol. XLIV (Dec. 3, 1912), 2222–25.
39. Ibid., 2325–34.
40. Ibid., 2336–41.
41. Ibid., 2357.

The next day, December 4, the Ulster Unionist members immediately seized upon Lloyd George's observation about the partisan nature of the lord lieutenant. They drafted an amendment to clause xxxi, which defined the lord lieutenant's role, to ensure that the lord lieutenant would be politically neutral in controversial matters, perhaps on the model of colonial governors.[42] As clause xxxi stood, a lord lieutenant would have important prerogative and executive powers. Acting on advice of his ministers, he would nominate the senate and appoint the administrative department heads and all Irish judges. Asquith pointed out that the Irish lord lieutenant's position was without precedent in the empire and that colonial models were not applicable. Nevertheless, he accepted the amendment and suggested the addition of "The Lord Lieutenant shall, in the discharge of the duties of his office, conform to the accustomed practice of Governors of His Majesty's Oversea Dominions."[43] Austen Chamberlain, the conservative member for East Worcester, then asked for a clarification of the duties of the minister who would be responsible to the House of Commons for Ireland.[44] Asquith stated that some high-ranking minister, perhaps called chief secretary or secretary of state, and perhaps holding cabinet rank, would be responsible.[45]

The debates on the civil service clauses, which were conducted on December 9–10, 1912, differed markedly from the debates of 1893. Morley had drafted the civil service clauses in 1893 expecting a large number of transfers, but Birrell, working some twenty years later, was free of this concern. Birrell met with several representative deputations of Irish civil servants and drafted clauses that guaranteed their salaries, pensions (which were set at a maximum of fifty percent of a salary), rights, and privileges. The terms covered virtually every civil service officer and official of the judicial establishment. Only some postal clerks and excise officials, members of two large Irish departments that were included in the reserved services, remained anxious about their positions, aware, perhaps, of Redmond's penchant for watching expenditure.[46] The Nationalist leader also declared early in the debates that

42. Ibid., 2391–95.
43. Ibid., 2395–98.
44. Ibid., 2398–2402.
45. Ibid., 2402–3; 2411–12.
46. See. H.L.R.O., Lloyd George Papers, 50/1/53, Memorandum re Associations of Irish Postal Clerks and Excise Officials; see also H.L.R.O., Law P., MS. 40/3/79,

the civil servants had nothing to fear from a Nationalist executive. He revealed that he too had met with representatives of every class of Irish civil servant and that he had left those meetings convinced that the Irish civil service personnel would be proud to serve a Nationalist executive. Redmond promised that any reduction of expenditure would not be made at the expense of Irish officials. He also acknowledged that the success of the new government depended in large part on an "efficient, content, and loyal" body of officials.[47]

The conservative and Ulster Unionist members were not convinced. They attacked clause xxxiii, which defined the continuation of service and compensation of civil servants, by raising initial questions about the teachers at the model schools and the Marlborough Street Training School, institutions that were detested by the Catholic hierarchy.[48] W. E. Hume-Williams, a conservative from Notts, Bassetlaw, offered an amendment designed to remove the power of dismissal of all Irish officers from the lord lieutenant and to transfer it instead to the Irish Civil Service Commission.[49] Birrell rejected the amendment and declared that the executive's power over its officials involved the entire question of home rule and that that power was "part and parcel of Irish Government, or any Government."[50] Conservative speakers replied that giving the power of dismissal to the lord lieutenant, who, they reminded the committee, would be acting on the advice of partisan Irish ministers, struck at the root of the contract that civil servants entered into with the imperial government. Finally, Charles Craig, the Unionist MP for South Antrim, stated the real difficulty, bluntly declaring that he and his colleagues simply did not trust the Nationalists. He suggested that no one would be able to stop the new ministry from dismissing high-level officials in the guise of reducing expenditure.[51] The closure rule terminated the debate and the clause passed, 289 to 176.

"Ireland Today" by "One who knows," and MS/40/3/80, "Civil Servants and Home Rule."

47. Commons, XLV:100–101. For Birrell's speech, see 90–96.

48. Ibid., XLIV:2438–39.

49. Ibid., 153–54. The Civil Service Commission—the lord chief justice of England, one member nominated by the Treasury, and one member nominated by the Irish executive—would settle questions of compensation, salary, and duties.

50. Ibid., 155–56.

51. Ibid., 167.

The following day, December 10, clause xxxvii, which concerned the constabulary, had a rapid passage. Healy, in a speech similar in tone to Redmond's remarks about the civil service, gave a vote of confidence to the constabulary.[52] Six Unionist speakers, however, took advantage of this last opportunity to make a point about potential discrimination against Unionist and Protestant personnel in government service and to predict that Nationalists would harass particular members of the constabulary. Birrell responded that although the Irish government was to have the power of dismissal in this reserved service, he had provided for dissatisfied constabulary officers on the same lines as the civil servants.[53]

The Home Rule Bill advanced successfully through the House of Commons but was rejected by the House of Lords in April 1913. The clauses of the Parliament Reform Act that limited the upper House's veto power were then invoked, and the bill began its second passage. Meanwhile, Ulster Unionists continued to prepare their provisional government. In the spring the standing committee of the provisional government combined the various Unionist paramilitary contingents into the 100,000-man Ulster Volunteer Force. In the autumn, as the Home Rule Bill completed its second passage, the structure of the provisional government took on a more definite shape. At a meeting of the Ulster Unionist Council, Carson was designated as the executive head of the seventy-seven members of the provisional government, and he was appointed chairman of each of its administrative branches and departments.[54] The provisional government included an executive committee, a military command, and a civil administration with departments for personnel, finance and business, railways, transport, supply, health, legal affairs, education, propaganda, customs, excise, post office, legal assessors, and chaplains. Carson declared that the provisional government was not merely a symbolic manifestation of Ulster's determination to resist home rule. On October 4, 1913, he told a group of Unionists in Armagh, "We have got the authority to set up a provisional government, and we are going straight ahead—day after day—perfecting all the arrangements which may be necessary."[55]

52. Ibid., 289–94.
53. Ibid., 307–12.
54. Colvin, *Carson,* pp. 187, 207–9.
55. Ibid., pp. 217–18.

Unionist leaders were confident that the provisional government could be launched without any fear of suppression by the police or the army.[56] The failure of the Liberal government to take disciplinary action against sixty mutinous army officers stationed at the Curragh, in County Kildare, when they declared that they would prefer dismissal from the service to coercing Ulster Unionists into submission to a home rule government, seemed to bear them out.[57] Moreover, Dublin Castle's control over the personnel in the branches of its administration in Ulster was suspect. Birrell knew that Carson could find civil servants who were opposed to home rule in Ulster's post offices, customs, and other government offices. Birrell also realized that the loyalty of the forces of law and order in Ulster would be a conditioning factor in any success Carson might have if he launched a provisional government. T. J. Smith, the highest-ranking police officer in Belfast, admitted to Birrell that violence was being prevented only by the firm grip Devlin and Carson had on their respective followers, and Birrell was worried because many of the police officers stationed in Belfast had signed the Ulster covenant.[58] Other observers thought that the Ulster Unionists' gunrunning activities, which were eventually capped on April 24, 1914, when forty thousand rifles were distributed at Larne Harbor, could only have taken place with the acquiescence of the military and the police.[59] Birrell was especially concerned about Sir Neville Chamberlain, the inspector-general of the Royal Irish Constabulary, who was, according to Birrell, a "true blue" Unionist.[60] Finally, the constabulary's complement of officers was depleted because the number of recruits had fallen off between 1910 and 1913 and because hundreds of officers resigned during a salary dispute in 1914.

In Dublin, Birrell faced another series of problems. In September 1913 the Dublin police force was hard-pressed during a bitter strike led by James Larkin. After he was arrested, a riot broke out and police discipline broke down. Many civilians were injured when the police attacked rioters and onlookers indiscriminately. Meanwhile, the radical

56. B. L., Bal. P., Add. MS. 49693, Law to Londonderry, Oct. 8, 1912.
57. Lyons, *Ireland Since the Famine,* pp. 308–9.
58. Ibid., p. 167.
59. Ibid., p. 289–94.
60. O'Broin, *The Chief Secretary,* p. 68.

Nationalists had organized the Irish Volunteers late in 1913 in response to the formation of the Ulster Volunteers. In July 1914 the Irish Volunteers landed a shipment of arms at Howth, County Dublin. When the assistant commissioner of the Dublin police, William Harrell, heard what was happening, he informed the under secretary, James Dougherty. They dispatched some Dublin police and constabulary officers to intercept the Volunteers. On his own authority Harrell also called on the army for support. The police succeeded in dispersing—although not in disarming—the Volunteers, but an angry mob harassed the soldiers on the quays of the River Liffey on their return from Howth. The soldiers opened fire, killing three and wounding about forty.[61]

As the Home Rule Bill began its third and final passage through Parliament, Redmond attempted to stabilize the situation in Dublin and meet some of the demands of the Unionists in Ulster. Redmond was alarmed at the rapid development of the Irish Volunteers, who enlisted over 100,000 men by mid-1914. He gained control of its governing body, but he did not know that some members of the Irish Republican Brotherhood were in league with other radical Nationalists who remained on the Volunteers' governing body. Meanwhile, he was thinking about ways to reach an accommodation with the Unionists. In November 1913 Redmond told Asquith that he might entertain a proposal to offer a large measure of administrative autonomy for Ulster under an Irish Parliament, if the proposal came from the other side, and then only at the last possible moment.[62] The cabinet decided to proceed along these lines, and in December Asquith met with Carson. The prime minister offered him "Home Rule within Home Rule" and conceded several of the points Unionists raised during the committee debates in 1912 on the shape and powers of the administration and judiciary. These included removing the police forces, post office, and customs from the control of the Irish legislature and permitting appeals of legislation and administrative action to judges who would be appointed by the imperial Parliament. Education and the local govern-

61. F. X. Martin, ed., *The Irish Volunteers, 1913–1915* (Dublin: James Duffy & Co., Ltd., 1963).

62. Bod. Lib., Asq. P., MS. 38, ff. 235–36, Birrell to Asquith, Oct. 16, 1914 [sic]; and MS. 39, ff. 23–26, Nov. 17, 1913, Asquith memorandum of meeting with Redmond. T.C.D., Dillon P., Memo of Redmond on meeting with Asquith, Lloyd George, and Birrell, Nov. 1913.

ment in Ulster would be administered by separate boards established for Ulster. Appointments in Ulster departments were to be specially provided for under a system that was yet to be formulated. Finally, Ulster was to be redefined geographically and could, if a majority of its members in the Irish Parliament agreed, be excluded from legislation affecting religion, land tenure, education, and industry, pending submission of the measure to the imperial Parliament. Carson was not moved by the concessions. He declared that the inclusion of Ulster under an Irish Parliament on any terms was impossible. He would only reach an agreement if it was based on the principle of total exclusion of Ulster from a home rule government.[63]

With the Home Rule Bill due to complete its final passage early in 1914, a compromise was essential to avoid a confrontation between the British government and the Ulster Unionists. Avoiding responsibility for an exclusion scheme was everything to the Irish Parliamentary party; the Liberal party's task was to find a satisfactory exclusion formula. The Unionist party hoped to block home rule altogether, perhaps by forcing another general election. In March the government devised a partition scheme, and the Nationalist leaders agreed, "as the price of peace," that individual Ulster counties, through county referendums, could opt out of home rule for a period of three years, when they would then automatically come under the Irish Parliament.[64] After a strong remonstrance from the king, who thought that three years was not sufficient, Redmond reluctantly agreed to a six-year exclusion period. The prime minister introduced the proposal as an Amending Bill to the Home Rule Bill on March 9, 1914, only to have Carson pronounce the measure a "sentence of death with a stay of execution for six years."[65] A week later Carson stalked out of the House of Commons, leaving many observers to conclude that he would set the provisional government in operation.[66]

The deadlock was still unresolved at the outbreak of the world war

63. Jenkins, *Asquith*, pp. 264–67.

64. Gwynn, *Life of Redmond*, pp. 253–54.

65. Colvin, *Carson*, pp. 294–301.

66. Ibid., pp. 310–21. Redmond, who doubted that Carson would activate the provisional government, nevertheless asked Birrell to remove from Belfast any police officers who were known to be disloyal. H.L.R.O., L.G. P., MS. C/7/3/no. 9, Redmond to Birrell, May 15, 1914.

in August 1914. After two adjournments of the House on the declaration of war and after several complaints from Redmond, who feared that the war would be used as a pretext to delay the home rule legislation, the bill, without any provision for partition, became law in September. It was accompanied by a Suspensory Act that prevented home rule from going into effect until the cessation of hostilities. Home rule was deferred to the conclusion of the war, which optimists expected would be a few months.

Redmond had the satisfaction of seeing home rule reach the statute book, but his party's chances of ever enjoying the fruits of its long labor now depended on how quickly their Liberal party allies could conclude the war. The War Office officials and generals, however, did not encourage Redmond's effort to assist them in winning the war. They refused to authorize special badges and regalia for Irish troops, to form an adequate Catholic chaplaincy corps, to exempt the bishops' correspondence with Rome from the censors, and to facilitate the awarding of army commissions for Irish Nationalists. At home Redmond faced another series of problems. He overcame some initial resentment that Parliamentary party members felt when he spontaneously committed them to the war effort in a speech in the House of Commons without consulting any of them. He also had to counteract Unionist charges that the Nationalists were not doing their fair share to help win the war. Recruiting statistics soon became as important to Redmond as figures relating to home rule finance. More ominously, some twelve thousand of the Irish Volunteers renounced his leadership in September 1914. The splinter group could not be considered a fighting force, but Irish Republican Brotherhood veterans and Clan na Gael men from America who espoused the use of physical force to establish an Irish republic as the solution to the Irish question joined the Volunteers who opposed Redmond.

While Redmond was experiencing new difficulties, Asquith decided that it was time to remedy an older problem. The prime minister was convinced that Dublin Castle personnel needed overhauling; in fact, he thought that a change was long overdue. Shortly after the Howth gunrunning incident in July 1914 he wrote that he "wished he had made a clean cut six months ago by removing Aberdeen and the whole crew. A weaker and more incompetent lot were never in charge of a leaky ship in stormy weather; poor old Birrell's occasional and fitful appearances at the wheel do not greatly improve matters."[67] The retirement of James Dougherty, the under secretary, in September 1914 gave him the opportunity to make the first change. With assistance from Lloyd George, now the minister of munitions, he appointed Sir Matthew Nathan, the chairman of the Board of Inland Revenue, as under secretary for Ireland. When his appointment was announced, Nathan, who was a Jew, was subjected to an anti-Semitic diatribe from the *Leader*, but the *Freeman's Journal* loyally defended the appointment on the basis of his outstanding record.[68] If the prejudice affected Nathan, he did not allow it to show. In fact, his handsome features and dashing manner attracted the attention of the Dublin Castle social set.

Birrell had three tasks for the new under secretary. He wanted Nathan to work with the heads of the constabulary and Dublin police to tighten the Castle's intelligence network. He also wanted him to find ways to reduce expenditures in the Irish administration to find more money for the war effort. Finally, he wanted Nathan to prepare the administration for the transfer to the home rule government. Nathan began at once. The Treasury remembrancer for Ireland, Maurice Headlam, assisted him in reducing expenditure by delegating the duties of officials who retired or enlisted to lower-ranking officials. This soon became standard practice because many civil servants enlisted and the government froze both promotions and entry in the civil service during the war. Nathan also began to confer with the heads of the police and the army about radical individuals, newspapers, and paramilitary organizations. He also began to seek transfers for a number of Irish civil servants who expressed pro-German sentiments.[69]

Nathan's most immediate problem was the command of the Dublin police. The assistant commissionership was vacant because William Harrell resigned after a royal commission investigating the Howth gunrunning incident criticized him for calling on the army to assist the police. The commission's findings enraged the chief commissioner, Sir

67. Cited in Jenkins, *Asquith*, p. 322. Birrell had offered his resignation to Asquith at least once before; see Bod. Lib., Asq. P., MS. 39, ff. 20–21, Birrell to Asquith, Nov. 13, 1913.

68. Leon O'Broin, *Dublin Castle and the 1916 Rising* (London: Sidgwick & Jackson, 1970), pp. 12, 14–15. *Leader*, Oct. 10, 1914; *Irish Times*, Oct. 5, 1914.

69. O'Broin, *Dublin Castle and the 1916 Rising*, pp. 24–26.

John Ross of Bladensburg, who had also been found derelict in his duty during the Howth affair. Ross also resigned, presumably out of loyalty to his second in command. Later, in a letter to Birrell, he defended Harrell's action during the incident and pointed out that the government's treatment of Harrell would shake the confidence of Irish civil servants in the administration.[70]

Nathan wanted to bring efficiency and economy to the higher ranks of the police. He recommended to Birrell that a new principle of vigorous selection of the best men from the ranks should guide them when they replaced Ross and Harrell.[71] Birrell was glad Nathan had taken the police business in hand, but he advised his under secretary to proceed cautiously. "These police appointments," Birrell wrote, "must be made on personal knowledge without outside interference, for in such matters those outside, however well-intentioned, have no real information. Who is your new man? R. C. or Protestant? I have no sort of confidence in Neville Chamberlain—his judgment is nil."[72] Birrell then explained that there was no need for quick action because two Royal Irish Constabulary officers, one Protestant and one Catholic, would take over the Dublin police on an interim basis.

Meanwhile, Asquith decided that it was time for the lord lieutenant to step down. Lord Aberdeen had served in Ireland for nine years, longer than any viceroy since the Act of Union. Although Aberdeen and his energetic wife won the affection of many Irish men and women, they often annoyed Birrell by meddling in the distribution of patronage. Neither viceroy nor vicereine wanted to leave—Lady Aberdeen had set several war-relief projects in motion—but they yielded to the prime minister's request.[73] Birrell used Aberdeen's departure to illuminate some of the dark corners involved in making Irish appointments for Nathan. "There is a pertinacity about the Kildare Street Club type of man which is very noticeable," Birrell observed while discussing the pressures that would be exerted during the selection of a successor. "They crop up with their suggestions at critical moments and always

70. Bod. Lib., Asq. P., MS. 41, ff. 1–148, Ross to Birrell, Jan. 12, 1915.

71. Bod. Lib., Nat. P., MS. 462, ff. 36–40, Nathan to Birrell, Oct. 20, 1914.

72. Ibid., MS. 449, ff. 27–28, Birrell to Nathan, Nov. 10, 1914.

73. Bod. Lib., Asq. P., MS. 46, ff. 97–100, Asquith to Aberdeen; Asquith to Lady Aberdeen, Oct. 8, Dec. 2, 1914.

with the same object—to cripple the Home Rule movement. It is hard not to get almost as suspicious as John Dillon of these men."[74] Birrell learned from Redmond that the Nationalists interpreted the Aberdeens' departure as a sign of a flagging in the Liberals' determination to press forward with home rule. The chief secretary was confident that another home ruler would be appointed, but what he wanted most was a lord lieutenant who would keep out of administrative matters.[75] After a short search, Asquith selected a young Liberal peer, Lord Wimbourne. The appointment seemed to be just what Birrell had hoped for. "I am not anxious to interfere in matters of administration," the new viceroy wrote, "but I should be glad to be informed generally in current events."[76]

As the search for a new lord lieutenant closed, Birrell and Nathan were obliged to return to a consideration of the Dublin police vacancies because the constabulary officers Birrell had appointed on a temporary basis had not taken the force firmly in hand. Modifying his earlier advice to Nathan about relying too much on personal knowledge when making police appointments, the chief secretary now advised him to contact Dillon.[77] Birrell then informed Dillon of Nathan's instructions. "I have impressed upon Nathan," Birrell wrote on November 22, 1914, "the importance of giving the D.M.P. whatever promotion they can fairly get, and how unfair it is to put the R.I.C. continually over their heads. He is alive to this and will take no steps until he has seen the men you name and looked them over."[78] The chief secretary assured Dillon that there could not be any divided responsibility in making the appointments and that the goodwill of the force was of primary importance in the troubled times that lay ahead.

Nathan and Dillon soon met at a neutral site, Land Commissioner Bailey's home, because Dillon would not go inside Dublin Castle. They discussed candidates for the chief positions in the Dublin police, and Dillon suggested that the under secretary search for prospective police officers in England. Nathan subsequently asked the Home Office

74. Bod. Lib., Nat. P., MS. 449, ff. 50–55, Birrell to Nathan, Dec. 14, 1914.
75. H.H. MS. 1/5, M. S. Green to Aberdeen, May 28, 1918.
76. Bod. Lib., Nat. P., MS. 448, ff. 69–70, Wimbourne to Nathan, May 9, 1915.
77. T.C.D., D.P., Birrell to Dillon, Oct. 14(?), 1914.
78. Ibid., Birrell to Dillon, Nov. 22, 1914.

whether an Irish Catholic officer were available.[79] Home Office officials recommended J. B. Wright, a Presbyterian serving in Newcastle who had previous service in Belfast while in the constabulary.[80] When he learned about this candidate, Dillon complained to Nathan that Wright was probably an Ulster Unionist, "and after all that has occurred during the last year, to appoint an Ulster Unionist to the head of the Dublin Police would create the worst possible feeling."[81] He asked Nathan to consider what would happen if a Catholic were appointed to lead the Belfast police. The appointment was not entirely a question of religion, Dillon explained, but appointing an Ulster Protestant whose record was unknown to the people of Dublin and to the Nationalist leaders would be "in a sense, putting Sir Edward Carson in control of the Dublin police."[82] Dillon concluded by suggesting two candidates who had his confidence and that of Redmond and Devlin. Nathan interviewed them but he settled instead on a third candidate, Lt. Col. Walter Edgeworth-Johnstone, a Protestant army officer from Londonderry who had received support from Assistant Under Secretary O'Farrell and from Max Sullivan Green.[83] For the second-in-command, Nathan promoted one of Dillon's candidates, Fergus Quinn, a Protestant, from the ranks of the Dublin police. Nathan reported to Birrell that Dillon was upset by his choices, "Though as you know, I consulted him, [but] I did not tell him which of his recommendations had been adopted."[84]

Birrell, meanwhile, tried to strengthen the supreme court bench and Law Office. The rapid promotions to the Law Office caused by the numerous vacancies on the bench forced Birrell to rely on inexperienced law officers during the recent turmoil in Belfast and Dublin. He began by selecting Stephen Ronan for a direct appointment to the Court

79. Bod. Lib., Nat. P., MS. 462, ff. 165–66, Nathan to Birrell, Nov. 26; ff. 195–96, Nathan to Birrell, Dec. 1; ff. 198–99, Nathan to L. Dunning (at the Home Office), Dec. 2, 1914.

80. Ibid., ff. 217–18, Nathan to Dillon, Dec. 6; f. 221, Nathan to Birrell, Dec. 7, 1914.

81. Ibid., MS. 450, ff. 224–27, Dillon to Nathan, Dec. 7, 1914.

82. Ibid.

83. Ibid., Ms. 462, f. 254, Nathan to Birrell, Dec. 10, and f. 286, Nathan to Birrell, Dec. 22, 1914; MS. 467, ff. 83–84. Memorandum of meeting with Dillon, Dec. 28, 1914.

84. Ibid., MS. 462, f. 346, Nathan to Birrell, Jan. 8, 1915. O'Broin, *Dublin Castle and the 1916 Rising,* p. 46.

of Appeal. It was a controversial appointment—Ronan was associated with Balfour in the attempt to link Parnell to the Phoenix Park murders—but Birrell explained to Nathan that he could no longer boycott Ronan at the bidding of the worst elements in the Irish Parliamentary party.[85] Redmond was disappointed that Justice Molony of the King's Bench Division was not promoted, but Dillon told T. P. O'Connor that they could use Ronan's appointment as leverage to prevent similar appointments in the future.[86] That tactic, however, did not work. In February 1915 Norway's term at the Dublin post office was extended by a new postmaster-general, Charles Hobhouse.[87] This broke the understanding that Redmond had reached with Herbert Samuel in 1912 about the promotion of James MacMahon. Hobhouse was pressed on the matter by Nathan, Devlin, Dillon, and Redmond, but he would not be bound by promises his predecessor made. His decision was that Norway would remain in place until home rule came into operation, whether that were one, two, or three years.[88]

By the end of 1914 Birrell was thoroughly worn out by the strains of his office, especially in the area of dispensing patronage. Moreover, he was deeply affected at this time by his wife's fatal illness.[89] When Lord Chief Justice Moriarty's health failed unexpectedly soon after Birrell weathered the storm blown up by Ronan's appointment, the chief secretary finally reached the breaking point. "The harpies," he snapped, "are already on the wing and are, no doubt, in telephonic communication with the Nursing Home. I wish I had some patronage in Hell."[90] He tried to tender his resignation but Asquith would not accept it. Birrell held on, dutifully overseeing more personnel changes on the bench. To reduce expenditures and to satisfy Redmond and Dillon, he transferred their protégé, Molony, from the King's Bench Division to Moriarty's position as lord justice of appeal. Molony's position was left vacant. This did not satisfy everyone. He observed that

85. Ibid., ff. 109–12, Birrell to Nathan, Jan. 21, 1915.

86. T.C.D., D.P., Dillon to T.P. O'Connor, Jan. 15, 1915.

87. Ibid., MS. 450, ff. 236–40, Dillon to Nathan, Feb. 21, 1915; MS. 467, ff. 151–52, Memorandum of meeting with Solicitor-General O'Connor, Feb. 12, 1915.

88. Ibid., MS. 454, ff. 137–38, Hobhouse to Nathan, Feb. 16, 1915.

89. O'Broin, *The Chief Secretary,* pp. 138–39; Bod. Lib., Nat. P., MS. 449, ff. 60–65, 67–70, Birrell to Nathan, Dec. 18, Dec. 21, 1914.

90. Ibid., ff. 152–58, Birrell to Nathan, Apr. 24, 1915.

the new vacancy was "a bitter pill, as the Lord Chancellor still hankers after McSweeney, either on the Bench or in the Law Room."[91]

With the chief secretary despondent, Nathan had a free hand when he set about the third task Birrell had assigned him—preparing for the transfer of the administration to a home rule government. Redmond and Dillon were eager to meet with the under secretary, and on February 4, 1915, Redmond visited Nathan at the Irish Office in London. Redmond stated that the administration should be transferred with as little structural change as possible. He was worried about maintaining the full financial sum that was to be transferred to the home rule government for operating the Irish administration. That amount was to be based on past expenditure, and he was concerned that Nathan and the Treasury officials might be too zealous in seeking war-time economies in the administration.[92] The two men also discussed the constitution of the future Irish ministry and the disposition of the departments that would be the responsibility of each of the new Irish ministers. At the conclusion of the session, Redmond eagerly suggested an ambitious schedule of three meetings a week with Nathan, perhaps at Dublin Castle where all the relevant documents were close at hand. Redmond realized that the transfer of the administration would require close attention. "It will certainly take us several sittings to deal with the matter," Redmond reported to Dillon on February 5, 1915. "The more I look at it, the more complicated it seems to me."[93]

Nathan arranged a series of meetings. The first one took place on February 17 at Dillon's house. Nathan, Dillon, and Redmond were in attendance. After deciding to keep the meetings a closely guarded secret and to include Devlin, Clancy, and some Irish Office officials at subsequent meetings, they discussed the major point on the agenda—the deployment of Irish administrative departments among the proposed Irish ministries. In addition to the prime minister, there would be ministers for finance, justice, local affairs and public health, agriculture and industries, lands and works, education, and posts and telegraphs. Later, Dillon proposed that a minister for industry and

91. Ibid., ff. 169–73, Birrell to Nathan, May 11, 1915.

92. Bod. Lib., Nat. P., MS. 467, ff. 133–40, Memorandum of meeting with Redmond, Feb. 4, 1915.

93. T.C.D., D.P., Redmond to Dillon, Feb. 5, 1915.

commerce should be independent of agriculture. He hoped this would allay Ulster Unionist fears that agricultural matters would overshadow industrial matters under a Nationalist government.[94]

When Nathan made plans for the next meeting, Birrell added his concern about maintaining secrecy in the enterprise. He wrote to Nathan on February 21, "I feel a little fidgetty about secrecy—if it gets about, as what does not get about in the most babyish of cities?—that a secret committee has been constituted and is on weekly sessions to arrange for Home Rule, there will be silly rumpus. . . . So I hope it will all be quite informal, and at the most casual conversations between interested parties, and that the records of the conversations will be kept in as few hands as possible."[95] On February 24 Nathan, Redmond, and Dillon met again. They agreed that the administration should be transferred with as little alteration as possible and that the administrative machinery should be assigned to the ministers who would be responsible for them before the home rule legislature began to operate. The Irish Office was to draw up the necessary transfer orders for the individual departments. Nathan promised to obtain memoranda from Irish department heads, who were not to be informed of the secret meetings, describing the operation of their respective departments. Turning from the bureaucracy to the Law Office, Redmond and Dillon stated that they would like to strip the lord chancellor of his political influence and make his position a purely judicial one. At the next meeting, on March 5, Nathan presented memoranda on the lord chancellorship and on several of the civil service departments. He also discussed the "composite departments," that is, those Irish offices that would remain under the imperial Parliament. Dillon was eager to avoid a conflict between the Irish and imperial parliaments on their account. The relationship of these departments and their personnel to the Irish ministry was not finalized, however, and the conferences came to a temporary halt to give Nathan time to gather more data from the Irish department heads.[96]

The administration that Nathan was preparing for Irish Nationalist

94. T.C.D., D.P., Notes on transfer of government departments.

95. Bod. Lib., Nat. P., MS. 449, ff. 126–27, 128–29, Birrell to Nathan, Feb. 21, Feb. 23, 1915.

96. T.C.D., D.P., Notes on transfer of government departments.

control had changed in two significant ways during the twenty-year period between the second and third home rule bills. First, the Irish civil service had become professionalized. Hundreds of rank and file officials who had obtained their positions prior to 1876 as first- and second-division clerks largely as a result of political influence had been replaced by men and women who had succeeded on open competition examinations.[97] These new officials worked hard under the supervision of competent staff officers and department heads. In Dublin Castle, three under secretaries had set the proper tone for the entire system. Indeed, it would be difficult to imagine three more capable bureaucrats than David Harrel, Antony MacDonnell, and James Dougherty. Each put his personal stamp on the administrative system. Harrel demanded and obtained efficiency in departments that had often been ridiculed in political speeches, popular literature, and humor magazines. Harrel's successor, MacDonnell, oversaw a substantial expansion of services in three areas: local government, agriculture and technical education, and land purchase. Dougherty's conviction that anyone who asked for assistance deserved a courteous and direct response established a model that guides the interaction of Irish civil servants with the public to this day.

The second change was in the religious and political character of the civil service personnel, from the rank and file officers in clerical positions to the members of the bureaucratic elite. The open competition examinations, in conjunction with the reform of the Irish intermediate education system in 1878 and the creation of the National University in 1908, were primarily responsible for this. By 1900, the change that had occurred in the clerical ranks was so sweeping that representatives of Catholic and Nationalist interests were able to contrast the clerks with the officials who were serving in staff positions and at the top of the system. The staff positions were slower to change because 80 percent of the vacancies in that echelon were filled by either direct nomination or limited competition examinations that included an interview with the department head. After 1908, however, the staff positions had also begun to change.

97. *Fourth Report of the Royal Commission on the Civil Service,* 1913, Chapter VIII, "Promotions," "Merit," pp. 57–58.

The period of Birrell's administration largely marked the greening of Dublin Castle. Irish civil servants were becoming more broadly representative of the people they served. The rank and file shared the popular enthusiasm for home rule. Indeed, some of the clerks were too enthusiastic. "The King's Health" was removed from a list of toasts to be drunk at the annual dinner of the Association of Irish Post Office Clerks in 1911.[98] In 1912, Birrell delayed the *Annual Report* from the Board of National Education until the resident commissioner, William Starkie, edited out home rule statements that Nationalist clerks had inserted into the text.[99] By 1912 Nationalists admitted that a significant change in attitude had also occurred at the center of the administration. Justin McCarthy, the former leader of the anti-Parnellites who had turned to writing history, pointed out in his *Irish Recollections* (1911) that Dublin Castle "represented in days gone by the domination of the conqueror, as a central garrison might do, and in more modern days it typified the ascendancy of the rulers of aristocratic society and fashion." "It had in our present time," McCarthy further observed, "lost or voluntarily surrendered much of its oppressive political power. One cannot now associate the presence of a Viceroy ruling at Dublin Castle with any idea of tyrannical dictatorship."[100]

The change in attitude was directly related to a change in the religious and political character of the bureaucratic elite. Birrell's distribution of appointments largely transformed the highest levels of the bureaucracy from a Protestant and Unionist preserve to one that began to reflect the Catholic and Nationalist preponderance in the country more accurately. In 1892, the top forty-eight administrative positions were monopolized, save three, by Protestant and Unionist officials. In 1914, these positions were divided between twenty Catholics—one Catholic was a Unionist—and twenty-eight Protestants, three of whom were Liberal home rulers. Ten of the top forty-eight bureaucrats were not native-born Irishmen.[101] These ten officials were evenly divided

98. Leon O'Broin, *Revolutionary Underground: The Story of the Irish Republican Brotherhood, 1858–1924* (Totowa, N.J.: Rowman and Littlefield, 1976), p. 137.

99. T.C.D., D.P., Starkie to Dillon, Sept. 23, 1912.

100. Justin McCarthy, *Irish Recollections* (London and New York: Hodder and Stoughton, 1911), p. 156.

101. R. B. McDowell, *The Irish Administration, 1808–1914* (London: Routledge & Kegan Paul, 1964), pp. 46–51.

between departments that were under Dublin Castle and the Irish branches of British departments. By every indication in 1914 members of the bureaucratic elite—Catholic and Protestant, Liberal, Nationalist, and Unionist alike—would stay in place when Redmond took control of the Irish administration. This was the real test of the professional civil servant.

It is also clear that Birrell's administration marked the greening of the Four Courts. The Supreme Court of Judicature and the lower levels of the judicial system underwent similar political and religious transformations. In 1892, the supreme court bench, including the judicial land commissioners and the lord chancellor, was divided between eighteen Protestants and three Catholics. The political affiliation of the justices was identical, eighteen Unionists and three Liberals. There was little net change under the Conservatives between 1895 and 1905. By 1914, however, the bench was evenly divided between Catholics and Protestants, Liberal home rulers and Unionists. Both of the law officers and two of the sergeants-at-law who were waiting in the wings for promotion were Catholic Nationalists. Birrell, advised by his Liberal and Nationalist law officers, also made significant changes in the religious complexion of the county court bench and the local magistracy. In 1909 the religious distribution of the sixteen county court judgeships and the five county court recorders stood at twelve Protestants and nine Catholics. By 1914 the same positions (augmented by one) stood at sixteen Catholics and six Protestants. When appointing justices of the peace, Birrell and Aberdeen appointed two Catholics for every Protestant. Between 1906 and 1914 Catholics rapidly closed the gap on the local bench. The distribution stood at four Protestants to one Catholic in 1892; in 1914 the ratio was reduced to slightly over three to two. Indeed, from justices of the peace to supreme court justices, Catholics were represented in legal positions far beyond what their share might be if the proportion of one Catholic lawyer for every three lawyers in Ireland had dictated these appointments.[102]

102. According to the *Annual Directory of the Incorporated Law Society of Ireland,* there were approximately seven hundred barristers in Ireland in 1909. In administrative positions in county and local judicial systems, the figures on the distribution of positions by religion were as follows: county court recorders, twelve Protestants and seven Catholics; resident magistrates, forty-three Protestants and

John Redmond expected to sit at the head of a Nationalist ministry that would govern Ireland, administer public services, and supervise the working of the judicial system. When the world war broke out the Home Rule Act was suspended, but the war did not reach the quick conclusion forecast by the optimists. Within a few months Asquith's abilities as a wartime leader were questioned by the military command and by political leaders of both British parties. Personal rivalries within his government hampered the development of a decisive policy. Political pressure, a press campaign, and lack of confidence of British public opinion in his leadership forced Asquith to break up the Liberal government in May 1915.

---

twenty-two Catholics; crown solicitors, twelve Protestants and ten Catholics; clerks of the crown and peace, nineteen Protestants and twelve Catholics; sessional crown solicitors, twenty-four Protestants and eight Catholics; district probate court registrars, ten Protestants and one Catholic. The *Irish Catholic* reported these figures on Nov. 19, 1909.

Chapter VII

Power without Responsibility, May 1915–December 1916

On May 18, 1915, Herbert Asquith invited the leaders of the Liberal, Conservative, and Irish Parliamentary parties to join with him in forming a Coalition government, which would be dominated by Liberals. The Conservative, Unionist and Labour party members who joined the cabinet were relegated to the less important posts. Edward Carson, who accepted the attorney-generalship of England, was among the Unionists who joined the cabinet, but John Redmond refused. He stated that the principles of the Parliamentary party prevented him from accepting office and that his efforts in assisting in bringing the war to a successful conclusion would be reduced if he did take office.[1] On May 20 Augustine Birrell, who retained his post as chief secretary, wrote to John Dillon, proposing that either Dillon or Joseph Devlin, the Parliamentary party MP for West Belfast, join the coalition in Redmond's stead.[2] Neither Dillon nor Devlin accepted Birrell's proposal and the Nationalists remained, true to their tradition, outside the government.

The Coalition government posed a threat to the influence that the Irish Parliamentary party had in Irish administrative affairs and in imperial affairs. Instead of holding the balance of power in the House of Commons, the Parliamentary party lost its leverage to the combined voting strength of the parties that joined the coalition. Since the war had to be ended before home rule would be placed in operation, the party could not take up a position of independent opposition. Indeed,

1. N.L.I., Red. P., MS. 15165 (5), Asquith to Redmond, May 18, 1915; and Redmond to Asquith, May 19, 1915.
2. T.C.D., D.P., Birrell to Dillon, May 20, 1915.

the political truce that had been observed since the outbreak of the war bound the Parliamentary party to work with the other parties to help win the war. The coalition also posed a threat to the historic Liberal-Nationalist political alliance. Asquith would have to take Conservative and Unionist party opinion into account when Irish policy and administration were under discussion. Birrell, as chief secretary and member of the cabinet, was likely to be affected by the change in the relationship between his own party and the Conservatives and Unionists. The key question was how far the Parliamentary party's influence in Irish affairs would be eroded by the Unionists and Conservatives who were members of the Coalition government.

Redmond was determined to find an answer to this question when he wrote to Asquith on May 22 to lodge a protest against Carson's inclusion in the cabinet. In the letter Redmond complained that Carson was the "leader of the Ulster revolters, who, the other day, was threatening hostilities to the forces of the Crown and the decision of Parliament."[3] Redmond also expressed his concern that the idea of including Unionists in the cabinet might be extended to Dublin Castle. "If it was sought to carry the Coalition into the government of Ireland by supplanting the existing Irish office-holders by Unionists, the greatest confusion would arise here in the public mind, and a state of perturbation, suspicion, and, I think, indignation would ensue. I think we may fairly ask that Mr. Birrell be given a free hand to carry on the government of Ireland as he has done in the past, and with the same officials."[4]

Birrell was also alarmed about the prospect of working with the Unionists who were now sharing power in the government. He had once called them the greediest pigs on record where patronage was concerned. "Suppose," he asked the under secretary, Matthew Nathan, "they begin listening to the hungry band of excluded lawyers and honor hunters—and pressing claims upon us, or criticising our modes and methods of administering Ireland during the next two or three years?"[5]

Unionists were in fact eager to extend the coalition to Dublin Castle and the Four Courts. "In any Coalition Government," James Campbell,

3. Bod. Lib., Asq. P., MS 27, ff. 192–93, Redmond to Asquith, May 25, 1915.

4. Cited in Gwynn, *Redmond,* p. 425, letter to May 27, 1915.

5. Bod. Lib., Nat. P., MS. 449, ff. 179–80, Birrell to Nathan, n.d.: See also., ff. 181–82, Birrell to Nathan, Whit Monday, 1915.

the former Unionist attorney-general pointed out to Bonar Law, "you must share in the responsibility for the government of Ireland, and you have a *right* to claim a share in it on that account."[6] Campbell saw the Coalition as his chance to attain his lifelong ambition, the Irish lord chancellorship. Carson thought that Hugh Barrie, a Scotsman with business interests in County Londonderry, deserved an administrative appointment and that John Gordon, a Liberal Unionist MP for South Londonderry since 1900, had the best claims for the Irish Law Office. Campbell agreed about Gordon's claims and told Law that William Moore was another Unionist worthy of an Irish Law Office appointment. Lord Lansdowne, meanwhile, speculated about replacing Birrell with "a good man for Irish Secretary."[7]

Birrell's and Redmond's fears about the extension of the coalition to Dublin Castle were justified. "The incomers," Birrell explained to Redmond shortly after returning from his first coalition cabinet meeting, "claimed their share in Ireland on the same terms as elsewhere."[8] Birrell reported that Asquith had decided to appoint Campbell as Irish lord chancellor, although he had been assured that the administration of Ireland would continue unaltered in his and the under secretary's hands. Birrell reported further that he told the cabinet that he was opposed to Campbell's appointment, knowing that Redmond and Dillon would also oppose it. Upon receiving this information the Parliamentary party leaders objected, not only to the man, but to the position offered. They pointed out what the Nationalist press had been emphasizing for two weeks: that Campbell held the position of legal assessor in Carson's provisional government and that he had signed the Ulster covenant.[9] Moreover, Redmond and Dillon wanted to protect the current Irish lord chancellor, Ignatius O'Brien.

Birrell's and Redmond's adverse reaction to Campbell's appointment forced the prime minister to inform Law that it had to be withdrawn.[10]

6. H.L.R.O., Law P., MS 50/3/3,8, Campbell to Law, May 19, May 20, 1915.

7. Ibid., MS 50/3/21, Carson to Campbell, May 21, 1915; MS 50/3/41, Landsdowne to Law, May 23, 1915; MS. 50/3/46, Campbell to Law, May 25, 1915; MS. 53/5/10, Carson to Law, n.d.

8. Gwynn, *Redmond,* pp. 426–27, citing letter from Birrell to Redmond, May 29, 1915.

9. *Irish News,* May 25, 1915; *Irish Catholic,* May 29, June 5, 1916; *Irish Independent,* May 29, June 5, 1915; *Leader,* June 5, 1915.

10. H.L.R.O., Law P., MS. 50/3/54, Asquith to Law, May 27, 1915.

Law, who was in communication with Campbell, accepted the reversal with dismay. He told Asquith, "it is not merely a question of disappointing Campbell, though that is serious to me after I had told him that he would receive the appointment; but it means that we have no voice in the Irish Administration and, therefore, no knowledge of what is being done." "If Campbell's appointment is impossible," he concluded, "then we must press either for the Chief Secretary or the Lord Lieutenant, for this is precisely the one subject in regard to which our Party is the most sensitive."[11] Law realized that if Redmond could block Unionist appointments, the Parliamentary party would be exercising an effective veto on the decisions of the coalition without joining it. A week later, in a letter to Lloyd George, Law warned that if the government yielded to the Nationalists on this issue, complaints from Unionist party members might force some Unionist cabinet members to resign. That, Law indicated, could wreck the coalition, and he concluded that the new government's buckling at the first breath of hostility did not auger well for its future.[12]

Campbell was angry and embarrassed that his appointment had been withdrawn. The embarrassment came when he told his family and friends that he had not received the position. The anger was evident in his letters to Asquith that recounted the scurrilous rumors that had appeared in the Nationalist press charging that he had sought the position only to collect its eight-thousand-pound salary and four-thousand-pound pension, to distribute patronage, and to control the administration. He declared that the Unionists had not received a judicial appointment since 1896 and that Birrell's recent appointments of Nationalists had been a scandal. Both grievances, Campbell believed, would be redressed through his appointment, although he drew the conclusion that the Nationalists could prevent him—or anyone else who did not favor home rule—from assuming a position in the Irish administration.[13]

Thinking that the matter was closed, Asquith asked Birrell to inform Redmond of the withdrawal of the appointment, and then he left for the front in France. Evidently Birrell failed to contact Redmond, and

11. Ibid., MS. 53/6/12, Law to Asquith, May 28, 1915.
12. Ibid., MS. 53/6/22, Law to Lloyd George, June 4, 1916.
13. Ibid., MS. 50/4/16, Campbell to Asquith, June 6, 1915.

the anxiety about the return of Unionists to Dublin Castle continued to grow in Nationalist circles. T. P. O'Connor told Dillon that if the appointment of Carson, and then F. E. Smith, who had signed the Ulster covenant as English solicitor-general "is to be followed-up by the appointment to Campbell, it looks to me like the end of all things." He urged Dillon to raise a question on the subject in the House of Commons.[14] This would break the political truce that had been in effect since the outbreak of the war. Dillon began to think about alternatives if it proved impossible to prevent Campbell's appointment. Campbell could, for example, be offered the existing vacancy on the Irish supreme court. At least this would prevent the disturbance of O'Brien.[15] Meanwhile, Michael Fogarty, bishop of Killaloe, wrote to Redmond to inform him that feeling in the country was running against the appointment of Campbell and against the party. "The people are full of indignation, but are powerless," he noted. "The Party, to my mind a great mistake, have taken the whole thing lying down, without a bit of fight."[16] And there was another point of view on the matter. Moderate Nationalists were worried that if Irish-American opinion were stirred up on this issue, it could adversely influence the American government's decision to join Britain in the war.[17]

Redmond was prepared to violate the political truce, but he hoped to avoid this by blocking the appointment through private channels. Once again he protested in a letter to Asquith on June 3. When he received no reply, he telegraphed, warning Asquith that if necessary, the Parliamentary party would fight the appointment on the floor of the House.[18] On receiving the telegram the prime minister immediately sent Redmond an explanation of the rationale for his disposition of the Irish offices. Asquith said that he had offered Campbell the lord chancellorship because he and Lloyd George thought it was the least political of the principal positions in Irish administration. He went on to explain that the Unionists had accepted the position before he realized that Birrell and the Parliamentary party leaders objected to Campbell.

14. T.C.D., D.P., T. P. O'Connor to Dillon, June 3, 1915; T. P. O'Connor to Asquith, June 3, 1915 (copy).

15. Ibid., Dillon to O'Connor, June 4, 1915.

16. Bod. Lib., Asq. P., MS 36, ff. 98–99, Fogarty to Redmond, June 3, 1915.

17. H.L.R.O., Law P., MS. 631/C/55, Spring-Rice to Lord Crew, June 8, 1915.

18. Gywnn, *Redmond,* p. 427.

Although the Unionist party leaders were trying to hold him to the appointment, Asquith reported that the Unionists would accept another position in the Irish administration if all parties could reach agreement on Campbell's fate and on the alternative position. "With the Viceroy, Chief Secretary, and the Law Officers, and the Vice-President of D.A.T.I. all our own men, and a sympathetic Under Secretary," Asquith reassured Redmond, "there could be no question of any change of policy." He concluded by telling Redmond, "a declaration of hostility from you or your friends would be all but fatal to the prospects of the new Government."[19]

Redmond rejected this explanation. He pointed out, somewhat disingenuously in view of the party's pledge, that Asquith had failed to make even the gesture of offering him a position in the Irish government. Worse, he had announced his intention to form the coalition without consulting his political allies in Ireland. Turning to the matter at hand Redmond stated that the Parliamentary party had scrupulously upheld the political truce, but he indicated again that if Campbell were appointed the truce would end. For good measure Redmond included the letter he had received from Bishop Fogarty.[20]

Redmond's protest did not prevent Asquith from extending the principle of coalition government to Dublin Castle. Although Campbell was not named lord chancellor, the prime minister appointed another Unionist, John Gordon, to the Irish attorney-generalship. Attorney-General Jonathan Pim was promoted to the vacancy on the King's Bench Division of the supreme court to make room for Gordon. Asquith also began to search for an alternate position for Campbell. In explaining his actions to Redmond on June 9, Asquith supposed that the entire arrangement was as unwelcome to Redmond as it was to him, but he hoped the decision would be accepted "in a spirit of patriotic self-abnegation."[21] A Parliamentary party resolution followed Asquith's suggested line of retreat. The party "learned with satisfaction that its protests have been successful in preventing the Lord Chancellorship of

19. Cited in Gwynn, *Redmond*, pp. 428–29.

20. Bod. Lib., Asq. P., MS. 36, ff. 89–97, Redmond to Asquith, June 7, 1915; and f. 96, Nationalist Party Resolution, June 7, 1915. See also N.L.I., MS. 12082, *Irish Parliamentary Party Minute Book,* June 7, 1915. The *Leader* reported on June 5, 1915, that Redmond had been offered the postmaster-generalship.

21. Gwynn, *Redmond,* p. 432.

Ireland being handed over under the Coalition Government to a Unionist, and especially a Unionist with the record of Mr. Campbell." "We abstain," the resolution concluded loyally, "in view of the extraordinary dangers of the present national crisis, from taking any hostile action against the new government in connection with the appointment of a Unionist to the Attorney-Generalship of Ireland."[22]

Although the principle of coalition had been recognized and implemented through one appointment, the Unionists were not entirely pleased. They had expected more, and they did not like being placed in the position of having to beg for what they thought was their due in the Coalition government. At a meeting of the South Belfast Unionist Association on June 11, James Chambers, the Unionist MP for South Belfast, pointed out that the Parliamentary party "had every other Irish office filled with Nationalists and sympathizers with Home Rule, and one would have thought that at least one office might have gone to a Unionist." "At the very moment it was suggested," Chambers asked, "what happened? The men who had fattened on the offices in this country for ten years raised a howl like a hyena."[23] The *Belfast News-Letter* also attacked the Parliamentary party for refusing to be generous when it had both the opportunity and the duty. On June 12 the newspaper expressed the long-standing Unionist fear that under home rule the Nationalists "might tolerate us if we were content to exist and speak and act with bated breath and humbleness, but as for having a share in the government of this country, we would not be given a single office."[24]

With the disposition of Irish offices finally settled, the chief secretary was ready to return to business as usual. "We seem to have withstood that most discreditable and discrediting storm," he wrote to his under secretary on June 10. "The Lord Chancellor is safe, the Attorney-General is evicted and rewarded with the Judgeship you had hoped to keep unfilled." "Campbell," he added amusingly, "is to have some glittering place in England, which plays the role Ireland used to play in the days when Royal Mistresses were placed on the Irish Civil Pension

22. Nat. Lib., MS. 12082, *Irish Parliamentary Party Minute Book,* June 10, 1915.
23. *Belfast News-Letter,* June 12, 1915.
24. Ibid.

List."[25] Two days later, Birrell wrote to Nathan to inform him that he had conferred with Redmond and found that they remained in accord on the desirability of Nathan's maintaining his close relationship with the Parliamentary party leaders.[26] Birrell was not going to let the formation of the Coalition government impede the preparations that were under way to transfer the Irish administration to a home rule government. The under secretary heeded his chief's suggestion. Within the week he wrote to Dillon informing him that a memorandum on the proposed Irish Department of Finance, which they had discussed at their last meeting before the formation of the coalition, was now ready for presentation at another of their secret conclaves.

The meeting was held at the under secretary's lodge in Phoenix Park on July 2. Nathan distributed a memorandum on the Finance Department, which met Dillon's approval. Maximum salaries for department heads were set at fifteen hundred pounds, and Dillon insisted on two thousand pounds for the permanent head of the Finance Department to attract the best candidates. They also agreed that it would be wise to retain the imperial Civil Service Commission's services for personnel decisions, at least temporarily. Recent events had indicated all too clearly that this area was likely to remain sensitive.[27]

The next meeting between Nathan and the Parliamentary party leaders was held in September. The agenda included a discussion of the transfer order that would be necessary for the establishment of Irish departments and for the appointment of the Irish cabinet officers: prime minister; ministers for finance, justice, trade, local affairs, lands, education; and postmaster general. The duties of each minister were adumbrated and the existing departments were tentatively apportioned among them. Ministerial power over subordinates was then defined along the lines that delimited English ministers; that is, it was absolute except where limited by Parliament.[28] The proposed organization of the Irish cabinet and administration revealed Redmond's and Dillon's vision of a reorganized, more coordinated administrative system. Ac-

25. Bod. Lib., Nat. P., MS. 449, ff. 189–90, Birrell to Nathan, June 10, 1915.

26. Ibid., 449, ff. 191–94, Birrell to Nathan, June 12, 1915.

27. T.C.D., D.P., "Notes on Transfer of Government Departments, Fourth Meeting." July 2, 1915.

28. Ibid., "Notes on Transfer of Government Departments," Sept. 1915.

cording to the scheme, three cabinet ministers—land, education, and local affairs—would bear responsibility for the administration of the thirty departments, offices, and agencies that were then responsible to the chief secretary. Ministers for finance, trade, and the post office would each bear responsibility for one department. The Law Office also had cabinet status. The only items missing from Dillon's copy of Nathan's memorandum listing the Irish ministries and departments were the names of those who would be the first ministers.

While preparations for the transfer of services to a Nationalist home rule government were completed, the results of the extension of the coalition principle to Dublin Castle became apparent. The new attorney-general quickly appointed William Moore as crown solicitor in Belfast. Birrell told Redmond he found the appointment very irritating, but later, when a judicial vacancy occurred in County Cork, he admitted to Nathan that Carson was correct when he argued that political priorities must be set in the making of appointments.[29] As a result, Birrell and Nathan tried to find a method to fill vacancies that would satisfy both Nationalists and Unionists. Nathan's first impulse was to leave positions vacant in the interest of wartime economy. If political interests were to prevail, he planned to neutralize them by devising a formula he could use in making all appointments. One of his formulas would maintain the status quo by filling vacated positions with candidates whose political and religious beliefs were identical to those of the previous official.[30] Another formula he suggested to Birrell was based on the aggregate political and religious complexion of all of the officials in a particular category. If this were a criterion, he and Birrell could continue to redress imbalances.[31] Birrell found the formulas undignified. He replied, "if the Coalition people really mean to divide the spoils, we must come to terms with them—turn them about or something of that sort, otherwise they will swamp us." He added that Unionists "are a grasping lot—and are not entitled to an equality—one in three is more like it."[32] His first impulse was to appoint the most

29. Bod. Lib., Nat. P., MS. 449, ff. 247–48, Birrell to Nathan, n.d. [between Sept. 8 and Sept. 13], 1915.
30. Ibid., MS. 464, ff. 439–41, Nathan to Birrell, Sept. 13, 1915.
31. Ibid., MS. 465, ff. 30–31, Nathan to Birrell, Oct. 11, 1915.
32. Ibid., 449, ff. 261–62, Birrell to Nathan, Oct. 12, 1915.

qualified man, taking into account local political conditions when necessary. He did not want to use a formula because it limited his options and amounted "to our handing over all the jobs to rank partisans on both sides." "I think," he concluded, "the Coalitionists must trust me, though it is a nuisance having both packs yelping at my heels each time a placeman dies."[33]

The Parliamentary party remained on guard to prevent the appointment of more Unionists. In October party members reacted vigorously to the rumor that a Unionist would be appointed to the position of clerk of the crown in County Down. Birrell assured Redmond and one of his Ulster lieutenants, Jeremiah MacVeigh, that no bargain had been struck with the Unionists over appointments. In fact, he told them what he had also told Carson—he hoped to appoint candidates on their merits and in a spirit of fairness to all parties.[34] But when the Ulster Nationalists remained unconvinced and even questioned his sincerity, he grew impatient. He asked Nathan to tell them, "There has been a change of government, and I am bound to recognize that fact not less in Ulster than elsewhere."[35]

Birrell eventually appointed a Catholic Nationalist to the County Down position. He told Nathan that this particular appointment had its own special guidelines, explaining that if he did not help occasionally in the north, the Nationalists there would "not be given a look in."[36] Obviously, this explanation won neither the confidence nor trust of Ulster Unionists. John Lonsdale, the unionist MP for Mid-Armagh, called the appointment an absolute scandal and said that it proved that the principle of coalition government did not apply to Ireland.[37] The *Belfast News-Letter,* observing that County Down was a Protestant Unionist county, complained that this was the eleventh successive time a Catholic Nationalist had been appointed clerk of the crown in Ireland since 1906. "If it could be urged," the *Newsletter* argued, "that this is an attempt on the part of the Castle to eliminate political considerations

33. Ibid.

34. N.L.I., Red. P., MS 15169 (4), Birrell to Redmond, and Birrell to MacVeigh (copy), Oct. 14, 1915.

35. Bod. Lib., Nat. P., MS. 449, ff. 263–64, Birrell to Nathan, Oct. 14, 1915.

36. Ibid., ff. 297–332, Birrell to Nathan, n.d. (filed between Birrell's letters to Nathan of Nov. 19 and Dec. 12, 1915).

37. *Northern Whig,* Dec. 1, 1915.

in the filling of such posts, there would be little ground for complaints. But as has been shown, the defense is impossible. 'The spoils to victors' is a principle the Nationalists have insisted shall be applied without exception—truce or no truce."[38]

The Unionists soon found two more instances of the Parliamentary party's maintaining its influence in administrative matters. The first instance involved James Campbell, who sent several proposals on appointments to Asquith during the autumn. Campbell, whose own interests were at the center of the plans, suggested the resignation of various Catholic justices, the promotion of Gordon to the bench, and his own appointment as either attorney- or solicitor-general. He realized that a position in the Law Office could lead to his appointment as lord chancellor, and would, in fact, enhance his claims.[39] The chief secretary was not seriously alarmed by Campbell's schemes. He told Nathan in October, "unless Redmond and Dillon agree, I don't think it can be done."[40] Redmond, however, was worried. He reminded Dillon that the party had set a precedent when they agreed that a Unionist might hold the attorney-general's position during the coalition.[41] Redmond wrote to Birrell on November 9, asking whether Campbell could be appointed directly to the bench. He warned that Campbell's appointment as attorney-general "would be regarded in Ireland as filling Carson's position in the Government with the next most objectionable Unionist."[42] After conveying Redmond's letter to the prime minister, Birrell discovered that Asquith was not ready to press forward, although the prime minister was sorry that he had broken his promise to appoint Campbell as lord chancellor in May. Asquith was also tiring of Parliamentary party pressure on the matter. In a terse letter he told Birrell that he did not want to ask the Nationalists' permission; rather, he simply wanted his Irish secretary to inform Redmond of what was proposed.[43] The next day, Birrell relieved Redmond's anxiety by in-

38. *Belfast News-Letter,* Dec. 7, 1915. Of a total of eighteen clerkships of the crown, Unionists held but five in 1915.

39. There are many letters from Campbell in both the Law Papers and the Asquith Papers that describe Campbell's various appointment schemes.

40. Bod. Lib., Nat., Nat. P., MS. 449, ff. 261–62, Birrell to Nathan, Oct. 12, 1915.

41. T.C.D., D.P., Redmond to Dillon, Nov. 8, 1915.

42. Ibid., Redmond to Birrell, Nov. 9, 1915 (copy).

43. Bod. Lib., Nat. P., MS. 449, ff. 282–88, Birrell to Nathan, Nov. 14, 1915.

forming him that since no fresh vacancy could be expected on the Irish bench, Campbell would be placed on the English bench before Christmas.[44]

The second occasion that Unionists used to allege continued Nationalist influence in Irish administrative matters involved the Treasury's appointment of a committee to identify wartime economies that could be made in public administration. At Birrell's request the committee extended its inquiry to Ireland, but he told Nathan in November that he hoped for a short inquiry that would not include the Irish departments under Treasury control or the Four Courts. As an added safeguard against too much interference from the Treasury, Birrell arranged for the committee to conduct its business from the Irish Office in London, not from Dublin Castle.[45] When Nathan began to collect memoranda on departmental expenditures rumors spread within the civil service that he envisioned slashing some £3 million from a total administrative expenditure of approximately £12.5 million. The rumors were fostered in part by Nathan's previous cutbacks of personnel on the Congested Districts Board, Land Commission, and police, as well as by a voluntary reduction in his own salary.[46] The Ulster Unionist press, which assumed that anything emanating from Dublin Castle must be the work of Redmond and Dillon, doubted that the Parliamentary party would agree to reduce Dublin Castle's budget. The *Northern Whig* charged that the Parliamentary party had only curtailed its criticism of the fiscal mismanagement in Dublin Castle because the party had secured so many positions for its supporters during the Birrell-Aberdeen regime.[47] The Nationalist press countered by charging that the committee would permit "fatted drones, party hacks, Freemasons, and nepotism to survive at the expense of those public servants who performed useful work in Ireland."[48]

Redmond initially favored the committee, and a member of the Parliamentary party, Thomas Boland, was selected to serve as a commis-

44. Ibid., Redmond to Dillon, Nov. 15, 1915.
45. Ibid., ff. 293–96, Birrell to Nathan, Nov. 19, 1915.
46. Ibid., MS 475, ff. 1–373. "Committee on Retrenchment in Public Expenditure: Irish Notes and Papers."
47. *Northern Whig*, Nov. 20, 1915.
48. *Irish News*, Nov. 27, 1915.

sioner. The extension of the scope of the committee's inquiry to Ireland, however, surprised Redmond. He thought that an inquiry into Irish administrative finance was a task best undertaken by a home rule government.[49] After conferring with Dillon, Redmond complained in a public letter to Birrell on November 30 that he had not been consulted about the expanded scope of the inquiry or about its personnel.[50] This was noteworthy because the party had been regularly consulted by the Liberal governments on the terms of reference for parliamentary commissions and on the selection of personnel. Redmond then warned that if his political allies were not going to cooperate with him, his party would not cooperate with them. He advised his followers to abstain from nominating members of the committee, and he instructed Boland to remove himself from the committee.

Unionist newspapers dismissed Redmond's attitude as hypocritical.[51] A letter to the editor of the *Belfast News-letter* from an anonymous Ulster Unionist MP made explicit what had previously been implicit in the Unionists' concern about Redmond's influence in the Irish administration. "It appears to us that he claims that he has a right to exercise the power which he would have if he were prime minister, and it follows that no step in Irish administration should be taken without his consent. But this is a claim no Unionist can concede." Birrell, the writer continued, had allowed the Nationalists to govern Ireland throughout his tenure, and it was apparent to them that this arrangement was continuing during the coalition. As a result, the letter concluded, the Unionists in the coalition "have responsibility without power, while Mr. Redmond has power without responsibility."[52] A week later the *Northern Whig* widened the scope of the attack on Nationalist influence in the administration by expressing its concern about the radical political opinions held by a number of civil servants appointed by Birrell. In the article "Mr. Birrell and Sedition" the newspaper suggested that the chief secretary should direct his attention toward Sinn

49. T.C.D., D.P., Redmond to Dillon, Nov. 24, 1915, and Dillon to Redmond, Nov. 25, 1915; Redmond to Dillon, Nov. 27, 1915.

50. N.L.I, Red. P., MS 15169 (4), Redmond to Birrell, Nov. 30, 1915.

51. *Belfast News-Letter,* Dec. 3, 1915.

52. Ibid., Dec. 4, 1915.

Feiners—the generic term for radical Nationalists since 1914—who were employed in government departments. "It is one of the many strange inconsistencies of the Nationalists," the *Whig* noted, "that those who are eating Government bread are generally the most disloyal. Under Mr. Birrell's unfortunate regime some of the Irish departments have been filled with men who are now obstructing recruiting."[53]

In fact, Birrell and Nathan worked assiduously to keep abreast of the anti-English, pro-German elements in Ireland. In addition to monitoring dissident civil servants,[54] the administration had to contend with politically charged theatrical productions at the Abbey Theatre and at Liberty Hall, the headquarters of James Larkin's Irish Transport and General Workers Union. The latter also served as headquarters for James Connolly's small Irish Citizen Army, whose members staged maneuvers in the Dublin streets that led up to a mock attack on Dublin Castle in October 1915. The activities of the Gaelic Athletic Association, the Gaelic League, the Irish Boy Scouts, and the Irish Volunteers were also monitored.

The chief secretary moved against the radicals only when it was deemed absolutely necessary. This strategy had the approval of the prime minister and the support of the Parliamentary party leaders, who advised Birrell not to enhance the reputations of men and newspapers with small followings by prosecuting them.[55] The under secretary and various Irish officials oversaw the tactical aspects of the plan. Nathan maintained communication with the constabulary and the army through Inspector-General Chamberlain and Major Ivor Price, who was on secondment to the army in Ireland; he used Local Government Board inspectors to report on political activity in the country; and he sounded out Land Commissioner Bailey about Dublin's intellectual circles. Nathan also interviewed Rev. Denis Coffey, the president of University College, Dublin, about the activities of students and professors. As for the civil servants, Nathan suggested to Birrell, who then

53. *Northern Whig,* Dec. 9, 1915.

54. See *The Spark,* Oct. 17, 1915, for a notice that "pro-Irish" civil servants were suspected of being "pro-German."

55. O'Broin, *Dublin Castle and the 1916 Rising,* pp. 38–42.

brought the matter to the attention of the cabinet, that all Irish officials should be forbidden, under pain of dismissal, to belong to the Irish Volunteers, to take part in its maneuvers, or to associate with its leaders.[56]

The administration's intelligence network also reported a marked decline in support for the Parliamentary party. The dissatisfaction centered on the party's loyal support of the war. Critics were especially vocal about the role the Parliamentary party leaders were playing in recruiting Irishmen into the British army. The increase in the number of armed Irish Volunteers was one indication of the dissatisfaction, but there were other indicators as well. For example, some parish priests and some bishops, such as Edward O'Dwyer, the bishop of Limerick, were expressing outright opposition to the war and to the party.[57] Redmond's problems in maintaining broad Nationalist support for the war were compounded when the cabinet decided to introduce conscription in January 1916. Redmond was able to prevent the extension of conscription to Ireland by promising that he would increase Irish recruiting, but he received no guarantee that conscription would not be extended to Ireland in the future.[58]

Sinn Fein's developing influence, the ebbing of episcopal and clerical support, and Redmond's failure to lay to rest the threat of conscription in Ireland all indicated that the party was losing its effectiveness. Its grip on Dublin Castle was also beginning to loosen. This became evident in April when Asquith finally appointed Campbell to the Irish attorney-generalship, in the place of Gordon, who succeeded to a vacant position in the King's Bench Division. Dillon told Nathan on April 13, 1916, that the appointment was "a very great outrage" and could "lead to very serious and deplorable consequences."[59] In fact, the appointment broke the political relationship between Asquith and Redmond. "I mean," Birrell explained to Nathan a week later, "they have

56. Bod. Lib., Nat. P., MS. 478, Nathan to Birrell, Jan. 16, 1916 (Cabinet Memorandum). Leon O'Broin, *Dublin Castle and the 1916 Rising* (New York University Press, 1971), pp. 32–37, on Nathan's investigations into civil servants who were thought to be disloyal.

57. Miller, *Church, State and Nation in Ireland, 1898–1921,* pp. 315–17.

58. Gwynn, *Redmond,* p. 465.

59. Bod. Lib., Nat. P., MS. 450–51, ff. 320–21, Dillon to Nathan, Apr. 13, 1916.

taken to their tents, and are pursuing their own policy. Redmond is, of course, furious about Campbell, and regards his appointment as a personal affront by the prime minister and as much as saying 'who needs you.' " "All of this is fostered," Birrell concluded, "by deliberately spread rumours that Campbell intends to instigate a new and sweeping policy of extermination and disarming of the Irish Volunteers, whose activities and seditions are busily being written up by those Irish Unionists who know no truce."[60]

When Nathan received this letter, he was preoccupied with a report that a German ship loaded with arms had been scuttled near Tralee, County Kerry. When he reported the incident to his chief, he expressed doubt about the other intelligence reports that indicated the weapons were going to be used in an uprising planned for some time around Easter. The cancellation, late on Holy Saturday, of Irish Volunteer maneuvers that were scheduled for Easter Sunday seemed to indicate that whatever might have been planned had been scrapped. Dillon, who was spending the Easter recess from Parliament with his family in Dublin, however, was worried. He wrote to Redmond on Easter Sunday morning indicating that Dublin was full of "the most extraordinary rumors, and I have no doubt that the Clan men are planning some devilish business." "What it is," he continued, "I cannot make out. It may not come off. But you must not be surprised if something very unpleasant and mischievous happens this week."[61]

The next day's events confirmed Dillon's suspicions and demonstrated that the administration's intelligence system had failed to penetrate the councils of the most militant Nationalists. On Easter Monday morning, April 23, 1916, Pearse, Connolly, and one thousand of their followers took up arms and fulfilled the Irish Republican Brotherhood's promise to rise up in rebellion before the end of the war. Pearse, acting as the commandant-general of an Irish republican army, which established its headquarters in the General Post Office in Dublin, proclaimed the foundation of an Irish Republic on behalf of an Irish provisional government. After two days of fighting the lord lieutenant declared martial law in Dublin and the surrounding area. Several days

60. Ibid., MS. 449, ff. 352–55, Birrell to Nathan, Apr. 22, 1916.
61. Cited in Gwynn, *Redmond,* p. 471.

later, the British army under the command of Sir John Maxwell forced the rebel forces to surrender.

Birrell realized at once that he must resign. In his last letter from Dublin Castle, on April 30, Birrell warned Asquith, "A good many 'loyalists' here are glad things have happened as they have, and look forward to a renewal of Protestant Ascendancy." "I hope (against hope)," he concluded, "that something better will eventuate from it."[62] For Birrell it was a heartbreaking farewell and a calamitous end to his chief secretaryship. For the Parliamentary party, it was the hail and farewell of the best friend they had ever had in Dublin Castle. The Unionists, however, were jubilant. Birrell's departure meant the end of nine years of "Birrellism." When Birrell tried to explain what had happened in Ireland to the House of Commons in a speech that marked the end of his career in government, several Unionist members disregarded his own personal tragedy and interrupted him with jeers about jobbery and corruption.[63] More important was their belief that his fall vindicated their charges that he had been an incompetent administrator and irresponsible in his policies regarding the radicals, and that Ireland would never be safe under any Nationalist administration.

Speculation about Birrell's successor was under way in London before the final shots were fired in Dublin. Bonar Law suggested to Asquith either Robert Cecil or Walter Long, arguing that a Unionist would have more success with a policy of leniency than a Liberal. After Asquith sounded out Redmond about Law's suggestions, Redmond wrote to Dillon on May 1 that he protested emphatically to Asquith "that it would be quite impossible for us to acquiesce in any way in the appointment of either Long or Cecil, which would mean, remembering that Campbell is Attorney-General, the installment of an Ulster Government in Dublin Castle."[64] The prime minister then shared Redmond's views with Law. Asquith indicated that the Liberal party would not stand for a Unionist chief secretary, adding that leniency, although important to him and to Redmond, was a subordinate consideration.[65]

62. Bod. Lib., Asq. P., MS. 36 ff. 141–44, Birrell to Asquith, Apr. 30, 1916.
63. *Parliamentary Debates,* House of Commons, 1916, LXXXII:31–39.
64. N.L.I., Red. P., MS 15182 (22), Redmond to Dillon, May 1, 1916.
65. H.L.R.O., Law P., MS. 53/2/1, Asquith to Law, May 1, 1916; ibid., MS. 53/2/3, Long to Law, May 2, 1916.

Dillon also had ideas about reconstituting the Irish executive. Replying to Redmond's letter of May 1, he stated that if Birrell were leaving, Nathan and Wimbourne should also resign. He regretted the prospect of Nathan's departure and, disregarding the pledge, told Redmond that when the time came, the new under secretary should be nominated for the position by the Parliamentary party leaders. Edwin Montague, given the unavailability of other Liberals, seemed to be as good as anyone else for chief secretary. Dillon then went on to suggest for viceroy either General Lord John French, who was the commander of the home forces, or Sir John Maxwell, who was in command of the forces that quelled the rebellion, if he were a home ruler. Passing from men to measures, Redmond's lieutenant advised him not to tolerate a patchwork settlement. "We should," Dillon declared, "state our terms—and if the Government won't accept them, wash our hands of all responsibility and warn the Government in the most emphatic terms that we shall be obliged to adopt a hostile attitude." An essential part of those terms, he added, was the removal of Campbell and the establishment of a home rule executive. He concluded his review of possible candidates for appointment by stating that he "would far rather face a frankly Tory Government than be dragged after a hybrid government for whose action you would be held responsible without having the power to control proceedings."[66]

There was speculation about Nathan's position because of his civil servant status. He squelched this talk when out of loyalty to Birrell he tendered his resignation on May 3. Wimbourne, however, was reluctant to resign, believing that such action would be interpreted as an admission that he had made erroneous judgments for which he was not responsible. At first the prime minister thought it would be best to leave Wimbourne at his post, but on May 7 he accepted the viceroy's resignation.[67] When Lord Chancellor O'Brien asked Asquith whether he should also resign, he was assured that he retained the government's confidence.[68] Two weeks later, Neville Chamberlain offered to

66. N.L.I., Red. P., MS. 15182 (22), Dillon to Redmond, May 2, 1916.

67. O'Broin, *Dublin Castle and the 1916 Rising,* pp. 120–21.

68. Bod. Lib., Asq. P., MS. 36, ff. 160–61 and 162–63, O'Brien to Asquith, May 8, 1916, and Asquith to O'Brien, May 9, 1916.

resign the inspector-generalship of the constabulary and Asquith accepted his resignation.[69]

With Wimbourne, Birrell, and Nathan gone, the direction of the Irish administration momentarily fell upon Attorney-General Campbell, who was also occupied with his legal duties of advising General Maxwell. When Montague refused the chief secretaryship, Asquith continued to look for an Irish secretary. Sir Robert Chalmers, the permanent secretary of the British Treasury, was appointed under secretary.[70] His immediate task was to direct the civil side of the administration until a chief secretary could be found. Two commissions of inquiry were also appointed. One, the Hardinge Commission, investigated the causes of the Rising; the second, the Sankey Commission, inquired into the problem of those civil servants who might have been involved in the rebellion.

Although basic public services were restored in a matter of days, Asquith needed a cabinet-level minister who would be responsible for the Irish administration. This problem was urgent because Irish public opinion, which was at first hostile to the rebels, was outraged by the post-Rising activities of Maxwell. He interned and deported suspected revolutionaries without due process of law; he extended the area under martial law; and he executed fifteen revolutionary leaders after secret court-martial trials.[71] The executions were confined to the Rising's leaders, but Maxwell failed to heed the cabinet's admonition to be quick about the work. The trials precipitated wild rumors in Dublin, and the executions secured for Pearse and his followers the martyrdom they desired.

The Parliamentary party expressed its anger over the declaration of martial law and the executions through a party resolution on May 8. Three days later in the House of Commons, Dillon, who was already very angry about a lack of consultation on the under secretary's position and about the lack of a responsible executive in Dublin Castle,

69. H.L.R.O., Law P., MS. 53/3/1, Carson to Law, June 16, 1916; MS. 53/3/2, Long to Maxwell, June 9, 1916.

70. Bod. Lib., Asq. P., MS. 36, ff. 164–65, Chalmers to Asquith, May 9, 1916.

71. Gwynn, *Redmond,* pp. 483, 485. One more man was executed in England later in the summer, bringing the total to sixteen.

challenged the government to identify the Protestant Irish officials who were advising Maxwell. He declared that there was no government in Ireland except Maxwell and the ascendancy in the Kildare Street Club.[72] Asquith responded that Maxwell had the confidence of the government, but he agreed with Dillon's description of the breakdown of the Irish executive. Asquith then told the House that he had decided to go to Ireland, where he would seek an arrangement for the future government of Ireland that would commend itself to all Irishmen and to the House.[73]

Asquith crossed over to Ireland and spent a week visiting Dublin, Belfast, and Cork. When he was in Dublin, the prime minister briefly took a hand in administrative business in order to help Chalmers. He also interviewed several Irish officials. Campbell made the most significant impression. Asquith found that the attorney-general concurred with his own vague idea that the lord lieutenancy and chief secretaryship should be abolished and replaced with some other type of responsible minister.[74] Campbell suggested Walter Long for this new position but did not press it.

During the visit Asquith became convinced that the Irish political leaders were disposed to settle the Irish question. He realized a resourceful person was needed to conduct the negotiations. Upon returning to England he offered the task and the chief secretaryship to David Lloyd George.[75] Lloyd George consulted both Law and Redmond. They each approved, but Redmond added the reservation that the appointment as chief secretary should only be temporary. Lloyd George eventually decided not to accept the appointment, although he told Asquith that he would attempt to secure a settlement.[76] After briefing the cabinet, Asquith returned to the House of Commons on May 25. He startled the members by stating bluntly that all of Dublin Castle's administrative machinery had broken down. This remark may have

72. N.L.I., MS. 12082, *Irish Parliamentary Party Minute Book,* May 9, 1916; *Parliamentary Debates,* House of Commons, 1916, LXXXII:935, 951.

73. Ibid., pp. 952–60.

74. Bod. Lib., Asq. P., MS. 44, ff. 113–15, Memorandum of meeting with Campbell, May 13, 1916.

75. H.L.R.O., L.G. P., MS. D/14/1/5, Asquith to Lloyd George, May 22, 1916.

76. Jenkins, *Asquith,* p. 399.

been intended merely as an introductory flourish. Nevertheless, it angered the officials serving in the Irish administration, and the remark became one of the most frequently quoted statements in subsequent discussions of Irish government. Asquith declared that if an agreement could be reached among the different interests in Ireland, the Home Rule Act would be put into operation at once. Lloyd George, he announced, would conduct the negotiations with that end in view.[77]

Lloyd George had a reputation as a consummate negotiator. He believed that the success of his mission depended upon Redmond's and Carson's willingness to agree to a partition of the country. After conducting separate negotiations, Lloyd George brought each of them to agree to accept the exclusion of six of Ulster's nine counties from the jurisdiction of a home rule government in the other twenty-six counties. The six-county area would be administered by a secretary of state through offices and departments with headquarters in Belfast. The six counties' bureaucracy would not be responsible to the home rule government in Dublin. Redmond and Carson agreed to the partition of Ireland on these conditions only because each came away from the negotiations with his own interpretation of the duration of partition.[78] Redmond thought, or was led to believe by Lloyd George, that partition would end after the war when Parliament or an imperial conference would bring about a permanent settlement. Carson thought the partition would be permanent and secured these terms in writing from Lloyd George. He compromised only because he thought, or was led to believe, that the Home Rule Act would go into effect without partition if an accommodation were not reached.

The three principals spent most of June and July trying to win approval for their interpretation of the settlement. Carson was able to persuade his followers to fall in behind him and accept partition. Redmond was able to secure approval of temporary partition from most of his followers, but he was unable to persuade the majority of Ulster's Catholic bishops to support a settlement on these lines. The bishops realized that a division of the offices that administered Irish education

77. *Parliamentary Debates,* House of Commons, 1916, LXXXII:2309–11.

78. Gwynn, *Redmond,* p. 503; Colvin, *Carson,* 3: 166–67, 173–78. Miller, *Church, State and Nation in Ireland, 1898–1918,* pp. 336–39.

would give the Protestant majority in Ulster control over the educational system within the partitioned area. This they would not abide, even temporarily. Meanwhile, Lloyd George met with several Unionist officials, including Attorney-General Campbell and Land Commissioner Wrench. They indicated that they would be comfortable serving under Redmond in a home rule administration. Some southern Unionists insisted that there was nothing fundamentally wrong with the administrative machinery; rather, their complaints centered on the former executive officers. They believed that if the Irish government were entrusted to a strong man like Redmond, and if the safeguards proposed during home rule debates in 1912 were adopted, the administration would respond without difficulty.[79] One thing was certain. Southern Unionists did not want partition. They were afraid that they would be a defenseless minority in the south under home rule. Their susceptibilities had been aroused by General Maxwell and Major Price, who maintained in their testimony to the Hardinge Committee that Sinn Fein would certainly supplant the Parliamentary party at the next election.[80]

On July 19 Asquith announced that the exclusion of six of Ulster's counties would be permanent.[81] This decision shocked Redmond, who was as frustrated at the loss of what he thought was an imperfect, temporary settlement as he was furious at being misled by Lloyd George. He told Asquith that the Parliamentary party would oppose legislation to implement permanent partition at every stage.[82] As the southern Unionists and the Parliamentary party expressed hostility to a settlement on these grounds, Asquith put an end to the negotiations.

The negotiations at least clarified issues and positions for both the Unionists and the Nationalists. The Ulster Unionists demonstrated that they were ready to act independently without the southern Unionists. The adoption of partition by the Liberal-dominated coalition cabinet

79. H.L.R.O., L.G. P., MS. D/14/1; D/14/2. "Memoranda concerning a settlement in Ireland, 1916." Buckland, *Irish Unionism,* I:62–64.

80. Great Britain, *Parliamentary Papers,* 1916, XI, Cd., 8311, *Royal Commision on the Rebellion in Ireland.* For Price's testimony, see "Minutes of Evidence," 56–60.

81. Buckland, *Irish Unionism,* I:63–81.

82. Gwynn, *Redmond,* p. 520.

showed the Parliamentary party that its continued adherence to their political alliance with the Liberal party had been a mistake. The Liberal government had done nothing about the Ulster Unionists' threat of civil war in 1914; now Asquith and Lloyd George yielded to that threat by offering to set up a legitimate Ulster government. When the Parliamentary party reluctantly agreed to permit a fundamental alteration of the home rule legislation when it accepted partition, even on a temporary basis, it was vulnerable to charges made by radical Nationalists that the party and its leader had exhibited a profound lack of political judgment. It appeared that Carson had confounded Redmond at a crucial moment.[83]

The weakness of the Parliamentary party's position became apparent when the prime minister moved to reconstruct the Irish executive in the wake of the failure to secure a solution. Asquith wrote to Redmond on July 28 stating that the Irish administration "should go back, for the moment, to the *status quo ante,* i.e., a Lord Lieutenant, a Chief Secretary, and the abrogation of the military regime."[84] Asquith thought that Lord Wimbourne should be recalled to the lord lieutenancy, pointing out that Wimbourne had been a popular viceroy and adding that the commission of inquiry had congratulated him for his actions during the insurrection. Asquith then declared that the new chief secretary must be a Unionist and that he had decided to appoint Henry Duke, a lawyer who was "'almost persuaded' to be a Home Ruler." Henry Wynne, a Unionist who had served as crown solicitor in Cork since 1905, was appointed to the chief crown solicitorship in Dublin. Asquith also appointed a member of Maxwell's staff, Brigadier General Sir Joseph Byrne, an Irishman, to lead the Royal Irish Constabulary (RIC). Byrne, who had been praised by Maxwell for his handling of the captured insurgents, was the first Catholic to become inspector-general in the R.I.C.[85]

The reconstitution of the executive in Dublin Castle on these lines

83. Stephen Gwynn, *John Redmond's Last Years* (London: Edward Arnold, 1919), pp. 239–40; Lyons, *Dillon,* pp. 401–3.

84. Gwynn, *Redmond,* pp. 521–22.

85. Bod. Lib., Asq. P., MS. 37, ff. 81–81, 93–94, Maxwell to Asquith, July 1, July 12, 1916.

did not please the members of the Parliamentary party, who indicated their displeasure through a resolution on August 1. The party protested "against the action of the Government in reviving the discredited system of Dublin Castle rule in Ireland, already condemned on all sides, and particularly by the Hardinge Commission and by the Prime Minister himself; and in our opinion, the appointment, at this moment, of a Unionist Executive to carry on that system is an outrage to the feelings of the Irish people."[86] Dillon told T. P. O'Connor a few days later that he was in favor of giving Duke fair play but regarded the appointment "as one of the most outrageous insults ever offered to our Party."[87] Although O'Connor had urged Dillon to see to it that Duke was surrounded with "the right people," Dillon replied he would not initiate any discussions with the new chief secretary.

Lord Wimbourne was worried about the Nationalists' reaction to his return and to Duke's appointment. He was especially alarmed when Duke announced in the House of Commons that his administration would enforce resolute government in Ireland.[88] Wimbourne decided that his own position must be strengthened. He sent a memorandum to the new chief secretary in an attempt to reverse the working relationship that had existed between viceroys and chief secretaries since the departure of Lord Cadogan in 1902, particularly with regard to all patronage. Duke, who knew nothing about Ireland, agreed and suggested that the lord lieutenant's relations with, and responsibility for, the administration's civil and military sides should be clarified to use the viceroy's office, status, and abilities in coordinating, directing, and regulating the public services.[89]

Three weeks later, on September 3, Wimbourne reported to Asquith, "I have taken on myself the task of assiduously coordinating the administration—which is deplorably loose jointed—in which I am cordially supported by the new grooms." "Nearly all of the old public

86. N.L.I., MS. 12082, *Irish Parliamentary Party Minute Book,* Aug. 1, 1916.

87. T.C.D., D.P., Dillon to O'Connor, Aug. 11, 1916.

88. Bod. Lib., Asq. P., MS. 37, ff. 113–14, Wimbourne to Asquith, Aug. 2, 1916.

89. Duke agreed to everything in Wimbourne's memorandum. The other points included emergency powers, clemency, minuting upon official papers, military powers, the chief secretary's responsibility and authority, and a public announcement about the lord lieutenant's position. Ibid., MS. 44, ff. 146–48, Duke to Wimbourne, Aug. 7, 1916.

officials," he continued, "have an acquired propensity to act independently on their own discretion, which is fatal to clear policy or concerted action."[90] Wimbourne then advised Asquith that General Maxwell "would be better gone, for himself, and for us, but it must be on promotion, otherwise it would be unfair to him and injurious here." "Price," he added, "is a still greater stumbling block." Next, he reported that Chalmers, the under secretary, had submitted his resignation. The lord lieutenant was eager to begin looking for an Irish official to replace Chambers, who had alienated many Irish department heads through an arrogant, ethnocentric attitude toward the country and its people.[91] Before he departed, Chalmers recommended the promotion of Edward O'Farrell, maintaining that the assistant under secretary had more ability than was made evident in Birrell's administration. Henry Robinson was another possibility for under secretary, but Wimbourne believed that the appointment of the vice president of the Local Government Board, "a Kildare Street Unionist," would emphasize the "Unionist Rule" that the Parliamentary party opposed. Wimbourne closed his report by observing that Nationalists "avoid me now, and say there can be no common ground between us: This is a pose, of course."[92]

Wimbourne's illusions were shattered six weeks later, on October 18, when Redmond moved a vote of censure on the Irish administration in the House of Commons. His resolution, which described Anglo-Irish relations in a wider context, declared, "The system of Government in Ireland was inconsistent with the principles for which the allies were fighting in Europe."[93] After recalling Asquith's statement about the breakdown of the Irish administration, Redmond protested that the prime minister had simply restored the old system, only in a more aggravated form under Duke and Campbell. Moreover, there had been

90. Ibid., MS. 37, ff. 119–26, Wimbourne to Asquith, Sept. 3, 1916. Duke, meanwhile, began to attempt to coordinate the seven independent intelligence systems operating in Ireland. See Charles Townshed, *The British Campaign in Ireland 1919–1921: The Development of Political and Military Policies* (Oxford: Oxford University Press, 1975), p. 2.

91. O'Broin, *Dublin Castle and the 1916 Rising,* p. 163; Robinson, *Memories: Wise and Otherwise,* p. 246.

92. Bod. Lib., Asq. P., MS. 37, ff. 119–26, Wimbourne to Asquith, Sept. 3, 1916.

93. Gwynn, *Redmond,* pp. 531–32.

no abrogation of the military regime—martial law continued under Maxwell and Price. Within a month Asquith responded to Redmond's pressure, but his decisions on Irish personnel also reflected the government's desire to calm Irish-American opinion, which had been greatly aroused by the Easter Rebellion and the executions. Maxwell, who Dillon initially thought was a good candidate for the lord lieutenancy, was transferred to the northern command. Sir Bryan Mahon, an Irishman and a Catholic who had assisted Redmond with Irish recruiting, was appointed his successor. Later that month the assistant secretary at the Home Office, Sir William Byrne, a Catholic Englishman who had assisted the Sankey Commission, was appointed under secretary.[94]

The Sankey Commission had, in fact, already begun to make recommendations about suspect civil servants. Two groups of civil servants were singled out, postal employees and excise tax collectors—employees of departments under the authority of British departments. The secretary of the Irish General Post Office, A. H. Norway, was alarmed by the number of what he thought were unwarranted transfers of his officials. He crossed over to England to lodge a protest with the postmaster-general, who was a cabinet minister.[95] The highest-ranking official in Dublin Castle to be dismissed in 1916 was J. J. MacElligott, a first-division clerk in the Chief Secretary's Office. Count George Noble Plunkett, the father of one of the leaders of the insurrection, lost his position as the director of the National Museum, presumably as a result of his son's political activities. There are no exact figures on the number of civil servants who were transferred or forced to resign immediately after the Rising, although approximately four hundred officials were discharged for political activity between 1916 and 1921.[96] Perhaps the recollections of M. F. Gallagher, who was a clerk in the Insurance Commission Office in 1916 and later the assistant secretary in the Irish Free State's Department of Agriculture, give an accurate description of the part some Irish officials played in the Rising. He

94. *Irish Catholic,* Oct. 28, 1916; Robinson, *Memories: Wise and Otherwise,* p. 257.

95. O'Broin, *Dublin Castle and the Rising,* p. 122; Healy, *Letters and Leaders,* 2:576.

96. M. F. Gallagher, "The Fateful Week," *Administration,* 14, no. 2 (Summer 1966), 171–85.

recalled that when he returned to work after the cease-fire order, "There were a few vacant seats belonging to colleagues who had taken part in the Rising and had been shipped off to England, and others who had been swept in the net on suspicion. The gaps were obvious; there were no surprises."[97]

James Campbell, the attorney-general, was concerned about disloyal officials and about maintenance of law and order. He argued that he needed to hold a more authoritative position than the attorney-generalship to be effective in combatting lawlessness. Asquith agreed; in November he obtained a promise from Justice Richard Cherry, who was in ill health, that he would soon retire from the lord chief justiceship. This allowed the prime minister to offer the position to Campbell, who wrote to Asquith on November 10 that he would accept on the condition that it would not jeopardize his claims to the lord chancellorship or to a potential escape route from Ireland—the first available law lordship in the House of Lords.[98] When Cherry retired, however, Asquith was no longer in a position to make good on his promise to Campbell. The prime minister's lack of effective domestic leadership had been demonstrated during the Irish negotiations in June and July. The enormous number of casualties incurred during the army's Somme offensive in 1915 and the navy's standoff at Jutland in May 1916 cast doubt on his ability as a war leader. After a furious press campaign, which was part of the political intrigue within the cabinet against Asquith and which effected a change in British public opinion, Lloyd George succeeded Asquith as prime minister on December 6, 1916. The first Coalition government had ended.

From its inception in May 1915, the Coalition government posed a serious threat to the Parliamentary party's influence in Dublin Castle. Initially, the threat was masked from public view by the momentum of the working relationship that had been established between Birrell and Redmond during the period 1907–15. The Unionists, who wanted the principle of coalition government fully extended to Dublin Castle, were at first limited to the attorney-generalship and to some local appointments. Birrell and Nathan continued to plan with Redmond and Dillon

97. Ibid.
98. Bod. Lib., Asq. P., MS. 28, ff. 54–55, Campbell to Asquith, Nov. 10, 1916.

for the expected transfer of the Irish administration. But the coalition principle soon began to have an effect on the Irish executive. Within three months of the formation of the coalition, Birrell hesitated when he made appointments; Nathan searched for a rule to follow when making appointments; and Redmond was not consulted on matters that would have an effect on financing the Irish administration under home rule. These matters did not immediately eclipse Nationalist influence in the administration, but they did indicate that the Parliamentary party was no longer the dominating factor in regard to the decisions made in, or affecting, Dublin Castle.

The Easter Rising of 1916 was the central event during the period of the first Coalition government that allowed the Unionists to break the Parliamentary party's grip on Dublin Castle. They seized upon the Rising to justify their charges that all Nationalists were potentially disloyal and that Birrell's administration, which they claimed was only a surrogate system for Redmond's exercise of power, had abetted that disloyalty. Birrell was replaced, first by a military regime and then by a Unionist executive. Within a few weeks of the Rising, the Parliamentary party's de facto control of the administration, at least at the top, had been broken. Dublin Castle was back in Unionist hands.

If the Parliamentary party had to struggle to contain both advanced Nationalist opposition and the Unionists immediately after the formation of the coalition, it appeared to have lost all of its influence in the months immediately after the Rising. Parliamentary party leaders might have understood the government's decision to execute the leaders of the Rising, considering that Britain was engaged in a war that they loyally supported, but the protraction of those executions over two weeks, combined with the arrest, internment, and detention of thousands of Irishmen without trials, galvanized all shades of Irish Nationalist opinion against English rule in Ireland. Redmond and Dillon were unable to prevent these gross violations of Irish civil liberties, and their failure in this regard was the first serious public indication that their influence was in real jeopardy. Later, when Redmond agreed to a temporary partition of Ireland and the establishment of a separate administrative system in the partitioned counties of Ulster—a concession that had been discussed in private after the home rule debates in 1914—he appeared to have been duped by the Ulster Unionists and Lloyd

George about the permanence of the arrangement. The period of the first Coalition government had been disastrous for the Parliamentary party. In December 1916 the party faced a second Coalition government under Lloyd George's leadership in the cabinet and with a Unionist executive in Dublin Castle.

Chapter VIII

The Hereditary Influence of the Governing Circles, December 1916–December 1918

When David Lloyd George became prime minister in the second Coalition government, his top priority was to bring the war to a successful conclusion. To achieve that objective, he knew it was necessary to avoid distractions in Ireland. One option at his disposal was to wait on the development of more favorable conditions in Irish politics. He had already tried to reach a compromise with the Parliamentary party and Ulster Unionists late in 1916. That attempt had failed and there was no apparent advantage to be gained by acting again as a middleman. Moreover, those negotiations damaged John Redmond's credibility as the spokesman for Nationalist Ireland, and there was no apparent advantage in negotiating with him unless he could reestablish his position. A second option was to design another home rule bill with administrative and legislative safeguards for either a whole or a partitioned Ireland. Keeping home rule alive had the advantage of keeping the Parliamentary party behind the government on one principal point, and he could retard or advance progress on a new home rule bill if either the Unionists or the Nationalists threatened his government's authority in Ireland. Because winning the war was a prerequisite for a settlement, Lloyd George could also tie home rule to the extension of conscription to Ireland. The prime minister's last option was to use a combination of conciliation and coercion in Ireland to keep the country quiet until the end of the war. The effectiveness of this option would depend on cooperation between the British government, the army command, the Irish executive, and the rank and file of the Irish bureaucracy and judicial system. Martial law could remain in effect to placate that part of British public opinion that was tired of revolutionary agitation in Ireland and to reassure Irish Unionists in the southern counties who feared another rising. If the Coalition government wanted to earn the goodwill of Nationalists, it could release some imprisoned Sinn Feiners; the Irish administration could then respond to Unionist pressure and put them back under arrest. Either way, men and women who espoused revolution would be harassed until the war ended.

Lloyd George's selection of cabinet ministers gave an early indication of which option he might adopt. The prime minister did not ask any of the Liberal party members of Herbert Asquith's coalition cabinet to serve under him. Instead, he balanced fifteen Unionists and Conservatives with a combination of Liberal and Labour MPs who were new to government office. The Conservatives monopolized the important departmental positions. H. E. Duke remained in the cabinet as chief secretary.[1] After Lloyd George and Duke met separately with Redmond early in December 1916, it was apparent that there was confusion between the prime minister and the chief secretary about the government's plans for Ireland. Lloyd George told Redmond on December 9 that he had no intention of reopening negotiations on the Irish question, but he stated that he would counteract any move by the Unionists to introduce conscription in Ireland by proposing home rule without partition. Lloyd George also told him that there would be no more changes in the personnel serving in the Irish administration. Four days later, however, Duke met with Redmond and indicated that the government planned to amend the Home Rule Act—without partition—and put it into operation at once.[2]

Where Redmond saw confusion, the Irish Unionists saw opportunity. They believed that under the second coalition they could recover the ground they had lost to the Nationalists between 1906 and 1915. They began their new drive by pressing Lloyd George to confirm James Campbell's claim on the lord chief justiceship. Edward Carson, Bonar Law, Walter Long, and Campbell wrote to the new prime minister ex-

1. Peter Rowland, *Lloyd-George* (London: Barie & Jenkins, Ltd., 1975), pp. 373–74, 377. Robert J. Scally, *The Origins of the Lloyd George Coalition* (Princeton: Princeton University Press, 1975), pp. 325–47.

2. Gwynn, *Redmond,* pp. 534–35.

plaining that Asquith had promised Campbell the position but had not followed through.[3] Lloyd George quickly reversed his position on Irish personnel and made good on Asquith's promise. The solicitor-general, James O'Connor, who was a Catholic Nationalist, succeeded Campbell as attorney-general. A few days later, when he was searching for candidates for O'Connor's place, Duke overlooked the two ranking sergeants-at-law, who were also Catholic Nationalists, and advised the prime minister that the best candidates for solicitor-general were James Chambers, the Unionist MP from Belfast, who was a Protestant, and Denis Henry, the Catholic Unionist MP from Londonderry.[4] Long advised Lloyd George that it seemed fair to appoint a Protestant as solicitor-general because the lord chancellor, attorney-general, under secretary, and assistant under secretary were Catholics. His candidate was the Unionist MP, William Moore, who also received support from the new lord chief justice.[5] When Lloyd George asked Carson for an opinion, the Ulster Unionist leader replied that Chambers had many years of experience in the House of Commons and that it would be better if both law officers were not Catholic.[6] The prime minister weighed the opinions of his Unionist advisors and selected Chambers. Throughout these negotiations, Carson and Lloyd George ignored Lord Lieutenant Wimbourne. Carson thought that the viceroy's recent attempt to supersede Duke in Irish appointments and administration was mischievous, and he told Lloyd George that he would rather consult Duke or the prime minister directly on appointments.[7] Wimbourne did not like being pushed out of the center of Irish affairs. He confided to Asquith that the Unionists were gaining ground in Irish affairs, "as in small matters of patronage, I detect Carson's hand."[8]

The Unionists did not make a complete sweep of every administrative appointment that was discussed during the first two months of the

3. H.L.R.O., L.G. P., MS. F/30/2/6, Law to Lloyd George, Dec. 23, 1916; ibid., Law P., MS. 81/1/12, 14, 44, 45, 56, 66, 74; and MS. 81/2/9, letters exchanged in December 1916 and January 1917 from Campbell, Carson, Long, and Law.

4. Ibid., MS. F/37/4/4, Duke to Lloyd George, Dec. 27, 1916.

5. Ibid., MS. F/32/4/17, Long to Lloyd George, Jan. 10, 1917.

6. Ibid., L.G. P., MS. F/6/2/8, 9, Lloyd George to Carson, Dec. 29, 1916; and Carson to Lloyd George, n.d.

7. Ibid., L.G. P., MS. F/6/2/4, Carson to Lloyd George, Dec. 12, 1916; MS. F/48/1/2, Wimbourne to Lloyd George, Dec. 21, 1916.

8. Bod. Lib., Asq. P., MS. 37, ff. 138–39, Wimbourne to Asquith, Mar. 13, 1917.

second Coalition. Late in December 1916 when A. H. Norway resigned as secretary of the Irish post office, the new postmaster-general, Albert Illingsworth, promoted the Catholic Nationalist assistant secretary, James MacMahon, to succeed him. J. J. Coonan, another Catholic Nationalist, succeeded MacMahon. These appointments redressed a long-standing grievance held by Catholic Nationalists who maintained that British postmasters-general had discriminated against them. Perhaps H. P. Pease, a Liberal who had relinquished the postmaster-generalship to Illingsworth and who was serving in the second coalition as assistant postmaster, assisted in securing MacMahon's and Coonan's advancement. He had worked closely with them after the Easter Rising to restore operations in the postal service. In another area of the bureaucracy, Duke and Lloyd George considered removing T. W. Russell from the Department of Agriculture and Technical Instruction, but they decided in February 1917 that the circumstances were not yet right for making a change.[9] There was, however, one significant change in the department. Professor W. G. S. Adams resigned as secretary of the department after seventeen years' service and joined Lloyd George's secretariat. He was replaced by J. P. Hooper, the son of a former Parliamentary party MP. His brother was the editor of the *Freeman's Journal.*

Neither Nationalists nor Unionists, however, were pleased when the new coalition appointed commissions to regulate Ireland's commercial, industrial, and agricultural resources for the war effort. Redmond had to exert great pressure on government ministers to secure Irish, not to mention Nationalist, representation on them. The Reconstruction Committee, which was planning for the transition from war to peace, was the most important new committee. It did not have an Irish representative on its staff for over five months.[10] Neither Duke nor Major James Downie, the director of munitions in Ireland, could convince the Treasury, the Munitions Department, the War Office, or the Air Ministry to use Ireland's resources.[11] Downie eventually resigned when

9. Ibid., MS. F/37/4/13, Duke to Lloyd George, Feb. 19, 1917.

10. H.L.R.O., L.G. P., MS. F/94/1/79, Hazelton to Lloyd George, Mar. 30, 1917; N.L.I., MS. 12082, *Irish Parliamentary Party Minute Book,* Apr. 23, 1917.

11. *Freeman's Journal,* Jan. 24, 1918; *Irish Times,* Feb. 14. 1918. H.L.R.O., L.G. P., MS. F/37/4/7, 21, Duke to Lloyd George, Jan. 10, Mar. 9, 1917 for Duke's recom-

the site of a proposed airplane factory in Ireland was moved to England for no apparent reason. Twenty Irish businesses lost contracts, and the English companies that received the contracts had to borrow equipment and materials from the disappointed Irish firms.

Lloyd George also would not take prompt action on the correlative matters affecting the administration. Duke pressed Lloyd George for honors for recently retired judges and officials unsuccessfully in February. He singled out three men: Chief Baron Palles, on the grounds that Irish Catholics would value the honor; Neville Chamberlain, the commander of the constabulary who had retired with his reputation darkened; and Chamberlain's second-in-command, W. A. O'Connell, who was also a Catholic.[12] Duke also advised Lloyd George to follow precedent and appoint the new attorney-general to the Irish Privy Council. Lloyd George did not act, and three weeks later Duke wrote again because the delay was embarrassing to O'Connell.[13] Meanwhile, Unionists who remembered the delay in securing Campbell's appointment as attorney-general in 1915 and 1916 waited anxiously for several weeks for the confirmation of Chambers's appointment as solicitor-general.[14]

If the government was dilatory in personnel matters, its inconsistent policy regarding the treatment of Irish revolutionaries confused and angered Nationalists and Unionists alike. Nearly six hundred Irish prisoners and internees who were released as a goodwill gesture in December 1916 were rearrested early in 1917. Unionists could not understand why the government released men who espoused treason during war. They expected their allies in Dublin Castle to use any pretext to arrest, or rearrest, anyone who supported the revolutionaries. Nationalists were critical of the policy for different reasons. They could not understand why the government condoned the activities of Irish officials who used coercion and unconstitutional methods to harass radicals. Sinn Fein turned the Coalition government's policy and Irish administration's actions to its own political advantage. They added

---

mendation of moderate Nationalists for the Wages Board and the Food Production Committee.

12. H.L.R.O., L.G. P., MS. F/37/4/4, 14, 15, Duke to Lloyd George, Dec. 27, 1916, Feb. 19, Feb. 20, 1917. Palles had retired in July 1916.

13. Ibid., MS. F/37/4/18, Duke to Lloyd George, Mar. 1, 1917.

14. Ibid., MS. F/37/4/19, Duke to Lloyd George, Mar. 5, 1917.

the issue of the blatant abridgment of their civil liberties to the Parliamentary party's failure to secure home rule. They used both issues as a means to consolidate their forces and win a by-election for the parliamentary seat in North Roscommon in January 1917. Count George Noble Plunkett, the recently dismissed director of the Science and Art Museum and the father of an executed Easter Rising leader, defeated the Parliamentary party's candidate, 3,022 votes to 1,708. Plunkett then embraced Griffith's philosophy and refused to take his seat at Westminster.[15] It was a stunning defeat for the Parliamentary party, and a sign that Sinn Fein could successfully use constitutional methods at the national level.

That the North Roscommon by-election could be a portent of things to come in the next general election was clear to the Parliamentary party leaders. On February 27 John Dillon moved for the adjournment of the House of Commons to focus attention on the administration's coercive actions and the continuation of martial law in Ireland.[16] He wanted to know who was responsible for the policy that was driving thousands of Irishmen into Sinn Fein's ranks. After parrying similar questions from other Parliamentary party members, Duke stated that General Byrne of the constabulary and General Mahon, the commander-in-chief of the army in Ireland, shared responsibility for the administration of law and order with the chief secretary.[17] Joseph Devlin rejected Duke's answer and blamed the chief intelligence officer, Major Ivor Price, for fostering the coercive policies. Devlin then surprised Unionist party members by revealing promises Asquith and Lloyd George had made to him in 1916 about removing Price from Ireland. He wanted to know when those promises would be kept.[18] A concluding speech by John O'Connor, the Parliamentary party member for North Kildare, reflected the disillusionment many Nationalists felt as they saw their political opponents benefit from what they thought were reactionary policies. "We thought that a revolution had taken place in Ireland and that the atmosphere of Dublin Castle had been changed,"

15. David Hogan, *The Four Glorious Years* (Dublin: Irish Press Ltd., 1920), pp. 8–18.

16. *Parliamentary Debates,* Fifth Series, House of Commons, Feb. 27, 1917, Vol. XC:1776–87.

17. Ibid., 1793–1802.

18. Ibid., 1802–7.

O'Connor lamented, "but it appears that it cannot be changed, and that a Chief Secretary, no matter how well disposed he may be, or how honourable the intentions with which he enters upon his office may be, if he falls under the hereditary influence of the governing circles in Ireland, he most assuredly shares the same fate as his predecessor."[19]

Two more by-election victories by Sinn Fein in March and Lloyd George's formation of a cabinet committee to draft a new home rule bill in April convinced the Parliamentary party leaders that they must do something to bolster their position in the country. When Redmond received an outline of the home rule bill in May, he rejected it but proposed a startling alternative plan. He suggested that a body of representative Irishmen should assemble and attempt to reach a settlement of the Irish question without outside interference. Redmond's proposal took the Irish question out of British politics and gave Irishmen the responsibility for finding a solution. Lloyd George may have been thinking along the same lines, and, in any case, it fit in well with his wait-and-see option. On May 21 he announced in the House of Commons that he would summon a convention that would be representative of Ireland's leading interests, classes, creeds, and political parties. He said that if the convention could reach substantial agreement on the character and scope of the constitution for the future government of Ireland, within the empire, the government would implement its recommendations.[20]

The full convention of 101 members, with Horace Plunkett as chairman, began the first stage of its deliberations on July 25, 1917 with a series of debates on Irish problems. Plunkett kept the topic "The existing system of Irish government and the best methods of improving it" off the agenda because he feared it might arouse too much antagonism.[21] During the second stage, begun in August, a grand committee of twenty members prepared seven proposals for the future government of Ireland.[22] When this work was completed in September the

19. Ibid., 1813–18.

20. R. B. McDowell, *The Irish Convention, 1917–1918* (London: Routledge & Kegan Paul, 1970), p. 77. Christopher Addison, *Politics from Within, 1911–1918* (London: Herbert Jenkins Ltd., 1924) 2:179, 184–85.

21. Ibid., pp. 127–28.

22. *Parliamentary Papers,* House of Commons, 1918, Vol. x, Cd. 9019, *Report of the Proceedings of the Irish Convention,* p. 10.

convention adjourned to allow the grand committee to draft a proposal that would meet the difficulties raised during the first two stages. The grand committee then divided into subcommittees, one of which, the subcommittee of nine, was to frame the entire plan. Plunkett asked Redmond, who lead the Nationalist contingent, to prepare a working scheme for the subcommittee, but Redmond had fallen seriously ill. He and Plunkett asked the bishop of Raphoe, Patrick O'Donnell, to chair the subcommittee.[23] Their choice was a critical one. O'Donnell was as opposed to establishing a separate administrative system in Ulster as he was to partitioning Ireland. The Ulster Unionists in the convention were equally insistent on demanding administrative autonomy for Ulster in any settlement that did not include partition.

From the Nationalist point of view, the need to reach a settlement based on an Irish consensus was growing even more urgent. While the convention deliberated the Parliamentary party continued to lose ground. The by-elections proved to be only one symptom of the decline of the party's strength. Lloyd George showed no regard for the historic Liberal–Parliamentary party alliance and continued to take advice on Ireland from Unionists and Conservatives. As a result the Unionists were largely successful in their effort to regain parts of the Irish administration piece by piece as the key positions became available. Lloyd George appointed T. J. Smith, the Belfast policeman whom the Parliamentary party leaders had prevented from assuming an office with a national scope of operations in 1915 and again in 1916, as the successor to W. A. O'Connell, the deputy inspector-general of the constabulary. When the government selected a new solicitor-general after Chambers died suddenly in June 1917, Denis Henry, the moderate Catholic Unionist from Ulster was passed over, as were the Nationalist sergeants-at-law. Instead, A. W. Samuels, a southern Unionist MP for Trinity College, Dublin, who was a Protestant and adept at using his knowledge of statistics to oppose home rule, was given the position in the Law Office. Meanwhile, Attorney-General O'Connor's reputation had suffered in Nationalist circles because he was a member of a coercive administration. He began to press his claims for an appointment to a vacancy in the King's Bench Division of the supreme court. Duke told O'Connor

23. Gwynn, *Redmond,* p. 566.

that the government had no plans to fill the vacancy, but he assured him that his claims would be recognized on the next vacancy.[24] Ten weeks later when Justice Dunbar Barton gave notice that he was ready to retire from the Chancery Division, Duke suggested to Lloyd George that another justice should be transferred to Barton's place. Lloyd George saw no need to fill Barton's place in Chancery, but he and Duke decided that William Moore should be appointed directly to the King's Bench Division.[25] Moore, who had hoped to succeed Barton, accepted the alternative offer. Moore's appointment to the supreme court sparked unfavorable comment in legal and political circles, but Duke assured Lloyd George that this would subside.[26]

These appointments stunned the Nationalists. T. M. Healy concluded that there was never a time when Orangemen were more dominant in Dublin Castle.[27] D. P. Moran of the *Leader* thought the success of the Unionists was a function of the uncertainty in Nationalist politics. "Nationalists," Moran wrote in his September 22, 1917, issue, "may go rotten on the placehunting tack, but we must see to it that every place of power and influence is not filled with an anti-national 'true blue.'" "In the present circumstances, with a strong reaction against the Party," he warned, referring to the recent by-elections, "we must watch out that the Ascendancy do not creep in under cover of the smoke of conflict and confusion."[28] A companion article noted that of the fifteen subdepartments in the Land Commission only one was now headed by a Catholic, and that since the deaths of Michael Finucane and William Bailey earlier that year, the tenants' cause was not represented. Although the *Leader* was satisfied with some recent promotions from the ranks in other departments, Moran urged his readers to be vigilant because the leader of the Sinn Fein party, Eamon De Valera, "would not think of interesting himself in the filling of vacancies of administrative importance under present political circumstances, and Devlin has heard so much oratory against jobbing and place-hunting that he

24. H.L.R.O., L.G. P., MS. F/37/4/27, Duke to Lloyd George, June 18, 1917.

25. Ibid., L.G. P., MS. F/37/4/32. Duke to Lloyd George, Sept. 3, 1917.

26. Ibid., Law P., MS. 82/6/3, Moore to Law, Nov. 4, 1917; L.G. P., MS. F/37/4/43, Duke to Lloyd George, Dec. 5, Dec. 9, 1917.

27. Healy, *Letters and Leaders of My Day,* 2:583.

28. *Leader,* Aug. 4, 1917.

and his friends would be chary of opening their mouths about a vacancy."[29]

Moran was correct when he stated that jobbery and place hunting were prominent topics in Nationalist politics during 1917. During the County Roscommon by-election, for example, Count Plunkett had been embarrassed by revelations that he had sought the under secretaryship in 1914. The *Freeman's Journal* also attacked the independent Nationalist Laurence Ginnell, who had been canvassing for the Sinn Fein candidates in other by-elections. Acting on information supplied by someone with access to Department of Agriculture and Technical Instruction records, the *Freeman's Journal* reported that Ginnell had sought positions in the department in 1899.[30] Meanwhile, William O'Brien renewed his attack on his former associates in the Parliamentary party, the Ancient Order of Hibernians, and those government officials who, he claimed, owed their titles and positions to party influence.[31] The Sinn Fein party reprinted Arthur Griffith's program with its demand for the creation of an Irish-speaking national civil service and the establishment of local arbitration courts that would obviate the ordinary courts.[32] A Sinn Fein pamphleteer declared that the policy of self-reliance was "a crushing indictment of the Parliamentary regime, reducing it to the level of a jobbery institution."[33] Another pamphleteer, when discussing Parliamentary party involvement with English politicians in the distribution of administrative patronage, asked the rhetorical question, "Is the Nationalist party Nationalist?"[34]

The Parliamentary party also lost ground in its attempt to convince the Irish administration to abandon its use of coercion. In May 1917 the government released most of the interned Volunteers and declared a general amnesty, that the convention could meet in a harmonious

29. Ibid., Sept. 29, 1917.

30. *Freeman's Journal,* May 28, 1917.

31. William O'Brien, M.P., *"The Party": Who They Are and What They Have Done* (Dublin and London: Maunsel and Company, Ltd., 1917), p. 4. See also, William O'Brien, M.P., *The Downfall of Parliamentarianism: A Retrospective for the Accounting Day* (Dublin and London: Maunsel & Company, Ltd., 1918), pp. 13–16.

32. *Sinn Fein in Tabloid Form: Sinn Fein Tract No. 1* (Dublin, Sinn Fein, 1917).

33. Anon., *Arthur Griffith: A Study of the Originator of the Sinn Fein movement* (Dublin: Cahill, n.d. [1917?]), pp. 20–21.

34. Anon., *Is the Irish Party Nationalist? Our Policy on the Parliamentary Question* (Dublin: The New Ireland Publishing Company, Ltd., 1918), pp. 1–3.

atmosphere. Many radical Nationalists immediately courted rearrest by making violent speeches. Dublin Castle's Unionist officials, who were under intense pressure from Unionists outside the administration, quickly resorted to the use of coercive methods to counteract Sinn Fein.[35] Those who were charged with a crime were denied political-prisoner status; others were detained or interned without being charged. The unconstitutional treatment of the prisoners had dire consequences in September 1917, when a radical Nationalist leader, Thomas Ashe, died after General Prisons Department officials attempted to force-feed him while he was on a hunger strike protesting the administration's refusal to treat him as a political prisoner.

Ashe's death prompted Redmond to move a resolution in the House of Commons, on October 23, condemning the Irish executive and military authorities for deliberately disrupting the favorable atmosphere that had existed during the early stages of the Irish convention. Redmond feared that coercive policies would push the country into a period of chaos and anarchy that it had not known for centuries.[36] During the ensuing debate, the Parliamentary party members summarized their views of why Dublin Castle was failing to act consistently and justly. The first reason they gave was that Dublin Castle was not in the hands of Irishmen; second, there were unconstitutional forces at work undermining the responsible authorities in Dublin Castle; and third, Lloyd George's Coalition government had placed Dublin Castle's officials in an impossible position by supporting coercion. William O'Brien blamed his former Nationalist colleagues, "a certain old gang of Members of Parliament in the House and the new gang of Castle officials whom they have established in power as their nominees," but he also declared that home rule should be implemented at once and suggested that well-intentioned Englishmen, like Duke, should no longer accept office in Ireland.[37] Thomas Lough, the English radical who was a longtime ally of the Parliamentary party, went further and brought to mind a phrase that O'Brien had used in 1892. He declared that the British officials should be cleared out of Dublin Castle, and he

35. Addison, *Politics from Within, 1911–1918,* 2: 180–84.
36. *Parliamentary Debates,* Fifth Series, House of Commons, 1917, Vol. XCVIII: 689–96.
37. Ibid., 721–30.

urged his old allies to take responsibility for the Irish administration by assuming the chief secretaryship.[38] William Anderson, the Labour member for Sheffield, maintained that there was a "hidden hand" or an "evil influence" behind the scenes that prevented Duke from implementing the high principles that the chief secretary had once told the House of Commons would guide his actions.[39] James Lardiner, the Parliamentary party member for North Monaghan, was perhaps more accurate in ignoring personalities and in blaming instead the overlapping of civil and military authority in Ireland, and by calling attention to the policemen and intelligence officers who were associated with the Ulster Volunteers.[40]

Dillon wound up the debate by tracing the lack of trust and confidence the Irish people now felt toward the Irish administration to the failure of British statesmanship.[41] After endorsing Anderson's "hidden hand" theory, he focused on the second coalition, which he believed was somehow, and for some unknown reason, conspiring to embarrass the convention by forcing Duke's administration to use coercion. He used the example of his own and other Nationalist members' experiences during the land war and plan of campaign in the 1880s to explain that Dublin Castle could not subdue a movement with policies that actually encouraged that movement's growth. Dillon concluded by asking two questions: was the government still pledged to act upon the recommendation of the convention, and would the government and Irish administration abandon coercion?

Lloyd George took his place on the front bench just in time to answer Dillon. He read extracts from De Valera's speeches and declared that the government would neither permit the militant nationalists to express cold-blooded incitements to rebellion nor permit preparations for another rebellion to continue. Further, he said that his government would never admit the legitimacy of Sinn Fein's demand for complete separation from Britain and the establishment of a sovereign Irish republic. Turning to Dillon's first question, the prime minister stated that the government would act on the convention's findings during the life

38. Ibid., 735–43.

39. See also the speeches of the Parliamentary party members A. A. Lynch and William Field, pp. 758–61 and 761–63, respectively.

40. Ibid., 752–58.

41. Ibid., 778–86.

of the present Parliament and that the settlement would be given immediate effect.[42]

Lloyd George's defense of the coercion policy and his promise to act on the convention's report made it clear to the Parliamentary party that the convention was their last hope for securing a native Irish executive in Dublin Castle and for outflanking Sinn Fein before the next general election. Redmond immediately returned to Ireland to join the subcommittee of nine, where the debate now centered on two areas: Irish finance and administrative safeguards for Ulster. Compromises were soon reached on the latter point. The position of all officials and judges remained fixed along the lines of the Home Rule Act.[43] Judges would be appointed by the Irish government, and legal appeals could be made to the Judicial Committee of the English Privy Council, which would include Irish judges. Both the lord chancellor and the lord lieutenant would no longer be political officers. When the Unionists expressed concern about administrative appointments, particularly the high-level administrative appointments and promotions that would affect Ulster, the subcommittee decided to recommend a revision in the Home Rule Act's provisions on the Irish Civil Service Commission. The act had called for the lord chancellor to act as chairman of the Civil Service Commission and directed him to nominate its two other members. The subcommittee suggested that two additional members should be named to the commission to participate in the appointment of officials for Ulster. The commissioners, the subcommittee decided further, were to follow the English Civil Service Commission's practice of using competitive examinations in making appointments. Moreover, the commission was to present the guidelines it would follow to the Irish Parliament before making any new appointments. It was also agreed

42. Ibid., 786–93.

43. The chairman of the General Committee of Irish civil servants, A. R. Barlas of the Local Government Board, informed Plunkett privately that the civil service, in general, was not satisfied by the provisions of the Home Rule Act regarding the terms for voluntary retirement or for compensation for loss of prospects. The committee wanted special facilities established to assist officials who wanted to transfer to the imperial service, and it wanted the procedures for admission to the Irish departments defined. P.F.C.S., P.L., MS. IRI./C. 1, Barlas to Plunkett, Oct. 17, 1917. Barlas also sent a memorandum for the convention's use to Plunkett on Dec. 12, 1917. There is a copy in N.L.I., Ir. 32341, p. 48. The main points are summarized in P.F.C.S., P.L., MS. IRI./C. 5.

that the lord lieutenant's exercise of patronage would be reviewed and that in the future there would be no unpaid magistrates. A timetable for the transfer of public services, including the police, to Irish control was reserved for further consideration.[44]

After the subcommittee reached agreement on administrative safeguards for Ulster, it turned to the question of Irish finance. The Nationalists, whose caucuses were chaired by O'Donnell when Redmond was too ill to attend, proposed complete fiscal autonomy for the Irish legislature. The Ulster Unionists, who were being led by Hugh Barrie, wanted the imperial Parliament to control Irish finance. The southern Unionists, led by Lord Midleton, offered a compromise: Great Britain would levy and collect customs duties using Irish officials, but in all other financial areas, including excise taxes, Ireland would be independent. The plan appealed to Redmond because it offered an opportunity to reach an agreement with the southern Unionists on finance. He hoped this would isolate the Ulster Unionists in the convention and thereby force them to compromise. However, the other Nationalists serving on the committee did not accept the compromise. O'Donnell convinced them that their demand for fiscal autonomy would force the government to legislate at least on the moderate lines of Midleton's proposal, and he hoped that the government would adopt a plan that fell between the Midleton proposal and that of the Nationalists.[45] The subcommittee reported to the grand committee, on November 21, 1917, that as a consequence of the divergence of views on the financial question, they had not succeeded in finding a basis for agreement. The grand committee attempted to break the deadlock, but when it did not succeed the committee adjourned for Christmas.[46]

During the adjournment, Redmond pressed his followers to accept Midleton's proposal. He was convinced that a compromise in the convention offered the only chance of settling the Irish question. Moreover, he was pleased that the convention had made great advances over previous home rule schemes. He wrote to a friend, "We are offered a Parliament for the whole of Ireland, with full and complete control over every purely Irish affair, both legislative and administrative, including

44. *Report of the Proceedings of the Irish Convention,* pp. 11–16.
45. Miller, *Church, State and Nation in Ireland, 1898–1918,* pp. 370–75.
46. *Report of the Proceedings of the Irish Convention,* pp. 16–17.

land, education, local government, old age pensions, insurance, police, judiciary, and everything else, with full and complete control over all internal taxation, both its collection and its imposition, including excise; that is to say, a Parliament infinitely better than was ever suggested by Butt, Parnell, or Gladstone."[47] O'Donnell and Devlin, however, refused to commit themselves until they were certain that the government would legislate on the lines of the compromise.

The split in the Nationalist ranks was disclosed on January 15, 1918, when the committee was back in session. Redmond was forced to withdraw an amendment he offered in support of Midleton's compromise because a majority of the Nationalist deputation would not support him. It was a humiliating defeat for the party leader whose power was now as broken as his health. From the moment Redmond was overruled by O'Donnell and Devlin, the movement for compromise was lost. Six weeks later, Redmond was dead. The Ulster Unionists interpreted Redmond's fall as a victory for clerical dominance in Nationalist politics and decided to wait for the best opportunity to press a resolution in the convention for the exclusion of the entire province of Ulster from home rule.[48] When the Nationalists in the convention gave Redmond what amounted to a vote of no confidence, they removed the linchpin that had held the home rule movement together for nearly twenty years. His death and the division of the Nationalist forces in the Irish convention marked the end of an era in Irish political history.

With the convention stymied, Sinn Fein maintained its offensive by implementing Griffith's ideas regarding administrative and judicial self-sufficiency. At first the effort seemed innocuous: appointing an ambassador to the United States, organizing food distribution, conducting livestock censuses in areas where food shortages were feared, and holding a referendum on whether Sinn Fein should send representatives to the peace conference when the war ended. In fact, Sinn Fein was doing in southern and western Ireland exactly what Carson said in 1914 he would do in Ulster—establishing an alternative administrative system. The *Irish Times* reported in January 1918 that Sinn Fein claimed it had established departments of government with "ministers

47. Cited in Gwynn, *Redmond,* pp. 592–93.

48. Miller, *Church, State and Nation in Ireland, 1898–1918,* p. 389; McDowell, *Irish Convention 1917–1918,* p. 134.

for each department—education, labor, food, etc., just as the English Government had its own Ministers."[49] Arbitration courts were established in Counties Mayo, Sligo, Roscommon, Kildare, and Galway. In Galway, a bridewell that was established was even provided with inmates serving out their sentences.[50] Sinn Fein's attempt to establish an administrative and judicial system was an important advance on its earlier by-election victories and on the militant talk of many of its followers. Nevertheless, from Dublin Castle's perspective Sinn Fein's administrative and judicial systems were illegal; the Castle was still the de facto and de jure power in the country.

Sinn Fein's programs and practices alarmed Unionists, who wanted the Coalition government and the Irish administration to take strong action. Campbell complained about Sinn Fein's illegal military drilling, raids for arms, land seizures, and hunger strikes on the one hand, and about the absence of Wimbourne and Duke from their offices and the demoralized police forces on the other. "The truth is," he told Bonar Law, "Duke is hopeless and has lost his nerve, if he ever had any."[51] The duke of Somerset said that the government should "get rid of the paying guest who has out-Birrelled Birrell, which one would have thought impossible, and govern Ireland instead of being governed by Sinn Fein and other such influence."[52] Meanwhile, Professor Adams informed Lloyd George that there was a strong feeling in Ireland that a complete change in the personnel of the Irish administration was required. He said that Lord Decies had the support of the *Irish Times* for viceroy and that General Joseph Byrne, the inspector-general of the RIC, would be an admirable under secretary in place of William Byrne, who, Adams believed, was not equal to the demands of the position. Adams reported further that there was a marked feeling that Duke had lost his grip and that a change was also required in the attorney-generalship.[53] On January 28 the *Northern Whig* declared, "the situation is bad, but unless the War Cabinet has the courage to remove Lord Wimbourne and Mr. Duke from offices which they have shown them-

49. *Irish Independent,* Jan. 8, Jan. 19, 1918; *Cork Constitution,* Jan. 14, 1918; *Irish Times,* Jan. 25, 1918.

50. *Daily Express,* Feb. 20, 1918; *Freeman's Journal,* Mar. 25, 1918.

51. H.L.R.O., Law P., MS. 82/9/10, Campbell to Law, Feb. 18, 1918.

52. *Daily Express,* citing *Morning Post,* Jan. 7, 1918.

53. H.L.R.O., L.G. P., MS. F/63/2/13, Adams to Lloyd George, Feb. 23, 1918.

selves incompetent to fill, we fear Ireland will have to pay for their folly in much blood and misery." "Mr. Duke," the newspaper concluded, "merits nothing but the severest condemnation for shirking his duty. His cowardice—we cannot find a more fitting word—is all the more reprehensible."[54]

Lloyd George tried to stabilize the Irish executive by asking Walter Long to go to Ireland as lord lieutenant. On March 1 Long replied that he could be more useful solving the problems related to the Irish government without taking an Irish office, but he told Lloyd George that he had some suggestions about recasting the Irish administration.[55] On March 4 Long forwarded his ideas, observing first that he was "convinced it is necessary to change the Irish Government from top to bottom."[56] He recommended Lord Londonderry for viceroy and noted that either Ian MacPherson, a Liberal MP of Irish extraction who was serving as under secretary in the War Office, or William Byrne was a good candidate for chief secretary. Long pointed out that Byrne's performance as under secretary in Dublin Castle had given him the confidence of the country. He also thought that Plunkett should be brought back to lead the Department of Agriculture and Technical Instruction, where he would be welcomed by everyone except Dillon, who had replaced Redmond as chairman of the Parliamentary party. Finally, Long suggested the establishment of a new Irish ministry, based on the model of the Oil and Munition ministries, that would cut across all the existing Irish departments and boards. Long did not recommend himself for the proposed ministry, but in a letter that he had written to Law a few days earlier, he maintained that Ireland could be governed under the scheme and predicted that the country would be quieted within six months.[57]

Rumors quickly spread about impending changes in Dublin Castle. The *Irish Independent* reported on March 12 that the government had decided to appoint joint chief secretaries, MacPherson and Long, with the latter to remain in England with a seat in the cabinet. The *Belfast News-Letter* reported on March 17 that the government intended to

54. *Northern Whig*, Jan. 28, 1918.
55. H.L.R.O., L.G. P., MS. F/32/5/9, Long to Lloyd George, Mar. 1, 1918.
56. Ibid., MS. F/32/5/10, Long to Lloyd George, Mar. 4, 1918.
57. Ibid., Law P., MS. 83/2/21, Long to Law, Mar. 1, 1918.

resuscitate the power of the viceroy, although it was certain that Dillon would "have quite a good deal to say about it."[58] Meanwhile, the prime minister was receiving reports from General Lord John French, who was the commander-in-chief of the home forces, about the state of the Irish countryside. After touring parts of Ireland, French wrote on March 2, "Duke seemed determined," and said that the situation in the countryside was improving.[59] Three days later French praised General Mahon who had predicted that law and order would soon be restored.[60] Later that month, Samuels, the Irish solicitor-general, sent the prime minister more advice. He suggested the appointment of an Irish MP or peer as secretary of state for Ireland in place of the chief secretary. The under secretary, he added, should also be an Irishman. Samuels then suggested the establishment of a council for Ireland, similar perhaps to the council of India, that would administer the country with the Irish department heads.[61] Finally, Lord Wimbourne tried to distance himself from his colleagues. The viceroy explained to Lloyd George that Duke had been too lenient during the convention and that this inaction had encouraged crime.[62] He was more alarmed, however, by the fact that Duke, Mahon, and Byrne often left Ireland without informing him, a situation that reminded the viceroy of the lack of administrative coordination that preceded the Easter rebellion. He also complained that his authority with the civil and military officials had been undermined because he had been ignored both in the making of Irish policy and in its administration. If this continued, Wimbourne stated, he would not be held responsible for anything that might happen.

The Parliamentary party also began to look forward to changes in the Irish executive. The *Freeman's Journal* began its campaign on February 20 by citing Cardinal Logue's recent assessment of Dublin Castle: there were forces "in Irish administration which were deliberately at work fostering the spirit of disorder with a view to compel the authorities to abandon even the most elementary forms of civil and

58. *Irish Independent,* Mar. 12, 1918; *Belfast News-Letter,* Mar. 17, 1918.
59. L.G. P., MS. F/48/6/4, French to Lloyd George, Mar. 2, 1918.
60. Ibid., MS. F/48/6/5, French to Lloyd George, Mar. 5, 1918.
61. Ibid., MS. F/44/9/1, Samuels to Lloyd George, Mar. 18, 1918.
62. Ibid., MS. F/48/1/6, 29, Wimbourne to Lloyd George, Feb. 23, Mar. 29, 1918.

constitutional administration and establish a purely military regime throughout the land."[63] Two days later Dillon renewed his attack on Major Price, who Dillon maintained "looked upon the Sinn Fein movement as a means of bringing back all that we have cursed in our youth, the Castle system [of the] dark and evil days of the past [that] took forty years of labor under the most experienced leaders to unloose."[64] When discussing potential successors to Duke two weeks later, the *Freeman's Journal* declared that Ian MacPherson was persona grata to the Nationalists because he was a staunch home ruler. The newspaper also thought that because MacPherson was a Scot and a Presbyterian, he would be acceptable to Ulster Protestants.[65] Joseph Devlin's Nationalist newspaper in Belfast, the *Irish News,* however, did little to assist the *Freeman's* campaign for MacPherson. It observed coolly that although "a Scots Gael" would be acceptable to the Gaelic League, the time when the personality of a chief secretary in Dublin Castle was a factor in the Irish situation had passed—and would never return.[66]

Speculation about changes in both the constitution of the Irish administration and the personnel serving in the executive offices was suspended when the Irish convention reconvened. The first order of business was to try to reach a compromise on Irish finances.[67] A resolution placed before the convention by Lord MacDonnell, the former under secretary, called for the postponement of the finance question for a maximum of seven years after the conclusion of the war, when a royal commission would be appointed to recommend a solution. The convention narrowly approved the resolution, thirty-eight to thirty-four. The convention then adjourned to allow its members to attend funeral and memorial services for John Redmond. When the convention reconvened, Barrie offered a plan to exclude Ulster from the authority of the Irish Parliament. He wanted a secretary of state to serve as the chief executive in Ulster; public services in Ulster to be administered by officers and departments that could be instituted by an order-in-council; and judicial authority in the province to be exercised by a

63. *Freeman's Journal,* Feb. 20, 1918.
64. Ibid., Feb. 22, 1918.
65. *Belfast News-Letter,* Mar. 12, 1918.
66. *Irish News,* Mar. 12, 1918.
67. McDowell, *The Irish Convention, 1917–1918,* pp. 162–63; *Report of the Proceedings of the Irish Convention,* pp. 20–23, 140.

new supreme court and by existing county courts.[68] An amendment embodying his plan was defeated, fifty-two to nineteen. Thereafter, the Ulster Unionists voted against every subsequent clause. On April 5, 1918, after eight months of deliberation, Plunkett proposed that the *Report of the Proceedings* ought to be adopted and the convention agreed, forty-four votes to twenty-nine.[69] Although the convention failed to reach substantial agreement on the financial question, it did on the report.[70]

The government could not give the report its immediate attention. The British army in France was suffering serious reverses; between March 21 and the end of April, over 300,000 men were killed or wounded in action. These appalling losses raised the question of extending conscription to Ireland. When Irish officials and politicians were sounded out by the cabinet, they were almost unanimous in their opposition to conscription. Lord Wimbourne explained that the Nationalists would not accept home rule if it were to be followed by conscription and that the extension of conscription to Ireland would not make home rule acceptable to the Ulster Unionists. If the two schemes were brought in simultaneously, he concluded, opposition would be general.[71] Carson agreed. He told Bonar Law and Lloyd George that the simultaneous introduction of both home rule and conscription would precipitate two agitations in Ireland.[72] Duke, however, thought that a home rule Parliament could enforce conscription, and Henry Robinson told the cabinet that if the government were firm, Ireland would accept conscription. The prime minister was convinced that home rule and conscription were bound together. On April 10 he introduced a military service bill that gave the government the power to extend conscription to Ireland if the necessity arose. He also pledged to introduce a home rule bill before conscription took effect. Three days later an eight-member cabinet committee under Long's chairmanship was appointed to draft yet another home rule bill.[73]

68. *Report of the Proceedings of the Irish Convention,* pp. 110, 116. McDowell, *Irish Convention, 1917–1918,* pp. 176–77.

69. Ibid., pp. 29, 179.

70. *Report of the Proceedings of the Irish Convention,* Covering Letter from Plunkett to Lloyd George, Apr. 8, 1918, pp. 3–7.

71. McDowell, *Irish Convention, 1917–1918,* p. 187.

72. Colvin, *Carson,* pp. 309–11, 325–27, 335–39.

73. Addison, *Politics from Within,* 2:244–46.

The prospect of conscription made a deeper impression on the Nationalists than another promise from Lloyd George on home rule. On April 16 the Parliamentary party withdrew from Westminster and returned to Ireland.[74] There, they attended a conference called by the lord mayor of Dublin where representatives of Sinn Fein, independent Nationalists, and labour pledged to resist conscription. Their action was reinforced by the Catholic bishops, who declared that conscription was an oppressive and inhuman law. This made resistance to conscription a matter of individual conscience. Two million Irishmen signed a pledge to resist conscription on April 21, and, on April 23 a one-day general strike was called in support of the pledge.[75] The withdrawal of the Parliamentary party from Westminster and the cooperation of its leaders with Sinn Fein in combatting conscription were a boon to the latter party. Although the Parliamentary party had withdrawn from Parliament many times during the party's forty-year history, their withdrawal in 1918 looked as if they were now adopting the policy of their Nationalist rivals. Moreover, the appearance of Sinn Fein leaders on platforms and the inclusion of their pictures on anticonscription propaganda leaflets with those of party leaders, bishops, and priests gave Sinn Fein respectability and, in a sense, equality with the party.

Anticonscription demonstrations and the cabinet committee's charge to develop a new home rule bill worried Unionist officials in Dublin Castle. Lord Chief Justice Campbell thought that neither policy should be put into effect during the war. He feared that he would be forced to preside at the trials of Ulster Unionists who might resist home rule by violent means. He sought to strengthen his position by renewing his quest for the lord chancellorship. He told Law that his claim for the chancellorship would be unanswerable if the potential viceroy, chief secretary, and under secretary were all going to be radicals and home rulers.[76] At least Attorney-General O'Connor did not have to face the dilemma of whether to follow the dictates of his conscience or prosecute conscription cases. He finally succeeded to the vacancy in the Chancery Division on April 8.[77] His successor, Samuels, was not so

74. Lyons, *Ireland Since the Famine,* pp. 392–93.
75. Hogan, *Four Glorious Years,* pp. 24–28.
76. H.L.R.O., Law P., MS. 83/2/3. Campbell to Law, n.d.
77. H.L.R.O., L.G. P., MS. F/37/4/48, Duke to Lloyd George, Apr. 7, 1918; *Freeman's Journal,* Apr. 8, 1918.

fortunate. The new attorney-general had pledged to his constituents that he would oppose home rule, but as an Irish law officer he would have to help pilot a home rule bill through the House.[78] His plight was not made any easier when Denis Henry publicly refused to take the solicitor-generalship on the ground that "acceptance of one of the Law Officerships would be an implication, at least, of his acquiescence in the Home Rule policy of the Government."[79] James Powell, a Catholic southern Unionist and a member of the convention who had voted with the minority for a clause in the convention's final report that endorsed compulsory military service, but with the majority for the adoption of the report, took up the position vacated by Samuels.[80] Now both law officers were Unionists.

The conscription issue also affected Nationalist officials in the country and in Dublin Castle. When Nationalist justices of the peace passed local resolutions defying conscription, Lord Chancellor O'Brien would not discipline them in the face of clerical and Parliamentary party opposition.[81] The chief secretary was worried that Sinn Fein would use the clergy's denunciation of conscription to subvert the largely Catholic police forces.[82] Byrne of the constabulary and Johnson of the Dublin police reported that they expected to receive many resignations from the police forces if conscription were introduced in Ireland.[83] In April, seventeen of the twenty king's counselors who were Catholics, led by Sergeant-at-Law A. M. Sullivan, signed a resolution supporting the bishops' resolution, and ten crown prosecutors who also signed the resolution declared that they would not prosecute cases involving conscription.[84] They were supported by another sergeant-at-law, George McSweeney. Finally, there was concern about the composition of the local tribunals that would have to be constituted to carry out conscription. On April 16 the *Irish Times* observed, "a majority of the

78. *Daily Express,* Apr. 24, 1918.
79. *Northern Whig,* Apr. 16, 1918.
80. *Irish Times,* Apr. 20, 1918.
81. H.L.R.O., Law P., MS. 83/2/4, Campbell to Law, Apr. 2, 1918.
82. Townshend, *The British Campaign in Ireland, 1919–1921,* p. 6, citing Duke memorandum of Apr. 21, 1918.
83. H.L.R.O., L.G. P., MS. F/48/6/8, French to Lloyd George, Apr. 18, 1918.
84. A. M. Sullivan, *Old Ireland, Reminiscences of an Irish K.C.* (Garden City, N.Y.: Doubleday, Doran & Company, Inc., 1928), pp. 216–17. *Freeman's Journal,* Apr. 25, Apr. 30, 1918; *Irish Times,* Apr. 27, 1918.

administrators of the Act in Ireland will be the very people who are now organizing resistance to it," and on April 17 the *Freeman's Journal* reported that it had received so many protests from local government bodies, who would have to supply the officials, that it could not print them all.[85] In Belfast, on April 18, the *Irish News* encouraged local magistrates to declare themselves against conscription and to let the government dismiss them "when they have done the work for Ireland that merits dismissal in the Castle's mind."[86]

The conscription crisis of April 1918 caught the Irish executive in a weakened position, as Campbell explained to Law on April 27.[87] He reported that Duke had resigned the chief secretaryship to assume the lord justiceship of appeal in England and that Wimbourne was preparing his resignation. Campbell then pointed out that Lord Chancellor O'Brien was "helpless at the best of times" and that in regard to conscription he was "hopelessly committed to his Bishop and to his Nationalist friends." Attorney-General Samuels, he continued, was being peppered by his constituents with questions about home rule. Powell had suffered a complete nervous breakdown within a week of accepting the solicitor-generalship, and he was, therefore, useless to the Irish administration. Under Secretary Byrne was the only member of the administration who had Campbell's confidence.

Rebuilding the Irish executive was now urgent. Lloyd George turned again to the former chief secretary, Walter Long, who agreed to act as a link between the cabinet and Dublin Castle and to hold "a watching brief" on Irish affairs. Next, Lloyd George asked Lord Midleton to accept the lord lieutenancy. After conferring with Lord French, Midleton told the prime minister that he would serve the government in Ireland, but only as one of three lord justices who would act as chief executives during the administration of conscription. This task, Midleton continued, would require firm administration and he wanted guarantees of cabinet support.[88] Although Lloyd George gave assurances on this point, Midleton asked Law to clarify Long's novel position. He wanted

85. *Irish Times,* Apr. 16, 1918; *Freeman's Journal,* Apr. 17, 1918.
86. *Irish News,* Apr. 18, 1918.
87. H.L.R.O., Law P., MS. 83/2/34, Campbell to Law, Apr. 27, 1918.
88. H.L.R.O., L.G. P., MS. F/29/2, Stanfordham to Lloyd George, Apr. 25, 1918; ibid., MS. F/38/1/12, Midleton to Lloyd George, Apr. 30, 1918.

it understood that the three lord justices must be included in policy-making decisions; and further, he must be included in cabinet discussions of home rule. When Midleton went on to state that he would not be bound by the "stand or fall" rule on cabinet decisions on either home rule or conscription, Lloyd George correctly refused to give him a position of power without responsibility.[89] Lloyd George then appealed to French, whose sense of duty would not permit him to refuse to fill the breach. But he also insisted upon laying down conditions. He told Lloyd George that neither conscription nor home rule could be carried out until the authority of the government had been reestablished; he wanted it "understood that it [was] proposed to set up a quasi-military government in Ireland with a soldier as Lord Lieutenant." The prime minister agreed to French's terms, and the general took up the lord lieutenancy.[90]

The new viceroy gave the Unionists some initial hope for a firm administration. He favored using airplanes armed with machine guns against Sinn Fein agitators.[91] They became alarmed, however, when French, who probably viewed himself as a Liberal, expressed his belief that the establishment of an Irish parliament was inevitable.[92] The Nationalists, on the other hand, believed that French's appointment was an indication that the government would drop all disguise in the administration of martial law and would rule Ireland by naked force.[93]

With the lord lieutenancy settled, Lloyd George searched for a new chief secretary. He selected Edward Shortt, a Liberal who had voted against the Irish clause in the Conscription Act but who had made a mark administering conscription in England. Shortt accepted the position, subordinate to the lord lieutenant but with a seat in the cabinet, on the basis of a promise he received from Lloyd George and Long that the government would continue to prepare its home rule bill.[94] Shortt received a cool reception from Nationalists and Unionists alike. The *Freeman's Journal* wondered whether Shortt knew anything about

89. Ibid., Law P., MS. 83/3/4, Midleton to Law, May 2, 1918. Earl of Midleton, *Records and Reactions, 1856–1939* (London: John Murray, 1939), pp. 249–52.
90. Ibid., L.G. P., MS. F/48/6/10, French to Lloyd George, May 5, 1918.
91. Ibid., MS. F/48/6/11, French to Lloyd George, Apr. 18, 1918.
92. *Belfast News-Letter,* May 6, 1918; Buckland, *Irish Unionism,* 1:132–33.
93. *Freeman's Journal,* May 6, 1918.
94. Addison, *Politics from Within, 1911–1918,* 2:245.

Ireland and stated in a May 1 editorial that his appointment might be good politics but was not statesmanship.[95] The *Northern Whig* observed on the same day that Shortt could not be worse than Duke, but then the newspaper remembered that it had once thought that Duke could not be worse than Birrell.[96]

When Lloyd George was finding men for the administrative side of the Irish executive, there was renewed concern about Lord Chancellor O'Brien, who would not take any action to discipline what Unionists called the seditious faction in the local magistracy.[97] Campbell wrote to Law, on May 4, to press his claims for the lord chancellorship, adding, however, that they would not be able to find any Irishmen worth having for the position who would not be opposed to conscription.[98] Long was also worried. He thought that O'Brien's political views were very extreme and that O'Brien would "hardly be likely to help the new government in the very difficult task which they have to perform."[99] Politics aside, Long pointed out that it was imperative that the new viceroy benefit from the best legal advice available. Because the attorney-general was not highly regarded as a lawyer, Long concluded by recommending Campbell for the lord chancellorship. Lloyd George finally decided to appoint Campbell, who upon fulfilling his lifelong ambition, promised that he would adhere to the condition laid down by Lloyd George—he would not resign over the conscription issue.[100] Campbell stated further that he accepted the Home Rule Act's and the convention's definition of the lord chancellor as a purely judicial officer. He would advise the lord lieutenant but would be free of administrative duties. O'Brien, who was sixty-one years old, yielded to the prime minister's request that he resign from the Irish executive.

With French, Shortt, and Campbell in place, General Mahon was replaced as commander-in-chief of the Irish command by Major General Sir Frederick Shaw. Although the Nationalist press assumed that Mahon resigned because he was unwilling to enforce conscription in

95. *Freeman's Journal,* May 1, 1918.
96. *Northern Whig,* May 1, 1918.
97. H.L.R.O., Law P., MS. 8/3/6, Samuels to Law, May 2, 1918.
98. Ibid., MS. 83/3/15, Campbell to Law, May 4, 1918. See also, ibid., MS. 83/3/16, Campbell to Law, May 6, 1918.
99. Ibid., L.G. P., MS. F/32/5/38, Long to Lloyd George, May 9, 1918.
100. Ibid., Law P., MS. 83/3/25, 31, Campbell to Law, May 11, May 17, 1918.

Ireland,[101] French wanted a man with whom he was familiar in command of the army in Ireland. Shaw had worked under French as director of the home defenses in the War Office and as the chief of staff of the home forces. French also secured the services of Edward Saunderson, an Ulster Unionist who was an inspector on the Local Government Board, for his private secretary; Shortt appointed Samuel Watt, who had been Henry Robinson's private secretary, as his private secretary. Nationalists realized that these appointments were further indications of a growing Unionist interest in Dublin Castle.[102]

On May 15 French began to act on the cabinet's instructions to suppress seditious speeches and to investigate alleged Sinn Fein intrigue with the Germans. Within one month, over one thousand Nationalists were arrested, including almost every Sinn Fein leader. French used the Crimes Act of 1887 to proclaim the Irish Volunteers, the Gaelic League, Cumann na mBan, and Sinn Fein as "dangerous associations," thereby making their meetings illegal. Although coercion curbed the agitation—in fact, there were indications that the Sinn Fein leaders allowed themselves to be arrested to influence public opinion in their favor—the administration's policy only drove the Sinn Fein movement underground where it became even more dangerous.[103]

There was, however, another side to French's strategy. "We must try, so far as we can," he advised the prime minister on May 18, "to get into closer touch with the Catholic hierarchy. I believe they are the best representatives of the really National aspirations of the country." French hoped that the appointment of Catholic Nationalists to bureaucratic and judicial positions would help him accomplish this task. He proposed to initiate the rapprochement by appointing Justice James O'Connor, who French thought was a "rigid Catholic and great friend of Cardinal Logue," to the vacant lord chief justiceship.[104] He also wanted to appoint the secretary in the General Post Office, James MacMahon, to the assistant under secretaryship in place of Edward O'Farrell, but he doubted that MacMahon could be induced to take the post.[105] In the

101. *Freeman's Journal,* May 10, May 11, 1918.

102. Robinson, *Memories: Wise and Otherwise,* p. 265.

103. Lyons, *Ireland Since the Famine,* pp. 395–97; Townshend, *The British Campaign in Ireland, 1919–1921,* pp. 9–10.

104. H.L.R.O., L.G. P., MS. F/48/6/12, French to Lloyd George, May 19, 1918.

105. Ibid., F/48/6/13, French to Lloyd George, May 30, 1918.

event, MacMahon surprised many observers when, instead, he replaced William Byrne as under secretary in July. Byrne had done everything the government had asked of him by clamping down on those who gave seditious speeches. He did not, however, support French's use of proclamations under the Crimes Act to prevent political meetings. This policy, he thought, only furthered the estrangement of the people from the Irish administration.[106] He placed his thoughts before the cabinet in a memorandum, and his open opposition to the lord lieutenant marked the end of his usefulness to French. He resigned and retired to private life.

MacMahon's appointment triggered other movements in the bureaucracy. When Postmaster-General Albert Illingsworth appointed S. G. Forsythe, an Irish postal official with thirty-three years' experience to succeed MacMahon, members of the Parliamentary party asked why J. J. Coonan, the Catholic Nationalist who was the assistant secretary in the General Post Office, was passed over. To them, Forsythe's appointment showed that Masonic Lodge influence was again at work in Irish personnel matters. Illingsworth defended the appointment and stated that he had a letter from Coonan protesting the interference of members of Parliament in his private affairs.[107] Apparently Coonan valued his reputation as a professional civil servant more than the politicians and editors who pressed for his appointment on political and religious grounds. Meanwhile, Long moved to balance MacMahon's appointment by securing the assistant under secretaryship for his former private secretary, J. J. Taylor, a Catholic Englishman and Unionist who had risen to the rank of principal clerk in the Chief Secretary's Office under Birrell. Assistant Under Secretary O'Farrell returned to the Estates Commission, where he assumed the judicial commissionership that had been vacant for eighteen months.

French's Unionist advisers could not prevent MacMahon's appointment as under secretary, but they were determined to block the appointment of O'Connor as lord chief justice or as justice on the Court of Appeal. Lord Chancellor Campbell wrote to Law, on July 3, stating that he agreed with French that political considerations demanded that

106. Townshend, *The British Campaign in Ireland, 1919–1921,* p. 10.
107. *Irish Independent,* Aug. 7, 1918; *Leader,* July 13, July 27, 1918.

a Catholic Nationalist must succeed him as lord chief justice, but he could not abide the selection of O'Connor. Campbell then told Shortt that it was impossible to appoint O'Connor because he was a junior member of the Irish bar and a second-rate lawyer without any judicial experience to boot. Campbell stated that Justice Thomas Molony was the only suitable Catholic judge for the lord chief justiceship. He argued that Molony had been a respectable judge on the King's Bench Division before he had been promoted to the Court of Appeal.[108] Campbell's advice was followed, and Lloyd George named Molony as lord chief justice.

Inevitably, this judicial appointment precipitated other adjustments on the bench and in the Law Office. Samuels pressed his claims as attorney-general to the vacancy in the Court of Appeal created by Molony's transfer.[109] Campbell understood the reasons behind the attorney-general's desire for security because home rule, under the present circumstances, would mean that Sinn Fein's leaders would probably assume positions in an Irish government. Campbell recommended that Samuels should be promoted to the King's Bench Division, which would then permit the transfer of Justice John Gibson to the appeals bench. Denis Henry, Campbell continued, could be named solicitor-general when Powell, who was recovering his health more rapidly than expected, was named attorney-general.[110] Lord French, however, was determined to place O'Connor on the appeals court as part of his plan to win the approval of Catholics; and Shortt wrote to Lloyd George complaining about Campbell's diatribes on appointments during discussions among members of the Irish executive.[111] Campbell defended himself in a letter to Law, observing that the English bench and bar thought that the Irish Court of Appeals was both discredited and a scandal. "I am, and was, prepared to back them up in every way in their Executive policy, but I cannot consent to be ignored, so long as I am Lord Chancellor, in judicial appointments or to allow my best judicial positions to be prostituted for political ends." "I have reason to know," Campbell continued, turning to those political ends, "that it

108. H.L.R.O., Law P., MS. 83/5/2, Campbell to Law, July 3, 1918.
109. Ibid., MS. 83/4/9, Samuels to Lloyd George, June 11, 1918.
110. Ibid., MS. 83/4/10, Campbell to Law, June 14, 1918.
111. Ibid., L.G. P., MS. F/45/6, Shortt to Lloyd George, July 4, 1918.

is part of some strange deal with Cardinal Logue, one turn of which has been the curious shuffle by which Sir William Byrne, a most competent and loyal official, has been replaced by MacMahon of the Post Office, whose real claim is that he is in the confidence of the Roman Catholic Bishops."[112] After railing next against Justice Stephen Ronan, who Campbell stated was becoming more hopeless each day on the appeals bench, and adding that O'Connor's presence on the Court of Appeals would make his position as president of the court impossible, the lord chancellor recommended Henry, or failing him, either Gibson or Ross for the appeals vacancy.

Law passed on Campbell's observations to Long, who took up the matter with the lord lieutenant. On July 6 French defended his appointment of MacMahon and denied Campbell's charge that the Irish executive was trying to secure Cardinal Logue's favor. He noted that the untrue report probably emanated from "Carson and his gang, who are just as bitter, obstinate, and aggressive as any other political body in Ireland."[113] Nevertheless, French continued to believe that the support of the Catholic clergy was a critical element in settling the troubled state of the country and that the vacillation of the Irish government on Molony's appointment as lord chief justice had greatly prejudiced and diminished the priests' and Catholic hierarchy's power to control their people. The viceroy told Long that O'Connor's record and ability were satisfactory and that his final decision to appoint him to the bench would not be revoked because that would only drive a deeper wedge between the church and the administration. French concluded by pointing out to Long that only four of the fifteen justices were now Catholics and that two of the judges recently appointed in the interest of Ulster Unionists were said to be the weakest lawyers who ever sat on the bench. French's perspective had no immediate effect on Campbell. When he met with French on July 8, he was prepared to resign. French dissuaded him by promising to consult him on future judicial appointments.[114]

More personnel changes on the supreme court and in the Law Office soon followed. In August some of the senior judges tried to secure the

112. Ibid., Law P., MS. 83/5/2, Campbell to Law, July 3, 1918.
113. Ibid., L.G. P., MS. F/48/6/15, French to Long (copy), July 6, 1918.
114. Ibid., Law P., MS. 83/5/7. Campbell to Law, July 8, 1918.

appointment of Denis Henry as O'Connor's successor in the Chancery Division. Their spokesman, Justice William Kenny, wrote to Lord Edward Talbot, the former Conservative chief whip, who was a Catholic Irishman, reviewing Denis Henry's political service as a Liberal-Unionist and his reputation as a lawyer, which had not been recognized because of his politics. "It may be said," Kenny wrote, "that this would be the third appointment of a Catholic to a judicial position within, I may say, a fortnight—but even so, it would, I can assure you, be in pleasing contrast to the two others."[115] When the position on the Chancery Division was filled in October, however, precedent was followed and Solicitor-General Powell, who had recovered his health, received the appointment. Attorney-General Samuels, who had not pressed his claims for the chancery position, then recommended the Unionist sergeant-at-law, Charles Matheson, for the Law Office, but Henry was appointed solicitor-general over the head of all the sergeants.[116] Perhaps the confidence that the Unionist justices had expressed in him helped Henry overcome his earlier predilections against joining a government that had a home rule bill in preparation.

Although French tried to balance the appointment and promotion of Unionist lawyers and civil servants with the appointment and promotion of Catholics, Nationalists were not mollified. One Nationalist official, T. P. Gill, wrote to Professor Adams, his former colleague in "The Department," "Insincere and incompetent men, from *all* sides have made a hash of this country, and I cannot see them doing anything else but shuffling along in the same way to the end."[117] Gill wondered whether Shortt exercised any real power and asked whether "he is not in a false position between French and Walter Long—a position in which no serious statesman (if he be a statesman) would place himself?" Turning from Shortt's vague status, Gill complained about "an indecent job-market, which is now in full blast. The whole thing with the French job at the top (including the kicking out of Mahon for French's pal) and Walter Long in the background, and James Campbell made Lord Chancellor in defiance of the Irish party and various other deals in prospect which are being discussed all over town, is all dom-

115. Ibid., MS. 83/6/26. Kenny to Talbot, Aug. 10, 1918.
116. Ibid., MS. 83/5/4, Samuels to Davidson (Law's secretary), July 5, 1918.
117. N.L.I., Gill P., MS. 13, 489(8), Gill to Adams, June 7, 1918.

inated by this spirit—the good old days of the Castle seem [to have] come back again." Gill concluded his gloomy letter by stating that he would "stand on duty by the only institution in which I am free to act, just on guard, carrying on." Nationalist civil servants throughout the bureaucracy must have been thinking along similar lines.

The Nationalist press was also not satisfied. The *Irish News* complained on July 3 that during "the last three months the personnel of the Irish Executive has been completely changed and every trace of Nationalism and almost every trace of Liberalism has been eliminated from its composition."[118] Campbell, readers were reminded, was still the chief legal adviser for Carson's provisional government, and Shortt did not deny this when he was asked questions in the House of Commons by some Parliamentary party members who had returned to Westminster.[119] The *Cork Examiner* criticized the new executive's continued persecution of radical Nationalists. "With the administrative powers of the country in its present hands, and [officers] chosen exclusively from the Ascendancy, such action by Dublin Castle might have been expected." "It is clear," the *Examiner* continued, "that Mr. Shortt's good intentions toward Ireland have been largely diluted since his arrival at Dublin Castle, and that the influences of the old gang have been too strong for the only alleged Home Ruler that now has any voice in the government of this country."[120] Finally, the *Freeman's Journal* declared on July 13 that Ireland was under the firm grip of a military dictatorship and that the revived ascendancy faction in Dublin Castle was more interested in using its power to destroy its opponents' political organization than in putting down treason.[121]

If Lord French's attempt to conciliate the Nationalists and the Catholic clergy through appointments failed, his problems were soon compounded by differences of opinion that emerged among his new colleagues in the Irish executive regarding Lloyd George's policy of linking home rule to conscription. The problems surfaced when Shortt stated in the House that the government had completed its draft of a home rule bill. The announcement alarmed Unionists and evoked a

118. *Irish News,* July 3, 1918.
119. Ibid., July 4, 1918; *Freeman's Journal,* July 4, 1918.
120. *Cork Examiner,* July 4, 1918.
121. *Freeman's Journal,* July 13, 1918.

sharp reply from Law, who told Shortt that Long's committee did not yet have a bill ready for the cabinet's deliberations.[122] Two days later Campbell declared in a speech in Dublin that he was in favor of home rule for a united Ireland and went on to state that conscription in Ireland was a dangerous policy that should be averted at any sacrifice.[123] The *Belfast News-Letter* sensed a betrayal and asked, on August 19, "Was it only when he had realized his own ambitions that he felt free publicly to assist the nationalists of Ireland to realize theirs?"[124] French moved quickly to inform a group of Unionists in Londonderry that, as viceroy, his utterances were the correct expressions of government policy.[125] These open differences of opinion alarmed the prime minister, but Walter Long reported to him that French was doing well, that he had won the confidence and respect of all, north and south, and that the state of the country was improving. "Shortt," he continued, "has done well, but he has made some bad mistakes. He and Campbell talk too much Home Rule and too little conscription." "I will not trouble you if I can help it," he concluded tactfully, "but if necessary I shall ask you to let me caution both these officials."[126] Early in September both French and Long reported to Lloyd George that harmony had been restored. French wrote on September 2 that differences of opinion did not prevent an effective working relationship, and Long reported that French had corrected Shortt's errors, adding incidentally that it was curious that with home rule on the statute book, the Parliamentary party would disappear at the next general election.[127]

The renewed harmony, however, was disrupted by fresh rumors about extending conscription to Ireland. Campbell wrote to Law on September 22 to warn that the courts would be overburdened with appeals because the bishops and priests had made resistance a question of conscience. MacMahon, he added, was in a state of absolute panic because he feared that priests might be shot by the police forces

122. H.L.R.O., Law P., MS. 84/7/61, Law to Shortt, Aug. 16, 1918. See also, Addison, *Politics from Within,* 2:187–88.

123. *Freeman's Journal,* Aug. 19, 1918.

124. *Belfast News-Letter,* Aug. 19, 1918.

125. Ibid., Aug. 22, 1918.

126. H.L.R.O., Law P., MS. F/33/1/18, Long to Lloyd George, Aug. 30, 1918.

127. Ibid., L.G. P., MS. F/48/6/18, French to Lloyd George, Sept. 2, 1918; MS. F/33/1/20, Long to Lloyd George, Sept. 1, 1918.

while leading resistance to conscription.[128] Three weeks later, the viceroy wrote to Lloyd George, admitting that he and Shortt were not compatible. "I feel," French began his analysis of the chief secretary, "that all his training and experience render him peculiarly incapable of arriving at just conclusions when dealing with people who nourish secret sedition and are in a state of veiled insurrection, which can only be held at bay by careful military vigilance."[129] After recalling that it was Shortt's inexperience that caused Lloyd George to give the viceroy administrative authority in Ireland, French declared that Shortt never recognized the viceroy's full responsibility. French was especially annoyed because he thought that the chief secretary was thwarting him merely to court the Irish vote in his home constituency. French reported further that Shortt had permitted MacMahon to telegraph to the cabinet an opinion on conscription that was in opposition to French's. French then added some sharp words about MacMahon, too: "a rigid Catholic, in close touch with the Catholic hierarchy, and simply the mouthpiece for the most rabid Irish priests, [whose] opinion the Chief Secretary thinks should influence H.M. Government." "The fact of the matter is," French concluded, "Mr. Shortt, in season and out of season, both openly and secretly, has opposed my policy from first to last, and I can only bring the matter before you to deal with as you think fit."

Lloyd George was not prepared to make a change in the chief secretaryship until after a general election; instead, he placated the lord lieutenant by supporting French's new idea, the formation of an Irish Advisory Council. In October French selected the six members for the council—all, he thought, "men of influence and power"—and appointed them to the Irish Privy Council. He wanted the Advisory Council to report periodically to him on the mood in their respective geographical areas and give advice on reforms that the viceroy would submit to them.[130] Walter Long supported the formation of a council. He wrote to Lloyd George on November 22 and declared that it could not be denied that there was great truth in the popular statement that

128. H.L.R.O., Law P., MS. 84/1/14, Campbell to Law, Sept. 22, 1918.
129. Ibid., L.G. P., MS. F/48/6/20, French to Lloyd George, Oct. 12, 1918.
130. Ibid., MS. F/48/6/19, French to Lloyd George, Sept. 7, 1918. The council included Lords French, Londonderry, Dunraven, and Granard and Stanley Harrington, MacMortough Kavanagh, and Thomas Stafford.

the Irish government was wholly divorced from the people.[131] After observing that the coalition was pledged to find a home rule solution, but that it could not move in that direction until the condition of the country was normalized, Long argued that the government had to do something to answer its critics and bridge the gap between the present situation and what he hoped would soon be the improved state of Ireland. He believed that Lord French's council, which had already met in private, would offer a rallying point for moderate Irish opinion and might even form the nucleus of a moderate Irish political party. Long also approved of French's plan to draft a bill to give the council statutory powers that would make it a cabinet for the government of Ireland. The chief secretary was more cautious. He forwarded his opinion in a memorandum to Lloyd George's secretariat. Shortt explained that the body was to be an "Advisory Committee" and not an "Executive Council." "His Excellency and I are agreed," Shortt continued, "that if something in the nature of a National Cabinet could be formed, it would be an important step in the direction of an Irish settlement. But I am not aware of any proposal to give statutory executive powers to a purely nominated body." "Personally," the chief secretary warned significantly, "I do not think that any such attempt could be either successful or desireable. No Irish Cabinet could command confidence or tend in any way to an Irish settlement unless it was composed of men who had been elected by their fellow citizens, either to Parliament or to County Councils."[132]

While schemes for potential Irish cabinets and councils were being discussed, the armistice was signed and the date of the general election was set for December 14, 1918. The issues were clear: the Parliamentary party stood for the establishment, within the empire, of national self-government for Ireland with complete executive, legislative, and fiscal powers; Sinn Fein demanded a sovereign Irish republic. The critical contest in the election was in East Mayo, where Dillon was challenged by De Valera, who was incarcerated in England. Dillon was, his biographer points out, "the Leader of a Lost Cause." He expected defeat and De Valera was returned, 8,843 votes to 4,451. Dillon was

131. Ibid., MS. F/33/1/35, Long to Lloyd George, Nov. 22, 1918.
132. Ibid., MS. F/67/1/50, Watt to Adams, n.d.

horrified, however, by the overall results of the general election.[133] Sinn Fein won seventy-three seats, the Unionist party twenty-six, the Parliamentary party only six. The Parliamentary party was virtually wiped out. On Christmas Day 1918, Dillon wrote to T. P. O'Connor and summarized the reasons for the fall.[134] First, he believed that the Asquith coalition's execution of the Irish Volunteer leaders in 1916 and Lloyd George's use of coercion against Sinn Fein in 1917 and 1918 had turned Irish cooperation in the war effort into hatred of England. Second, a large section of the Catholic clergy had thrown over the party in favor of Sinn Fein. Third, the party had made tactical mistakes. It had not kept in fighting trim; it had not taken a more aggressive stance against the government after the execution of the Easter Rising's leaders; and it had not taken the propaganda disseminated by the radical and independent Nationalists seriously enough.

Although Dillon did not elaborate on the content of the propaganda, allegations about Parliamentary party "jobbery" played a significant part in the party's fall. Much of the antiparty propaganda concentrated on the party members' acceptance of the parliamentary salary of four hundred pounds and on violations of the party pledge, which prohibited interference in appointments. On the latter point, the same cases were repeatedly cited as evidence of corruption: the appointment of the so-called Morley Magistrates in 1892–95, the appointment of county court judges and Land Commission officials by James Bryce and Augustine Birrell in 1906 and 1907, and the wholesale appointment of scores of Catholics and Nationalists by Augustine Birrell between 1907 and 1915. For propaganda purposes, even a few cases of Nationalists receiving appointments were all that Sinn Fein and independent Nationalists needed to portray the party as a corrupt organization. When Redmond and Dillon demanded in the House of Commons that they be given de jure responsibility for the conduct of Irish government, they could not admit that they had established any de facto administrative power without giving their critics, either Unionist or Nationalist, an open field for attack. Before the formation of the first Coalition government in May 1915, the party had to present an appearance of

133. Lyons, *Dillon,* pp. 437–53.
134. Ibid., pp. 454–55.

indifference where specific appointments were concerned, an appearance which most observers came to see as hypocritical and false.

The appointments that Lloyd George made in Ireland in 1917 and 1918, coming after the initial breach that the Unionists in the Asquith coalition made in the Nationalists' control of Dublin Castle in 1915, proved to be far more damaging to the Parliamentary party than the years of antiparty propaganda involving appointments. When the party was unable to prevent the second Coalition's appointment of Unionists and stop their use of coercion against Sinn Fein, it became obvious that their influence over the Irish executive had been completely broken. The party leaders dropped all pretext of not having de facto control over the administration and warned the House of Commons that the forty years of work they had invested in transforming the Dublin Castle system was being rapidly undermined by newly appointed Unionist officials.

It was conscription, however, not the loss of influence in Dublin Castle, that really broke the Parliamentary party in the country in 1918. Conscription had been the one issue around which all Irish Nationalists could rally after the Easter Rising, and Sinn Fein made that issue its own. Moreover, with the report of the Irish convention in favor of a home rule settlement buried in a committee headed by Walter Long, Sinn Fein's argument for the withdrawal of Irish members from Westminster seemed not only logical but irresistible. When the Parliamentary party did withdraw, Sinn Fein's initiative was, in effect, endorsed by the older generation of Nationalists. The younger generation then seized the moment in Irish Nationalist politics and drove their advantage home in the general election of 1918.

It is ironic that the conscription issue, which broke the Parliamentary party, also provided the occasion that demonstrated that the party's forty-year pursuit of a transformation in the Irish administration had not been in vain. The refusal of Catholic Nationalists officials—the lord chancellor, attorney-general, crown prosecutors, local authorities, justices of the peace, and police officials—to support conscription was a clear indication that personnel serving at all levels of the system were beginning to feel a deeper sense of loyalty to the wishes of Catholic and Nationalist Ireland than to the policies of the Coalition government. Although Lloyd George appointed Irishmen who he thought would support conscription at the executive level, he could not even obtain unanimous endorsement of conscription from them. When some opposed Lord French's coercion policy, the viceroy and his Unionist advisers fell back on unrepresentative and even unconstitutional devices such as the Advisory Council. Nevertheless, it was now apparent that Irish officials serving in all levels in the administration would be an important conditioning factor in the success or failure of any policy that the prime minister might advance to solve the Irish question.

Chapter IX

A Fair and Square Fight, 1919-22

After the general election of December 1918 Walter Long reflected on his forty years of experience in Irish affairs. He concluded that Sinn Fein was the most difficult movement to confront any government in his time. Sinn Fein's leaders, the former chief secretary observed in a letter that David Lloyd George brought before his cabinet on December 31, 1918, "were brave and fanatical men who feared neither prison nor death. They are not to be influenced by private negotiations with Bishops or Priests, or captured by getting the patronage of appointments, which has been the favorite instrument of the Irish Government since 1905." "It is," he declared, "a fair and square fight between the Irish Government and Sinn Fein as to who is going to govern the country."[1]

Lloyd George began his preparation for the impending struggle by making two changes in personnel in the Irish administration. Ian MacPherson, a Liberal MP, was appointed chief secretary in place of Edward Shortt. Two days later, Hugh Barrie, who had served as the leader of the Ulster Unionists in the Irish convention, was appointed vice president of the Department of Agriculture and Technical Instruction in place of T. W. Russell, who had lost his seat in the general election. Neither the Nationalists nor the Unionists were pleased by the change in the chief secretaries. Carson thought that any Liberal chief secretary would be in a difficult position in Dublin Castle. He told the *Morning Post* that Shortt had fallen under the influence of the Nationalist-packed civil service, and he feared that MacPherson would also

1. Cited in Townshend, *The British Campaign in Ireland, 1919–1921,* p. 14, Cabinet memorandum from Long, Dec. 31, 1918.

be misled.[2] Joseph Devlin's *Irish News* declared that MacPherson, and for that matter, any government official, became ipso facto an agent and instrument of tyranny.[3] The *Freeman's Journal* announced MacPherson's appointment without comment, but it called Barrie's appointment a scandal. Under the leader "TIGHTENING THEIR GRIP," the newspaper noted that Barrie was one of Carson's strongest supporters and had demonstrated a violent hostility to the great majority of Irish people throughout his career.[4] Six weeks after taking office, Barrie assured an Ulster Unionist audience that Unionist party members who occupied many of the high offices of state would resign if Lloyd George were even tempted to fulfill his home rule pledges.[5]

The lord lieutenant, Lord John French, also prepared for the test of strength with Sinn Fein. He wanted to reorganize the executive branch of the Chief Secretary's Office, appoint resident magistrates in place of the local justices of the peace, and administer a loyalty oath to all government officials.[6] Lord Chancellor James Campbell gave his support to French by recommending the immediate removal of all officials and magistrates who embraced Sinn Fein principles.[7] The *Belfast News-Letter* also endorsed these proposals, observing, "Under Lord Morley and the Radical Chief Secretary who succeeded him, the Bench was packed with Nationalists, many of whom refuse to administer the law, so that the offenders who are brought before them are as safe from punishment as they are when they are tried by Nationalist juries."[8] French was unable to implement his own proposals because an illness prevented him from working for several months. When MacPherson arrived, he was forced to attend to other administrative problems in Dublin Castle. These ranged from filling approximately eight hundred vacancies in the civil service to combatting charges of nepotism when Lord Chancellor Campbell's son, Gordon, was appointed secretary to the Irish department of the Ministry of Labor. A strike by officials at the Labor Exchanges was especially worrisome to MacPherson because

2. *Freeman's Journal,* Jan. 11, Jan. 20, 1919.
3. *Irish News,* Jan. 11, 1919.
4. *Freeman's Journal,* Jan. 14, Feb. 28, 1919.
5. Ibid., Feb. 28, 1919.
6. Ibid., Jan. 20, 1919.
7. H.L.R.O., Law P., MS. 84/4/21, Campbell to Law, Dec. 28, 1918.
8. *Belfast News-Letter,* Jan. 21, 1919.

thousands of returning Irish veterans were seeking employment. Finally, he was quickly immersed in a completed, and eventually ill-fated, bill to reorganize the Irish school systems.

Sinn Fein's preparations to gain control of the country were far more ambitious. After the general election its leaders invited all of Ireland's parliamentary representatives to Dublin to attend the first session of Dáil Eireann, or Irish Parliament. When the Dáil convened on January 21, 1919, the twenty-nine Sinn Fein representatives who were able to attend—because they were not under arrest—elected Cathal Brugha to act as president of the Dáil in Eamon De Valera's absence. They also constructed part of the executive branch of their government. The executive was to consist of a prime minister, who was to be chosen by the Dáil and who would act as its president, and four other ministers: finance, home affairs, foreign affairs, and defense. Each minister was to be nominated by the prime minister and subject to the Dáil's approval.[9] About fifty Sinn Fein representatives were present when Dáil Eireann met again on April 1. The second session of the first Dáil aimed to make Sinn Fein's rule effective throughout Ireland. Brugha resigned the presidency and De Valera, who had been released, formed his first ministry. The Dáil hoped to nullify Dublin Castle's administration by encouraging passive resistance to its departments and by operating an alternative bureaucracy and judiciary in its place. The Dáil had both a right and a duty to do this, according to a leading Sinn Fein official, P. S. O'Hegarty, who was also a civil servant in the postal service. "England had a *de facto* government here," he admitted, "but it had not, and it never had a *de jure* one. She held Ireland by force and by guile, never by consent or by legal or moral authority. It was within the powers of the Dáil to declare a Republic, and to give it such *de facto* and *de jure* existence as it could."[10]

Two obstacles handicapped the Dáil's effort to establish its administration. First, only 10 percent of the deputies had any practical experience in government and that experience was largely at the local level.[11] Second, the Dáil's administration would have to supplant a sys-

9. Brian Farrell, *The Founding of Dáil Eireann* (Dublin: Gill and Macmillan, 1971), pp. 55–61, 78, 80–84.

10. P. S. O'Hegarty, *A History of Ireland Under the Union, 1801–1922* (London: Methuen & Co., Ltd., 1952); pp. 729, 735.

11. Lyons, *Ireland Since the Famine,* p. 405.

tem that would not easily relinquish its authority and that could substantiate its power by delivering services to the people. Nevertheless, the Dáil's ministers had some factors in their favor. First, they had laid the foundation of their system in 1918, and one part of that system, the arbitration courts, already had gained the confidence of some solicitors in the country. Second, many of the Irish civil servants who had been dismissed after the Rising in 1916 and many of the officials who refused to take the new loyalty oath were eager to join the administration. Approximately nine hundred officials eventually served in Sinn Fein's administration.[12] These officials understood that the proper procedural techniques were important in legitimizing the Dáil's system for people who were reluctant to use an alternative system.[13] Third, and perhaps most important, the Coalition government failed to respond to the Dáil's activities for five months. Lloyd George, who was in Paris negotiating the peace treaty, did not give the Irish executive any guidance about restricting the Dáil.[14]

Although some of the Dáil's administrative system was window dressing—establishing makeshift goals, declaring an arbor day, appointing a fisheries minister with an insignificant budget, and employing youths on bicycles as a postal system—the Dáil's ministers made every effort to convince the Irish people that their system worked. Countess Constance Markievicz, the minister of labor and the first woman to hold a cabinet-level position in a European government, developed a cooperative milk-distribution scheme that benefited poor families in Dublin. Her good offices were used to arbitrate industrial disputes, and Dáil civil servants on her staff established conciliation boards and set wage and price guidelines.[15] The minister of agriculture, Robert Barton, established a Land Bank that negotiated land purchase loans with landless men in the west of Ireland. He also established a

12. S.P.O., *Minute Book of the Irish Free State, Second Executive Council,* Vol. 1, No. C. 2/49, Feb. 9, 1924, and No. C. 2/130, Sept. 27, 1924; Vol. 2 (G. 2/4), No. C. 2/159, Jan. 2, 1925 (S.P.O. file no. S. 3406).

13. Conor A. Macguire, "The Republican Courts," *Capuchin Annual,* 1969, 378–88. The National Archives, State Paper Office, in Dublin Castle has a collection of Dáil Eireann files pertaining to its administrative and judicial systems in series DE 2.

14. Rowland, *Lloyd George,* p. 545.

15. Van Voris, *Constance de Markievicz,* pp. 260–61, 269–70.

Land Commission to administer a scheme of land acquisition and distribution.[16] Barton did not, however, interrupt payments to the Irish Land Commission because he knew that the farmers feared they would lose their land by default. Barton's programs were made possible, in part, by Michael Collins, the minister for finance, who raised the Dáil Eireann national loan of £358,000, an oversubscription of £125,000. At the Ministry of Local Government, William Cosgrave began to conduct business with local government bodies whose members supported Sinn Fein. The judicial system continued to develop. Austin Stack and Conor Maguire augmented the original arbitration courts with a court system that consisted of parish courts, for hearing small civil and criminal cases; district courts, for trying more important cases and for hearing appeals; four special sessions of the district courts with unlimited civil and criminal jurisdiction; and a supreme court for both appeals and cases of original jurisdiction. Special land courts were established by the minister for agriculture. A police force was formed to execute the decrees of the courts and to perform the duties that were usually conducted by the constabulary and Dublin police.[17] Finally, the Dáil sent representatives to the peace conference in Paris and envoys to several foreign capitals. De Valera traveled to the United States to seek recognition of the Irish Republic from the United States government and to float a loan through the sale of bonds. Later, in October 1919, the Dáil discussed the formation of ministries for education and the Irish language, two issues that interested the Catholic bishops, who had not yet endorsed Sinn Fein or reaffirmed the clerical–Parliamentary party political alliance.[18]

At the Ministry of Defense, Brugha faced a different challenge. While other ministers were attempting to administer public services in the country, Brugha was trying to establish the Dáil's authority over Sinn Fein's militant wings: the Irish Republican Brotherhood (IRB) and the Irish Volunteers. In January 1919 isolated bands of Volunteers began to wage a guerrilla war against Irish officials and policemen who were deemed to be doing political work for Britain in Ireland. The IRB's

16. Lyons, *Ireland Since the Famine,* p. 407.

17. Dáil Eireann, *The Constructive Work of Dáil Eireann, No. 1: The National Police and Courts of Justice* (Dublin: Talbot Press, 1921).

18. Miller, *Church, State and Nation in Ireland, 1898–1921,* p. 441.

constitution sanctioned their activity and called the Dáil's authority into question as well. The constitution provided that the Supreme Council of the IRB was the sole government of the Irish Republic until Ireland secured absolute national independence and established a permanent government.[19] The conflict over the locus of constitutional authority was compounded by a conflict in personalities between Brugha and Collins, who was also a secret member of the IRB's governing body. Moreover, De Valera had aroused the IRB during the Dáil's April session when he declared that the police were the eyes and ears of the enemy and were guilty of treason.[20] To many Volunteers, this was a declaration of war on the police forces. After several police officers were assassinated, moderate Nationalists began to remind the Dáil government of its responsibilities. The Irish people had a right to an account of the Dáil's ministers' stewardship, according to the *Irish Statesman,* a new weekly edited by George Russell. "If the minister responsible for checking outrages cannot discharge his duty," the weekly observed on July 19, "he ought either to resign his portfolio or to speak plainly both as to his views on assassination and as to the reason why he is unable to put an end to it."[21]

In August the Dáil approved Brugha's resolution requiring all members of the Dáil and all Irish Volunteers to take the same oath of allegiance. The oath implied that the Dáil was ultimately responsible for the actions of its military forces. In the months that followed, however, it is not clear how far the Supreme Council of the Irish Republican Brotherhood developed its strategy and tactics independently of the Dáil, which did not declare war on the British government until March 1921. Nevertheless, a soldier in the Irish Republican Army (IRA), as the Irish Volunteers were now called, who fought against Britain's attempt to weaken the authority of the Dáil did so, again according to O'Hegarty, as an agent of a de jure government. He was no longer an insurgent, a rebel, a protester; his actions were legal, and it was his opponent's actions that were illegal.[22]

In May the Irish executive officers took steps to combat the Dáil.

19. Lyons, *Ireland Since the Famine,* pp. 410–11.
20. Dáil Eireann, *Minutes of Proceedings,* Apr. 10, 1919, pp. 67–69.
21. *Irish Statesman,* July 19, 1919.
22. O'Hegarty, *Ireland Under the Union, 1801–1922,* pp. 735–37.

MacPherson and Campbell decided that the chief secretary should remain in Dublin and that the attorney-general should attend to Irish business in London. This division of labor meant that they would have to find a way to strengthen the Law Office. Campbell, who was eager to promote Attorney-General Samuels to the supreme court, was worried because neither Denis Henry, who as solicitor-general would probably succeed Samuels, nor a new solicitor-general had enough experience in the Law Office. Therefore, on May 3 Campbell wrote to Bonar Law, who as chancellor of the Exchequer could sanction the extraordinary personnel moves that the lord chancellor had in mind. Campbell recommended that Daniel Wilson, the Unionist MP for the Western Division of County Down, should be trained immediately as a colleague and understudy to Henry. Campbell explained that the chief secretary required a trained and courageous lawyer at his elbow, adding that MacPherson had requested the services of a brilliant Liberal barrister, William E. Wylie, whose uncle was a judicial land commissioner. "In the old Land League and Fenian days," Campbell recalled, "there was always a lawyer of this kind attached to the Castle and known as the Law Advisor. In effect, the proposal is to revive this appointment for a specific time, say two or three years, though it is quite unnecessary to describe Wylie by that or any other title if it is not deemed advisable." In concluding, Campbell stated that MacPherson was displaying "great courage, as well as wisdom, in being anxious to stick to his post here, as I am convinced that French, he and indeed myself carry our lives in our hands from day-to-day."[23]

MacPherson and French also hoped to implement other new policies. They wanted to outlaw Sinn Fein newspapers, Sinn Fein clubs, the Irish Volunteers, Cumann na mBan, and the Gaelic League.[24] MacPherson wrote bluntly to Law on May 16, declaring that if the cabinet approved, "it means *open war* with all its horrible consequences."[25] Law was reluctant to endorse these proposals. He wrote to Lloyd George stating that the issue of suppressing Sinn Fein should not be raised in the cabinet until the prime minister had time to consider it.

23. H.L.R.O., Law P., MS 97/3/4, Campbell to Law, May 3, 1919.

24. Ibid., L.G. P., MS. F/180/3/2, French and MacPherson memorandum, May 15, 1919.

25. Ibid., Law P., MS. 97/3/24, MacPherson to Law, May 16, 1919.

Law noted that the cabinet was "too inclined to jump at what they call the strong line" and that Carson agreed with him that "to proclaim Sinn Fein [as an illegal organization] means, in effect, putting an end to the whole political life of Southern Ireland, and that could not be effectively done." Law concluded his letter by stating that MacPherson would consult further with French and Carson about proclaiming the Dáil and possibly the Irish Volunteers.[26] Two weeks later, Walter Long, the cabinet's link to the Irish executive, was sent to Ireland. His visit prompted the inevitable rumors that personnel changes were imminent, but Long was satisfied with the current executive personnel. He reported to Lloyd George on May 27 that the lord lieutenant was succeeding in straightening up the Castle and that the chief secretary was doing splendid work. Long thought that the Irish government could enforce a ban on the Dáil and on individual Sinn Fein clubs, but that the Dublin police's Special Crimes Branch and the Irish constabulary needed overhauling, processes that might take months to complete. The chief police officers, he declared, were either incompetent or worn out, and he recommended that they should be either pensioned or retired with some special consideration. Inspector-General Joseph Byrne of the RIC, Long explained, had lost his nerve. He suggested T. J. Smith, the commissioner of the Belfast police, as a possible successor.[27]

The cabinet followed Long's advice. The Irish executive was allowed to proclaim only local Sinn Fein clubs until the police forces and the Law Office were strengthened. Campbell and MacPherson took immediate action on the latter by promoting the attorney-general to the bench. There was no question about Denis Henry's succeeding to the attorney-generalship, but several candidates were mentioned for the solicitor-generalship.[28] These candidates included Sergeants-at-Law Matheson and Sullivan, as well as Wylie, who had not yet been given an appointment, and two Ulster Unionists, T. W. Brown and Daniel Wilson. Each candidate had supporters and detractors. MacPherson thought that Matheson, a Unionist who was one of Campbell's favorites, was too old for the position. Sullivan, the Nationalist who was French's favorite

26. Ibid., L.G. P., MS. F/30/3/63, Law to Lloyd George, May 18, 1919.

27. Ibid., L.G. P., MS. F/32/2/45, Long to Lloyd George, May 21, 1919.

28. Ibid., Law P., MS. 97/3/34, 36, MacPherson to Law, May 25, 1919; Campbell to Law, May 27, 1919.

and the least attractive candidate in Campbell's and Law's eyes, told the lord lieutenant that he would not take the position. MacPherson then wrote to Law on May 31, suggesting, "If it becomes a question between Brown and Wilson, a word from Carson might help."[29] Wilson was given the appointment, but MacPherson, who knew about former Solicitor-General Powell's nervous breakdown, was uneasy about Wilson's health, even though Wilson produced two doctor's certificates attesting to his fitness. Because Henry would be stationed in London and Wilson would have sole charge of the Castle's legal work, MacPherson pressed Law to expedite Wylie's appointment as law adviser. "He is a first-rate lawyer with no political attachments," the chief secretary wrote of the Ulster Liberal, adding that Wylie did most of the court martial work during the rebellion.[30] Law raised no objection and Wylie's appointment as law adviser was announced in July.

With new Law Office personnel in place, the Irish executive was ready to respond to the Dáil's activities in its assembly and in the country. The Dáil's adoption of the oath for its members and military forces provided the legal justification to suppress the Dáil. When a group of English soldiers was attacked near Fermoy, County Cork, on September 7, 1919, by the Irish Republican Army, the Irish executive proclaimed the Dáil as an illegal organization. "We had to allow these members to sit together *in consultation* if they wished," MacPherson explained to Law on September 13, but when they "conspired by executive acts to overthrow the duly constituted authority, then we could act."[31]

Strengthening the police forces became the executive's top priority. There were two immediate problems: recruitment—the constabulary was approximately fifteen hundred men short of its full complement—and leadership of the forces.[32] General Frederick Shaw, the commanding general-in-chief of the army in Ireland, thought that either Inspector-General Byrne should recruit non-Irishmen into the constabulary,

29. Ibid., MS. 97/3/40, MacPherson to Law, May 31, 1919.

30. Ibid., MS. 97/4/20, MacPherson to Law, June 21, 1919.

31. Ibid., Law P., MS. 98/3/12, MacPherson to Law, Sept. 13, 1919; Townshend, *The British Campaign in Ireland, 1919–1921,* p. 31.

32. Richard Hawkins, "Dublin Castle and the Royal Irish Constabulary, 1916–1922," in *The Irish Struggle, 1916–1922,* ed. by Desmond Williams (London: Routledge & Kegan Paul, 1966), pp. 167–82.

or the government should raise a force of discharged soldiers and place them under the command of the police forces. Neither Inspector-General Byrne of the Royal Irish Constabulary (RIC) nor Chief Commissioner Edgeworth-Johnson of the Dublin Metropolitan Police (DMP) embraced these alternatives. The former argued that the proposed force could not be expected to obey the constabulary's discipline code; the latter contended that the army was not needed in Dublin and agreed with Byrne that the proposed force would be difficult to control.[33] The civil service was also viewed as a potential source of police officers. The personnel shortage became so serious that in December the Irish executive sent a circular to civil service department heads in Ireland asking for officials from their departments to assist the RIC and DMP as special constables.[34] Dublin's civil servants had little trouble explaining their reasons for refusing the invitation. Some feared a social boycott from their neighbors, while others declared that Irish civil servants had enough problems of their own to solve, including collecting their war bonuses and securing their right, as workers, to organize.[35]

In December 1919 French made changes in the leadership positions in the constabulary. "I have sent Byrne on a month's leave and placed Smith to act as I.G.," French wrote to MacPherson. He explained that Byrne's temperament and methods were unsuited to the demands of the times; and he disclosed, "as I knew he would not take leave voluntarily, I have given the order that he should do so." "I feel sure," the viceroy concluded, "it will be necessary to increase considerably the numbers of people to be sent away for the benefit of their health."[36] Lloyd George supported the change. "Byrne," the prime minister wrote to Law on December 30, "clearly has lost his nerve. It may, of course, very well be that the task in Ireland is a hopeless one and that Byrne has simply the intelligence to recognize it. However, until we are through with Home Rule, a man of less intelligence and more stolidity would be a more useful instrument to administer in the interregnum." "Smith," Lloyd George concluded, "is very highly spoken of by all who know him best. Carson has a high opinion of him."[37]

33. Townshend, *The British Campaign in Ireland, 1919–1921,* pp. 29–30.
34. *Freeman's Journal,* Dec. 15, 1919.
35. *Irish Independent,* Dec. 15, 1919.
36. Bod. Lib., Strath P., MS. c. 490, f. 171, French to MacPherson, Dec. 10, 1919.
37. H.L.R.O., L.G. P., MS. F/31/1/15, Lloyd George to Law, Dec. 30, 1919.

Chief Commissioner Edgeworth-Johnson looked for help to strengthen the Dublin police's Detective Branch and the Intelligence Division, which was being systematically liquidated by a squad of Irish Republican Army soldiers. He wrote to J. J. Taylor, the assistant under secretary, on December 1, declaring that police work had increased "by no less than 1000%," and that there was "too much for the Chief Commissioner and one superintendent to oversee."[38] He wanted the Treasury to sanction the permanent appointment of a second assistant commissioner, preferably a constabulary officer of proven experience and ability. Before the Treasury could act, French placed W. C. F. Redmond, a native of County Down who had been a detective in Belfast's constabulary office for fifteen years, in charge of the Dublin Metropolitan Police's criminal investigation and detective branch.[39] A. P. Waterfield, an official in the Treasury Office, balked at the transfer. He declared in a memorandum on December 24 that the police problems could be alleviated by replacing Assistant Commissioner Quinn. "The truth is," the memorandum elaborated, "the DMP is thoroughly rotten—first because the Home Rule Act of 1914 handed them over to Dublin Corporation, and it has since been in their interest to stand well with that body, i.e., against the Government." Returning to the request at hand, Waterfield noted that it was a tradition to have one of the heads of the Dublin police a Catholic and the other a Protestant. Redmond, he warned, was a Protestant and if he were appointed charges of bigotry and Protestant ascendancy could be expected from Nationalists.[40] Waterfield's objections were overruled by Lloyd George, and Redmond was promoted to the rank of assistant commissioner. Within days of his appointment, Redmond was assassinated, and Byrne returned to Dublin. French then instructed Taylor to inform Byrne that the Irish government had concluded, "with regret, that the interests of the Service require that you should vacate the office." Byrne, who was aware of no serious and unanswerable cause of complaint, asked to be furnished with detailed reasons for his dismissal. In reply Taylor stated simply that the Irish government had concluded that Byrne was "unequal to that active discharge of all the essential duties of Inspector-General."[41]

38. P.R.O., T. 162/28/E, 1915, Edgeworth-Johnson to MacMahon, Dec. 1, 1919.
39. Ibid., Taylor to secretary of the Treasury, Dec. 20, 1919.
40. Ibid., Waterfield memorandum, Dec. 24, 1919.
41. H.L.R.O., L.G. P., MS. F/7/4/33, Memorandum on Joseph Byrne.

French and MacPherson also began to reorganize the executive branch of the Chief Secretary's Office. This had become urgent because of the political and personal rivalry that had developed between the under secretary, James MacMahon, and the assistant under secretary, Taylor. Politically, MacMahon was at the center of a group of Nationalist civil servants in Dublin Castle who urged the executive officers to follow a moderate course in combatting Sinn Fein and the Dáil. Taylor was a Unionist and a proponent of vigorous action against Sinn Fein and the Dáil. Taylor, moreover, was trying to concentrate administrative, business, financial affairs, criminal investigations, and appointments in his own hands.[42] MacMahon, in turn, disrupted Taylor's centralizing tendencies and hampered the work of French's Advisory Council, which had met several times after the general election of 1918.[43] These activities angered the viceroy, who confided to MacPherson on December 11 that MacMahon and his personal staff were in contact with Sinn Fein leaders and radical priests. "The anomalous position of MacMahon and Taylor," French continued, "is causing me a great deal of worry. Efficient government is quite impossible as things are at present, and steps must be taken at once to cut MacMahon off from any access to papers or documents which really matter." French went on to state that the only thing to do was to separate the duties of the under secretary and assistant under secretary. "This is the only means," he concluded, "by which we can possibly remedy the terrible state of things existing now at the Castle. The place seems to be honeycombed with spies and informers and men who cannot be trusted."[44] MacPherson then reversed the duties of his subordinates: Taylor was given exclusive control over all matters dealing with the local magistracy, the police, crime, prisoners, and the employment of demobilized soldiers; MacMahon was given the administration of routine office matters.[45]

Taylor did not, however, relinquish his control of the routine business, and he further undermined MacMahon's position in police business. Taylor used his new authority to collaborate with his friend, Chief

42. "Periscope," G. C. Duggan, "The Last Days of Dublin Castle," *Blackwood's Magazine,* 222 (July 1922), 136–90.

43. Bod. Lib., Strath. P., MS. C. 490, f. 149, Saunderson to Watt, Nov. 10, 1919.

44. Ibid., MS. c. 490, f. 173, French to MacPherson, Dec. 11, 1919.

45. Ibid., MS. c. 470, f. 175, n.d., Memorandum on Duties of Assistant Under Secretary.

Crown Solicitor Henry Wynne, on the Criminal Inquiries Act, which aimed to curtail the Dáil's local government administration by withholding financial grants from local government bodies that cooperated with the Dáil. In addition, Taylor and Wynne prepared the way for a possible revocation of trial by jury in troubled areas by reviewing a clause in the Act for the Prevention of Crime in Ireland (1882) that allowed the lord lieutenant to appoint a commission of three judges to try cases without a jury.[46]

While the executive officers in Dublin Castle made their personnel decisions, the cabinet turned its attention to home rule. This was necessary because the Home Rule Act of 1914 was scheduled to come into effect after the negotiation of the last treaty of the war. On October 7, 1919, the cabinet appointed a committee, under Long's chairmanship, to review several alternative approaches to home rule, including granting dominion status to a united Ireland, excluding Ulster from any settlement, and giving Ulster special status within an all-Ireland Parliament.[47] The committee decided on a federal solution with two home rule Parliaments, one in Dublin, the other in Belfast. A Council of Ireland, made up of members of both Irish Parliaments, would administer common affairs and provide the way for possible unification. The cabinet was not enthusiastic about partition or about the prospect of Sinn Fein's dominating the Southern Parliament, and some cabinet members doubted that a unified Irish Parliament could evolve from the federal scheme. Ulster Unionists convinced the cabinet that the territory under the Northern government would be defined by the six counties of Tyrone, Fermanagh, Antrim, Down, Londonderry, and Armagh. In terms of the results of the general election of 1918, this geographic configuration would give them a permanent working majority in the Northern Parliament, whereas if all nine of Ulster's counties were included, they would hold only a precarious one-vote majority.[48] Long was instructed to supervise the drafting of new home rule legislation, which was named the Better Government of Ireland Bill.[49]

The bill's principal points were laid before the House of Commons

46. Duggan, "Last Days of Dublin Castle," pp. 141, 161.
47. Townshend, *The British Campaign in Ireland, 1919–1921,* pp. 34–37.
48. Colvin, *Carson,* 3:383–384; Buckland, *Irish Unionism,* 2:115–21.
49. Petrie, *Walter Long and His Times,* p. 214.

in December 1919 and it moved to the second reading on March 29, 1920. MacPherson, the government's spokesman on the bill, told the House that the measure was based on two principles: that northeast Ulster desired self-government free from the rest of Ireland and that the separation of any part of Ireland from the imperial connection with the United Kingdom would never be tolerated.[50] As in the Government of Ireland Act of 1914, Ireland was to send forty-two representatives—elected by the existing parliamentary counties, boroughs, or divisions—to the imperial Parliament. MacPherson explained that the Council of Ireland would be an advisory body of forty members, twenty from each Irish Parliament, with a president who would be appointed by the imperial government. MacPherson said the council would assume the administration of all common services, whether transferred or reserved.

The bureaucracy and the judicial system were MacPherson's next topics. Personnel matters were a central concern because the civil servants and judges did not know what might happen to them under the new governments. MacPherson declared that the imperial government would safeguard the pension rights of all loyal servants of the crown in Ireland and indicated that the bill's improvements over the Home Rule Act for safeguarding officials were framed by suggestions that had been offered to him by Irish civil servants. These safeguards included extending the voluntary retirement period from five to seven years and granting up to two-thirds (instead of one-half) salary as the basis for determining pensions for those officers who either were forced into retirement or retired voluntarily. MacPherson then turned to the judicial systems. He told the House that because each Parliament would have sovereign authority in its own territory, it was necessary that each should have the signs and symbols of its authority, namely the courts of law. This meant that the existing judicial system would be abolished and replaced by separate Supreme Courts of Judicature for both Southern and Northern Ireland. Each system, MacPherson explained, would have a High Court and a Court of Appeal. The Southern High Court would consist of a lord chief justice and six other judges; the Northern High Court would consist of a lord chief justice and two other judges.

50. *Parliamentary Debates,* Fifth Series, House of Commons, 127:925–43.

The Court of Appeal, in both instances, would consist of the lord chief justices and two lords justices of appeal. The bill also proposed to establish a link between the two supreme courts by proposing a High Court of Appeal for the whole of Ireland, consisting of the lord chancellor, the two lord chief justices, and two additional justices, one from each supreme court. Each judge would be allowed to choose where he wished to serve. The judicial land commissioner would serve in each system because the Land Commission was a reserved matter. Unlike the 1914 act, this bill provided that judicial appointments would remain an imperial responsibility for three years, except in the case of the lord chancellor, whose appointment would be a permanent imperial responsibility. The court's administrative offices and personnel would also remain a reserved matter until the union of Southern and Northern Ireland. Finally, all members of the Irish bar and all solicitors would have the right to an audience in both court systems.

During the ensuing debate, opposition to the bill emerged from Asquith's followers, who supported the 1914 act, and from the Conservative back-benchers, who were alarmed by the disturbed state of Ireland and were, therefore, wary of embarking on constitutional experiments. Labour party members proposed a six-month postponement of the measure and the cessation of coercion in Ireland. Southern Unionists expressed concern about their position as a small minority in southern Ireland. Ulster Unionists said they would not vote for home rule but that they would not obstruct the measure. T. P. O'Connor, the Irish Nationalist MP for Liverpool, spoke for the few remaining members of the Irish Parliamentary party. He observed dryly that the bill would probably be carried in the House without a single Irishman's vote in its favor. Next, O'Connor stated that the conflicting and overlapping authorities in Ireland would not be conducive to better government but would instead increase disorder and thereby paralyze government. O'Connor was especially critical of the duplication of administrative offices and courts. He predicted that these new institutions would create vested interests that would make partition permanent. In his peroration, he declared that the Government of Ireland Act of 1914 was regarded in Ireland as a solemn act of reconciliation between the peoples of England and Ireland. If the government succeeded in repealing that act, O'Connor concluded, Ireland would regard it "as one of the most perfidious betrayals which she has ever had to endure at the hands of England."[51]

On March 31, 1920, the bill passed its second reading, 348 to 94, and was sent to a standing committee for debate on individual clauses. Several clauses concerning administrative matters were adopted without debate. Clauses relating to the lord lieutenant and lord chancellor were no longer controversial. The government used the guillotine rule on the clauses concerning the police forces to prevent a debate while Ireland was in a disturbed state. There was, however, debate on clause 36 and on clauses 52 through 61, which related to the establishment of separate judicial and civil service systems. The debate on clause 36 began on June 22.[52] Robert Cecil, Conservative member for Hitchen, moved to reject the entire clause, which he called silly and grotesque. He argued that two judicial systems would be costly and even inconvenient for litigants and that the present system was not objectionable to people in the north or in the south. The division of the judiciary, he predicted, would cause distrust and would make partition definite and permanent.[53] Another Conservative, W. E. Guinness, an Irishman who represented the Bury St. Edmunds division of Suffolk, agreed that the courts had the confidence of all classes of people, and he read a resolution passed by the legal profession's leading organization in Ireland, the Council of the Incorporated Law Society, which disapproved of the duplication of the judicial system.[54] A supporter of the Ulster Unionists, J. R. P. Newman, Conservative member for Finchley, however, was adamant that the north must have its own judges. He stated that Unionists would not trust judges nominated by Dáil Eireann.[55] J. M. Kenworthy, the Liberal member for Central Hull, responded by pointing out that the efficient administration of the Sinn Fein courts demonstrated that good could come from any court set up in the south of Ireland.[56] Cecil's motion was rejected, and the clause was adopted, 181 to 29.

The debate on the clauses concerning the Irish civil service was conducted on June 28. After approving clause 52, which guaranteed Irish officials' pensions, the standing committee debated clause 53,

51. Ibid., 966–79.
52. Ibid., 130:2099–2100.
53. Ibid., 2074–79.
54. Ibid., 2080–82.
55. Ibid., 2082–84.
56. Ibid., 2084–85.

which established the Civil Service Committee.[57] The committee's most important duty would be to determine—finally and conclusively—the claim or question that any Irish official might raise about his or her tenure. The government accepted an amendment from Sir Laming Worthington-Evans, minister without portfolio, that was suggested to him by Irish officials. The Irish civil servants wanted to have two representatives, instead of one as proposed in the clause, on the Civil Service Committee: one from Northern Ireland and one from Southern Ireland. As amended, the committee consisted of the two Irish civil servants, a Treasury representative, the lord chief justice of England, and a representative from each Irish Parliament.[58]

After adopting clauses 54 and 55—concerning pensions for judges, police officers, and certain civil servants—the select committee moved on to clause 56, allocation of existing officers between Southern and Northern Ireland.[59] The government intended that officers who were employed solely in the north would be allocated to the Northern Parliament; those employed solely in the south would be allocated to the Southern Parliament; the allocation of officials whose work was conducted in both areas would be decided by the Civil Service Committee with due regard for the wishes of the officials. Major R. W. H. O'Neill, the Unionist MP for Mid-Antrim, began the debate by moving an amendment that aimed at giving the respective Parliaments a veto on the Civil Service Committee's decisions. He argued that the Northern government might be strapped with officials it did not want. On one hand, he maintained that Dublin Castle's incompetent and elderly officials might move north because they feared serving under a Sinn Fein government. On the other, O'Neill declared, "it is well-known that to a large extent, the Civil Service in Dublin—not, perhaps, in the case of the highest officials—is imbued with the doctrines which find acceptance among the majority of the people in that part of the country. . . . It would really be asking for the breakdown of government in the northern part of Ireland if a large number of those gentlemen [were] sent up to the Government in the North."[60] Solicitor-General Wilson admitted that there would be difficulties in making the allocations, but

57. Ibid., 131:76–82.
58. Ibid., 82–85.
59. Ibid., 85–90.
60. Ibid., 91–92.

he refused the amendment, explaining that the civil servants had confidence in the proposed Civil Service Committee, which, he added, would have representatives from both Parliaments.[61] This explanation did not satisfy Carson, who used the post office as an example to reinforce O'Neill's statement about Sinn Feiners permeating the civil service.[62] Carson wanted to have the police and the civil service dissolved so each official, regardless of current assignment, could choose freely which Parliament he or she preferred. Thomas Moles, the Unionist MP for Belfast, went further than Carson, declaring "the majority of the officials in any government department was in sympathy with Sinn Fein."[63] Wedgwood Benn, Liberal member for Leith, then accused the Ulster Unionists of attempting "to sack all the Sinn Feiners employed in the service" or "everybody who does not agree with them politically."[64] As he spoke, several members interrupted him with cries of "Why not?" and "Sack the lot!" The next speaker, Lord Hugh Cecil, Conservative member for Oxford, supported the Unionists by pointing out that political partisanship was not the question; rather, it was a question of disaffected civil servants being sent to northern Ireland and organizing revolution.[65] P. W. Raffin, Liberal member for Leigh, concluded the debate by charging that the Ulster Unionists' desire to prevent non-Unionists—regardless of ability—from serving in northern Ireland was unfair to the substantial Catholic Nationalist minority who lived in the north.[66] The amendment was refused and the clause was adopted without a division.

The comments in the House of Commons about the Irish judges and the civil servants from Unionists and Conservatives provided an interesting counterpoint to the Dáil's administrative and military actions in the country. Although its ministers were driven underground by the ban issued by Dublin Castle, they continued to deliver services and mete out justice. Dáil ministers who were arrested were promptly succeeded by others who conducted business "on the run." After Sinn Fein's sweeping victory in the local government elections in January and June 1920, the Dáil asked local government bodies to break off their connections with the existing Local Government Board, and by

61. Ibid., 93.
62. Ibid., 94–96.
63. Ibid., 98–100.
64. Ibid., 100–102.
65. Ibid., 102.
66. Ibid., 102–7.

October 1920 practically all of them outside northeast Ulster had done so.[67] The Dáil's court system was equally successful. By July 1921 over nine hundred parish courts and over seventy district courts were in operation. The Dáil's Land Commission's and arbitration courts' decisions on land purchase prices were giving satisfaction to purchasers and sellers alike.

Meanwhile, the IRA conducted a guerrilla war. Between January and June 1920 thirty-three courthouses were destroyed; almost five hundred constabulary barracks were either damaged or destroyed; sixty-six policemen were killed and forty-one wounded; five soldiers were killed and two wounded.[68] In addition to the assassination of Assistant Commissioner Redmond, there were other sensational incidents. The first was the lord lieutenant's narrow escape in December 1919 from assassination in Phoenix Park. In March 1920 Alan Bell, a resident magistrate who was assisting Taylor by investigating Sinn Fein's bank accounts, was assassinated, and in July Frank Brooke, an Irish railroad company executive who was a member of Lord French's Advisory Council, was assassinated presumably because of his political work for Dublin Castle. During the spring assizes, however, the justices on every circuit heard only trivial cases because prospective jurors would not serve and witnesses would not testify.[69]

It was obvious that French's, MacPherson's and Campbell's administrative reorganization had not helped them to regain control of the country. More changes, therefore, were in order. MacPherson told the prime minister that the demands of the Irish chief secretaryship were more than his physical constitution could bear, and when the committee debates on the Better Government Bill were completed at the end of March, he resigned. MacPherson's successor was Hamar Greenwood, a Canadian-born Liberal who had been seeking the chief secretaryship since 1916.[70] This change in Dublin Castle's executive

67. Lyons, *Ireland Since the Famine,* pp. 407–8. Of 127 corporations and town councils, Sinn Fein completely controlled 72 and shared authority with other Nationalists in twenty-six others.

68. I. O. [Cecil Street], *The Administration of Ireland, 1920* (New York: E. P. Dutton & Co., 1921), pp. 62, 92.

69. *Parliamentary Debates,* Fifth Series, House of Commons, 127:959, for statements citing Justices Moore, Molony, Gibson, and O'Connor.

70. N.L.I., Red. P., MS. 15192 (5), Greenwood to Redmond, May 9, 1916.

alarmed Ulster Unionists, including the owner of the *Belfast News-Letter,* who thought that Lloyd George was driving loyal officials like MacPherson out of Ireland to placate Sinn Fein.[71] Law assured Carson that the government would not sacrifice its friends to please its enemies, but Long did not favor Greenwood's appointment.[72] Lloyd George decided to follow up the change in the executive with a change in military leadership. He wanted to replace General Shaw as a commander of the army in Ireland with a military man who was familiar with police operations. The prime minister believed that Ireland's civil administration, using its legal departments and police forces, must be responsible for restoring order. He selected General Sir Nevil Macready, who had made his mark in the war before becoming the commissioner of the London Metropolitan Police.[73]

While Greenwood familiarized himself with the Government of Ireland Bill in London, Macready turned his attention to the police forces. The new army commander wrote to Lord French on April 23 that the Dublin police required drastic remodeling from top to bottom and that many Irish constabulary officers were not suited for the positions they occupied. This assessment included Chief Commissioner Edgeworth-Johnson, who Macready believed did not have a grip on police work, and Inspector-General Smith, who Macready found was a political partisan. Although Macready rejected the notion of amalgamating the two police forces, he thought that a tested organizer should be appointed to a superposition over both the inspector-general of the constabulary and the chief commissioner of the Dublin police. Macready observed that it would be wise to have a Catholic Irishman for the position and recommended Lt. Gen. Sir Edward Bulfin.[74] Bulfin refused the position, but he did send Macready some books on Irish history.[75] During his study of the police forces, Macready concluded that no effective coordination of the police and army could take place in Ireland until the civil administration was placed on a more businesslike footing.[76]

71. H.L.R.O., Law P., MS. 98/9/1, 2, R. J. Lynn to Carson, and Lynn to Law, Apr. 1, 1920. Lynn was the owner of the *Belfast News-Letter.* See also MS. 98/9/7, Sinclair to Law, Apr. 2, 1920.

72. Ibid., L.G. P., MS. F/31/1/20, Law to Lloyd George, Apr. 3, 1920.

73. Macready, *Annals of an Active Life,* 2:446–48.

74. H.L.R.O., Law P., MS. 103/2/16, Macready to French, Apr. 23, 1920. See also MS. F/31/1/20, Macready to Long, May 1, 1920.

75. Macready, *Annals of an Active Life,* 2:453.

76. Ibid., p. 449.

Lord French agreed with Macready's assessment; he wrote to Law on April 17, suggesting that a small committee, constituted of two or three government officials and one representative of the Irish civil service, should assess Dublin Castle administration.[77] French and Macready intimated to Law and Long, respectively, what they thought a committee might find. French wrote to Law on April 18, 1920, stating, "administration in Ireland is, I believe, as bad as it is possible for it to be." The Viceregal Council, he continued, had not been encouraged by either Shortt or MacPherson, and worse, MacPherson had completely ostracized MacMahon. French went on to state that he had urged MacPherson either to replace MacMahon with an official the chief secretary could trust or restore him to his duties. "But MacPherson would do neither one thing nor the other; and this is really the cause of the frightful mistakes which are constantly made." "However," French concluded, "I am quite determined that the Irish Government shall be handed over to Hamar Greenwood in as efficient as a condition as is now possible, and I am reinstating MacMahon and making him responsible for everything that goes on in the Castle in the absence of the Chief Secretary."[78] A few days later Macready wrote to Long, stating that he was flabbergasted by the administrative chaos. He reported that the lord lieutenant was performing the duties of a departmental junior because no other officials were willing to take responsibility even in small matters. Macready believed that this was the result of the impasse created by Taylor's centralizing tendencies, which French was now correcting. "I sincerely hope," he concluded, "that the committee which His Excellency has asked for will come over and put the administrative details of the Castle right, because until that is done, I am convinced that the most brilliant Chief Secretary you may send here must be a failure."[79]

Law thought that Sir Warren Fisher, the permanent head of the Treasury, was the best choice to head the committee. After Winston Churchill, Sir Herbert Creedy, and the former under secretary for Ireland, David Harrel, declined to undertake the task, Law secured Fisher's services, as well as those of Alfred Cope, an Irish official serving as

77. H.L.R.O., Law P., MS. 103/2/9, French to Law, Apr. 17, 1920.
78. Ibid., MS. 103/2/11, French to Law, Apr. 18, 1920.
79. Ibid., L.G. P., F/34/1/19, Macready to Long, Apr. 23, 1920.

the second secretary in the Ministry of Pensions.[80] When Fisher's committee visited Dublin Castle during the first week in May, Cope and another Treasury official, R. E. Harwood, inspected the under secretary's office, the constabulary offices, and the general headquarters of the Irish command. Within the week they reported to Fisher that the under secretary's office had lost its grip on the civil government of the country and that the office's relationships with the Law Office, the police, and the military authorities were in general confusion. MacMahon, they reported, was a weak official who did not hide his friendly relations with avowed Sinn Feiners. They noted, however, that MacMahon was very popular and that it would be impolitic to remove him.[81] Taylor, their report continued, was highly unpopular and this was a serious disadvantage to an important public official in the present circumstances. They recommended that Taylor and his principle clerk, W. P. J. Connolly, who had assisted Taylor in overcentralizing the Castle's work, should be encouraged to resign. They did not recommend the promotion of any of the office's first-class clerks to fill these vacancies. Rather, they recommended the temporary appointment of a small number of officers from English departments. Turning next to their findings on the police, the two investigators reported that Inspector-General Smith told them that he wished he could return to Belfast. Cope concluded that Smith was not equal to the responsibilities of his position. Finally, the two officials reported that they had heard contradictory opinions about the role the military had played in assisting the constabulary, but they agreed with Smith's assessment that, in general, the army was a hindrance.

Fisher submitted Cope's report with his own observations to Chamberlain and Law, who forwarded both documents to Lloyd George on May 12. Fisher's report began with the strong assertion "The Castle Administration does not administer. On the mechanical side it can never have been good and it is now quite obsolete; in the infinitely more important sphere (a) of informing and advising the Irish Gov-

80. Ibid., MS. 102/5/3, 4, Law to Greenwood, Apr. 17, Apr. 20, 1920; MS. 103/2/10, 15, Law to French, Apr. 17, Apr. 23, 1920. See also, 103/5/2, Long to Law, Apr. 20, 1920, for Long's approval of Fisher.

81. Ibid., L.G. P., MS. F/31/1/32, Cope and Harwood memorandum to Sir Warren Fisher, forwarded to Lloyd George by Law on May 12, 1920.

ernment in relation to policy and (b) of practical capacity in the application of policy it simply has no existance."[82] Fisher endorsed Cope's recommendation, which Macready had already seconded, that MacMahon should remain in Dublin Castle, where he was a source of satisfaction to the Catholic hierarchy. Moreover, Fisher warned that MacMahon's superiors must not leave him "outside the pole of any confidence, as the only effect of this must be to offend the hierarchy." Fisher also noted that MacMahon "holds views more in keeping with 20th century sentiment than those expressed by the Ascendancy party and the supporters of indiscriminate coercion, and, so far as it counts, his advice would be on the side of judicious moderation." Still, Fisher thought that the under secretary's office needed more attention. He recommended the appointment of Sir John Anderson, the chairman of the Board of Inland Revenue, as joint under secretary (pro tem). Fisher went on to suggest that Taylor be retired, and he recommended Cope as successor. Fisher suggested that picked men from London who were experts in administrative finance should be placed in subordinate positions under Anderson and Cope. He pointed out that this would provide Greenwood with first-class civilian advisers. Fisher concluded his treatment of the administrative side of Dublin Castle with the suggestion "At the earliest possible date I would remove the Irish Administration from the Castle, the associations of which are a heavy sentimental handicap."

Turning next to the forces of law and order, Fisher reported that from all accounts the condition of the police was very unsatisfactory. The heads of the RIC and DMP, he explained, were mediocrities; the morale of the former force was shaken, and that of the latter was entirely lost. Fisher recommended drastic overhauling in terms of personnel and organization, and he approved of Macready's efforts to secure a man who could supervise and modernize both forces. Fisher noted that he was in agreement with Macready: "The soldier stands by to assist civil authority (unless and until martial law is proclaimed) but is not a substitute for it."

Fisher reinforced his report on the Irish administration with a private letter to Law on May 15. He stated that the Irish situation would

82. Ibid., MS. F/31/1/32, Fisher memorandum, May 12, 1920.

be far from hopeless if Macready and Anderson were working together. Fisher, who had been reading the books that General Bulfin had sent to Macready, also offered some thoughts on Irish politics to Law. Dublin Castle, he reported, "listens solely to the Ascendancy party and (previous to General Macready's arrival) it never seemed to think of the utility of keeping in close touch with opinions of all kinds. The phrase 'Sinn Fein' is a shibboleth with which everyone not a 'loyalist' is denounced, and from listening to the people with influence you would certainly gather that Sinn Fein and outrage are synonymous." Fisher went on to discuss the Sinn Fein movement at greater length and acknowledged the successes of the Dáil's courts. He concluded the portion of his letter that dealt with politics by advising that Sinn Fein should not be proclaimed and that the Irish people should be allowed to think and vote Sinn Fein without being accounted murderers or criminals. Returning to administrative reform, Fisher noted one small change that he believed would have a psychological effect out of all proportion to its intrinsic importance: the abolition of the lord lieutenancy. "This post," Fisher observed, "with its atmosphere of pinchbeck royalty, has associations which do nothing but harm in the tenacious memories of the Irish people; and its abolition would have a spectacular touch which appeals to their temperament."[83]

On May 14 Law sent Fisher's recommendations on the reorganization of the Dublin Castle to Greenwood, stating that if the chief secretary wanted them carried out, he (Law), would do his best to have them brought into effect at once.[84] Greenwood endorsed the proposals, and within a week an official communiqué announced that Sir John Anderson was to be joint under secretary with MacMahon. Anderson was also given the authority of a secretary of the Treasury. Cope was appointed assistant under secretary in place of J. J. Taylor, who learned from the communiqué that he had been retired. The method was reminiscent of the one he used to announce Inspector-General Byrne's mysterious retirement only a few months earlier. Mark Sturgis, an Inland Revenue official who had once been assistant private secretary to Asquith, was also sent to Ireland. Sturgis was given the title of special

83. H.L.R.O., L.G. P., MS. F/31/1/33, Fisher to Law, May 15, 1920.
84. Ibid., Law P., MS. 103/3/8, Law to Greenwood, May 14, 1920.

commissioner of income tax, but he acted as an assistant under secretary to Anderson. In line with Cope's recommendations, eight other English officials were transferred to Ireland: three from the Treasury, two from the Home Office, and one each from the Privy Council Office and Pensions. A journalist was named director of information.[85] As recommended by Fisher, the English officials set up their offices in Dublin Castle but decided not to reside in the Castle, choosing instead a hotel in Kingstown, a suburb of Dublin.

When the new band of officials was in place, the Irish administration in Dublin Castle came to have four key groups, as defined by their personnel: military officers, politicians, Irish civil servants in the Chief Secretary's Office, and English civil servants on loan to Ireland. As defined by objectives, individual group members were divided into those who wanted to defeat Sinn Fein and those who hoped for a negotiated settlement. Most of the military officers wanted to take a strong offensive against Sinn Fein and introduce martial law. They were in favor of issuing identity cards, restricting the movement of Sinn Feiners, transferring Irish prisoners to English prisons, and removing Sinn Fein sympathizers who were postal workers.[86] The Irish civil servants urged moderation, and Wylie, the law adviser, as well as newcomers such as Anderson, Cope, and General Macready, agreed that although an increase in coercion might dampen lawlessness, it would not lead to a solution of the Irish question.[87] The coercive policy also posed a problem for the officials who had to carry it out. "Ireland is not like it was in the old days," Greenwood explained to Mark Sturgis, because "now every man carried arms, and the Civil Servants went in danger of their lives."[88] French was also worried about what the future would hold for Irish officials. He wanted to retire to the land his family owned in County Roscommon and he understood how a remark Wylie had made—"I have got to live there"—had "colored the opinions of many men of great ability," including Justice Ross and Campbell.[89] Law

85. John W. Wheeler-Bennett, *John Anderson, Viscount Waverly* (New York: St. Martin's Press Inc., 1962), pp. 56, 59–63.

86. Townshend, *British Campaign in Ireland, 1919–1921,* pp. 99, 101.

87. H.L.R.O., L.G. P., MS. F/36/2/14, Macready to Frances Stevenson, May 25, 1920.

88. P.R.O., *Sturgis Diary,* 30/59/part 1, July 23, 1920.

89. H.L.R.O., L.G. P., MS. F/48/6/37, French to Lloyd George, July 27, 1920. See also, Gerald French, *The Life of Field-Marshall Sir John French* (London: Cassell and Company, Limited, 1931), pp. 366–67.

had a slightly different perspective on the relationship between the Irish civil servants and coercion. He reminded his conservative colleagues in the cabinet, "you can go so far as your instruments will hit," recalling, perhaps wistfully, "there was no mixture of Home Rulers in the [Irish] Government in Mr. Balfour's time."[90]

Within a week of Fisher's report, Macready began to revamp the police forces. Winston Churchill assisted him in the search for a special adviser for both police forces. Macready interviewed two candidates and selected Major-General Hugh Tudor, a friend of Churchill's who wanted the position.[91] Tudor's first concern was the constabulary, in which resignations were running at nearly two hundred per month, against about twenty-five per month before the war. To counteract this drain in personnel, Tudor encouraged the recruitment of former servicemen, a process that Assistant Under Secretary Taylor had initiated on a modest scale before his removal from Dublin Castle. The great majority of these recruits were British. Known as Black and Tans, they soon became synonymous with terror because they reacted to attacks upon the police with reprisals.[92] The constabulary was also reinforced by an Auxiliary Division that was made up of recently discharged army officers. The two new units raised the police forces to some twelve thousand men. Tudor also brought efficient secretaries into the RIC's offices and secured better means of transportation for the police. Attempts to coordinate the activities of the intelligence systems of the army, RIC, DMP, and London police did not succeed. This task was complicated by civil servants and police officials who passed on information to Collins and the IRA.[93] Macready and Tudor were unable to bring the constabulary and the army into a more cooperative relationship throughout the remainder of 1920 and into 1921. Tudor would not discipline his new units and he resisted Macready's attempts to subject recruits to military discipline.[94]

90. H.L.R.O., L.G. P., MS. F/19/2/18, Wylie to Anderson, Aug. 3, 1920, and Thomas Jones, *Whitehall Diary,* ed. Keith Middlemas, Vol. 3 *Ireland, 1918–1925* (London: Oxford University Press, 1971), p. 27.

91. Wheeler-Bennett, *John Anderson,* p. 63.

92. Townshend, *The British Campaign in Ireland, 1919–1921,* pp. 92–95; 209.

93. Sean Kavanagh, "The Irish Volunteers' Intelligence Organization," *Capuchin Annual,* 1969, pp. 354–67.

94. Townshend, *British Campaign in Ireland, 1919–1921,* pp. 55–59.

In August legislation was enacted to expand the power of courts-martial. The Restoration of Order (Ireland) Act expanded the jurisdiction of the courts-martial and substituted secret tribunals for the coroners' inquests that had frequently decided that the British government and the Irish executive officers were guilty of murder in cases involving Sinn Feiners. Because Lloyd George worried that British and Irish public opinion might object to the use of courts-martial in peacetime, he wanted these courts in civilian hands. Anderson warned the cabinet that any civilian who served on a court-martial would require police protection. The Irish justices and law officers did not object to the formation of the courts-martial because they did not supersede the jurisdiction of the existing courts, but Denis Henry thought correctly that no Irish judge would serve.[95]

Greenwood was primarily concerned with the reorganization of the civil side of Dublin Castle. He believed that responsibility for the conduct of the Irish administration could not be divided and that the lord lieutenant was the chief obstacle in the way of a united executive. Greenwood used the opportunity of William Starkie's resignation as resident commissioner of national education to begin to assert his authority. On June 21 Greenwood wrote to French declaring that the chief secretary should make recommendations on appointments; that any information in the lord lieutenant's possession about an appointment should be sent directly to the chief secretary; and that, in fact, all communications should be sent directly to the chief secretary.[96] Greenwood also began to undermine Walter Long's influence on Irish affairs. He informed Long that work on Taylor's and Wynne's proposed three judges bill, which Long supported, would now go slowly. Although the chief secretary stated tactfully that he had no intention of advising against the special tribunal, he pointed out that the Irish judges were against the scheme (one had called it a "bloody assize"), and that in any case Lord Chief Justice Molony and Wylie, the law adviser, had assured him that juries would do their duties.[97] Lord Chan-

95. Ibid., pp. 32–34.

96. C.S.O., R. P., 1921, no. 3397, Greenwood to French, June 21, 1920.

97. H.L.R.O., L.G. P., MS. F/34/1/27, Long to Lloyd George, June 18, 1920; ibid., MS. F/34/1/28, Greenwood to Long, June 28, 1920; ibid., MS. F/17/1/2, 6 and Fisher to Lloyd George, June 17, 1920, July 21, 1920.

cellor Campbell was Greenwood's next target. The chief secretary cut Campbell's access to all important documents and excluded him from executive meetings. By November 1920 Campbell was ready to resign the lord chancellorship, which was to be reduced in status under the divided judicial system. He began yet another quest for promotion, this time hoping to succeed Justice John Atkinson as a law lord in the House of Lords.[98] Finally, Greenwood secured the transfer of the Treasury remembrancer, Maurice Headlam, to the Treasury Office in England. Headlam was an outspoken Unionist who later recorded in his memoirs that he had passed his views on Irish politics to Conservative politicians during times of political crisis. Anderson took over Headlam's duties; his removal pleased the Nationalist officials in Dublin Castle.[99]

John Anderson's major responsibility was to improve the performance of, and human relations in, Dublin Castle. Fisher, who stayed abreast of his colleagues' work, reported to Lloyd George on June 17, "Both Wylie and MacMahon tell me they are convinced that people are holding the opinion that the Castle is improving. Anderson is satisfied there is some improvement and that the offices show that a spring clean is in operation." "Brennan and Duggan now smile," Fisher concluded, referring to the two clerks in the Chief Secretary's Office, "and I shall soon be happy—but only so far as office machinery goes."[100] Anderson was also cautious. He found that many people in Ireland believed that the reconstituted executive stood for a more generous policy, but he believed that there was still much spadework to do in correcting administrative problems. He wrote to Greenwood on July 20 that resignations continued to weaken the constabulary and he was worried about maintaining discipline among the new recruits. The prisons, moreover, were structurally unsound, and prison officials, from governors downward, were unequal to the strain. The military, he concluded, were useless to the civil authority. He warned Greenwood that any hasty conclusions drawn about the state of the administrative ma-

98. Ibid., Law P., MS. 99/7/2, 12, Campbell to Law, Nov. 15, Nov. 30, 1920; ibid., MS. 99/8/6, Campbell to Law, Dec. 5, 1920.

99. John McColgan, *British Policy and the Irish Administration, 1920–22* (London: George Allen & Unwin, 1982), pp. 11–13.

100. H.L.R.O., L.G. P., MS. F/17/1/2, Fisher to Lloyd George, June 17, 1920.

chine from a comparison of the statistics of outrages or of any other manifestations of Sinn Fein power would be absolutely illusory.[101]

A few days later Anderson looked deeper into the overall administrative system and summarized his findings in a cabinet memorandum. "The Local Authorities, where over a wide sphere are the agents of the Central Government, are profoundly disaffected. The machinery of the Courts has been brought virtually to a standstill and rival Courts are functioning openly, and, where forcibly suppressed, will continue to function in secret." "The Local Civil Service," he continued, "composed entirely of Irishmen, while in a sense not disloyal, is politically alienated, and exposed as it is to every kind of pressure, and in many cases, of intimidation, cannot be relied upon in the execution of a vigorous policy." The constabulary, on the other hand, could still be relied upon, but he concluded that the force had already performed well beyond what could have been expected of it.[102]

The continuing violence in the country had a profound effect on the administrative personnel. In Dublin, several leading civil servants, Law Office officials, and police officers moved their families into Dublin Castle for protection. High-ranking officials who did not, or could not, avail themselves of the Castle's sanctuary went about their work under armed police protection. Because the IRA maintained the distinction between officials who were doing normal administrative duties and those who were doing political work, civil servants and judges were not attacked. Those deemed to be doing political work—especially the constabulary and Dublin police detectives, tax collectors, and legal officials like Sergeant-at-Law Sullivan, who survived two attempts on his life—were considered legitimate targets.[103] Greenwood wrote to Law in May that he directed a nervous civil service, in which everyone was more or less frightened.[104] This problem was compounded by a sag in morale, and then resentment, when Irish officials learned that the temporary English officials received larger salaries, additional dan-

101. P.R.O., John Anderson Papers, C.O., 904, 188(1), Anderson to Greenwood, July 20, 1920.

102. Ibid., C.O., 904, 188(1), "Irish Situation, Note by Sir John Anderson to Cabinet," July 25, 1920.

103. *Second Annual Report of the Council of the Institute of Professional Civil Servants,* Dublin, Mar. 31, 1922.

104. H.L.R.O., Law P., MS. 103/3/1, Greenwood to Law, May 8, 1920.

ger allowances, police protection day and night, as well as the safe domicile in Kingstown.[105] In the country, local officials, resident magistrates, and field-based civil servants, especially those who served in the revenue departments, received no police protection and, if not attacked physically, were subjected to intimidation. If the danger (real or imagined) to an official's person was not enough, his place of employment was not safe. This was demonstrated on two occasions: on Easter Sunday 1920 nearly one hundred local Inland Revenue offices were destroyed simultaneously by the IRA; and on May 25, 1921, Dublin's Custom House, which housed the central revenue departments and the Local Government Board offices, was destroyed by the IRA.[106]

In spite of the reorganization of Dublin Castle's personnel and the qualified success of the Restoration of Order in Ireland Act (approximately 600 of the 1,800 suspects arrested late in 1920 were convicted by the expanded courts-martial), outrages in Ireland continued unabated between July and December 1920. Of the 432 policemen who were attacked during this period, 127 were killed and 192 wounded. Of the 246 soldiers who were attacked, 47 were killed and 118 wounded. One hundred thirteen civilians were killed and hundreds more were wounded.[107] IRA losses for the worst part of 1920 amounted to 43 killed.[108] The total number of outrages reached a high point during the first two weeks of September. November and December were less violent, but they were marked by several sensational events. One was the execution of Kevin Barry, a youth who had participated in a deadly attack on a squad of British soldiers in Dublin but had not fired his revolver. Barry's case aroused widespread sympathy, as did the death of the lord mayor of Cork, Terence MacSwiney, after a seventy-four-day hunger strike that began when the Irish executive refused to give him political-prisoner status. Late in November Brugha and Collins sanctioned a simultaneous attack on British intelligence officers living in Dublin that killed 14 and wounded 4 others. Black and Tans avenged

105. Robinson, *Memories: Wise and Otherwise,* pp. 293–94, 303, 310–18. See also P.R.O., 30/59, *Sturgis Diary,* for the fears about attacks on civil servants and intimidation of civil servants; and Duggan, "Last Days of Dublin Castle," pp. 173–75.

106. E. Holt, *Protest in Arms* (London: Putnam, 1960), p. 205.

107. I. O., *The Administration of Ireland, 1920,* pp. 97, 342–53.

108. Townshend, *British Campaign in Ireland, 1919–1921,* pp. 175, 179, 210–12.

these deaths when they opened fire on the crowd and players at a football match in Croke Park, Dublin, killing 12 and wounding 60. Within a week the IRA ambushed two lorries carrying Auxiliaries near Cork, killing every policeman but 1. Martial law was then declared in County Cork, but the Auxiliaries took their revenge by setting fire to the city center of Cork on December 10. Between January and July 1921 a total of 223 policemen were killed, 428 were wounded, and 326 others were fired upon; 94 soldiers were killed, 210 were wounded, and another 141 were fired upon. Seven more counties in the south and west were placed under martial law.[109]

The IRA's guerrilla war and the Dáil's expansion of its administrative authority slowly turned Irish and English public opinion against the government's coercion policy. For example, the British press defended the owner and editor of the *Freeman's Journal* in 1920 when they were jailed on the charge of printing a false report.[110] The *London Times,* which had been a defender of past governments' use of coercion in Ireland, began to criticize the policy early in 1920.[111] The report of a Labour party commission to Ireland in January 1921 was especially critical of the conduct of the army, the Black and Tans, and the Auxiliary Division. In February General Hubert Gough, the leader of the so-called Curragh mutiny in 1914, condemned the use of reprisals by the police in *Review of Reviews,* and County Clare's judge, Matthew Bodkin, condemned reprisals and stirred English public opinion with a pamphlet entitled *On the Lawlessness of the Forces of the Crown in Ireland.*[112] Throughout 1921 other organizations and commissions took evidence in Ireland and reported that not only had British policy in Ireland failed but Sinn Fein had achieved a large measure of de facto administrative and military control of the country.[113]

109. C. J. C. Street, *Ireland in 1921* (London: Philip Allan & Co., 1922), pp. 6–7.

110. Macready, *Annals of an Active Life,* 2:476; Townshend, *The British Campaign in Ireland, 1919–1921,* pp. 158–59.

111. Jones, *Whitehall Diary,* 3:44.

112. Matthew Bodkin, *A County Court Judge on the Lawlessness of the Forces of the Crown in Ireland* (London: Peace with Ireland Council, 1921).

113. See *Interim Report of the American Commission on Conditions in Ireland,* Dublin, 1921. See also, Peace with Ireland Council, *Pamphlets* (London: Caldonian Press, Ltd., 1921) in N.L.I., Pamphlets, 1921, Ir. 94109, p. 24; and D. G. Boyce, *Englishmen and Irish Troubles: British Public Opinion and the Making of Irish Policy, 1918–1922* (London: Jonathan Cape, 1972).

By summer 1920 many southern Unionists were convinced that rule by Sinn Fein in a divided Ireland promised more peace and stability than continued British rule.[114] They, too, were impressed by the Dáil's court system, which they found had administered justice impartially and prevented criminals from taking advantage of the guerrilla war. In August 1920 the southern Unionists organized a peace conference that was attended by moderate Nationalists and Unionists, as well as by John Sweetman, a founder of the Sinn Fein movement, and Sergeant-at-Law Henry Hanna, Horace Plunkett, and Antony MacDonnell. The conference passed one resolution recognizing northeast Ulster's rights as a free contracting party in future negotiations with the rest of Ireland, and a second one demanding for the rest of Ireland "complete administrative, fiscal and financial independence, [which] is the decisive test and characteristic of National self-government."[115] With these resolutions, the southern Unionists severed their ties with the Ulster Unionists and moved to protect their own interests.

Ulster Unionists now realized that it was in their interest to prepare for home rule along the lines of the Government of Ireland Bill, which was scheduled to reach the statute book in December. Sir James Craig was the most likely candidate for prime minister of Northern Ireland. He wrote to Bonar Law on September 1 to complain about some immediate problems: Dublin Castle's lenient treatment of Sinn Feiners, the attempts of central and local government officials to disarm loyalists, and the recent promotion of Catholic constabulary officers stationed in Ulster.[116] In a separate memorandum Craig outlined some measures that he thought would reestablish the north's confidence in the Coalition government, if not Dublin Castle. The first thing to do, he explained, was give the Ulster Unionists de facto control of the administration and police in northeast Ulster before the de jure transfer of power. Craig recommended the appointment of an under secretary for Ulster, one "embued with the spirit of Ulster," to represent the government and be responsible for the maintenance of law and order. Craig also thought that the Ulster secretary should have an office staff

114. Law P., MS. 102/5/30, Long memorandum to Irish Situation Committee, June 30, 1920; Buckland, *Irish Unionism,* 1:195, 212–218.

115. Street, *Administration of Ireland, 1920,* pp. 120–27.

116. H.L.R.O., Law P., MS. 102/10/3, Craig to Law, Sept. 1, 1920.

to arrange transfer of the administration of services. "Nothing," Craig declared, "would do more to restore the confidence of the Loyalists in the North than the knowledge that the Government was taking essential anticipatory steps of this nature."[117] Craig then went on to discuss the forces of law and order in Ulster, where sectarian violence of a political nature had left twenty dead in Derry and sixty-two dead in Belfast between June and September 1920. He recommended the appointment of a commissioner of the constabulary for Ulster, and he thought that a special constabulary force of two thousand men should be put in that officer's charge. He also hoped that the army would conduct its business in northeast Ulster with the new commissioner, perhaps Inspector-General Smith, and without reference to Dublin Castle. In the event of an emergency, Craig continued, the special constabulary could be augmented by a reserve force that could be raised from the Ulster Volunteers. Finally, Craig wanted the government to remove all civil servants and local officials who refused to take the oath of allegiance.

Macready, Anderson, and Sturgis opposed Craig's recommendations. Macready thought that the use of the Ulster Volunteers would complicate the problems already facing the police forces.[118] Sturgis and Anderson opposed the appointment of another under secretary on the ground that the administration already had too many officials standing in the way of unified command.[119] Nevertheless, Law and Churchill thought that Craig's suggestions had merit, and on September 13, 1920, the government announced that Sir Ernest Clark had been appointed assistant under secretary for the six counties of northeast Ulster. Clark, who had worked under Anderson at the Board of Inland Revenue, was technically subordinate to Anderson and MacMahon, but he quickly established his own office in Belfast. During the autumn approximately one hundred civil servants were transferred to Belfast to help Clark construct the administrative apparatus of the new Ulster state.[120] Clark

117. Ibid., MS. 102/10/3, Craig memorandum, "Suggested Steps of Government Action," Sept. 1, 1920; ibid., Draft Statement of the Ulster Unionist Council, Sept. 14, 1920.

118. P.R.O., And. P., C.O., 904/188(1), Macready to Anderson, June 18, 1920; H.L.R.O., Law P., MS. 102/7/1, Anderson to Law, Sept. 2, 1920. Macready, *Annals of an Active Life,* 2:488–89.

119. P.R.O., *Sturgis Diary,* 30/50/part 2, Sept. 13, Sept. 14, Sept. 15, Sept. 16, 1920.

120. McColgan, *British Policy and the Irish Administration,* pp. 32, 59.

immediately gained the confidence of wary Ulster Unionists when he attempted to settle a strike by some eight thousand Catholic shipyard workers. Clark demanded that the strikers sign a declaration disclaiming adherence to Sinn Fein before they could return to work. Craig's request for a special police force was filled in October. The Special Constabulary for Ulster was placed under the command of the existing Irish constabulary. It consisted of three classes, A, B, and C, according to the terms of service: full time, occasional duty, and reserves.[121]

The first steps toward establishing a de jure Unionist administration in northeast Ulster had been taken. According to historian John McColgan, when the Government of Ireland Act reached the statute book on December 23, 1920, "the administration of Ireland was already partitioned at its centre bureaucratically and even ideologically, and the administrative machinery was installed to make Home Rule and partition a reality."[122] The Ulster Unionists took the next step. In January 1921 James Craig agreed to accept nomination by the Ulster Unionist Council as premier of Northern Ireland.[123] Craig selected a speaker and chief whip for the Northern Parliament and began to look for men to serve in his first cabinet.

The topic of shaping the North's administrative system came before the cabinet in January. Greenwood submitted a memorandum recounting his search for persons to serve on the Joint Exchequer Board, on the Civil Service Committee, and as lord chief justice of Northern Ireland.[124] In April Sturgis began to compile lists of officials who were available for transfer to Northern Ireland. Clark wanted the names forwarded to him in Belfast at the earliest possible date. He told Sturgis that without this information "the unfortunate representatives of the North would be blindfolded, and perforce compelled to accept those officers whom the South might feel inclined to propose for assignment." "To expect that the South would freely offer us to their best," he added, "would be to expect more than poor human nature is ca-

121. Street, *Administration in Ireland, 1920,* pp. 296–98, 351–52.

122. McColgan, *British Policy and the Irish Administration,* p. 32.

123. Ervine, *Craigavon,* pp. 370–72. The appointment was in the hands of the lord lieutenant; the Ulster Unionists sought his "ratification."

124. P.R.O., And. P., C.O., 904, 188 (2), Cabinet memorandum of Greenwood, C.P. 2444, with appendix (copy), Jan. 12, 1921.

pable of."[125] Clark followed up this request on April 12 by suggesting a schedule for establishing Northern Ireland's administration. The thirteen-point schedule, which was to begin on April 19 and continue until June 21, 1921, included appointing the lord chief justice for Northern Ireland; establishing the court system; appointing ministers, department heads, and privy councilors; and nominating the North's civil service committee representative.[126] Anderson replied that before the schedule could begin, the individual points would have to be negotiated in consultation with both of the new governments. He did not think that the first transfers of personnel could occur before September.[127] Two weeks later Anderson wrote to Clark and explained, "As regards lists of staffs we have had practically nothing, nor do I think it is likely that men will be found willing to commit themselves long in advance of the actual date." He concluded by falling back on the standard method of selecting high-level officials for both appointment and promotion in the Irish bureaucracy. Anderson thought that most of the department heads for the North's system would be selected from the existing departments and they would, therefore, have personal knowledge of other officials who would be willing to move to the North. "The most prudent course," he advised, "will be for the Northern Government first to decide upon the person who is to be the permanent head of each Department, and then rely mainly on him to see that the North is not prejudiced in the allocation."[128]

With preparations for the launching of the Northern Ireland government under way, Lloyd George turned to the south, where the police forces were finding the pursuit of military victory costly. Lloyd George decided to open negotiations with Sinn Fein, but he refused to accept the idea of a truce because that term implied belligerent status, and thereby, legitimacy, for the Republicans.[129] Meanwhile, weekly totals of casualties reached a new high in March 1921, and in June the Dáil's ministers considered taking direct action against particular individuals serving in the Irish administration and judicial system. The targets

125. P.R.O., And. P., C.O., 904, 188 (2), Clark to Sturgis, Mar. 20, 1921.
126. Ibid., Clark to Anderson, Apr. 12, Apr. 14, 1921.
127. Ibid., Anderson to Clark, Apr. 12, 1921.
128. Ibid., Anderson to Clark, Apr. 23, 1921.
129. P.R.O., 30/59/part 3, *Sturgis Diary,* Jan. 1, Jan. 14, Jan. 26, 1921, for Cope's, Anderson's, and Macready's attempts to open the peace process.

included Dublin Castle bureaucrats, privy council members, justices of the supreme court, court administrators, crown prosecutors, sheriffs, and tax collectors. Officials who were perceived as administrators of services, including post office and education officials, were not to be disturbed.[130]

To improve the climate for negotiations, Lloyd George used his appointment power to make some last-minute changes in the Irish executive. Lord French, who had become the most vigorous proponent of coercion in Dublin Castle, reluctantly agreed when Lloyd George asked him to give up the lord lieutenancy. He asked to be appointed a temporary under secretary, pending the outcome of the conflict, but his request was refused.[131] The new viceroy was Lord Edmund Talbot, Viscount Fitzalan, the first Catholic to hold the position since the seventeenth century. Although the Nationalist press ridiculed the appointment because of Talbot's record in Parliament as chief whip of the Conservative party,[132] Greenwood told Lloyd George that the appointment was a master-stroke that would appeal to public opinion in the dominions and in America.[133] Greenwood used Fitzalan's Catholicism for propaganda purposes by filming the viceroy for "Movies of the World" newsreels. A second significant change in personnel occurred when Greenwood and Anderson pressed Lloyd George to seek Lord Chancellor Campbell's resignation. They cited Campbell's refusal to act as one of the lords justices earlier in November and December 1920 as sufficient grounds. Campbell had claimed that serving in that capacity would be a conflict of interest, but Greenwood thought that his refusal had been a clear case of dereliction of duty.[134] Greenwood convinced Lloyd George and Campbell acquiesced. This time, Campbell received no promises about future appointments for him or his son.[135] The new lord chancellor was Justice John Ross, the only Irish judge who had Greenwood's complete confidence. Ross assumed the position in June; his position on the Chancery bench was not filled.

130. McColgan, *British Policy and the Irish Administration,* p. 70.
131. H.L.R.O., Law P., MS. 107/3/21, Anderson to Law, Mar. 10, 1921.
132. *Freeman's Journal,* Apr. 2, 1921; *Leader,* Apr. 9, 1921.
133. H.L.R.O., L.G. P., MS. F/19/3/7, Greenwood to Lloyd George, Apr. 3, 1921.
134. Ibid., MS. F/10/4/8, Greenwood to Lloyd George, May 10, 1921; Campbell to Lloyd George, Apr. 30, 1921.
135. Ibid., Lloyd George to Campbell, May 10, 1921. See also, ibid., Law P., MS. 107/1/23, Campbell to Law, May 13, 1921.

On May 3, 1921, the first provisions of the new Government of Ireland Act went into effect. All executive powers in the North were delegated to the lord lieutenant, who in turn established seven departments of government: the prime minister's department and ministries of finance, home affairs, labor, education, commerce, and agriculture. Collectively these ministers would be like a cabinet, although the act styled them the Executive Committee of the Privy Council of the Northern Ireland Parliament. The elections for the Northern Parliament, which were fought on the issue of partition, were held on May 24. The Unionists won forty of the fifty-two seats. The Irish Parliamentary party and Sinn Fein divided twelve seats.[136] On May 31, Prime Minister Craig announced the names of his executive committee. All of its members were Unionists, although none of them had ministerial experience and most had no parliamentary experience.[137] The North's House of Commons assembled on June 7, without Irish Parliamentary party and Sinn Fein members in attendance.

In the elections for the Southern Parliament, which Sinn Fein used chiefly as a means of choosing the members of the second Dáil Eireann, 124 Sinn Fein candidates were returned unopposed in every constituency except Trinity College, which returned four Unionist members.[138] Southern Ireland's Parliament was scheduled to meet on June 28, and the Government of Ireland Act had provided that if fewer than half of the members attended, which now seemed likely, the Southern Parliament was to be dissolved and Southern Ireland would be ruled as a crown colony, presumably under martial law.[139] Macready submitted a plan for martial law that he and Anderson thought would work to govern the country, but, they warned, only with the most dire consequences for Ireland and the Coalition government.[140]

The government, therefore, redoubled its effort to open official negotiations with De Valera. On June 24 Lloyd George withdrew demands that to begin negotiations the IRA must surrender its arms and that

136. Buckland, *Irish Unionism,* 2:129–31.

137. Ervine, *Craigavon,* pp. 378–84.

138. Lyons, *Ireland Since the Famine,* p. 425.

139. A council of existing executive officers and British department heads would administer Southern Ireland with existing Irish department heads. Responsibility to Parliament would lie with the ministers responsible for a given department.

140. Townshend, *The British Campaign in Ireland, 1919–1921,* pp. 181–90.

certain Sinn Feiners, including Collins, must be barred from the conference table.[141] Cope took a letter with this information to Dr. Edward Mulhern, the bishop of Dromore, who had been looking for a way for the Catholic bishops to reach an accord with De Valera. Mulhern delivered the letter to De Valera, who insisted that a truce must precede negotiations. He also insisted on consulting the representatives of the southern Unionists before he would meet Lloyd George. The prime minister agreed, and De Valera met with Lord Midleton on July 5, then with Macready on July 8.[142] They negotiated a cease-fire, which came into effect on July 11, 1921. A truce and preliminary talks followed later that month. The negotiators considered two major questions in the preliminary talks. First, would southern Ireland, styled as the Irish Free State, remain in the empire as a dominion, or in "external association" as the Irish Republic? Second, what would be Ulster's status in the final settlement?[143] A subordinate topic but one that had posed difficulties in the past concerned the future compensation and treatment of officials and judges. Lloyd George made it clear from the outset that the Irish government, and not the Treasury, would have to pay the pensions of any officials who were discharged or forced to retire as a consequence of a change in government.

With negotiations under way, the Treasury officials serving in Dublin Castle prepared the Irish administration for the transfer of services. The Treasury was given responsibility for handing the administration over to the new government in good working order. One problem was that several Irish department heads, including Gill, Robinson, O'Farrell, Stevenson, LeFanu, MacMahon, and several others, had reached retirement age. A. P. Waterfield, the Treasury official in Dublin Castle who was supervising the transfer, realized that he could not replace these men with new officials and still effect the smooth transfer that he desired.[144] He knew, moreover, that the total losses in key personnel

141. P.R.O., 30/59/part 4, *Sturgis Diary,* May 4, May 19, June 4, June 25, 1921; Jones, *Whitehall Diary,* 3:79–82; Lyons, *Ireland Since the Famine,* p. 427.

142. Earl of Longford and T. P. O'Neill, *Eamon De Valera* (London: Hutchenson and Co., Ltd., 1970), pp. 129–32; Buckland, *Irish Unionism,* 1:236–46; Macready, *Annals of an Active Life,* 2:571–76.

143. Longford, *De Valera,* pp. 132–46.

144. P.R.O., T. 158/4, Waterfield to Scott, Aug. 3, 1921. See also C.S.O., R.P., 1921–22, nos. 2602, 2638, 2692, 2700, 2807, 3039, 3279, and 3621 for a sampling of problems in several departments due to the retirement of leading officials.

were going to be severe because a large proportion of what he thought were the best men in subordinate positions were also at the retirement age. Waterfield could not find any English officials who were willing to transfer to Ireland, even temporarily, to replace those Irish department heads who wanted to retire, and he did not believe that any lower-level Irish officials in the departments had the requisite ability or experience to merit promotion to the top positions. He decided that the best means of fulfilling his department's responsibility was either to leave vacancies unfilled (as in the case of the resident commissioner of national education and the inspector-general of the constabulary), or appoint "acting" department heads from the ranks, or ask officials not to retire as a matter of public duty. Although he eventually employed all three techniques, Waterfield relied mainly on the third alternative. This option also prevented the payment of higher pensions by either the British or Irish Treasury, in the event that the potential replacements for these officials were to take the promotion and then immediately take advantage of special retirement provisions. He also had to solve other personnel problems involving demands for salary increases and pension disputes. Waterfield also had to attend to an audit of the financial records of the Office of Arms when he discovered that Sir Henry Burtchaell kept that office's fees in his own personal bank account.[145]

Finding officials to serve in Northern Ireland's civil administration proved to be the most difficult task undertaken by the Treasury officials in Ireland. Only some three hundred Irish bureaucrats eventually volunteered for service in the North. These officials were nearly all Protestants and Unionists, and the Coalition government failed in its attempt to place even a handful of Catholic or Nationalist officials in positions of authority in the North's civil service.[146] Because the shortage of officials in key positions remained acute, Clark secured approximately thirty officials from England on a temporary basis to begin the administration of services.[147] Waterfield then decided to try to reorganize the North's departments as a way to solve the problem. Prime Minister Craig resisted this proposed solution, arguing that the Northern gov-

145. P.R.O., T. 158/4, 5, Waterfield's correspondence, Aug.–Oct. 1921.

146. McColgan, *British Policy and the Irish Administration,* pp. 60–61.

147. P.R.O., T. 158/5, Waterfield to Anderson, Sept. 21, 1921. For loans of officials to the Northern government, see T. 162/72/E. 6471 and T. 162/78/E. 7735.

ernment should have the right to shape its own departments.[148] Still, he could not shape those departments until he had the requisite personnel. On September 22 he wrote to Greenwood urging him to facilitate the staffing process. In the letter Craig complained that his government was being left in midair by the shortage of civil servants. He explained that he was having difficulty maintaining the confidence of the people in the North and that he was especially worried about controlling the police.[149] Craig wrote again on September 27 urging the government not to wait for the Irish Civil Service Committee to allocate experienced civil servants. Instead, he revived Anderson's earlier proposal that the Northern and Southern department heads should meet and, in conjunction with Anderson, draft a circular inviting civil servants to choose where they wished to serve. Craig believed that this plan would provide at least a sufficient nucleus of officials to justify the takeover of the administration of services. Although he had received some sixteen hundred applications from persons seeking civil service positions, he pointed out that his plan was better than "ordering personnel here and there, possibly saddling on the North men who had no desire to come and whom the North were not particularly anxious to have."[150]

Greenwood took the letters to the cabinet. He told his colleagues that although he sympathized with Craig, the plan would require complicated legislation. Greenwood declared further that providing the Northern government with its administrative staff might jeopardize the success of the treaty negotiations that were scheduled to start in November.[151] The order-in-council to transfer services to the government in Northern Ireland was issued on November 9, but the Civil Service Committee that was to protect the tenure of Irish officials was not

148. Ibid., T. 162/108/E. 13539, "Reorganization of Anglo-Irish Departments prior to the transfer of services." Waterfield wanted to reorganize fourteen Irish departments. Customs and Excise was the most troublesome because of the 400 customs officials, 326 volunteered for service in the South, and there was a question about forcing the remaining officials, who were Scottish and English and apparently Unionists, to serve in the South. See also, ibid., T. 162/87/E. 9764, letter from Glasgow Unionist Association to Sir John Gilmore, Nov. 21, 1921, about this matter.

149. P.R.O., And. P., C.O., 904, 188 (2), Craig to Greenwood, Sept. 22, 1921.

150. Ibid., Craig to Greenwood, Sept. 27, 1921.

151. Ibid., Cabinet memorandum on civil servants for the Northern government, Oct. 1921.

convened until December 8. The Irish Civil Service Alliance, which represented all of the staff officers' professional organizations, promptly brought suit against the committee on the grounds that, as constituted, its personnel could not adequately represent the Irish officials' interest. The two representatives of the staff officials refused to sit on the committee until the suit was resolved. On December 12, 1921, some fifteen hundred civil servants who represented all levels and every professional organization in the Irish civil service passed a resolution endorsing the suit and protesting that the committee's "real function is to facilitate a political manoeuvre."[152] Although the suit was not upheld, the Alliance's legal action effectively stopped the further transfer of Irish civil servants to the North.

The establishment of the judicial system in Northern Ireland, however, proceeded on schedule. The Treasury was also pledged to transfer the court's administrative system in good working order. Again, Waterfield wanted to reshape the court's offices before the transfer of authority, but he quickly discovered that the supreme court justices, and Lord Chancellor Ross in particular, were reluctant to allow the Treasury officials even to recommend reorganization and retrenchment in the Four Courts.[153] Nevertheless, some permanent reductions were made in the judges' staffs in October 1921 when the Irish supreme court was divided.[154]

The Supreme Court of Judicature in Ireland was divided on religious and ideological lines. Of the fourteen justices who were sitting in 1921, six Liberal justices and two Unionist justices chose the South; one Unionist justice chose the North; the other justices and the lord chancellor retired. The judicial land commissioner, William Wylie, the law advisor, who had also succeeded his uncle in that position in 1920, transferred to the South. The Southern bench had six Catholic justices and two Protestant justices.

Craig secured Denis Henry, the attorney-general, for lord chief justice of Northern Ireland. This appointment attracted attention because

152. McColgan, *British Policy and the Irish Administration,* pp. 83–84.

153. P.R.O., T. 162/108/E. 13769, Ireland, Legal Departments Committee of Enquiry—correspondence.

154. Ibid., T. 162/68/E. 5784/1, 2, Legal Departments in Ireland, staff and organization.

Table 1. Supreme Court of Northern Ireland and the Irish Free State 1921–24

Northern Ireland
Lord chief justice
Lords justices of appeal (2)
Justices of the High Court (2)
Irish Free State
Chief justice
Lord justices of appeal (2)
Justices of the High Court (5)

Adapted from: V. T. M. Delany, *Christopher Palles: Lord Chief Baron of Her Majesty's Court of Exchequer in Ireland, 1874–1916* (Dublin: Allen Figgis & Co., Ltd., 1960).

Henry was a Catholic.[155] The other four justices in the North were Protestants. Justice William Moore also chose to serve in the North, as one of the lord justices of appeal. James Andrews, a nephew of the former justice William Andrews of the King's Bench Division, became the other lord justice for Northern Ireland. (See Table 1 for the structure of the courts.) Daniel Wilson resigned the solicitor-generalship in June to become recorder of Belfast and county court judge of Antrim; in October he was appointed as a justice of the High Court. Richard Best, Unionist MP for County Armagh, was named attorney-general for Northern Ireland. The new solicitor-general in Dublin Castle was Thomas Watters Brown, the Unionist MP for North Down. He then advanced to the attorney-generalship after serving as solicitor for only a few weeks. In November Brown gave Anderson notice that he intended to resign the attorney-general's position. He was appointed a justice of the High Court in Northern Ireland early in 1922. In its dying days, the system that had produced law officers and judges on demand for more than one hundred years still worked smoothly. The Law Office in Dublin Castle was now vacant. There was virtually no legal work to do during the truce.[156]

The formal treaty negotiations began in November. During the negotiations issues involving the Irish administration played only a very

155. Ervine, *Craigavon,* pp. 439, 498; Buckland, *Irish Unionism,* 2:135.
156. H.L.R.O., L.G. P., MS. F/20/1/13, Greenwood to Lloyd George, Dec. 29, 1921.

small part. The Irish deputation, which was led by Griffith and Collins, missed an opportunity to use the transfer of services and division of the judicial system as negotiable points. The British representatives, who were led by Lloyd George, proposed that the Irish Free State pay fair compensation to all judges, officials, members of the police forces, and any other public officials who might be discharged or forced to retire.[157] The Irish deputation won a small concession. Clause 10 in the Articles of Agreement eventually declared that the Free State would not have to pay compensation to the auxiliary police force or to other persons who had been recruited in Britain for the Irish constabulary since 1919; the British government assumed responsibility for their compensation and pensions.[158] On the larger issues Lloyd George offered the Dáil's negotiators a modified dominion status for Ireland with full fiscal powers. The members of the Irish deputation were reluctant to affix their signatures because they had not won recognition of the Republic. However, Lloyd George's threat of war within three days if they did not sign and the belief, in Collins's words, that the treaty gave Ireland the potential to achieve ultimate freedom, convinced them to sign the Articles of Agreement for a Treaty on December 6, 1921.[159]

The treaty had a rapid passage through Parliament, but there was a serious difference of opinion about it in the Dáil. The members of the Irish deputation were opposed by De Valera. The debate centered on two questions: the oath of allegiance to the constitution of the Irish Free State, with its declaration of faithfulness to the king, and the failure of the Irish deputation to gain recognition of the Irish Republic. The protreaty forces challenged the antitreaty forces to present a viable alternative, but De Valera was unable to explain an alternative constitutional relationship to the satisfaction of most of the Dáil's deputies. When the vote was taken on January 7, 1922, the protreaty forces had the majority, sixty-four to fifty-seven.[160]

157. Jones, *Whitehall Diary,* 3:178; Dorothy Macardle, *The Irish Republic* (Dublin: Irish Press Ltd., 1951), p. 576.

158. Ibid., pp. 952, 954; Lord Longford, *Peace by Ordeal* (London: Sidgwick & Jackson, 1972), pp. 204, 298. H.L.R.O., L.G. P., MS. F/21/1/2, Ross to Greenwood, Dec. 7, 1921, and Greenwood to Lloyd George, Dec. 9, 1921.

159. Dáil Eireann, *Official Report: Debate on the Treaty Between Great Britain and Ireland Signed in London on December 6, 1921* (Dublin: Talbot Press, 1922), p. 32.

160. Ibid., pp. 345–46.

De Valera resigned the presidency of the Dáil, but not the presidency of the Republic. Griffith succeeded him and formed a ministry. Clause 17 of the treaty, which provided for the constitution of a Provisional Government until new elections could be held in Ireland, was then invoked. The British government promised in this clause to assist the Provisional Government in preparing for the transfer of powers and machinery requisite for the discharge of its duties.[161] The Provisional Government, which was a separate entity from Griffith's government, was chaired by Collins. The fact that Collins and several other men figured in both governments—Griffith's cabinet and the Provisional Government held several joint meetings—facilitated the eventual transfer of power. The transfer process began officially on January 16, 1922, when Michael Collins accepted the keys to Dublin Castle from Lord Fitzalan in the presence of every Irish department head.[162]

Sinn Fein achieved de jure power in Ireland for two reasons. First, the Irish Republican Army was able to maintain a stalemate with the British army and Irish police forces. The coordination and reinvigoration of Dublin Castle's civil and legal branches did not tip the balance in Britain's favor. The only way the Coalition government could have broken this stalemate was by a larger commitment of troops and the extension of martial law and concomitant suspension of civil liberties throughout Ireland. British public opinion would not, however, sanction a war with Ireland. Second, the Republicans demonstrated to Irish Nationalists and southern Unionists, as well as to interested British observers, that above all else they were a constitutional party and not simply the party of physical force. Sinn Fein displaced the Irish Parliamentary party through the electoral process in 1918 and went on to establish Dáil Eireann in 1919. The Dáil's ministers conducted their affairs in a businesslike manner throughout the period 1919–1921, and they showed due regard for the political conventions that were the constitutional legacy they inherited from the Irish Parliamentary party. The Irish Nationalist electorate endorsed Sinn Fein's conduct in two local government elections in 1920 and in the election for the second Dáil in 1921.

161. Lyons, *Ireland Since the Famine,* p. 451. Macardle, *The Irish Republic,* p. 956; Ernest Blythe, "Birth Pangs of a Nation," *Irish Times,* Nov. 19–20, 1968.

162. Duggan, "Last Days of Dublin Castle," pp. 187–90; P. R. O., 30/50/part 5, *Sturgis Diary,* Jan. 15, Jan. 18, 1922.

Sinn Fein's constitutionalism was perhaps best demonstrated by the successful conduct of its administrative and judicial systems. The systems gave satisfaction to Nationalists and southern Unionists alike, and they convinced British public opinion that Sinn Fein could conduct the administration of services with due regard for property and minority rights. As far as the existing system was concerned, Sinn Fein used rhetoric to discredit Dublin Castle's administration, and the IRA used force to destroy its facilities in the country. Nevertheless, Sinn Fein's distinction between those officials who were administering services and those who were performing political work demonstrated that the Republicans appreciated the transformation that had taken place in the character of the Irish administration's personnel. During the truce negotiations and treaty debate in the Dáil, the position of the Irish officials whom the new government was about to inherit was not a controversial topic. This was because the majority of officials were Nationalists—perhaps even in northeast Ulster, as Craig discovered when he began to establish his administration. Although Craig eventually obtained the type of personnel for Northern Ireland that he wanted—its officials were predominantly Unionist and Protestant from top to bottom—only some three hundred officials volunteered to go to Northern Ireland, including just five members of the bureaucratic elite and about twenty professional staff members. The vast majority of Irish civil servants wanted no connection with the Northern government.

The Dáil's leaders realized that the officials they inherited were professionals who would play an essential part in the successful administration of the new state's business. The day after they assumed control of the Irish administration, the Provisional Government issued a proclamation banning any further transfer of officials. The anti-Castle rhetoric, which had served Sinn Fein and their Nationalist forebears so well, stopped. The bureaucrats, in turn, were prepared to serve the new generation of politicians loyally in the years that lay ahead.

Epilogue

According to the treaty the Free State was to come officially into being on December 6, 1922. From the outset of the transfer, Michael Collins, the chairman of the Provisional Government and minister for finance in the prospective Free State ministry, used issues relating to the Irish civil administration to stabilize his government politically and to hamper the further development of the civil administration in Northern Ireland. The Provisional Government's first step in this direction was to indicate that it was in de facto and de jure control of the administration, the courts, and all personnel. On January 17, 1922, the Provisional Government ordered all courts, corporations, councils, departments of state, boards, judges, officers of the peace, and all public servants and functionaries from the old regime to continue to carry out their functions "unless and until otherwise ordered by us. . . ."[1] The order went on to prohibit new appointments and alterations of the employment status of any officer, servant, employee, or functionary of the state without the specific authority of the Provisional Government or a minister who acted on its authority. The proclamation concluded with a prohibition against removing, tampering with, or destroying records in Irish departments and their branch offices. The following day Collins distributed the responsibility for the Irish administration among six ministers of state: home affairs, economic affairs, agriculture, education, local government, and labour. Later in the year, Timothy Healy, the former member of the Irish Parliamentary party who had switched his allegiance to Sinn Fein after 1918, was named the first governor-general of the Irish Free State. With the exception of W. T. Cosgrave, the minister for local government, the new ministers had no experience in civil administration. The ministry established its headquarters in Leinster House.

1. The complete proclamation is cited in McColgan, *British Policy and the Irish Administration, 1920–1922,* pp. 96–97.

The transfer of services was a complex process because it involved several interest groups, each with its special concerns.[2] The British Treasury officials in Dublin were led by A. P. Waterfield, who worked diligently to solve technical, legal, and constitutional problems related to the transfer of individual Irish departments from British departments and Dublin Castle to the control of Irish ministers in the Free State and Northern Ireland. Preparations for the transfer also involved A. W. Cope and, to a lesser extent, James MacMahon. Joseph Brennan, the first division clerk in the Chief Secretary's Office, became the comptroller and auditor-general for the Provisional Government, and eventually was named permanent secretary of the Department of Finance. James Craig and Ernest Clark remained the chief spokesmen for the North's fledging administration; Dawson Bates, the North's minister for home affairs, played an important role in selecting its personnel.[3]

Waterfield was at the center of the transfer. His chief task in regard to Northern Ireland was to prevent that government from exercising its option to opt out of the Free State before December 6. During 1922 Craig's government continued to have difficulty in securing civil service personnel. Although the handful of civil servants who volunteered for service in the North made their way to Belfast in March, thereby bringing the total number of volunteers to about 350, Collins refused to sanction any further allocation of staff to the North. Moreover, his Provisional Government did not participate in any joint tribunals that worked on the transfer of services. In May the Irish ministers for agriculture and education prepared obstructive and noncooperative policies to undermine Northern Ireland's control over its schools and its ability to conduct land transactions. Clark complained about Collins's intransigence on administrative matters, but Waterfield kept the transfer on schedule.[4] By the end of the year the Northern government began to constitute its civil service from the ground up. Using the transferred officials as a nucleus, Craig and his ministers turned to the applications they had received in 1921 to fill the rank and file positions.

2. Ibid., pp. 90–131.

3. Ronan Fanning, *The Irish Department of Finance, 1922–58* (Dublin: Institute of Public Administration), pp. 30–58; Patrick Buckland, *Factory of Grievances: Devolved Government in Northern Ireland, 1921–39* (Dublin: Barnes and Noble, 1979), p. 205.

4. McColgan, *British Policy,* pp. 110–21.

Many of the North's new civil servants received rapid promotions because of the lack of experienced officials.[5] Nevertheless the administrative system that developed in the North was well organized and its officials were efficient.[6]

There was, however, a consistent pattern of deliberate discrimination against Catholics in the North's administrative appointments and promotions at all levels. Although Craig hoped to appoint some Catholics to the civil administration, the bureaucracy became almost the exclusive preserve of Protestant officials. Once in place the members of the new bureaucratic elite in the North followed the long tradition in the Irish civil administration of selecting their subordinates. Given that the nucleus of the North's bureaucratic elite was overwhelmingly Protestant and Unionist, the top subordinates and the professional staff officers were bound to reflect these two characteristics. Rank and file administrative positions were also filled largely by Protestants. Studies conducted as early as 1927 and later, in 1959, found that 94 percent of Northern Ireland's civil servants in clerical ranks, from the grade of deputy to assistant principal, were Protestants, although Protestants made up about 65 percent of the total population in northeast Ulster.[7] Exact figures for the rank and file positions after 1960 are difficult to determine, but current estimates of the percentage of Catholic civil servants vary between twelve and twenty percent of the whole.[8] Protestants increased their hold on all the senior positions—permanent, second, and assistant secretaries—from 89 percent to 96 percent between 1927 and 1959.[9] The figure for Protestant department heads was

5. Government of Northern Ireland, Command Papers, Cmd. 117, 1930, *Report of the Ministry of Finance* (1927–1929), 35–47; Government of Northern Ireland, Command Papers, Cmd. 116, 1930, *Report of the Departmental Committee on Civil Service Re-Grading*, 1–11.

6. Government of Northern Ireland, Command Papers, Cmd. 66, 1926, *Report of Sir R. R. Scott on the Civil Service of Northern Ireland*, 2–5.

7. John Darby, *Conflict in Northern Ireland: The Development of a Polarized Community* (Dublin: Gill and Macmillan, 1976), p. 66. For similar figures for the period 1935–50 see, All-Party Anti-Partition Conference, *Discrimination: A Study in Injustice to a Minority* (Dublin: All-Party Anti-Partition Conference, 1950).

8. *Chicago Reader*, Oct. 12, 1984, "Northern Ireland," citing an independent agency in the North, the Fair Employment Agency, p. 38.

9. Darby, *Conflict in Northern Ireland*, pp. 66. A press notice from the Northern Ireland Office in 1973 reported that Catholics held about 15 percent of the senior positions in the civil service.

92 percent in 1983.[10] Appointments to the judicial system in the North have followed the same pattern, although charges of religious or political bias in the criminal justice system are generally leveled more against the police than the judges and court officers.[11] Fighting this sort of discrimination has been a prominent part of the Catholic civil rights movement in Northern Ireland. It will take either a substantial measure of so-called reverse discrimination against Protestant officials or a long period of fair employment and promotion practices before Catholics are represented in the civil administration in numbers that approximate their position in the population.

Approximately twenty-one thousand officials remained in the Free State. Nearly fifteen thousand of these were postal clerks, subpostmasters, and postmen. About fifteen hundred more were part-time and temporary officers. The remainder, some forty-five hundred, formed the bulk of what is generally called the civil service.[12] During 1922 control over the departments was loose and day-to-day administration remained firmly in the hands of the department heads and their staffs.[13] However revolutionary the transfer of services was to be in conditioning the political development of the state, the Provisional Government did not cause any immediate disturbance of any fundamental kind in the daily work of the average civil servant.[14] Maintaining the delivery of services was especially important to the Provisional Government because from May 1922 through May 1923 it was combatting anti-Treaty forces in the Irish civil war.

The bureaucratic elite, which included about sixty-five individuals in 1921, remained largely intact and in place. Forty-nine of these officials retained their positions. Five others had transferred to Northern Ireland, and four had returned to England. There were seven vacancies, including three important ones: the resident commissionership of national education, the vice presidency of the Local Government Board, and the secretary of the General Post Office. The first two had not been

10. *Reader,* "Northern Ireland," p. 38.

11. Darby, *Conflict in Northern Ireland,* pp. 63–65.

12. Saorstat Eireann, *Commission of Inquiry into the Civil Service, 1932–35,* II, "Memoranda of Evidence, General Memorandum furnished by the Department of Finance on the Civil Service," 13–14.

13. McColgan, *British Policy and the Irish Administration,* pp. 99–104.

14. *Commission of Inquiry into the Civil Service,* 3:61–65.

filled, but the Provisional Government's postmaster general appointed P. S. O'Hegarty, a former postal clerk and a Sinn Fein publicist, to the secretary's position early in 1922.[15] The appointment alarmed the British Treasury officials, and, no doubt, many Irish civil servants who feared that men without meaningful experience would be rewarded for their political activities rather than for their administrative talents and professional achievements. Their apprehension probably increased when some two hundred of the approximately eight hundred Dáil civil servants were merged into the existing civil service.[16]

The bureaucratic elite began to break up shortly after the official transfer took place. Of the forty-nine top officials who served under the Provisional Government during 1922, twelve had reached retirement age. They left public service when Cosgrave's government, which defeated its rivals in the civil war, reorganized the Irish bureaucracy in 1923. Fourteen more members of the old elite either retired or died in office between 1924 and 1932, the year of the first change of government in the Free State. About half of the members of the old bureaucratic elite continued to serve beyond 1932. Personnel lists in Irish directories reveal that as the members of the bureaucratic elite retired, they were replaced by men from within their respective departments.

Turning to the middle and lower echelons of the civil service, only 39 officials retired in consequence of the initial change to the Provisional Government in January 1922. Within two years, however, nearly 900 of the 21,000 officials retired: 689 in 1923 and 209 more in 1924.[17] Many of them were past age sixty-five, and they were ready to retire now that the transition period was completed. For others, the Free State's reorganization of the administration in 1923 provided an excellent opportunity to bow out and still take advantage of the enhanced pension terms offered to officials who retired because of the change in government under the Government of Ireland Act and the treaty.

15. McColgan, *British Policy and the Irish Administration,* pp. 97–98.

16. State Paper Office, Ireland, *Minute Book of the Irish Free State, Second Executive Council,* Vol. 1, No. C. 2/49, Feb. 9, 1924, No. C. 2/130, Sept. 27, 1924; Vol. 2 (G. 2/4), No. C. 2/159, Jan. 2, 1925, S.P.O. file number S. 3406.

17. Saorstat Eireann, *Commission of Inquiry into the Civil Service, 1932–35,* I, "Third Appendix to the Final Report, (a) Number of Retirements Under Article 10 of the Treaty during each of the five years 1922 to 1934," 138. When the Free State Government declared in 1929 that it would not honor any more claims from civil servants who wished to retire under Article 10, 286 more officials retired.

Working conditions were difficult for the officials who served in the Irish Free State during the 1920s and 1930s. There were bans on hiring and promotions. No compensation was paid to them for work performed that was beyond one's grading, and there were decreases in the civil service bonus. Salary increments were low and failed to keep pace with increases in the cost of living. Finally, the Whitley Councils, which had been established in 1919 to protect the rights of public employees, were abolished in the Irish civil service in 1924.[18]

The reorganization of the bureaucracy in 1923 placed additional burdens on civil servants in several departments. For example, when the intermediate and primary schools' education departments were consolidated, the officials revised curriculum and overhauled examination procedures.[19] At the Land Commission, officials took on additional responsibilities when the Congested Districts Board was abolished and when new land legislation created some eighty thousand additional peasant proprietors. The commission conducted an average of ten thousand transactions a year after 1922, an annual addition of some two thousand purchases over previous years.[20] The Department of Posts and Telegraphs, which remained the largest department, was reduced by 1931 to some twelve thousand workers.[21] Four other old departments, the Local Government Board, the Department of Agriculture and Technical Instruction (DATI), the Dublin Metropolitan Police, and the Royal Irish Constabulary, were abolished. DATI officials were reassigned to the new Department of Agriculture and to the new Department of Fisheries.[22] DATI educational functions were given to Irish universities. Local Government Board officials were also transferred to a new department, the Department of Local Affairs. The work load was enormous in that new department because of the sweeping reforms instituted in the management of local government bodies, hospitals, and facilities for the poor.[23] The constabulary was disbanded

18. *An Peann,* 1, No. 1 (Sept. 1927), 1. *An Peann* was the official organ of the Civil Service Clerical Association. *Scientific Service: Journal of the Institute of Professional Civil Servants,* 1, no. 1 (Spring 1950), reprinted the Second and Third Annual Reports of the Council of the Institute of Mar. 31, 1922 and Mar. 28, 1923, 39–41.

19. "Saorstat Eireann, Irish Free State, 1921–1931, A Decade of Progress," supplement to the *Irish Times,* Jan. 21, 1932. See pp. 43–44.

20. Ibid., p. 21.

21. Ibid., p. 49.

22. Ibid., pp. 13–15, 22.

23. Ibid., p. 39.

early in 1922. The Provisional Government organized an unarmed police force, Garda Siochana, which began recruiting its officers in February 1922. The Dáil set its complement at approximately sixty-four hundred officers and men in 1924. The Dublin police force was amalgamated into the Garda in 1925 and the combined body of some seventy-two hundred officers and men were placed under one commissioner.[24]

The position of minorities in the Irish Free State's civil administration was secure. The top forty-nine officials who transferred to the Free State in 1922 were about evenly divided between Catholics and Protestants, perhaps with the Catholics holding a slight majority. The professional staff of some sixteen hundred positions was also about evenly divided, perhaps with Protestants enjoying a slight majority. The rank and file positions were largely occupied by Catholics. In 1924 the Civil Service Commission, which included the speaker of the Dáil and two high-ranking civil servants, devised regulations for appointing officials. The system has been fair, although on occasion government ministers who are going out of power have helped members of their staff advance to important positions in the civil service and in the judicial system.[25]

The transfer of the judicial system and the justices and court officials to the Irish Free State was also part of the transition process. During the treaty negotiations the British promised to hand over the judicial system to the new government in good working order. During 1922 the Treasury officials worked with the Provisional Government to achieve a smooth transfer. The Dáil dissolved its judicial system. Within weeks of the transfer date, the Free State appointed a commission to recommend changes in the judicial system it had inherited, which it characterized as "a standing monument to alien government."[26] In 1924 the Supreme Court of Southern Ireland was reorganized. Six of the eight judges who had transferred to the Free State retired, and the other two retired the following year. Ten new men were appointed. All but one, a law professor, had been associated with the old legal system

24. Eire, *Commission on the Garda Siochana, Report on Remuneration and Conditions of Service,* Prl. No. 933, 1970, pp. 23–24.

25. Mark Osborne, "Machinery of Government—No. 3," *The Bell,* 13 (1946–1947), 23–24; *Hibernia,* "Full Patronage Tally," "Liam Congrave's Galley of Greed," July 22–Aug. 4, 1977, pp. 1, 4–5.

26. Cited in Delany, *Christopher Palles,* p. 2.

as county court judges, recorders, or court officers. Two were descendants of former Irish justices; one had served the old regime as judicial land commissioner. Eight of the ten new justices were Catholics, a ratio that was maintained for at least fifty years.[27] The court's ten leading administrative officers, who had all transferred to the Free State in 1922, remained in their places after the reorganization.

In 1926 the Free State instituted more judicial reforms. The old method of appointing the court's top administrative officers through the Law Office's patronage was abolished and replaced by open competition examinations, as in the civil service.[28] Henceforth officers in the Free State's court system reported to the minister of justice instead of the chief justice of the supreme court, who had replaced the lord chancellor at the time of the transfer. The reorganization of the system was extended to local and county courts, too. Circuit courts replaced the county courts, and some two thousand district courts replaced the old petty sessions courts, which had been under the control of the resident magistrates and justices of the peace. Salaries were cut throughout the system—judges' salaries were reduced by about one thousand pounds per annum—and other economies were effected by abolishing selected positions as vacancies occurred. Court officials, along with the thousands of other civil servants who decided to transfer to the Free State, crowded into classrooms to meet a requirement that all public officials must learn the Irish language. Finally, much of the nineteenth-century court ritual was abolished, although the Free State government moved quickly to rebuild the Four Courts building, which had been destroyed in the opening phase of Irish civil war.[29] The rebuilt structure was less than faithful to the original and much of the majesty of the old building was lost. Nevertheless, in the years after independence a body of Irish case law took shape in the Four Courts.[30] Administrative law and land law have been important parts of the shaping of a new legal tradition in the Republic.[31]

27. J. M. Kelly, Review of V. T. H. Delany's *Administration of Justice in Ireland,* in *Administration,* 11 (Spring 1963), 88–90.

28. "Saorstat Eireann," in the *Irish Times,* pp. 8–10.

29. Ibid., p. 10.

30. G. M. Golding, *George Gavin Duffy, 1882–1951* (Dublin: Irish Academic Press, 1982).

31. T. J. Barrington, "Resolving Disputes in Ireland," a review of Ronald M. Stout's

Between 1892 and 1914 Irish administrative personnel were transformed in ways that had a direct bearing on the development of the modern Irish state. The administrative personnel had become professionalized, in that they were prepared to serve the legally constituted government. The administration itself had largely overcome the two most divisive factors in Irish life, religion and politics. This transformation was important to the Irish Free State, and later, to the Irish Republic. In any democratic state administrative personnel must obey rules of procedure and be fair and impartial; they must be competent and effective in solving problems and preserving human rights; and they must do all of these things with the support and participation of the citizens.[32] The slow change in the religious affiliation and political orientation of Irish civil servants, from Protestant to Catholic, and from Unionist to Nationalist, conditioned the development of these imperatives for the operation of a civil administration in a participatory Irish democracy. As professionals, the Irish officials were as ready to serve a home rule government in 1914, when it appeared that John Redmond would become the first Irish prime minister, as they were in 1922, when the overwhelming majority of them transferred to the Irish Free State. They served loyally under its first ministers, and when Eamon De Valera and the Fianna Fáil party succeeded Cosgrave and the Cumann na nGaedheal (the protreaty party) in March 1932, there was no disruption of the Irish officials.[33] The transformation was complete.

Administrative Law in Ireland (Dublin: Institute of Public Administration, 1986), in *Irish Literary Supplement,* Fall 1987; New Ireland Forum, "The Legal Systems, North and South," pp. 16–36.

32. T. J. Barrington, *The Irish Administrative System* (Dublin: Institute for Public Administration, 1980), pp. 1–29, 199–208, 221. See also Barrington, "Public Administration, 1927–1936," in *Administration,* 13, No. 4 (1965), 316–23.

33. Terrence de Vere White, "Social Life in Ireland," in *Years of the Great Test, 1926–1939,* ed. Francis MacManus (Cork: Mercier Press, 1967), pp. 19–29; T. Desmond Williams, "De Valera in Power," in *The Years of the Great Test,* p. 39; *An Peann,* V, 6 (March 1932), 320.

Bibiliography

Unpublished Manuscript Sources

Ireland

Dublin Diocesan Archives, Dublin

William Walsh Papers

King's Inns Library, Dublin

"The Reminiscences" of Lord Shandon, Lord Chancellor of Ireland (Ignatius O'Brien)

National Library of Ireland, Dublin

Bodkin Papers
Bryce Papers
Gill Papers
Green Papers
O'Brien Papers
Redmond Papers
Sheehy-Skeffington Papers
Minute Book of the Irish Parliamentary Party

Public Record Office, Dublin

Index of Wills

State Paper Office, Dublin

Chief Secretary's Office Files and General Register
Minute Book of the Provisional Government and Irish Free State Executive Council

Trinity College, Dublin

Dillon Papers
Minute Book of the Irish Parliamentary Party

England

British Library, London

Balfour Papers
Campbell-Bannerman Papers
Gladstone Papers
Ripon Papers

House of Lords Record Office, London

Ashbourne Papers
Cadogan Papers
Law Papers
Lloyd George Papers

London School of Economics, London

Harrel *Autobiography*

Public Record Office, London

Anderson Papers
Cabinet Office files and minutes
Colonial Office files
Diary of Mark Sturgis
Treasury Outletters (Ireland)

Bodleian Library, Oxford

Asquith Papers
Birrell Papers
Bryce Papers
MacDonnell Papers
Nathan Papers
Strathcarron Papers

Plunkett Foundation for Cooperative Studies, Oxford

Diaries of Sir Horace Plunkett
Plunkett Papers

Scotland

Haddo House, Tarves

Aberdeen Papers

National Library of Scotland, Edinburgh

Rosebery Papers

Scottish Record Office and General Register House, Edinburgh

Index to Balfour Papers at Whittinghame

Public Documents

Chief Secretary for Ireland. *Memorandum as to the organization and staff of the Chief Secretary's Office and other Departments connected with the Irish Government.* Dublin: HMSO, 1913.

Chief Secretary's Office, Dublin Castle. *Irish newscuttings with some annotations, 1880–1920.* Dublin: Bound by the National Library of Ireland.

Dáil Eireann. The constructive work of *Dáil Eireann.* No. 1. The National Police and Courts of Justice. (Ministry of Home Affairs.) No. 2 (In three sections) I.—The Department of Agriculture and the Land Settlement Commission. II.—The Commission of Inquiry into the resources and industries of Ireland. III.—The Department of Trade and Commerce. Edited by Erskine Childers. Dublin: Talbot Press, 1921.

———. *Official Report: Debate on the Treaty Between Great Britain and*

Ireland Signed in London on December 6, 1921. Dublin: Talbot Press, 1922.

Eire. Commission on the Garda Siochana. *Report on Remuneration and Conditions of Service.* Prl. No. 933, 1970.

Government of Northern Ireland. *Report of Sir R. R. Scott on the Civil Service of Northern Ireland.* Cmd. 66, 1926.

———. *Report of the Ministry of Finance (1927–1929).* Cmd. 117, 1930.

———. *Report of the Departmental Committee on Civil Service Re-Grading.* Cmd. 116, 1930.

Great Britain. *Parliamentary Debates* (Fourth Series, Fifth Series).

———. *Parliamentary Papers.* 1907, Vol. 22, H. C. paper 45. "Return setting forth the name, age, length of service, and official position, of all salaried officials in the various government departments in Ireland who have been appointed (a) by nomination without examination; (b) by nomination with limited competition; (c) by nomination with a qualifying examination."

———. 1912–13, Vol. 2, Bill 347. "Government of Ireland Bill (As Amended in Committee and on Report)."

———. Vol. 56, H. C. Paper 104. "Return showing as regards public service departments in Scotland and Ireland, and departments stationed in England which deal wholly with Scottish or Irish affairs, the number of established and unestablished officials employed on the 31st of March, 1911, together with the number of such officials in receipt of salaries of 160 per annum or more, with a note showing what departments are partially engaged in Scottish or Irish affairs by means of officials having their headquarters in England."

———. *Parliamentary Papers.* 1912–13, Vol. 56, H. C. paper 454. "Return setting forth the name, age, date of appointment, salary, address at time of appointment and occupation for the five years preceding the appointment, of each person appointed without competitive examination to any position in the public service during the period from the 29th day of June 1895 to the 5th day of December 1905, with an annual salary of 100 and upwards, specifying separately the appointments for England, Wales, Scotland, and Ireland."

———. Vol. 56, H.C. papers 454, 455, and 528. "Return setting forth the name, age, date of appointment, salary, address at time of appointment, of each person appointed without competitive examination to any position in the public service from the 5th day of December 1905, with an annual salary of 100 and upwards, specifying separately the appointments for England, Wales, Scotland, and Ireland."

———. 1914, Vol. 16, H.C., Cmd. 7340. Royal Commission on Civil Service, 4th Report, "Minutes of Evidence."

———. 1916, Vol. 11, Cmd. 8311. Royal Commission on the Rebellion of Ireland, "Minutes of Evidence and Appendix of Documents."

———. 1918, Vol. 10, Cmd. 9019. "Report of the Proceedings of the Irish Convention."

Saorstat Eireann. *Commission of Inquiry into the Civil Service, 1932–35.* R./54.

Newspapers and Periodicals

An Claideamh Soluis
Belfast Morning News
Belfast News-Letter
Catholic Bulletin
Cork Constitution
Cork Examiner
Daily Express
Dublin Figaro
Dublin Opinion
Freeman's Journal
Hibernia
Irish Catholic
Irish Figaro
Irish Independent
Irish Life
Irish Statesman
Irish Times
Leader
Lepracaun
Lyceum
Nation
New Ireland Review
New Irish Jurist and Local Government Review
Northern Star
Sinn Fein Weekly
Spark
Times (London)
United Irishman

Miscellaneous Periodicals, Directories, and Yearbooks

An Peann
Capuchin Annual
Civil Service Review
Civil Service Staff Officer
Dictionary of National Biography
Freemason's Calendar for Ireland
Palmer's Index to the Times Newspaper
Scientific Service: Journal of the Institute of Professional Civil Servants
Thom's Irish Who's Who
Thom's Official Directory
Who Was Who

Books and Articles by Contemporaries

Addison, Christopher. *Politics from Within, 1911–1918.* Vol. 2. London: Herbert Jenkins, Ltd., 1924.

All-For-Ireland League. *Home Rule by Consent, the Proposals of the All-For-Ireland League, Speeches by . . . Dunraven . . . O'Brien . . . Healy . . . in City Hall, Cork, March 1, 1913.* No city, n.d.

American Commission on Conditions in Ireland. *Interim Report.* (British Edition.) London: Harding & Moore, Ltd., 1921.

The Ancient Order of Hibernians. *The Irish Party, Its Records and Achievements.* Dublin: The Ancient Order of Hibernians Press Bureau, 1919.

Arthur Griffith, A Study of the Originator of the Sinn Fein Movement. Dublin: Cahill [1917].

Askin, Paul. *Orangeism, What it is, and What it is not: A Lecture.* Dublin: Church of Ireland Printing and Publishing Co., Ltd., 1896.

Atkinson, John. *Speeches on Devolution.* Dublin: Irish Unionist Alliance, 1904.

Bagenal, Philip. *The Priest in Politics.* London: Hutchinson and Co., 1893.

Ball, F. Elrington. *The Judges in Ireland, 1221–1921.* London: John Murray, 1926.

Barker, Ernest. *Ireland in the Last Fifty Years.* Oxford: Clarendon Press, 1917.

Berkeley, G. F. M. "The Present System of Government in Ireland" in J. H. Morgan, ed., *Home Rule Problems.* London: P. S. King & Son, 1911.

Birrell, Augustine. *Things Past Redress.* London: Faber & Faber, Ltd., 1937.

Blunt, Wilfred Scawen. *My Diaries, Being a Personal Narrative of Events, 1888–1914.* 2 vols. New York: Alfred A. Knopf, 1921.

Bodkin, Mathew. *A County Court Judge on the Lawlessness of the Forces of the Crown in Ireland.* London: Peace with Ireland Council, 1921.

Brooks, Sydney. *The New Ireland.* Dublin: Maunsel & Co., Ltd., 1907.

Campbell, James. "Judiciary" and "Police" in *Against Home Rule: The Case for Union.* London: Frederick Warne & Co., 1912.

Childers, Erskine. *The Home Rule Bills of 1886 and 1893 Compared and Explained.* Westminster: Irish Press Agency, 1893.

Clancy, John J. *Six Months of "Unionist" Rule.* London: The Irish Press Agency, 1887.

Colles, Ramsay. *In Castle and Court House, Being Reminiscences of 30 Years in Ireland.* London: T. Werner Laurie, 1911.

Conlon, Lil. *Cumann na mBan and the Women of Ireland.* Kilkenny: Kilkenny People, Ltd., 1969.

Connolly, James. *The Re-Conquest of Ireland.* Dublin: Liberty Hall, 1915.

Davitt, Michael. *The Fall of Feudalism in Ireland.* Dublin: Macmillan & Co., 1904.

———. "The Irish National Assembly (Session of 1910)." *Independent Review* 5 (April 1905): 284–98.

Dicey, A. V. *A Leap in the Dark or Our New Constitution.* London: John Murray, 1893.

Does Home Rule Mean Rome Rule? By "R. J. S." London: Harrison and Sons, 1892.

Donovan, Robert. "The Situation in Ireland." *Independent Review* 7 (March 1906): 306–12.

Dowden, Edward. *Irish Unionists and the Present Administration.* Dublin: Irish Unionist Alliance, 1904.

Duggan, C. J. "The Last Days of Dublin Castle." *Blackwood's Magazine* 222 (August 1922): 137–90.

Dunraven, Earl of. *Past Times and Pastimes.* Vol. 2. London: Hodder and Stoughton, Ltd., 1921.

———. *The Outlook in Ireland.* Dublin, 1904.

"Editorial on the appointment of Mr. Duke as Chief Secretary for Ireland and the re-establishment of the Dublin Castle Regime." *Catholic Bulletin* 6 (November 1916): 581–87.

Emmet, T. A. *Ireland Under English Rule, or a Plea for the Plaintiff.* 2 vols. New York and London: G. P. Putnam's Sons, 1903.

Field, William. "How Ireland Suffers Under Centralized Departments." *The New Ireland Review* 20 (February 1904): 338–48.

———. *Ireland and Imperial Expenditure: More Light on the Financial Relations Questions: How Ireland Is Drained Through Government Departments: Suggested Economies, Remedies, Reforms.* Dublin: *An Clo-Cumann,* Ltd., 1906.

———. *Treasury Tactics.* Dublin: James Duffy and Co., Ltd., 1907.

Filleul, P. V. M. *Mr. Gladstone's Home Rule Bill.* Weston-Super-Mare: Lawrence and Lawrence, 1893.

Fitzgerald, Percy. *Recollections of Dublin Castle & of Dublin Society, by "A Native."* London: Chatto & Windus, 1902.

Friends of Irish Freedom. *Ireland's elected government, a History of Dáil Eireann.* Washington: Friends of Irish Freedom National Bureau of Information, August 1920.

Gallagher, Frank [Hogan, David]. *The Four Glorious Years.* Dublin: Irish Press, Ltd., 1953.

Gallagher, M. F. "The Fateful Week." *Administration* 14 (Summer 1966): 171–85.

Gavan Duffy, Charles. *Young Ireland.* Dublin: M. H. Gill & Son, 1884.

General Committee of Irish Civil Servants. *Statements as by the General Committee of Irish Civil Servants as to their position in view of the further legislation affecting the government of Ireland.* Dublin: Printed at the Committee's expense, 1917.

Good, James Winder. *Ulster and Ireland.* Dublin and London: Maunsel and Co., Ltd., 1919.

Green, Alice Stopford. "The Case of Sir Antony MacDonnell." *Independent Review* 6 (July 1905): 12–26.

———. *Ourselves Alone in Ulster.* Dublin and London: Maunsel & Company, Ltd., 1918.

Grievances in Ireland. By "One of the Tolerant Majority." Dublin: James Duffy & Co., Ltd., 1913.

Griffith, Arthur. *The Resurrection of Hungary: A Parallel for Ireland.* Dublin: James Duffy & Co., Ltd., 1904.

———. *The Sinn Fein Policy.* Dublin: James Duffy & Co., Ltd., 1906.

Gwynn, Stephen. *John Redmond's Last Years.* London: Edward Arnold, 1919.

Harding, Clement. *Under the Papal Crown; or "Birrellism in Ireland."* London: Drane's, 1915.

Healy, Maurice. *The Old Munster Circuit.* Dublin: The Mercier Press, 1979.

Healy, T. M. *Why Ireland Is Not Free, A Study of Twenty Years in Politics.* Dublin: *Nation* Office, 1898.

———. *Letters and Leaders of My Day.* 2 vols. London: T. Butterworth, Ltd., 1928.

Henry, H. M. *The Evolution of Sinn Fein.* New York: B. W. Huebsch, Inc., 1920.

Hobson, Bulmer. *The Creed of the Republic.* Belfast: The Republican Press, 1907.

———. *Defensive Warfare: A Handbook for Irish Nationalists.* Belfast: The West Belfast Branch of Sinn Fein, 1909.

Hocking, Joseph. *Is Home Rule Rome Rule?* London: Ward, Lock & Co., Ltd., 1912.

Hogan, J. F. "The Essays of Augustine Birrell." *Irish Ecclesiastical Record* 21 (1907): 267–68.

Home Rule Union. *Pamphlets.* London: Home Rule Union, 1893.

Imperial Protestant Federation. *Grievances from Ireland.* Vol. 2, No. 17. London: Imperial Protestant Federation, June 1906.

Ireland a Nation! The Diary of an Irish Cabinet Minister: Being the History of the First (and Only) Irish National Administration, 1894. By "Phineas O'Flannagan." Belfast: Olley & Company, Ltd. 1893.

Ireland from one or two neglected points of view from the author of "Hints to Country Bumkins. (London: Hatchards, 1889).

Irish Centre Party. *The Irish Centre Party: Objects of the Party.* Dublin: Irish Centre Party, 1919.

The Irish National Ideal: An Open Letter. By "Devonia." London: *Grievances from Ireland* Office, 1907.

Irish Press Agency. *What Home Rule Means and Other Leaflets Issued by the Irish Press Agency.* Vols. 1–2. Dublin: Maunsel & Co., Ltd., 1912.

Irish Unionist Alliance. *The Irish Unionist Alliance: Its Work and Organisation.* Dublin: IUA, 1893.

———. *The New Home Rule and Its Contemporary Associations and Considerations.* Dublin: IUA, 1906–7.

———. *Pamphlets, 1906–1911.* Vols. 1–2. Dublin: IUA, 1906–11.

———. *Ireland and the Union: A Short Sketch of the Political History of Ireland.* Dublin: IUA, 1914.

Is the Irish Party Nationalist? Our Policy on the Parliamentary Question. Dublin: The New Ireland Publishing Co., Ltd., 1918.

Jones, Thomas. *Whitehall Diary,* Vol. 3: *Ireland, 1918–1925.* Edited by Keith Middlemas. London: Oxford University Press, 1971.

Kavanagh, Sean. "The Irish Volunteers' Intelligence Organisation." *Capuchin Annual* (1969), pp. 354–67.

Kay, D. L. [D. L. Kelleher]. *The Giant of Dublin.* Dublin: The Talbot Press, Ltd., 1918.

Law, Hugh A. "The Irish Question: An Essay in Explanation." *Independent Review* 12 (March 1907): 311–21.

Lecky, W. E. H. *Clerical Influences: An Essay on Irish Sectarianism and English Government.* Edited with an Introduction by W. E. G. Lloyd and F. Cruise O'Brien. Dublin: Maunsel and Co., Ltd., 1911.

Leech, H. Brougham. *A Handbook for Unionist Speakers.* Dublin: Hodges, Figgis & Co., 1910.

Lysaght, Edward E. *Sir Horace Plunkett and His Place in the Irish Nation.* Dublin and London: Maunsel & Co., Ltd., 1916.

McCarthy, Justin. *Irish Recollections.* London and New York: Hodder and Stoughton, 1911.

McCarthy, Michael J. F. *Five Years in Ireland.* London: Simpkin, Marshall, Hamilton, Kent & Co., Ltd., 1901.

———. *Priests and People in Ireland.* Dublin: Hodges, Figgis & Co., Ltd., 1902.

———. *Irish Land and Irish Liberty: A Study of the New Lords of the Soil.* London: Robert Scott, 1911.

MacNeil, J. G. Swift. *What I Have Seen and Heard.* London: 1925.

Macready, Nevil. *Annals of an Active Life.* Vol. 2. London: Hutchinson & Co., 1924.

Mahaffy, J.P. "The Romanization of Ireland," in *The Nineteenth Century and After,* 50 (July 1901): 31–43.

Micks, William L. *An Account of the Congested Districts Board for Ireland, from 1891–1923.* Dublin: Eason & Son, Ltd., 1925.

Midleton, Earl of. *Records & Reactions, 1859–1939.* London: John Murray, 1939.

Morgan, John H. *John, Viscount Morley, An Appreciation and Some Reminiscences.* London: John Murray, 1924.

Morley, John. *Recollections.* 2 vols. London: Macmillan and Co., Ltd., 1921.

Morris, William. *Present Irish Questions.* London: Grant Richards, 1901.

National Organizations in Ireland: Their Origin, Development, and Aims. London: Offices of the *Outlook,* 1907.

A New Spirit in Irish Administration, and the King: An Invitation. By "A Constitutional and Loyal Home Ruler." Westminster: P. S. King & Son, 1903.

Next Year's Ministry. By "An Irish Cabinet-Maker." Dublin: Printed by Ponsonby and Gibbs at the University Press, 1913.

Nugent, J. D. *The A.O.H. and its Critics.* Dublin: P. P. Curtis, 1911.

O'Brien, R. Barry. *England's Title in Ireland: A Letter Addressed to His Excellency the Lord Lieutenant of Ireland.* London: T. Fisher Unwin, 1905.

———. *Dublin Castle and the Irish People.* 2nd ed. London: Kegan Paul, Trench, Tribner & Co., Ltd., 1912.

O'Brien, William. *Irish Ideas.* London and New York: Longmans, Green, and Co., 1893.

———. *The Irish National Question and the Land Act.* Dublin: *Irish People* Office, 1903.

———. *Recollections.* New York and London: The Macmillan Company, 1905.

———. *Sinn Fein and Its Enemies.* Dublin and London: Maunsel & Company, Ltd., 1917.

———. *"The Party": Who They Are and What They Have Done.* Dublin and London: Maunsel and Company, Ltd., 1917.

O'Brien, William. *The Downfall of Parliamentarianism: A Retrospect for the Accounting Day.* Dublin and London: Maunsel & Company, Ltd., 1918.

O'Connor, James. *History of Ireland, 1798–1924.* 2 vols. London: Edward Arnold & Co., 1926.

O'Donnell, F. Hugh. *Paraguay on Shannon.* London: P. S. King & Son, 1908.
———. *Political Priests and Irish Ruin: Paraguay on Shannon Up-to-Date.* London: P. S. King & Son, 1910.
O'Hegarty, P. S. *History of Ireland Under the Union, 1801–1922.* London: Methuen & Co., Ltd., 1952.
O'Mahony, Charles. *The Viceroys of Ireland.* London: John Long, Ltd., 1912.
Our Judges. By "Rhadamanthus." Dublin: *Irish Society* Office, 1890.
Peace with Ireland Council. *The Situation in Ireland: A Short History.* London: Peace with Ireland Council, 1921.
———. *Some Moderate and Non-Party Views on Affairs in Ireland.* London: Caledonian Press, Ltd., 1921.
Peel, George. *The Reign of Sir Edward Carson.* London: P. S. King & Son, 1914.
Permanent Civil Servants of the Crown Serving in Ireland. *Supplementary Statement on behalf of the Permanent Civil Servants of the Crown Serving in Ireland with Suggested Amendments to the Government of Ireland Bill, 1893.* Dublin: 1893.
Phillips, Ernest. *Irish Grievances Answered.* London: Chas. J. Thynne, 1920.
Phillips, W. Allison. *The Revolution in Ireland, 1906–1923.* London: Longmans, Green and Co., 1923.
Pim, Frederic W. *Home Rule Through Federal Devolution.* London: T. Fisher Unwin, Ltd., 1919.
Pim, Herbert Moore. *Ascendancy While You Wait.* Dublin: Irish Publicity League, [1915].
Plunkett, Horace. *Ireland in the New Century.* Popular Edition, with an Epilogue. New York: E. P. Dutton and Company, 1905.
Provincial Self-Government versus Home Rule. By "An Irish Democrat." London: Sir Isaac Pitman, 1913.
Redmond, John. *Some Arguments for Home Rule: Being a Series of Speeches Delivered in the Autumn of 1907.* Dublin: Sealy, Bryers, and Walker, 1908.
Redmond-Howard, L. G. *John Redmond, the Man and the Demand.* London: Hurst and Blackett Ltd., 1910.
Robinson, Henry. *Memories: Wise and Otherwise.* London: Cassell and Company, Ltd., 1923.
Russell, Richard. *Officialism Rampant: The Primary Antagonist of Home Rule.* London: William Reeves, 1889.
Ryan, W. P. *The Pope's Green Island.* London: James Nisbet & Co., Ltd., 1912.
Sheehan, D. D. *Ireland Since Parnell.* London: Daniel O'Connor, 1921.
Sheehy-Skeffington, F. "Michael Davitt's Unfinished Campaign, by one of his disciples." *Independent Review* 10 (July–September 1906): 298–312.
Sherwell, Arthur. *Two Years of Liberal Government, 1906–7.* London: The Liberal Publications Department, 1908.
Sinn Fein in Tabloid Form. Tract No. 1, 1917.
Smith, R. J. *Ireland's Renaissance.* Dublin: Hodges, Figgis & Co., Ltd., 1903.
Street, Cecil John Charles. *The Administration of Ireland, 1920.* New York: E. P. Dutton & Co., 1921.

———. *Ireland in 1921*. London: Philip Allan & Co., 1922.
Sullivan, A. M. *Old Ireland: Reminiscences of an Irish K.C.* Garden City, N.Y.: Doubleday, Doran & Company, Inc., 1928.
———. *The Last Sergeant*. London: MacDonald, 1952.
Synan, Arthur. "Home Rule for Beginners." *New Ireland Review* 22 (December 1904): 193–99.
———. "Half Way to Home Rule." *New Ireland Review* 24 (February 1906): 321–33.
———. "Government by Disreputables." *New Ireland Review* 25 (April 1906): 81–86.
Through Corruption to Dismemberment: A Story of Apostasy and Betrayal. By "Red Hand." Derry: Jos. Chambers [1916].
Ulster's Opportunity: A United Ireland. By "An Irish K.C." Dublin: James Duffy & Co., Ltd., 1917.
Unionist Association of Ireland. *Irish Unionist Pocket Book: Containing Radical Questions and Unionist Answers Regarding Home Rule*. Dublin and Belfast: Unionist Association of Ireland, 1911.
The Unknown Power Behind the Irish Nationalist Party. London: Swan Sonnenschein & Co., Ltd., 1907.
Wells, Warre B., and Marlowe, N. *The Irish Convention and Sinn Fein*. New York: Frederick A. Stokes Company, 1919.
Wells, Warre B. *John Redmond: A Biography*. London: Nisbet & Co., Ltd., 1919.
———. *Irish Indiscretions*. Dublin: Maunsel & Roberts, Ltd., 1923.
White, Albert C. *Self-Government and Sectarianism, Being Some Reflections on the Religious Aspects of Home Rule*. Slough: I. Day, 1914.
Wileman, William. *Rome Rule in Ireland and Civil War*. London: William Wileman, Publisher of Gospel and Protestant Literature, 1893.
Williams, Basil, ed. *How Far Ireland Is Already Separately Governed*. London: P. S. King, 1911.
———. *Home Rule Problems*. London: P. S. King, 1911.
Young, Filson. *Ireland at the Cross Road: An Essay in Explanation*. 2nd ed. London: Grant Richards, 1904.

Selected Later Works on Irish Administrative and Judicial History

Barrington, T. J. "Public Administration, 1927–1936." *Administration* 13 (1965): 316–23.
———. *The Irish Administrative System*. Dublin: The Institute for Public Administration, 1980.
Baylen, J. O. "'What Mr. Redmond Thought': An Unpublished Interview with John Redmond, December, 1906." *Irish Historical Studies* 19 (September 1974): 69–89.
Bowden, Tom. "The Breakdown of Governability in Ireland, 1919–1921." In *The Dynamics of Public Policy: A Comparative Analysis*. London: SAGE, 1976.

Boyce, D. G., and Hazelhurst, Cameron. "The Unknown Chief Secretary: H. E. Duke and Ireland, 1916–1918." *Irish Historical Studies* 20 (March 1977): 286–311.

Briggs-Davidson, John. *George Wyndham: A Study in Toryism.* London: Hodder and Stoughton, 1951.

Buckland, Patrick. *Factory of Grievances: Devolved Government in Northern Ireland, 1921–39.* London and Dublin: Barnes & Noble, 1979.

Cohan, A. S. *The Irish Political Elite.* Dublin: Gill and Macmillan Ltd., 1972.

Colvin, Ian. *Carson: The Statesman.* Vols. 2 and 3. New York: The Macmillan Company, 1935.

Curran, Joseph. *The Birth of the Irish Free State, 1921–1923.* Tuscaloosa: University of Alabama Press, 1980.

Curtis, L. P. *Coercion and Conciliation in Ireland, 1880–1892: A Study in Conservative Unionism.* Princeton, N.J.: Princeton University Press, 1963.

Darby, John. *Conflict in Northern Ireland: The Development of a Polarized Community.* Dublin: Gill and Macmillan, 1976.

Delany, V. T. H. *Christopher Palles, Lord Chief Baron of Her Majesty's Court of Exchequer in Ireland, 1874–1916.* Dublin: Allen Figgis & Co., Ltd., 1960.

Fanning, Ronan. *The Irish Department of Finance, 1922–58.* Dublin: The Institute for Public Administration, 1978.

Farrell, Brian. *The Founding of Dáil Eireann.* Dublin: Gill and Macmillan, 1971.

Flanagan, Kieran. "The Chief Secretary's Office, 1853–1914: A Bureaucratic Enigma." *Irish Historical Studies,* Vol. XXIV, no. 94 (November 1984): 197–225.

French, Gerald. *The Life of Field-Martial Sir John French.* London: Cassell and Company, Ltd., 1931.

Hepburn, A. C. "The Irish Council Bill and the Fall of Antony MacDonnell, 1906–1907." *Irish Historical Studies* 17 (September 1971): 474–90.

Hogan, Daire. *The Legal Profession in Ireland, 1789–1922.* Dublin: The Incorporated Law Society of Ireland, 1986.

Hyland, Aine. "The Treasury and Irish Education, 1850–1922: The Myth and The Reality," in *Irish Educational Studies,* Vol. 3, No. 2 (1983): 57–82.

Kelly, J. M. Review of V. T. H. Delany's *Administration of Justice in Ireland. Administration* 11 (Spring 1960): 88–90.

McColgan, John. "Implementing the 1921 Treaty: Lionel Curtis and Constitutional Procedure." *Irish Historical Studies* 20 (March 1977): 312–33.

———. *British Policy and the Irish Administration, 1920–22.* London: Allen & Unwin, 1982.

McDowell, R. B. *The Irish Administration, 1801–1914.* London: Routledge & Kegan Paul, 1964.

MacKail, J. W., and Guy Wyndham. *Life and Letters of George Wyndham.* 2 vols. London: Hutchinson & Co., 1925.

Mathuna, S. O. "The Christian Brothers and the Civil Service." *Administration* 3 (1955): 69–74.

New Ireland Forum. *The Legal Systems: North and South.* Dublin: Stationery Office, 1983.

O'Broin, Leon. *Dublin Castle and the 1916 Rising.* Dublin: Helicon Ltd., 1966.

———. *The Chief Secretary: Augustine Birrell in Ireland.* London: Chatto & Windus, 1969.

———. *Revolutionary Underground: The Story of the Irish Republican Brotherhood, 1858–1924.* Totowa, N.J.: Rowan and Littlefield, 1976.

———. "Joseph Brennan, Civil Servant Extraordinary." *Studies* 65, no. 261 (Spring 1977): 25–37.

O'Halpin, Eunan. *The Decline of the Union: British Government in Ireland, 1892–1920.* Dublin: Gill and Macmillan, 1987; Syracuse: Syracuse University Press, 1988.

Osborne, Mark. "The Machinery of Government—No. 3, The Civil Service." *The Bell* 13 (October 1946): 19–28.

Petrie, Charles. *Walter Long and His Times.* London: Hutchinson & Co., 1936.

Sheehy, Eugene. *May It Please the Court.* Dublin: C. J. Fallan, 1951.

Townshend, Charles. *The British Campaign in Ireland, 1919–1921: The Development of Political and Military Policies.* Oxford: Oxford University Press, 1975.

Index

Abbey Theatre, 34, 206
Abercorn, Duke of, 73, 74–75, 80
Aberdeen, Lady Ishbel, 40–41, 150, 155, 183
Aberdeen, Lord (John Campbell), 4, 39–40, 150, 155; appointed lord lieutenant, 124–25; resigns, 183
Act for the Prevention of Crime (1882), 271, 285
Act of Union (1801), 28, 39
Adams, Richard, 145, 237
Adams, W. G. S., 225, 251
administrative departments, *see* Irish administrative departments; Irish administration, branches of British departments in Ireland
Agriculture and Technical Instruction Act, 81
Ancient Order of Hibernians, 148, 231
An Claidheamh Soluis, 138, 149
Anderson, John, 281, 282, 286–87, 295, 300; and James Craig, 291; and Clark, 293
Anderson, Robert, 49, 61
Anderson, William, 233
Andrews, James, 300
Andrews, William, 300
anti-clerical writers, 51, 149–50
anti-Parnellites, 38, 91
army, British, in Ireland, 209, 267–68, 281; and guerrilla war, 284, 286, 288–89
Ashbourne, Lord, 71, 98; and appointments, 71, 74, 86, 88–89, 120; and judicial reform, 72, 73–74
Ashe, Thomas, 232
Asquith, Herbert H., 158, 192, 219, 228; and Birrell, 181–82; and Campbell, 195, 197–98, 207; and Carson, 179–80; and Dublin Castle administration, 181–82, 212–13; and first Coalition government, 192, 256; and Redmond, 159, 179, 193–94, 196–98, 207–8, 212, 214, 215; and reform of Parliament, 159–60. *See also* Birrell; Campbell; Carson; Coalition government (first); Redmond
assistant land commissioners, *see* Land Commission, appointments
assistant under secretaryship, 65
Association of Clerks in the Second Division, 25
Association of Post Office Clerks, 190
Atkinson, John, 71, 74, 77, 87, 89, 117, 120
attorney-generalship, 8–10
Auxiliary Division (of RIC), 284, 289

Bagwell, Richard, 80
Baily, William, 102, 128, 141, 157, 184, 206, 230
Balfour, Arthur, 49–50, 51, 57, 61, 77, 83, 136, 154; and Dudley, 118–19; and home rule debates, 172; and Long, 118–19; and Wyndham, 115–17
Balfour, Gerald, 83, 89, 95, 142; and judicial appointments, 74; and judicial reform, 75–76; and Land Act of 1896, 72–74; and local government reform, 77–78; appointed chief secretary, 71; local government appointments 80, 154; Nationalist opinion of, 77–78, 95; Unionist opinion of, 95
Balfour, Lady Betty, 82, 97
Barrie, Hugh, 195, 259–60
Barrington, T. B., x, 312n
Barry, Charles, 75
Barry, Kevin, 288
Barry, Redmond, 125, 161, 162
Barton, Dunbar Plunket, 71, 87, 89, 230
Barton, Robert, 262–63
Bates, Dawson, 305
Beard, Charles, 163
Beatty, William, 90
Belfast-Newsletter, on appointments

Belfast-Newsletter (*continued*)
before first Coalition government, 15, 150, 199; on appointments after first Coalition government, 202–3, 205, 238–39, 260, 278
Bell, Alan, 277
Benchers of the King's Inns, 10, 36
Benn, Wedgewood, 276
Best, Richard, 300
Bewley, Edmund, 87
Birrell, Augustine, appointed chief secretary, 133–34; and appointments during 1907–09, 140, 144–45, 155, 256; and appointments during 1910–15, 160–61, 185–87, 256; and appointments during first Coalition, 201–3; and Easter Rising, 209; and formation of first Coalition government, 193, 199–200; and home rule debates in 1912, 175–76; and Irish Council Bill, 134–36; legislative record, 145, 156; and Nathan, 182, 183–84, 203, 207–8; and radical Nationalists, 206–7; and Redmond, 145, 194–95, 201, 203–4; resigns, 209; and Unionists, 150–51; and university reform, 141–42. *See also* Coalition government (first); Nathan; Redmond
Birrellism, 158, 209
Black and Tans, 284, 288–89
Board of Public Works, 19, 25, 63, 112
Bodkin, Matthew, 129, 145, 146, 289
Boland, Thomas, 204–5
Bourke, Charles, 63
Boyd, Walter, 75, 76
Brennan, Joseph, 286, 305
Brooke, Frank, 277
Brown, Thomas W., 266–67, 300
Brugha, Cathal, 261, 263, 288
Bryce, James, appointed chief secretary, 124; and appointments, 125; and Irish Council Bill, 126, 131; and MacDonnell, 126–27; relationship with Nationalists, 130–31; resignation, 133
Bulfin, Edward, 278
bureaucratic elite, 10–16, 27, 35; in Irish Free State, 11, 307–8, 310; in Northern Ireland, 11, 306; political and religious characteristics in 1892, ix, 111, 306; in 1914, 190–91; in 1922, ix, 11, 307; positions held by the elite, listed, 12–13; relationship with staff, 14–15; service on boards and commissions, 27; social life, 15–16, 33; testimony at Royal Commission on the Civil Service, 25–26; training of, 14
Burtchaell, Henry, 297
Butler, William, 162
Butt, Isaac, 46n
Byrne, Joseph, 215, 227, 237, 243, 266, 267–68, 269
Byrne, William, 218, 237–38, 244, 248, 282

Cadogan, Lord, 78, 80; appointed lord lieutenant, 70–71; appointment of magistrates, 86; and appointments, 86, 89–91; and DATI, 83; and royal visits, 98; resignation, 98; and Wyndham, 96–98
Cambridge University, 14, 24
Campbell, Gordon, 260, 294
Campbell, J. H. M., 88, 89, 137, 171, 211, 283; appointed solicitor-general, 107, 108; appointed attorney-general by A. J. Balfour, 120, by Asquith, 207; appointed lord chancellor, 246; appointed lord chief justice, 224; and Asquith, 212, 219; and conscription, 242; and first Coalition government, 194–95, 196, 197–98, 203–4; and French, 249–50, 260; and Greenwood, 286, 294; and Lloyd George, 214, 224; and MacPherson, 265, 266; resigns, 294; and second Coalition government, 223–24, 237, 244, 248–49, 253–54. *See also* Asquith; French; MacPherson
Campbell, John, 85
Campbell-Bannerman, Henry, 50, 124–25, 133, 158
Carson, Edward, 71, 72, 116n, 117, 177; and first Coalition government, 193, 196, 201; and home rule debates in 1912–13, 172, 173, 174; and Government of Ireland Act (1920) debates, 276; and second Coalition government, 223, 241, 259–60, 266–67, 278; as leader of Unionist party, 170, 180; and partition talks, 213–14, 215; on proposed provisional government for Ulster, 170, 177, 180. *See also* Asquith

Catholic Association, 104, 107
Catholic bishops, 91, 138, 176, 213–14, 247, 250, 281; as board and commission members, 28; attack discrimination in appointment matters, 105–6; oppose conscription, 242, 253; and Sinn Fein, 263
Catholic officials, 68–69, 84–85, 149, 163, 189, 203, 257–58; discrimination against, 36–37, 103–5, 122–23, 147, 306–7; salaries of, 19; success on competitive examinations, 26, 37, 121–22, 189. *See also* civil servants; Nationalist officials
Cecil, Hugh, 276
Cecil, Robert, 274
Chalmers, Robert, 211, 217
Chamberlain, Austin, 175
Chamberlain, Joseph, 55
Chamberlain, Neville, 96, 178, 183, 206, 210–11, 226
Chambers, James, 199, 224, 226, 229
Cherry, R. R., 125, 162, 219
chief crown solicitorship, 10
chief secretaryship, 5–8, 11, 14
Chief Secretary's Office, clerks, in 1920–21, 286; organization of, 6–8; under French, 260, 270
Church of Ireland, 90
Churchill, Lord Randolph, 57–58
Churchill, Winston, 279, 284
civil servants, British, in Dublin Castle, 282–83, 287–88, 305, 308
civil servants, Irish, 268, 283; allocation between North and South, 275–76; and Easter Rising, 218; and guerrilla war, 268, 283–87, 294; and home rule bill (1893), 52–54; and home rule bill (1912), 175, 175n, 176; and Irish Convention (1918), 234n; and Irish Volunteers, 207; and loyalty oath, 260, 261, 291; opposed to home rule, 178; political activity of, 18, 26, 205–7, 218, 260; transfer to the Irish Free State, 304–5, 307–10; transfer to the North, 291, 297, 303; and world war, 182. *See also* bureaucratic elite; Catholic officials; Nationalist officials; professional staff officers; Protestant officials; rank and file officials; Unionist officials
Civil Service Commission, 112, 167, 200; in 1924, 310
Civil War, Irish, 307, 308, 311
Clancy, J. J., 58
Clan na Gael, 181, 208
Clark, Earnest, 291, 292–93, 297, 305
clergy, as board and commission members, 28, 45
clerkships of the crown, 203n
Coalition government, first, formed, 193–94; summarized, 219–21. *See also* Asquith; Birrell; Dillon; Redmond
Coalition government, second, formed, 222–23; summarized, 257–59. *See also* Dillon; Lloyd George; Redmond
Coercion and Arms Acts, 6, 145, 156
Coercion and Conciliation policy, 70
Coffey, Rev. Denis, 206
Collins, Michael, 263, 264, 301, 302; and civil servants, 305; and I.R.A., 284, 288; and Provisional Government, 304
Commission of National Education, 33
Commissioners of Charitable Donations and Bequests, 33
Commissioners of Intermediate Education, 33
committees of inquiry, under Balfour, 72; under Bryce, 127, 130; under Cadogan, 72; under first Coalition government, 204–5, 211; under Irish Free State, 310; under Morley, 43, 49, 72; under Northern Government, 306n; under second Coalition government, 225–26
Congested Districts Board, 45–46, 69, 204, 309
Connolly, James, 110, 206, 208
Connolly, W. P. J., 280
conscription, 222–23, 241–42, 252, 253, 256
Conservative government, and appointment of Catholics, 70, 107, 121; of 1895–1900, 91, 93–94; of 1900–05, 95, 107–9, 120–21
Conservative party, 38–39, 70, 87, 159, 160, 194; MPs in home rule debates in 1912–13, 175–76; and second Coalition government, 223
Considine, T. I., 163
Coonan, J. J., 225, 248
Cope, Alfred (Andy), 279–81, 282, 305
Cork Examiner, 252
Cosgrave, William, 263, 304, 312

county councils, 131–32, 138, 255
county courts and judges, 9, 36, 173, 191, 256, 311
court officers, clerks, ix, 37, 74, 77; clerk of the crown and hanaper, 35; listed, 34–35; masters of the courts, 32, 35; method of appointment, 35, 37; permanent secretary to the lord chancellor, 35; receivers, 35; registrars, 35; salary of, 35; social status, 35–36; taxing masters, 35; transfer to Irish Free State, 309–10; training, 35–36. *See also* Supreme Court of Judicature officials
courts-martial, 211, 285
Craig, Charles, 116, 176
Craig, James, and establishment of Northern Ireland administration, 290–92, 297–98, 305–6; and home rule debates in 1912–13, 172, 174; as prime minister of Northern Ireland, 292, 295, 305
Creedy, Herbert, 279
Criminal Inquiries Act (1919), 271
Cumann na mBan, 247, 265
Cumann na nGaedheal, 103; political party, 312
Curragh Mutiny, 178
Custom House, Dublin, 288

Dail Eireann, 303, 310, first Dail, 261–62, 276–77, 294, 302; second Dail, 295, 301; treaty debates, 301
Dail Eireann, civil administration, 261–64; officials of, 262
Dail Eireann, judicial system of, 263, 274, 277, 287, 310
DATI, *see* Department of Agriculture and Technical Instruction
Davitt, Michael, 44, 48, 76–77, 137
Dawson, W. R., 163
Deasy, James, 48
Dennehy, W. F., 150
Department of Agriculture and Technical Instruction (DATI), 17, 81, 84, 109, 309
Department of Fisheries, 309
Department of Local Affairs, 309
Department of Posts and Telegraphs, 309
deputy lord lieutenants of the counties, 3, 10, 28
De Valera, Eamon, 230, 255–56, 312; and negotiations to end guerrilla war, 295–96; as president of Dail Eireann, 261, 263, 264, 301; and treaty, 301
Devlin, Joseph, 146, 147, 178, 186, 193, 227, 230, 236
devolution crisis, 113–18
Dicey, A. V., 52
Dickie, Mary, 166
Dillon, John, 146, 157, 165, 186; as anti-Parnellite leader, 38, 65, 92, 93; and Bryce, 125–26, 128–29, 130; and devolution, 113; and Easter Rising, 208, 211–12; and first Coalition government, 193, 197, 216, 256; and Healy, 92–93; and judicial reform, 76–77; as leader of Irish Parliamentary party, 238, 240, 255–56; and MacDonnell, 99, 140; and Morley, 48; and Nathan, 184–85, 187–88, 200–1; and Plunkett, 141, 238; and Redmond, 93, 127–28, 130, 139, 200–1, 205, 209–10; and second Coalition government, 227, 233, 256. *See also* Nathan; Redmond
Dodd, William, 41, 125, 129, 140
Doran, Henry, 157
Dougherty, James, 15, 66, 144, 157, 182, 189
Downie, James, 225–26
Doyle, Daniel, 155
Dublin Castle, 2, 6, 68, 302
Dublin Metropolitan Police, 8, 17, 183–85, 204, 269, 309. *See also* police, Irish
Dudley, Lord Edward, 127; appointed lord lieutenant, 98; and devolution crisis, 113–18; and Long, 118–20
Duffy, Charles Gavin, 46n
Duggan, George, 286
Duke, Henry E., 215; and second Coalition government, 223, 225–27, 229–30, 238; and Wimbourne, 216
Dunraven, Lord, 101, 112–14

Easter Rising, 208–9, 220
Edgeworth-Johnson, Walter, 185, 243, 268, 269, 278
Edinburgh University, 14
Education, departments, 6, 8, 106; intermediate, 105, 109; national (primary), 64, 90

Edward VII, 159
Egerton, Reginald, 164
Emmet, Thomas Addis, 110–11
Ennis, Edward, 65, 144
Estates Commission, 30, 102
estates commissioners, 31, 101
Evening Telegraph, 145
examinations for the civil service, 86; open competition, 15, 21, 23, 37, 73; results of open competition, 26, 37, 104, 111, 121, 142, 189; qualifying (limited competition) examinations, 14–15, 73, 111
executive officers, Irish, *see* attorney-generalship, chief secretaryship, lord chancellorship, lord lieutenancy, solicitor-generalship

Fianna Fail party, 312
Field, William, 111–12
Finucane, Michael, 102, 128, 140, 230
Fisher, Warren, 279–82
Fitzalan, Lord, *see* Talbot
Fitzgerald, Gerald, 128
FitzGibbon, Gerald, 90, 120, 161
Flinn, D. E., 162
Fogarty, Bishop Michael, 197
Four Courts, 6, 311
Franks, John, 67, 101, 163
Freeman's Journal, comments on appointments before first Coalition government, 15, 114, 138, 145, 153, 182; comments on appointments after first Coalition government, 239–40, 245–46, 252, 289
Freemasons, *see* Masonic lodges
French, Lord John, 210; appointed lord lieutenant, 245; and appointments, 247, 249, 268, 269; and Advisory Council, 254–55, 258, 270, 277, 279; and Campbell, 249–50; and conscription; 252–53; and Lloyd George, 227, 239, 245, 253, 255; and MacMahon, 247, 254, 270, 279; and MacPherson, 265, 270, 279; and Macready, 278–79; resigns, 294; and Sinn Fein, 245, 247; and Shortt, 254–55, 279

Gaelic Athletic Association, 206
Gaelic League, 18, 138, 206, 247, 265
Gallagher, M. F., 218–19
Garda Siochana, 310
general election of 1892, 38
general election of 1895, 70
general election of 1900, 95
general election of 1906, 124
general election of 1910, 158–59, 160
general election of 1918, 255–56
General Post Office, 164, 208
General Prisons Board, 64
General Register Office, 18, 25
George V, 159
Gibbons, James, 63, 163
Gibson, John, 249
Gill, T. P., 82–86, 138, 251–52, 296
Ginnell, Laurence, 231
Gladstone, William E., 38–41, 49; and administrative reform in Ireland, 39; and Home Rule Bill (1893–94), 54, 57, 59; resigns, 61; and Ridgeway crisis, 59–61
Glynn, Joseph, 165–66, 167
Gordon, John, 195, 198, 207
Gough, Hubert, 289
Government of Ireland Act (1914), *see* Home Rule Bill (1912–14)
Government of Ireland Act (1920), 271; civil service clauses debated, 272, 274–76; introduced, 271; judicial clauses debated 272, 274; Long's committee, 252–53, 271; reaches Statute Book, 290, 293; takes effect, 295
grand jury reform, 27, 77, 107
Green, Alice Stopford, 143
Green, Max Sullivan, 145, 163, 185
Greenwood, Hamar, 282–83, 292, 294; and Anderson, 286–87, 294; appointed, 277; and Craig, 298; and French, 285; and Talbot, 294
Greer, Edward, 43
Griffith, Arthur, 92, 103, 110, 148–49, 227, 231, 236, 301–2
Guinness, W. E., 274
Gunrunning, 178, 179

Hanna, Henry, 290
Hanson, Philip, 109
Hardinge Commission, 211, 214, 216
Harrel, David, 50, 98, 100, 109, 189, 279
Harrell, William, 179, 182, 183
Harrison, Michael, 74
Harwood, R. E, 280
Headlam, Maurice, 164, 182, 286

Healy, Timothy, 122, 125, 147, 150, 164, 230; anti-Parnellite leader, 38, 77, 93; and appointment of Nationalists, 48, 92; appointed governor-general, 304; and home rule debates in 1912–13, 173, 177; and reform of judicial system, 76
Healyites, 76, 81
Hemphill, Charles H., 41
Henry, Denis, 224, 229, 249–50, 251, 265
Hewby, Thomas, 164
hierarchy, *see* Catholic bishops
Hobhouse, Charles, 186
Hobson, Bulmer, 103, 138, 148–49
Hogan, Rev. John, 106
Home Office, 184–85
Home Rule Bill (1886), and civil servants' opposition to, 53
Home Rule Bill (1893–94), 54–59; and civil service clauses, 54, 56–57; and judicial clauses, 56; and lord lieutenancy, 55–56; Nationalist approach to, 55, 57; reserved powers and services, 54; Unionist approach to, 55–56
Home Rule Bill (1912–14), Government of Ireland Act (1914), 171–77, 179–81, 274; civil service clauses, 175–77; judicial clauses, 172–73; and the lord lieutenancy, 174, 175; Nationalists attitudes, 172; and reserved services, 171, 172; suspended, 180; Unionist attitudes toward, 172
honors for officials and judges, 16, 20, 66, 98, 226
Hooper, J. P., 225
Houghton, Lord, 41, 66
Houlihan, George, 166
House of Commons, 58, 139, 152, 157, 158
House of Lords, 38, 59, 134, 135, 158, 159, 160, 177

Illingsworth, Albert, 225, 248
Incorporated Law Society of Ireland, 274
Independent Irish party, 46n
Inland Revenue, offices of, 288
Intermediate Education Office, 17, 18, 105
intermediate education reform, 23, 121, 189
Irish administration, branches of British departments in Ireland, listed, 7–8. *See also* names of individual departments
Irish administrative departments, listed, 7–8. *See also* names of individual departments
Irish Boards and Commissions, 26–28; appointment to, 27; listed, 26; personnel, 27–28; political and religious characteristics of members, 27
Irish Catholic, 18, 36, 84, 104, 150, 161
Irish Christian Brothers schools, 23
Irish Citizen Army, 206
Irish Civil Service Alliance, 299
Irish Civil Service Commission, convened, 299; proposed, 176, 234–35, 275, 292, 298
Irish Convention (1917–18), 227–28, 234–35, 240–41
Irish Council Bill (1908), 126–27, 131–39; and Birrell, 135–36; and Bryce, 131n, 132–33; introduced in House, 136; and MacDonnell, 131, 132, 136; and Nationalists, 138–39; and Redmond, 131–33, 134, 139–40; rejected, 139; and Unionists, 136, 137–38
Irish executive officers, *see* attorney-general; chief secretary; lord chancellor; lord lieutenant; solicitor-general
Irish Figaro, 43
Irish Free State, government of, 301, 304, 312; administrative reform, 308–10; and civil servants, 308, 310; judicial system reformed, 311; judges in, 310–11; transfer of officials to, 304–5, 307–10
Irish Independent, 147, 238
Irish Independent Party, 46n, 156
Irish-Ireland movement, 103
Irish language, 24, 107, 126, 148, 311
Irish National Convention, 136, 139
Irish News, 240, 244, 252, 259. *See also* Devlin
Irish Office, 187–88, 204
Irish officials, *see* bureaucratic elite; Catholic officials; civil servants, Irish; professional staff officers; Protestant officials; Unionist officials; rank and file officials
Irish Parliamentary party, 9, 40, 55, 93, 110, 128, 130, 169, 211, 302; and

conscription, 207, 242; and Dublin Castle administration, 151–52; and election for Northern Parliament, 295; and first Coalition government, 193, 198–99, 202, 207–8, 215, 216; and home rule negotiations in 1914, 180; and Irish Council Bill, 138; and Liberal party alliance, 62, 69, 124, 194, 215, 229; and party pledge, 46–47, 84, 99, 146, 147, 154, 156, 169, 198; position in 1916; 207, 220–21; position in 1917–18, 229–30, 253, 256; position after 1918, 256, 273–74; position in Ulster, 295; and recruitment, 207; and second Coalition government, 231
Irish Privy Council, 2, 26, 27–28, 33
Irish Reform Association, 113, 114
Irish Republic, 208, 264, 296, 301, 302, 312
Irish Republican Army, 264; conducts guerrilla war, 268, 277, 288–89, 296, 302–3
Irish Republican Brotherhood, 179, 181, 208, 263
Irish Rosary, 104
Irish Times, 15, 150, 236–37, 243–44
Irish Unionist Alliance, 151
Irish Volunteers, 179, 206, 207, 247, 263, 265

Johnson, Swift Paine, 105
Jones, J. J., 51
Joyce, James, "Ivy Day in the Committee Room," 92
judicial appointments, at local and regional level, 36
judicial circuits, 32
judicial land commissioners, 28–29, 34, 42
justices, *see* Supreme Court of Judicature, justices
justices of the peace, *see* magistracy

Kaye, William Squire Baker, 65
Keenan, P. J., 64
Kenny, William, 71, 74, 86, 251
Kent, Pierce, 166
Kenworthy, J. M., 274
Keogh, William, 46n, 150, 167
Kildare Street Club, 16, 34, 87, 183, 212, 217
King's Inns, 32, 34, 36
Kinnear, Walter, 166

Labor Exchanges, 20, 166, 260
Labour party, 223, 289
Land Act (1896), 72
Land Act (1903), 101, 122
Land Act (1909), 156
Land Commission, 25, 30, 56, 58, 72–73, 101, 102, 110, 204, 309; appointments on, 128–30, 139–40, 256
land commissioners, 31, 101, 128–30
Land Registry, 18
Lansdown, Lord, 99, 116, 117, 195
Lardiner, James, 233
Larkin, James, 147, 179, 206
Law, Bonar, 195–96, 209, 283–84; and second Coalition government's Irish policy, 223, 265–66, 279–84, 291
Law Office, in Dublin Castle, 9; patronage in, 311, 312
Law officers, 8–10. *See also* attorney-generalship; sergeants-at-law; solicitor-generalship
Lawyers, benchers of the King's Inns, 10; Catholic and Protestant lawyers, 36, 191; in Ireland, 31–32, 34–37; as placehunters, 10
Leader, comments on appointments before 1910, 18, 23, 27, 103–4, 109, 114, 138, 146; comments on appointments after 1910, 165, 182. *See also* Moran
Leathes, S. M., 24
Lecky, W. E. H., 90
Leech, H. Brougham, 150–51, 155
Le Fanu, W. R., 296
Leinster House, 304
Liberal government, of 1892–95, 38; of 1906–10, 124, 130, 134–35; of 1910–15, 159–60, 177, 192, 215
Liberal-Nationalist alliance, 62, 69, 124, 194, 215, 229
Liberal party, 38, 54, 55, 60, 158, 180, 193, 223, 273
Liberals, Irish, 9, 66
Liberal-Unionists, 71, 251
Lloyd George, David, appointments in 1918, 223–24, 229, 244, 246, 257; appointments, 1919–21, 259, 268, 269, 277–78, 294; and Dail Eireann, 262; and French, 227, 245, 253, 255; and home rule debates of 1912–13, 174, 175, 182; and Irish Convention

Lloyd George (*continued*) (1917–18), 228–29; negotiates to end guerrilla war, 293, 294, 296; and partition talks, 212–14; and Redmond, 213–14, 223; and second Coalition government's Irish policy, 222–24, 226, 233–34, 241, 285
local government, administration of, 27, 47–48, 78–79, 106–7, 136, 148, 151, 153, 173; after the Easter Rising, 244, 263, 271, 277, 287, 309; in Ulster, 154, 171
Local Government Act (1898), 77–78
Local Government Board, 18–19, 78–80, 309
Logue, Cardinal Michael, 105, 164, 239–40
London Times, see Times, London
London University, 14, 31
Londonderry, Lord, 72, 109–10, 171
Long, Walter, 137, 170, 209, 259; appointed chief secretary, 117; and Better Government of Ireland Bill (1920), 241; and cabinet committee on home rule, 271; and Dudley, 118–20; and Greenwood, 285; and MacDonnell, 117–18; and second Coalition government's Irish policy 223–24, 238, 246, 248, 253, 254–55, 266
Lonsdale, John, 202
Lord Lieutenant of Ireland, 2–5, 8–10, 26–27, 98; expenses, 4; household staff, 3, 66, 118; Irish indifference to, 98; private secretary, 3, 63, 145; proposed abolition of, 4, 212, 282; social role, 3
Lough, Thomas, 232–33

McCarthy, Justin, 38, 190
McCarthy, M. J. F., 42, 149
McColgan, John, x, 292
MacDermott, Charles, 109, 163
MacDermott (The), Hugh, 41, 68, 88
MacDonnell, Antony, 107, 108, 118, 134, 189, 240, 290; appointed, 99–100; appointments, 125, 128–30; and Bryce, 125; and devolution crisis, 112–17; and Irish Council Bill, 131, 132, 134–36; and Nationalists, 143; resignation, 143; and Royal Commission on the Civil Service, 15; and Unionists, 113–17, 118; and university reform, 143; and Wyndham, 115–16
MacDonnell, Dr. M. A., 99
McDowell, R. B., x
MacElligott, J. J., 218
MacMahon, James, 164, 186, 225, 296, 305; as under secretary, 247, 280, 291; impasse with Taylor, 270, 279
MacNeill, Eoin, 24
MacPherson, Ian, 238, 243; appointed chief secretary, 259–60; and appointments, 265–67; and Chief Secretary's Office staff, 270; and Government of Ireland Act, 272–73; resigns, 277
Macready, Nevil, 278, 283, 284, 291
MacSweeny, George, 162, 243
MacSwiney, Terence, 288
MacVeagh, Jeremiah, 202
Magistrates, 3, 6, 9, 28, 47–48, 191, 243, 246; and Morley, 48–49
Maguire, Conor, 263
Maguire, William, 166
Mahaffy, John, 106–7
Mahon, Bryan, 218, 246
Markievicz, Countess Constance, 262
martial law, 209, 211, 218, 223, 283, 285, 289, 295
Masonic lodges, 16, 34, 108, 248
masters of the court, 32
Matheson, Charles L., 161, 171, 251, 266
Maunders, Richard, 155
Maxwell, John, 209–11, 214, 215, 217, 218
Meredith, Richard E., 87, 101, 128
Methodists, 107, 155
Micks, William L., 45–46, 50, 62, 79, 80
Midleton, Lord, 235, 244–45
Miller, Stearne Ball, 75
Moles, Thomas, 276
Molony, Thomas F., 151, 186, 249, 285
Monroe, John, 68, 74
Montague, Edwin, 210, 211
Moore, William, 101n, 120, 136, 195, 201, 224; appointment to bench, 230; and home rule debates of 1912–13, 172, 173; transfers to Northern Ireland, 300
Moran, D. P., 103–4, 122, 146–47, 230–31. *See also, Leader*
Moriarty, John F., 161, 186
Morley, John, 40–42, 62–69, 134, 142; and anti-Parnellites, 43, 48; ap-

pointed chief secretary, 39–40; appointments of, 42–46, 63–66; and Gladstone, 39–41, 59–61; and Home Rule Bill (1893–94), 51, 56; and "Morley Magistrates," 49, 69, 256; and Parnellites, 43, 48; and Redmond, 44, 158; relationship with officials, 42, 62, 63, 67–68; and Ridgeway, 49–50, 59–61; and Rosebery, 61–62, 67
Morris, William O'Connor, 108
Mulhall, John, 163
Murphy, James, 109
Murphy, William Martin, 104

Nathan, Matthew, 182, 186, 194, 204, 208, 210; and appointments, 184, 201–2; and Birrell, 206–7; and Dillon, 184, 187–88, 200–201
Nation, 81, 87, 92
National Health Insurance Act (1911), 165
National Health Insurance Commission, 17, 18, 20, 166
Nationalist officials, 252, 303; appointment of, 69, 166; and conscription, 243–44, 257–58. *See also* bureaucratic elite; Catholic officials; civil servants, Irish; professional staff officers; rank and file officials
Nationalist party, *see* anti-Parnellites; Irish Parliamentary party; Parnellites
Nationalists, 16; and the Conservative governments of 1895–1905, 122–23; and DATI, 81; and judicial reform, 76–77; and land legislation, 72; and Liberal government's appointments, 69; and local government reform, 77–79; position in 1892, 38; in 1900, 93; radical, 205–7, 215, 232; and second Coalition government, 226. *See also* Irish Parliamentary Party; Sinn Fein movement; Sinn Fein party
National University, 14, 24, 142, 189
nepotism, 16, 25
Norman, F. H., 25
North, *see* Northern Ireland, government
Northern Ireland, administration of, 297, 305–6; bureaucratic elite, 306; religious and political characteristics of civil servants, 297, 303, 306–7
Northern Ireland, government of, 295; plans to launch, 292–93; Supreme Court and judicial system, 299–300, 307
Northern Whig, 204, 205–6, 237, 246
Norway, A. H., 164, 218, 225

O'Brien, Ignatius, 161, 162, 195–96, 210, 243, 244, 246
O'Brien, J. R., 162
O'Brien, Morrough, 42, 44–45, 101
O'Brien, Peter, 75, 76, 162
O'Brien, R. Barry, 1, 123, 152
O'Brien, William (justice), 87
O'Brien, William (Nationalist MP), 76, 100, 147, 231, 232; and "Cleaning out the Castle," 47, 57; cooperates with Unionists, 113, 122; and Dillon, 45; and Morley, 43; on patronage abuses of Irish Parliamentary party, 167, 168
O'Broin, Leon, x
O'Connell, Daniel, 148, 156
O'Connell, W. A., 226, 229
O'Conner, Charles, 129, 130, 140, 162
O'Conner, T. P., 133, 134, 151, 186, 216, 273–74
O'Conor Don (The), 87–88
O'Connor, James, 224, 229–30, 242, 247, 249, 250
O'Connor, John, 227–28
O'Donnell, Bishop Patrick, 45, 229, 236
O'Donnell, F. H., 149
O'Dwyer, Bishop Edward, 207
O'Farrell, Edward, 144–45, 185, 217, 247, 296
O'Halpin, Eunan, x
O'Hara, Rev. Denis, 45
O'Hegarty, P. S., 261, 264, 308
O'Neill, R. W. H., 275, 276
Office of Arms, 155, 297
Office of Inspectors of Fisheries, 81, 85
Old Age Pensions Act (1908), 155
Owen-Lewis, A. F., 163–64
Oxford University, 14, 24, 31

Palles, Christopher, 33, 76, 226
Parliament, Northern, 271, 295
Parliament, Southern, 271, 295
Parliament Act (1911), 160, 177
Parliamentary party, *see* Irish Parliamentary party

Parnell, Charles Stuart, 38, 46n, 65, 91, 169
Parnell myth and appointments, 92
Parnellites, 38, 91
partition talks, in 1914, 179–80; in 1916, 213–14
Pearse, Padriac, 138, 149, 208, 211
Pease, H. P., 225
People's Budget, 158, 159
Phoenix Park murders, 51, 65, 186
Pigott forgeries, 89
Pim, Jonathan, 162, 198
Pittman, H. E., 162
pledge (against placehunting), *see* Irish Parliamentary party
Plunket, D. R., 55
Plunkett, George Noble, 218, 227, 231
Plunkett, Horace, 72, 97, 117, 125, 126, 138, 238, 290; and the Department of Agriculture and Technical Instruction, 82–85; and *Ireland in the New Century,* 110, 126; and the Irish Convention (1917–18), 228–29, 241; and Nationalists, 125–26; and Parliamentary party, 141; and the Recess Committee, 72; and Wyndham, 97
police, Irish, 6, 57, 96–97, 233, 243, 266, 278, 281, 284; and guerrilla war, 288–89, 309–10. *See also* Dublin Metropolitan Police; Garda Siochana; Royal Irish Constabulary
Poor Law Guardians, 79
Porter, A. M., 129
Powell, James, 243, 244, 249, 251
Presbyterians, and appointments, 41, 66, 75, 90
Price, Ivor, 206, 214, 217, 227
prison system, 19, 163, 286
Privy Council, Irish, 2, 26, 27, 28, 294
professional staff officers, 16–20, 33–34; appointment of, 17–18; number of, 16–17; political and religious characteristics in 1907, 18–19, in 1922, 310; salary of, 18–19; social characteristics, 19–20; transfer to Irish Free State, 310; typical career path, 17–18. *See also* civil servants, Irish
Protestant ascendancy, 52n, 57, 108–9, 212, 230, 252, 218–82; in Northern Ireland, 297, 303
Protestant (and Unionist) officials, 57, 157; alleged discrimination against, 51–52, 110–11, 137, 148–49, 167, 172, 177
Provisional Government, and civil servants, 303, 304–5, 307–10; established, 302
provisional government for Ulster (proposed), 170–71, 177, 180, 252
Public Record Office, 86

Queen's Colleges, at Belfast, Cork, and Galway, 14, 31, 90, 141–42
Quinn, Fergus, 185, 269

Raffin, P. W., 276
rank and file officials, 20–26; by department, 21–22; entry to civil service, 20, 22; first division (class I) clerks, 23–24; number of, 21–22; patronage appointments, 24–26; political influence on appointments, 24–25; religious and political characteristics, ix, 23; salary level, 20; second division (class II) clerks, 22–23; transfer to Irish Free State, 310; women officials, 22. *See also* civil servants, Irish
Recess Committee, 72
Redington, Christopher, 64–65, 89
Redmond, John, 100, 112, 123, 124, 164; and appointments of civil servants, 186; and Asquith, 193–94, 196–98, 207–8, 209, 212; and Birrell, 145, 195–96, 202–4; and Bryce, 127–28, 130–31; and devolution crisis, 116; and Dillon, 93, 127–28, 130, 139, 200–201, 205, 209–10; and Dublin Castle and judicial administration, 152–54, 217; and formation of first Coalition government, 193–94, 197–98; and Gill, 83; and Home Rule Bill (1893–94), 57; and Home Rule Bill (1912–14), 172, 175–76; and Irish Convention (1917–18), 228–29, 234–36; and Irish Council Bill, 135–36, 139–40; and local government matters, 77; and Lloyd George, 213–14, 223; and MacDonnell, 99, 116, 132, 134, 136; and Morley, 44, 48, 158; and Parnellites, 38; as Parnellite leader, 38, 44, 48, 77, 93; as party leader, 93, 181; and patronage, 44; and partition talks, in 1914, 179–80; in 1916, 213–14, 215; and party

pledge, 154, 157; and second Coalition government, 223, 225–26, 232; and transfer of services talks with Nathan, 187–88, 200–201; and Volunteers, 179; and world war, 181
Redmond, W. C. F., 269, 277
Registrar-General Office, 155
resident commissioner of National Education Board, 27, 64
resident magistrates, 9, 10, 36, 260, 288
Restoration of Order Act (1920), 285, 288
Ridgeway, Joseph West, 49–50, 59–61, 62, 98
Ripon, Lord, 100
Robinson, Henry, 78–79, 97, 98, 117, 157, 217, 241, 296
Rosebery, Lord, 1, 48, 59, 60–61; as prime minister, 61–63
Ronan, Stephen, 75, 89, 185–86, 250
Ross, John, 74–75, 87, 250, 283, 294, 299
Ross, John of Bladensburg, 96, 183
Royal Commission on the Civil Service, 15, 23–26, 79, 85, 102
Royal Irish Constabulary, 8, 16, 96–97, 118, 177, 178, 204, 206; abolished, 309; in guerrilla war with Sinn Fein, 267, 284, 286–87; Special Constabulary for Ulster, 291–92. *See also* police, Irish
Royal University, 14, 24
Russell, George, 264
Russell, T. W., 58, 100, 137, 141, 225, 259

Sadlier, John, 46n, 150, 167
Salisbury, Lord, 70–71, 91, 95, 98
Samuel, Herbert, 164
Samuels, A. W., 229, 239, 242–43, 244, 251, 265
Sankey, George, 63
Sankey Commission, 211, 218
Saunderson, Edward, 247
Scanlon, Thomas, 174
sergeants-at-law, 8–10
sessional crown solicitors, 36
Sexton, Thomas, 56
Shaw, Frederick, 246–47, 267
Shaw, T. B., 85
Shortt, Edward, 245–46, 249, 252–55, 259
Sinn Fein judicial system, 237
Sinn Fein movement, 103, 169, 205–6, 214, 226–27, 240; after 1919, 259, 265, 281, 302–3
Sinn Fein party, 148, 227–28, 231; and conscription, 242, 243, 257; and election of 1920, 276; and election for second Dailand Northern Parliament, 295; establishes alternative administrative and judicial system, 236–37; and general election of 1918, 255–56
Sinn Fein Weekly, 138, 148, 164, 167, 168
Skeffington, J. B., 146
Smith, R. J., 108
Smith, T. J., 178, 229, 268, 278, 280, 291
social clubs, 16, 34, 35. *See also* Kildare Street Club
social welfare legislation, for Ireland, 130, 155, 158, 165, 172
Society of Friends, 107, 162
solicitor-generalship, 8–10
Sommerville, William, 85
Spencer, Earl, 39–40, 60
Spotswood-Green, Rev. William, 85
Stack, Austin, 263
Stafford, T. J., 80
Starkie, William, 90, 190, 285
Stationery Office, 162
Stead, W. T., 145
Stevenson, George, 296
Sturgis, Mark, 282–83, 291, 292
Sullivan, A. M., 147, 162, 243, 266, 287
Supreme Court of Judicature, Ireland, 28–34; appointment to, 10; divided in 1921, 299; judicial positions, listed, 29, 30; structure of in 1877 and in 1897, 28–30; in 1920, 287. *See also* Supreme Court of Judicature justices; Supreme Court of Judicature officials
Supreme Court of Judicature (Ireland) Act of 1877, 28, 74
Supreme Court of Judicature (Ireland) Act of 1897, 29, 75–77
Supreme Court of Judicature justices, 31–34, 294; education, 31; family connections, 33; intellectual contributions, 34; legal training and career path, 31–32; religious and political characteristics of justices in 1881, 42, 88; in 1886, 88; in 1892, ix, 30;

Supreme Court of Judicature (*cont.*) in 1910, 160–61; in 1914, 31, 190; in 1918, 250; in 1921, 30, 299; in 1924, 311; service on boards and commissions, 27; social background, 31; social life, 34; transfer to Northern Ireland and Southern Ireland, 299
Supreme Court of Judicature officials, 34–37, 74, 294; court officials listed, 34–35; education and legal training, 35; family connections, 35; and judicial reform of 1897, 77; and open competition examinations, 37; patronage, 37; rank and file staff, 37; religious and political characteristics, ix, 36–37; selection by justices, 35; social life, 35–36; transfer to Irish Free State, 310, 311. *See also* court officials
Supreme Court of Northern Ireland, 272–73, 299–300
Supreme Court of Southern Ireland, 272–73, 299–300, 310
Swain, George, 80
Sweetman, John, 290
Sweetman, R. M., 162

Talbot, Lord Edward, 251, 294, 302
Taylor, J. J., 248, 269, 270, 271, 279–80, 281, 282, 284
Thompson, William, 155
Times, London, 15, 88, 114
Townshend, Charles, x
Townshend, John, 68
Treasury, control over the Irish administration, 6, 26, 63, 112, 187, 269; officials in Ireland; regulations on political activity of civil servants, 18, 26; Retrenchment Committee, 204–5; transfer of officials to North and to the Irish Free State, 296, 299
Treaty of 1921, 300–302, 304
Trinity College, Dublin, 141; and the education of officials and judges, 14, 24, 31, 35
Tudor, Hugh, 284

Ulster, appointments proposed for in 1914, 179–80; political geography of, 180, 213, 271–72; violence, 291
Ulster covenant, 171, 178
Ulster Liberals, 41, 66
Ulster Unionist Council, 171, 177, 292
Ulster Unionists, 83, 88, 170, 173, 178, 188, 236, 271, 273, 290, 292. *See also* Unionists, Northern
Ulster Volunteers, 177, 233, 291
under secretaryship, 8, 11
Unionist officials, *see* Protestant (and Unionist) officials
Unionist party, 128, 170, 180, 194, 198, 295; and elections for Northern Parliament, 295; and second Coalition government, 260
Unionists, 9, 16, 38–39, 66, 114, 160; attitude toward the Irish administration and judicial system in 1892, 58; attitude toward local government, 78, 114, 136; and Birrell, 150–51, 169–70; and DATI, 81–83; and first Coalition government, 194, 202–4, 219–20; and Home Rule Bill (1893–94), 51–52, 55–59; and land legislation, 72, 101; and Long, 119–20; moderate Unionists, 121–22; oppose devolution, 114–18, 122; oppose Irish Council Bill, 136–38; and second Coalition government, 223–24, 226, 229–30, 232. *See also* Unionists, Northern; Ulster Unionists; Unionists, Southern
Unionists, Northern, 120, 170, 214–15; and DATI, 83; and devolution crisis, 114–18; and Dudley, 114–18; and home rule, 38–39; and Home Rule Bill (1893–94), 55–59; and Home Rule Bill (1912–14), 172–74; and Irish Convention (1917–18), 236; and Land Commission appointments, 72–73, 102; and Long, 117, 137; and MacDonnell, 114–17, 118; and Wyndham, 115–17. *See also Belfast Newsletter*; *Northern Whig*; Ulster Unionists
Unionists, Southern, 170, 214, 223, 295; and Dail courts, 290; and home rule, 38–39; and Irish Convention, 235, and negotiations with De Valera, 296
United Irish League, 145, 147
university reform, 105, 141

Vicars, Arthur, 155

Walker, Samuel, 41, 48, 68, 128, 140, 157; appointed lord chancellor in

1892, 41; re-appointed lord chancellor, 125; appointment of justices of the peace, 48; retires, 161
Walsh, Archbishop William J., 90–91, 141
Warren, Robert, 86
Waterfield, A. P., 269; and the Irish Free State's officials, 305; and the North's officials, 297; and transfer of officials, 296–97
Watt, Samuel, 247
Whitley Councils, 309
Wilkinson, N. R., 155
Wilson, Daniel, 265, 266, 275, 300
Wimbourne, Lord, 184, 210, 215–17; and second Coalition government, 224, 237, 239, 241, 244
World War I, 180–81, 241, 255
Worthington-Evans, Laming, 275
Wrench, John, 50, 101–2, 214
Wright, George, 89, 109
Wylie, James, 130
Wylie, William, 265–67, 283, 284, 299
Wyndham, George, 154; appointed, 95–96; appointments of, 96; and Cadogan, 96–98; and devolution crisis, 112–17; and Land Act (1903), 101; and proposed Department of Education, 106; relationship with officials, 97; resignation, 117
Wynne, Henry, 215, 271

Yeo family, 35
Young, Filson, 108–9
Young Ireland, 46n